Official Google Cloud Certified

Associate Cloud Engineer

Study Guide

Official Google Cloud Certified
Associate Cloud Engineer
Study Guide

Dan Sullivan

A Wiley Brand

Development Editor: Stephanie Barton
Technical Editors: Stacy Véronneau and Manjeet Dadyala
Google Technical Reviewers: Jake Bednard, Brian Rice, Teresa Hardy, Grace Mollison, Tanay Buddhdev, Richard Rose, Jasen Baker, Jim Rambo, Varsha Datta, Mylene Biddle, Evan Jones, Samar Bhat, Josh Koh, Jeff Sherman, Kuntal Mitra, Michael Arciola and Lisa Guinn
Senior Production Editor: Christine O'Connor
Copy Editor: Kim Wimpsett
Content Enablement and Operations Manager: Pete Gaughan
Production Manager: Kathleen Wisor
Associate Publisher: Jim Minatel
Book Designers: Judy Fung and Bill Gibson
Proofreader: Louise Watson, Word One New York
Indexer: Johnna VanHoose Dinse
Project Coordinator, Cover: Brent Savage
Cover Designer: Wiley
Cover Image: Getty Images Inc. / Jeremy Woodhouse

to Katherine

Acknowledgments

A book is a team effort—more so for this book than any I've written before.

I am fortunate to have had the opportunity to work with Jim Minatel, associate publisher at John Wiley & Sons, and Carole Jelen, VP of Waterside Productions. Carole and Jim shared their vision for this book and invited me into their endeavor. They have been through the entire, sometimes time-challenged, writing of this book. Their knowledge and experience led to an improved book over the one you might otherwise be reading.

I am especially grateful for Stephanie Barton's help shaping the manuscript into its finished form. Stephanie edited the text, deciphered awkward grammatical contortions, and helped me think through the pedagogy of question design.

Thank you to Christine O'Connor for shepherding this book through the production process, which had more moving parts than I could track. Thanks to Kim Wimpsett for getting the text into final shape and suitable for the public.

I appreciate the careful attention and close reading by the technical editors, whose efforts made the text more precise and accurate.

I am fortunate to work in a stimulating professional environment where the culture supports who we are as individuals and enables a level of collaboration I've never experienced before joining New Relic. Thank you to my director, Cathy Rotering, who has a talent for seeing what makes people tick and helping them get where they want to go.

Like any accomplishment that might look like my doing, this book is possible because of those closest to me: Meg; all five of my children, particularly James and Nicholas, who were my first readers; and most importantly my wife, Katherine. For the 35 years we've been together, Katherine has engaged life with joy. Her own demanding work in literary publishing and poetry is changing lives, but Katherine is always present for those she loves, especially me.

About the Author

Dan Sullivan is a principal engineer and software architect at New Relic. He specializes in streaming analytics, machine learning, and cloud computing. Dan is the author of *NoSQL for Mere Mortals* and several LinkedIn Learning courses on databases, data science, and machine learning. Dan has certifications from Google and AWS along with a Ph.D. in genetics and computational biology.

Contents at a Glance

Contents

Introduction

Google Cloud Platform (GCP) is a leading public cloud that provides its users with some of the same software, hardware, and networking infrastructure used to power Google services. Businesses, organizations, and individuals can launch servers in minutes, store petabytes of data, and implement global virtual clouds with GCP. It includes an easy-to-use console interface, command-line tools, and application programming interfaces (APIs) for managing resources in the cloud. Users can work with general resources, such as virtual machines (VMs) and persistent disks, or opt for highly focused services for Internet of Things (IoT), machine learning, media, and other specialized domains.

Deploying and managing applications and services in GCP requires a clear understanding of the way Google structures user accounts and manages identities and access controls; you also need to understand the advantages and disadvantages of using various services. Certified Associate Cloud Engineers have demonstrated the knowledge and skills needed to deploy and operate infrastructure, services, and networks in Google Cloud.

This study guide is designed to help you understand GCP in depth so that you can meet the needs of those operating resources in Google Cloud. Yes, this book will, of course, help you pass the Associate Cloud Engineer certification exam, but this is not an exam cram guide. You will learn more than is required to pass the exam; you will understand how to meet the day-to-day challenges faced by cloud engineers, including choosing services, managing users, deploying and monitoring infrastructure, and helping map business requirements into cloud-based solutions.

Each chapter in this book covers a single topic and includes an "Exam Essentials" section that outlines key information you should know to pass the certification exam. There are also exercises to help you review and reinforce your understanding of the chapter's topic. Sample questions are included at the end of each chapter so you can get a sense of the types of questions you will see on the exam. The book also includes flashcards and practice exams that cover all topics you'll learn about with this guide.

What Does This Book Cover?

This book describes products and services in GCP. It does not include G Suite administration topics.

Chapter 1: Overview of Google Cloud Platform In the opening chapter, we look into the types of services provided by GCP, which include compute, storage, and networking services as well as specialized services, such as machine learning products. This chapter also describes some of the key differences between cloud computing and data center or on-premise computing.

Chapter 2: Google Cloud Computing Services   This chapter provides an overview of infrastructure services such as computing, storage, and networking. It introduces the concept of identity management and related services. It also introduces DevOps topics and tools for deploying and monitoring applications and resources. GCP includes a growing list of specialized services, such as machine learning and natural language processing services. Those are briefly discussed in this chapter. The chapter introduces Google Cloud's organizational structure with a look at regions and zones. The chapter concludes with a discussion of Cloud Launcher for deploying packaged applications.

Chapter 3: Projects, Service Accounts, and Billing   One of the first things you will do when starting to work with GCP is to set up your accounts. In this chapter, you will learn how resources in accounts are organized into organizations, folders, and projects. You will learn how to create and edit these structures. You will also see how to enable APIs for particular projects as well as manage user identities and their access controls. This chapter describes how to create billing accounts and link them to projects. You will also learn how to create budgets and define billing alerts to help you manage costs. Finally, the chapter describes how to create Stackdriver accounts, which are used as part of the monitoring system in GCP.

Chapter 4: Introduction to Computing in Google Cloud   In this chapter, you will see the variety of options available for running applications and services in GCP. Options include Compute Engine, which provides VMs running Linux or Windows operating systems. App Engine is a platform as a service (PaaS) option that allows developers to run their applications without having to concern themselves with managing VMs. If you will be running multiple applications and services, you may want to take advantage of containers, which are a lightweight alternative to VMs. You will learn about containers and how to manage them with Kubernetes Engine. This chapter also introduces Cloud Functions, which is for event-driven, short-running tasks such as triggering the processing of an image loaded into Cloud Storage. You will also learn about Firebase, a set of services well suited for providing backend infrastructure to mobile applications.

Chapter 5: Computing with Compute Engine Virtual Machines   In this chapter, you will learn how to configure VMs, including selecting CPU, memory, storage options, and operating system images. You will learn how to use GCP Console and Cloud Shell to work with VMs. In addition, you will see how to install the command-line interface and SDK, which you will use to start and stop VMs. The chapter will also describe how to enable network access to VMs.

Chapter 6: Managing Virtual Machines   In the previous chapter, you learned how to create VMs, and in this chapter you will learn how to manage individual and groups of VMs. You will start by managing a single instance of a VM using the GCP console and then perform the same operations using Cloud Shell and the command line. You will also learn how to view currently running VMs. Next, you'll learn about instance groups, which allow you to create sets of VMs that you can manage as a single unit. In the section on instance groups, you will learn the difference between managed and unmanaged instance groups. You will also learn about preemptible instances, which are low-cost VMs that may be shut down by Google. You will learn about the cost-benefit trade-offs of preemptible instances. Finally, the chapter closes with guidelines for managing VMs.

Chapter 7: Computing with Kubernetes   This chapter introduces Kubernetes Engine, Google's managed Kubernetes service. Kubernetes is a container orchestration platform created and released as open source by Google. In this chapter, you will learn the basics of containers, container orchestration, and the Kubernetes architecture. The discussion will include an overview of Kubernetes objects such as pods, services, volumes, and namespaces, as well as Kubernetes controllers such as ReplicaSets, deployments, and jobs.

Next, the chapter turns to deploying a Kubernetes cluster using GCP console, Cloud Shell, and SDK. You will also see how to deploy pods, which includes downloading an existing Docker image, building a Docker image, creating a pod, and then deploying an application to the Kubernetes cluster. Of course, you will need to know how to monitor a cluster of servers. This chapter provides a description of how to set up monitoring and logging with Stackdriver, which is Google's application, service, container, and infrastructure monitoring service.

Chapter 8: Managing Kubernetes Clusters   In this chapter you will learn the basics of managing a Kubernetes cluster, including viewing the status of the cluster, viewing the contents of the image repository, viewing details about images in the repository, and adding, modifying, and removing nodes, pods, and services. As in the chapter on managing VMs, in this chapter you will learn how to perform management operations with the three management tools: GCP console, Cloud Shell, and SDK. The chapter concludes with a discussion of guidelines and good practices for managing a Kubernetes cluster.

Chapter 9: Computing with App Engine   Google App Engine is Google's PaaS offering. You will learn about App Engine components such as applications, services, versions, and instances. The chapter also covers how to define configuration files and specify dependencies of an application. In this chapter, you will learn how to view App Engine resources using GCP console, Cloud Shell, and SDK. The chapter also describes how to distribute workload by adjusting traffic with splitting parameters. You will also learn about autoscaling in App Engine.

Chapter 10: Computing with Cloud Functions   Cloud Functions is for event-driven, serverless computations. This chapter introduces Cloud Functions, including using it to receive events, evoke services, and return results. Next, you'll see use cases for Cloud Functions, such as integrating with third-party APIs and event-driven processing. You will learn about Google's Pub/Sub service for publication- and subscription-based processing and how to use Cloud Functions with Pub/Sub. Cloud Functions are well suited to respond to events in Cloud Storage. The chapter describes Cloud Storage events and how to use Cloud

Functions to receive and respond to those events. You will learn how to use Stackdriver to monitor and log details of Cloud Function executions. Finally, the chapter concludes with a discussion of guidelines for using and managing Cloud Functions.

Chapter 11: Planning Storage in the Cloud   Having described various compute options in GCP, it is time to turn your attention to storage. This chapter describes characteristics of storage systems, such as their time to access, persistence, and data model. In this chapter, you will learn about differences between caches, persistent storage, and archival storage. You will learn about the cost-benefit trade-offs of using regional and multiregional persistent storage and using nearline versus coldline archival storage. The chapter includes details on the various GCP storage options, including Cloud Storage for blob storage; Cloud SQL and Spanner for relational data; Datastore, Bigtable, and BigQuery for NoSQL storage; and Cloud Firebase for mobile application data. The chapter includes detailed guidance on choosing a data store based on requirements for consistency, availability, transaction support, cost, latency, and support for different read/write patterns.

Chapter 12: Deploying Storage in Google Cloud Platform   In this chapter, you will learn how to create databases, add data, list records, and delete data from each of GCP's storage systems. The chapter starts by introducing Cloud SQL, a managed database service that offers MySQL and PostgreSQL managed instances. You will also learn how to create databases in Cloud Datastore, BigQuery, Bigtable, and Spanner. Next, you will turn your attention to Cloud Pub/Sub for storing data in message queues, followed by a discussion of Cloud Dataproc, a managed Hadoop and Spark cluster service, for processing big data sets. In the next section, you will learn about Cloud Storage for objects. The chapter concludes with guidance on how to choose a data store for a particular set of requirements.

Chapter 13: Loading Data into Storage   There are a variety of ways of getting data into GCP. This chapter describes how to use the command-line SDK to load data into Cloud SQL, Cloud Storage, Datastore, BigQuery, BigTable, and Dataproc. It will also describe bulk importing and exporting from those same services. Next, you will learn about two common data loading patterns: moving data from Cloud Storage and streaming data to Cloud Pub/Sub.

Chapter 14: Networking in the Cloud: Virtual Private Clouds and Virtual Private Networks
In this chapter, you'll turn your attention to networking with an introduction to basic networking concepts, including the following:

- IP addresses
- CIDR blocks
- Networks and subnetworks
- Virtual private clouds (VPCs)
- Routing and rules
- Virtual private networks (VPNs)
- Cloud DNS

- Cloud routers
- Cloud interconnect
- External peering

After being introduced to key networking concepts, you will learn how to create a VPC. Specifically, this will include defining a VPC, specifying firewall rules, creating a VPN, and working with load balancers. You will learn about different types of load balancers and when to use them.

Chapter 15: Networking in the Cloud: DNS, Load Balancing, and IP Addressing In this chapter, you will learn about common network management tasks such as defining subnetworks, adding subnets to a VPC, managing CIDR blocks, and reserving IP addresses. You will learn how to preform each of these tasks using Cloud Console, Cloud Shell, and Cloud SDK.

Chapter 16: Deploying Applications with Cloud Launcher and Deployment Manager Google Cloud Launcher is GCP's marketplace of preconfigured stacks and services. This chapter introduces Cloud Launcher and describes some applications and services currently available. You will learn how to browse Cloud Launcher, deploy applications from Cloud Launcher, and shut down Cloud Launcher applications. The chapter will also discuss Deployment Manager templates to automate the deployment of an application and launch a Deployment Manager template to provision GCP resources and configure an application automatically.

Chapter 17: Configuring Access and Security This chapter introduces identity management. In particular, you will learn about identities, roles, and assigning and removing identity roles. This chapter also introduces service accounts and how to create them, assign them to VMs, and work with them across projects. You will also learn how to view audit logs for projects and services. The chapter concludes with guidelines for configuring access control security.

Chapter 18: Monitoring, Logging, and Cost Estimating In the final chapter, we will discuss Stackdriver alerts, logging, distributed tracing, and application debugging. Each of the corresponding GCP services is designed to enable more efficient, functional, and reliable services. The chapter concludes with a review of the Pricing Calculator, which is helpful for estimating the cost of resources in GCP.

Interactive Online Learning Environment and TestBank

Studying the material in the *Official Google Certified Associate Cloud Engineer Study Guide* is an important part of preparing for the Associate Cloud Engineer certification exam, but we provide additional tools to help you prepare. The online TestBank will help you understand the types of questions that will appear on the certification exam.

The sample tests in the TestBank include all the questions in each chapter as well as the questions from the assessment test. In addition, there are two practice exams with 50 questions each. You can use these tests to evaluate your understanding and identify areas that may require additional study.

The flashcards in the TestBank will push the limits of what you should know for the certification exam. There are 100 questions provided in digital format. Each flashcard has one question and one correct answer.

The online glossary is a searchable list of key terms introduced in this exam guide that you should know for the Associate Cloud Engineer certification exam.

To start using these to study for the Google Certified Associate Cloud Engineer exam, go to www.wiley.com/go/sybextestprep and register your book to receive your unique PIN. Once you have the PIN, return to www.wiley.com/go/sybextestprep, find your book and click Register or Login, and follow the link to register a new account or add this book to an existing account.

Exam Objectives

The Associate Cloud Engineer certification is designed for people who create, deploy, and manage enterprise applications and infrastructure in GCP. An Associate Cloud Engineer is comfortable working with Cloud Console, Cloud Shell, and Cloud SDK. Such individuals also understand products offered as part of GCP and their appropriate use cases.

The exam will test your knowledge of the following:

- Planning a cloud solution using one or more GCP services
- Creating a cloud environment for an organization
- Deploying applications and infrastructure
- Using monitoring and logging to ensure availability of cloud solutions
- Setting up identity management, access controls, and other security measures

Objective Map

The following are specific objectives defined by Google at https://cloud.google.com/certification/guides/cloud-engineer/.

Section 1: Setting up a cloud solution environment

1.1 Setting up cloud projects and accounts. Activities include:

- Creating projects
- Assigning users to predefined IAM (Identity and Access Management) roles within a project
- Linking users to G Suite identities

- Enabling APIs within projects
- Provisioning one or more Stackdriver accounts

1.2 Managing billing configuration. Activities include:

- Creating one or more billing accounts
- Linking projects to a billing account
- Establishing billing budgets and alerts
- Setting up billing exports to estimate daily/monthly charges

1.3 Installing and configuring the command-line interface (CLI), specifically Cloud SDK (e.g., setting the default project)

Section 2: Planning and configuring a cloud solution

2.1 Planning and estimating GCP product use using the Pricing Calculator

2.2 Planning and configuring compute resources. Considerations include:

- Selecting appropriate compute choices for a given workload (e.g., Compute Engine, Kubernetes Engine, App Engine)
- Using preemptible VMs and custom machine types as appropriate

2.3 Planning and configuring data storage options. Considerations include:

- Product choice (e.g., Cloud SQL, BigQuery, Cloud Spanner, Cloud Bigtable)
- Choosing storage options (e.g., Regional, Multiregional, Nearline, Coldline)

2.4 Planning and configuring network resources. Tasks include:

- Differentiating load balancing options
- Identifying resource locations in a network for availability
- Configuring Cloud DNS

Section 3: Deploying and implementing a cloud solution

3.1 Deploying and implementing Compute Engine resources. Tasks include:

- Launching a compute instance using Cloud Console and Cloud SDK (gcloud) (e.g., assign disks, availability policy, SSH keys)
- Creating an autoscaled managed instance group using an instance template
- Generating/uploading a custom SSH key for instances
- Configuring a VM for Stackdriver monitoring and logging
- Assessing compute quotas and requesting increases
- Installing the Stackdriver Agent for monitoring and logging

3.2 Deploying and implementing Kubernetes Engine resources. Tasks include:

- Deploying a Kubernetes Engine cluster
- Deploying a container application to Kubernetes Engine using pods
- Configuring Kubernetes Engine application monitoring and logging

3.3 Deploying and implementing App Engine and Cloud Functions resources. Tasks include:

- Deploying an application to App Engine (e.g., scaling configuration, versions, and traffic splitting)
- Deploying a Cloud Function that receives Google Cloud events (e.g., Cloud Pub/Sub events, Cloud Storage object change notification events)

3.4 Deploying and implementing data solutions. Tasks include:

- Initializing data systems with products (e.g., Cloud SQL, Cloud Datastore, BigQuery, Cloud Spanner, Cloud Pub/Sub, Cloud Bigtable, Cloud Dataproc, Cloud Storage)
- Loading data (e.g., command-line upload, API transfer, import/export, load data from Cloud Storage, streaming data to Cloud Pub/Sub)

3.5 Deploying and implementing networking resources. Tasks include:

- Creating a VPC with subnets (e.g., custom-mode VPC, shared VPC)
- Launching a Compute Engine instance with custom network configuration (e.g., internal-only IP address, Google private access, static external and private IP address, network tags)
- Creating ingress and egress firewall rules for a VPC (e.g., IP subnets, tags, service accounts)
- Creating a VPN between a Google VPC and an external network using Cloud VPN
- Creating a load balancer to distribute application network traffic to an application (e.g., global HTTP(S) load balancer, global SSL proxy load balancer, global TCP proxy load balancer, regional network load balancer, regional internal load balancer)

3.6 Deploying a Solution using Cloud Launcher. Tasks include:

- Browsing the Cloud Launcher catalog and viewing solution details
- Deploying a Cloud Launcher marketplace solution

3.7 Deploying an Application using Deployment Manager. Tasks include:

- Developing Deployment Manager templates to automate deployment of an application
- Launching a Deployment Manager template to provision GCP resources and configure an application automatically

Section 4: Ensuring successful operation of a cloud solution

4.1 Managing Compute Engine resources. Tasks include:

- Managing a single VM instance (e.g., start, stop, edit configuration, or delete an instance)
- SSH/RDP to the instance
- Attaching a GPU to a new instance and installing CUDA libraries
- Viewing current running VM inventory (instance IDs, details)
- Working with snapshots (e.g., create a snapshot from a VM, view snapshots, delete a snapshot)
- Working with images (e.g., create an image from a VM or a snapshot, view images, delete an image)
- Working with instance groups (e.g., set autoscaling parameters, assign an instance template, create an instance template, remove an instance group)
- Working with management interfaces (e.g., Cloud Console, Cloud Shell, Cloud SDK)

4.2 Managing Kubernetes Engine resources. Tasks include:

- Viewing current running cluster inventory (nodes, pods, services)
- Browsing the container image repository and viewing container image details
- Working with nodes (e.g., add, edit, or remove a node)
- Working with pods (e.g., add, edit, or remove pods)
- Working with services (e.g., add, edit, or remove a service)
- Working with management interfaces (e.g., Cloud Console, Cloud Shell, Cloud SDK)

4.3 Managing App Engine resources. Tasks include:

- Adjusting application traffic splitting parameters
- Setting scaling parameters for autoscaling instances
- Working with management interfaces (e.g., Cloud Console, Cloud Shell, Cloud SDK)

4.4 Managing data solutions. Tasks include:

- Executing queries to retrieve data from data instances (e.g., Cloud SQL, BigQuery, Cloud Spanner, Cloud Datastore, Cloud Bigtable, Cloud Dataproc)
- Estimating costs of a BigQuery query
- Backing up and restoring data instances (e.g., Cloud SQL, Cloud Datastore, Cloud Dataproc)
- Reviewing job status in Cloud Dataproc or BigQuery
- Moving objects between Cloud Storage buckets

- Converting Cloud Storage buckets between storage classes
- Setting object lifecycle management policies for Cloud Storage buckets
- Working with management interfaces (e.g., Cloud Console, Cloud Shell, Cloud SDK)

4.5 Managing networking resources. Tasks include:

- Adding a subnet to an existing VPC
- Expanding a CIDR block subnet to have more IP addresses
- Reserving static external or internal IP addresses
- Working with management interfaces (e.g., Cloud Console, Cloud Shell, Cloud SDK)

4.6 Monitoring and logging. Tasks include:

- Creating Stackdriver alerts based on resource metrics
- Creating Stackdriver custom metrics
- Configuring log sinks to export logs to external systems (e.g., on premise or BigQuery)
- Viewing and filtering logs in Stackdriver
- Viewing specific log message details in Stackdriver
- Using cloud diagnostics to research an application issue (e.g., viewing Cloud Trace data, using Cloud Debug to view an application point in time)
- Viewing GCP status
- Working with management interfaces (e.g., Cloud Console, Cloud Shell, Cloud SDK)

Section 5: Configuring access and security

5.1 Managing Identity and Access Management. Tasks include:

- Viewing account IAM assignments
- Assigning IAM roles to accounts or Google Groups
- Defining custom IAM roles

5.2 Managing service accounts. Tasks include:

- Managing service accounts with limited scopes
- Assigning a service account to VM instances
- Granting access to a service account in another project

5.3 Viewing audit logs for project and managed services

Cloud Computing Components

- Compute resources
- Storage
- Networking
- Specialized services

Difference between Cloud Computing and Data Center Computing

- Rent instead of own resources
- Pay-as-you-go-for-what-you-use model
- Elastic resource allocation
- Specialized services

Assessment Test

92%

1. Instance templates are used to create a group of identical VMs. The instance templates include:
   - **A.** Machine type, boot disk image or container image, zone, and labels
   - **B.** Cloud Storage bucket definitions
   - **C.** A load balancer description
   - **D.** App Engine configuration file

2. The command-line command to create a Cloud Storage bucket is:
   - **A.** gcloud mb
   - **B.** gsutil mb
   - **C.** gcloud mkbucket
   - **D.** gsutil mkbucket

3. Your company has an object management policy that requires that objects stored in Cloud Storage be migrated from regional storage to nearline storage 90 days after the object is created. The most efficient way to do this is to:
   - **A.** Create a cloud function to copy objects from regional storage to nearline storage.
   - **B.** Set the MigrateObjectAfter property on the stored object to 90 days.
   - **C.** Copy the object to persistent storage attached to a VM and then copy the object to a bucket created on nearline storage.
   - **D.** Create a lifecycle management configuration policy specifying an age of 90 days and SetStorageClass as nearline.

4. An education client maintains a site where users can upload videos, and your client needs to assure redundancy for the files; therefore, you have created two buckets for Cloud Storage. Which command do you use to synchronize the contents of the two buckets?
   - **A.** gsutil rsync
   - **B.** gcloud cp sync
   - **C.** gcloud rsync
   - **D.** gsutil cp sync

5. VPCs are _____ resources.
   - **A.** Regional
   - **B.** Zonal
   - **C.** Global
   - **D.** Subnet

6. A remote component in your network has failed, which results in a transient network error. When you submit a `gsutil` command, it fails because of a transient error. By default, the command will:

   A. Terminate and log a message to Stackdriver

   B. Retry using a truncated binary exponential back-off strategy

   C. Prompt the user to decide to retry or quit

   D. Terminate and log a message to Cloud Shell

7. All of the following are components of firewall rules except which one?

   A. Direction of traffic

   B. Action on match

   C. Time to live (TTL)

   D. Protocol

8. Adding virtual machines to an instance group can be triggered in an autoscaling policy by all of the following, except which one?

   A. CPU utilization

   B. Stackdriver metrics

   C. IAM policy violation

   D. Load balancing serving capacity

9. Your company's finance department is developing a new account management application that requires transactions and the ability to perform relational database operations using fully compliant SQL. Data store options in GCP include:

   A. Spanner and Cloud SQL

   B. Datastore and Bigtable

   C. Spanner and Cloud Storage

   D. Datastore and Cloud SQL

10. The marketing department in your company wants to deploy a web application but does not want to have to manage servers or clusters. A good option for them is:

    A. Compute Engine

    B. Kubernetes Engine

    C. App Engine

    D. Cloud Functions

11. Your company is building an enterprise data warehouse and wants SQL query capabilities over petabytes of data, but does not want to manage servers or clusters. A good option for them is:

    A. Cloud Storage

    B. BigQuery

    C. Bigtable

    D. Datastore

12. You have been hired as a consultant to a startup in the Internet of Things (IoT) space. The startup will stream large volumes of data into GCP. The data needs to be filtered, transformed, and analyzed before being stored in GCP Datastore. A good option for the stream processing component is:

    A. Dataproc

    B. Cloud Dataflow

    C. Cloud Endpoints

    D. Cloud Interconnect

13. Preemptible virtual machines may be shut down at any time but will always be shut down after running:

    A. 6 hours

    B. 12 hours

    C. 24 hours

    D. 48 hours

14. You have been tasked with designing an organizational hierarchy for managing departments and their cloud resources. What organizing components are available in GCP?

    A. Organization, folders, projects

    B. Buckets, directories, subdirectories

    C. Organizations, buckets, projects

    D. Folders, buckets, projects

15. During an incident that has caused an application to fail, you suspect some resource may not have appropriate roles granted. The command to list roles granted to a resource is:

    A. `gutil iam list-grantable-roles`

    B. `gcloud iam list-grantable-roles`

    C. `gcloud list-grantable-roles`

    D. `gcloud resources grantable-roles`

16. The availability of CPU platforms can vary between zones. To get a list of all CPU types available in a particular zone, you should use:

    A. `gcloud compute zones describe`

    B. `gcloud iam zones describe`

    C. `gutil zones describe`

    D. `gcloud compute regions list`

17. To create a custom role, a user must possess which role?

    A. `iam.create`

    B. `compute.roles.create`

    C. `iam.roles.create`

    D. `Compute.roles.add`

18. You have been asked to create a network with 1,000 IP addresses. In the interest of minimizing unused IP addresses, which CIDR suffix would you use to create a network with at least 1,000 addresses but no more than necessary?

   A. /20

   B. /22

   C. /28

   D. /32

19. A team of data scientists have asked for your help setting up an Apache Spark cluster. You suggest they use a managed GCP service instead of managing a cluster themselves on Compute Engine. The service they would use is:

   A. Cloud Dataproc

   B. Cloud Dataflow

   C. Cloud Hadoop

   D. BigQuery

20. You have created a web application that allows users to upload files to Cloud Storage. When files are uploaded, you want to check the file size and update the user's total storage used in their account. A serverless option for performing this action on load is:

   A. Cloud Dataflow

   B. Cloud Dataproc

   C. Cloud Storage

   D. Cloud Functions

21. Your company has just started using GCP, and executives want to have a dedicated connection from your data center to the GCP to allow for large data transfers. Which networking service would you recommend?

   A. Google Cloud Carrier Internet Peering

   B. Google Cloud Interconnect – Dedicated

   C. Google Cloud Internet Peering

   D. Google Cloud DNS

22. You want to have GCP manage cryptographic keys, so you've decided to use Cloud Key Management Services. Before you can start creating cryptographic keys, you must:

   A. Enable Google Cloud Key Management Service (KMS) API and set up billing

   B. Enable Google Cloud KMS API and create folders

   C. Create folders and set up billing

   D. Give all users grantable roles to create keys

23. In Kubernetes Engine, a node pool is:

    A. A subset of nodes across clusters

    B. A set of VMs managed outside of Kubernetes Engine

    C. A set of preemptible VMs

    D. A subset of node instances within a cluster that all have the same configuration

24. The GCP service for storing and managing Docker containers is:

    A. Cloud Source Repositories

    B. Cloud Build

    C. Container Registry

    D. Docker Repository

25. Code for Cloud Functions can be written in:

    A. Node.js and Python

    B. Node.js, Python, and Go

    C. Python and Go

    D. Python and C

Answers to Assessment Test

1. **A.** Machine type, boot disk image or container image, zone, and labels are all configuration parameters or attributes of a VM and therefore would be included in an instance group configuration that creates those VMs.

2. **B.** gsutil is the command line for accessing and manipulating Cloud Storage from the command line. mb is the specific command for creating, or making, a bucket.

3. **D.** The lifecycle configuration policy allows administrators to specify criteria for migrating data to other storage systems without having to concern themselves with running jobs to actually execute the necessary steps. The other options are inefficient or do not exist.

4. **A.** gsutil is the command-line tool for working with Cloud Storage. rsync is the specific command in gsutil for synchronizing buckets.

5. **C.** Google operates a global network, and VPCs are resources that can span that global network.

6. **B.** gcloud by default will retry a failed network operation and will wait a long time before each retry. The time to wait is calculated using a truncated binary exponential back-off strategy.

7. **C.** Firewall rules do not have TTL parameters. Direction of traffic, action on match, and protocol are all components of firewall rules.

8. **C.** IAM policy violations do not trigger changes in the size of clusters. All other options can be used to trigger a change in cluster size.

9. **A.** Only Spanner and Cloud SQL databases support transactions and have a SQL interface. Datastore has transactions but does not support fully compliant SQL; it has a SQL-like query language. Cloud Storage does not support transactions or SQL.

10. **C.** App Engine is a PaaS that allows developers to deploy full applications without having to manage servers or clusters. Compute Engine and Kubernetes Engine require management of servers. Cloud Functions is suitable for short-running Node.js or Python functions but not full applications.

11. **B.** BigQuery is designed for petabyte-scale analytics and provides a SQL interface.

12. **B.** Cloud Dataflow allows for stream and batch processing of data and is well suited for this kind of ETL work. Dataproc is a managed Hadoop and Spark service that is used for big data analytics. Cloud Endpoints is an API service, and Cloud Interconnect is a network service.

13. **C.** If a preemptible machine has not been shut down within 24 hours, Google will stop the instance.

14. **A.** Organizations, folders, and projects are the components used to manage an organizational hierarchy. Buckets, directories, and subdirectories are used to organize storage.

15. B. `gcloud` is the command-line tool for working with IAM, and `list-grantable-roles` is the correct command.

16. A. `gcloud` is the command-line tool for manipulating compute resources, and `zones describe` is the correct command.

17. C. `iam.roles.create` is correct; the other roles do not exist.

18. B. The /22 suffix produces 1,022 usable IP addresses.

19. A. Cloud Dataproc is the managed Spark service. Cloud Dataflow is for stream and batch processing of data, BigQuery is for analytics, and Cloud Hadoop is not a GCP service.

20. D. Cloud Functions responds to events in Cloud Storage, making them a good choice for taking an action after a file is loaded.

21. B. Google Cloud Interconnect – Dedicated is the only option for a dedicated connection between a customer's data center and a Google data center.

22. A. Enabling the Google Cloud KMS API and setting up billing are steps common to using GCP services.

23. D. A node pool is a subset of node instances within a cluster that all have the same configuration.

24. C. The GCP service for storing and managing Docker containers is Container Registry. Cloud Build is for creating images. The others are not GCP services.

25. A. Node.js 6, Node.js 8, and Python are the languages supported by Cloud Functions.

Chapter

1

Overview of Google Cloud Platform

THIS CHAPTER COVERS THE FOLLOWING OBJECTIVE OF THE GOOGLE ASSOCIATE CLOUD ENGINEER CERTIFICATION EXAM:

✓ **1.0   Setting up a Cloud Solution Environment**

Google Cloud Platform (GCP) is a public cloud service that offers some of the same technologies used by Google to deliver its own products. This chapter describes the most important components of GCP and discusses how it differs from on-premise data center–based computing.

Types of Cloud Services

Public cloud providers such as Google, Amazon, and Microsoft offer a range of services for deploying computing, storage, networking, and other infrastructures to run a wide array of business services and applications. Some cloud users are new companies that start in the cloud. They have never owned their own hardware and software. Other cloud customers are enterprises with multiple data centers that use public clouds to supplement their data centers. These different kinds of users have different requirements.

A company that starts on the cloud can choose services that best fit its application and architectural needs without having to consider existing infrastructure. For example, a startup could use GCP's Cloud Identity and Access Management services for all authentication and authorization needs. A company that has already invested in a Microsoft Active Directory solution for identity management may want to leverage that system instead of working solely with the cloud's identity management system. This can lead to additional work to integrate the two systems and keep them synchronized.

Another area of concern for enterprises with their own infrastructure is establishing and maintaining a secure network between their on-premise resources and their public cloud resources. If there will be high-volume network traffic between the on-premise systems and the public cloud, the enterprise may need to invest in dedicated networking between its data center and a facility of the public cloud provider. If the volume of traffic does not justify the cost of a dedicated connection between facilities, then the company may use a virtual private network that runs over the public Internet. This requires additional network design and management that a company that is solely in the cloud would not have to address.

Public cloud providers offer services that fall into four broad categories.

- Compute resources
- Storage
- Networking
- Specialized services such as Machine Learning Services

Cloud customers typically make use of services in more than one of these categories.

Compute Resources

Computing resources come in a variety of forms in public clouds.

Virtual Machines

Virtual Machines are a basic unit of computing resources and a good starting point for experimenting with the cloud. After you create an account with a cloud provider and provide billing information, you can use a portal or command-line tools to create VMs. Google Cloud Platform offers a variety of preconfigured VMs with varying numbers of vCPUs and amounts of memory. You can also create a custom configuration if the preconfigured offerings do not meet your needs.

Once you create a VM, you can log into it and administer it as you like. You have full access to the VM, so you can configure file systems, add persistent storage, patch the operating system, or install additional packages. You decide what to run on the VM, who else will have access to it, and when to shut down the VM. A VM that you manage is like having a server in your office that you have full administrator rights to.

You can, of course, create multiple VMs running different operating systems and applications. GCP also provides services, such as load balancers, that provide a single access point to a distributed back end. This is especially useful when you need to have high availability for your application. If one of the VMs in a cluster fails, the workload can be directed to the other VMs in the cluster. Autoscalers can add or remove VMs from the cluster based on the workload. This is called *autoscaling*. This helps both control cost by not running more VMs than needed and ensure that sufficient computing capacity is available when workloads increase.

Managed Kubernetes Clusters

Google Cloud Platform gives you all the tools you need to create and manage clusters of servers. Many cloud users would rather focus on their applications and not the tasks needed to keep a cluster of servers up and running. For those users, managed clusters are a good option.

Managed clusters make use of containers. A container is like a lightweight VM that isolates processes running in one container from processes running in another container on the same server. In a managed cluster, you can specify the number of servers you would like to run and the containers that should run on them. You can also specify autoscaling parameters to optimize the number of containers running.

In a managed cluster, the health of containers is monitored for you. If a container fails, the cluster management software will detect it and start another container.

Containers are good options when you need to run applications that depend on multiple micro services running in your environment. The services are deployed through containers, and the cluster management service takes care of monitoring, networking, and some security management tasks.

Serverless Computing

Both VMs and managed kubernetes clusters require some level of effort to configure and administer computing resources. Serverless computing is an approach that allows developers and application administrators to run their code in a computing environment that does not require setting up VMs or kubernetes clusters.

Google Cloud Platform has two serverless computing options: App Engine and Cloud Functions. App Engine is used for applications and containers that run for extended periods of time, such as a website backend, point-of-sale system, or custom business application. Cloud Functions is a platform for running code in response to an event, such as uploading a file or adding a message to a message queue. This serverless option works well when you need to respond to an event by running a short process coded in a function or by calling a longer-running application that might be running on a VM, managed cluster, or App Engine.

Storage

Public clouds offer a few types of storage services that are useful for a wide range of application requirements. These types include the following:

- Object storage
- File storage
- Block storage
- Caches

Enterprise users of cloud services will often use a combination of these services.

Object Storage

Object storage is a system that manages the use of storage in terms of objects or blobs. Usually these objects are files, but it is important to note that the files are not stored in a conventional file system. Objects are grouped into buckets. Each object is individually addressable, usually by a URL.

Object storage is not limited by the size of disks or solid-state drives (SSDs) attached to a server. Objects can be uploaded without concern for the amount of space available on a disk. Multiple copies of objects are stored to improve availability and durability. In some cases, copies of objects may be stored in different regions to ensure availability even if a region becomes inaccessible.

Another advantage of object storage is that it is serverless. There is no need to create VMs and attach storage to them. Google Cloud Platform's object storage, called Cloud Storage, is accessible from servers running in GCP as well as from other devices with Internet access.

Access controls can be applied at the object level. This allows users of cloud storage to control which users can access and update objects.

File Storage

File storage services provide a hierarchical storage system for files. File systems storage provides network shared file systems. Google Cloud Platform has a file storage service called Cloud Filestore, which is based on the Network File System (NFS) storage system.

File storage is suitable for applications that require operating system–like file access to files. The file storage system decouples the file system from specific VMs. The file system, its directories, and its files exist independent of VMs or applications that may access those files.

Block Storage

Block storage uses a fixed-size data structure called a *block* to organize data. Block storage is commonly used in ephemeral and persistent disks attached to VMs. With a block storage system, you can install file systems on top of the block storage, or you can run applications that access blocks directly. Some relational databases can be designed to access blocks directly rather working through file systems.

In Linux file systems, 4KB is a common block size. Relational databases often write directly to blocks, but they often use larger sizes, such as 8KB or more.

Block storage is available on disks that are attached to VMs in Google Cloud Platform. Block storage can be either persistent or ephemeral. A persistent disk continues to exist and store data even if it is detached from a virtual server or the virtual server to which it is attached shuts down. Ephemeral disks exist and store data only as long as a VM is running. Ephemeral disks store operating system files and other files and data that are deleted when the VM is shut down. Persistent disks are used when you want data to exist on a block storage device independent of a VM. These disks are good options when you have data that you want available independent of the lifecycle of a VM, and support fast operating system– and file system–level access.

Object storage also keeps data independent of the lifecycle of a VM, but it does not support operating system– or file system–level access; you have to use higher-level protocols like HTTP to access objects. It takes longer to retrieve data from object storage than to retrieve it from block storage. You may need a combination of object storage and block storage to meet your application needs. Object storage can store large volumes of data that are copied to persistent disk when needed. This combination gives the advantage of large volumes of storage along with operating system– and file system–based access when needed.

Caches

Caches are in-memory data stores that maintain fast access to data. The time it takes to retrieve data is called *latency*. The latency of in-memory stores is designed to be submillisecond. To give you a comparison, here are some other latencies:

- Making a main memory reference takes 100 nanoseconds, or 0.1 microsecond
- Reading 4KB randomly from an SSD takes 150 microseconds
- Reading 1MB sequentially from memory takes 250 microseconds

- Reading 1MB sequentially from an SSD takes 1,000 microseconds, or 1 millisecond
- Reading 1MB sequentially from disk takes 20,000 microseconds, or 20 milliseconds

Here are some conversions for reference:

- 1,000 nanoseconds equal 1 microsecond.
- 1,000 microseconds equal 1 millisecond.
- 1,000 milliseconds equal 1 second.

These and other useful timing data are available at Jonas Bonér's "Latency Numbers Every Programmer Should Know" at https://gist.github.com/jboner/2841832.

Let's work through an example of reading 1MB of data. If you have the data stored in an in-memory cache, you can retrieve the data in 250 microseconds, or 0.25 millisecond If that same data is stored on an SSD, it will take four times as long to retrieve at 1 millisecond. If you retrieve the same data from a hard disk drive, you can expect to wait 20 milliseconds, or 80 times as long as reading from an in-memory cache.

Caches are quite helpful when you need to keep read latency to a minimum in your application. Of course, who doesn't love fast retrieval times? Why don't we always store our data in caches? There are three reasons.

- Memory is more expensive than SSD or hard disk drive (HDD) storage. It's not practical in many cases to have as much in-memory storage as persistent block storage on SSDs or HDDs.

- Caches are volatile; you lose the data stored in the cache when power is lost or the operating system is rebooted. You can store data in a cache for fast access, but it should never be used as the only data store keeping the data. Some form of persistent storage should be used to maintain a "system of truth," or a data store that always has the latest and most accurate version of the data.

- Caches can get out of synchronization with the system of truth. This can happen if the system of truth is updated but the new data is not written to the cache. When this happens, it can be difficult for an application that depends on the cache to detect the fact that data in the cache is invalid. If you decide to use a cache, be sure to design a cache update strategy that meets your requirements for consistency between the cache and the system of truth. This is such a challenging design problem that it has become memorialized in Phil Karlton's well-known quip, "There are only two hard things in computer science: cache invalidation and naming things." (See https://martinfowler.com/bliki/TwoHardThings.html for riffs on this rare example of computer science humor.)

 Real World Scenario

Improving Database Query Response Time

Users expect web applications to be highly responsive. If a page takes more than 2 to 3 seconds to load, the user experience can suffer. It is common to generate the content of a page using the results of a database query, such as looking up account information by customer ID. When a query is made to the database, the database engine will look up the data, which is usually on disk. The more users query the database the more queries it has to serve. Databases keep a queue for queries that need to be answered but can't be processed yet because the database is busy with other queries. This can cause longer latency response time, since the web application will have to wait for the database to return the query results.

One way to reduce latency is to reduce the time needed to read the data. In some cases, it helps to replace hard disk drives with faster SSD drives. However, if the volume of queries is high enough that the queue of queries is long even with SSDs, another option is to use a cache.

When query results are fetched, they are stored in the cache. The next time that information is needed, it is fetched from the cache instead of the database. This can reduce latency because data is fetched from memory, which is faster than disk. It also reduces the number of queries to the database, so queries that can't be answered by looking up data in the cache won't have to wait as long in the query queue before being processed.

Networking

When working in the cloud, you'll need to work with networking between your cloud resources and possibly with your on-premise systems.

When you have multiple VMs running in your cloud environment, you will likely need to manage IP addresses at some point. Each network-accessible device or service in your environment will need an IP address. In fact, devices within GCP can have both internal and external addresses. Internal addresses are accessible only to services in your internal GCP network. Your internal GCP network is defined as a virtual private cloud (VPC). External addresses are accessible from the Internet.

External IP addresses can be either static or ephemeral. Static addresses are assigned to a device for extended periods of time. Ephemeral external IP addresses are attached to VMs and released when the VM is stopped.

In addition to specifying IP addresses, you will often need to define firewall rules to control access to subnetworks and VMs in your VPC. For example, you may have a database server that you want to restrict access to so that only an application server can query the database. A firewall rule can be configured to limit inbound and outbound traffic to the IP address of the application server or load balancer in front of the application cluster.

You may need to share data and network access between an on-premise data center and your VPC. You can do this using one of several types of *peering*, which is the general term for linking distinct networks.

Specialized Services

Most public cloud providers offer specialized services that can be used as building blocks of applications or as part of a workflow for processing data. Common characteristics of specialized services are as follows:

- They are serverless; you do not need to configure servers or clusters.
- They provide a specific function, such as translating text or analyzing images.
- They provide an application programming interface (API) to access the functionality of the service.
- As with other cloud services, you are charged based on your use of the service.

These are some of the specialized services in Google Cloud Platform:

- AutoML, a machine learning service
- Cloud Natural Language, a service for analyzing text
- Cloud Vision for analyzing images
- Cloud Inference API, a service for computing correlations over time-series data

Specialized services encapsulate advanced computing capabilities and make them accessible to developers who are not experts in domains, such as natural language processing and machine learning. Expect to see more specialized services added to Google Cloud Platform.

Cloud Computing vs. Data Center Computing

Although it may seem that running VMs in the cloud is not much different from running them in your data center, there are significant differences between operating IT environments in the cloud and an on-premise or colocated data center.

Rent Instead of Own Resources

Corporate data centers are filled with servers, disk arrays, and networking equipment. This equipment is often owned or leased for extended periods by the company, a model that requires companies to either spend a significant amount of money up front to purchase equipment or commit to a long-term lease for the equipment. This approach works well when an organization can accurately predict the number of servers and other equipment it will need for an extended period and it can utilize that equipment consistently.

The model does not work as well when companies have to plan for peak capacity that is significantly higher than the average workload. For example, a retailer may have an average load that requires a cluster of 20 servers but during the holiday season the workload increases to the point where 80 servers are needed. The company could purchase 80 servers and let 60 idle for most of the year to have resources to accommodate peak capacity. Alternatively, it could purchase or lease fewer servers and tolerate the loss in business that would occur when its compute resources can't keep up with demand. Neither is an appealing option.

Public clouds offer an alternative of short-term rental of compute capacity. The retailer, for example, could run VMs in the cloud during peak periods in addition to its on-premise servers. This gives the retailer access to the servers it needs when it needs them without having to pay for them when they are not needed.

The unit cost of running servers in the cloud may be higher than that of running the equivalent server in the data center, but the total cost of on-premise and short-term in the cloud mix of servers may still be significantly less than the cost of purchasing or leasing for peak capacity and leaving resources idle.

Pay-as-You-Go-for-What-You-Use Model

Related to the short-term rental model of cloud computing is the pay-as-you-go model. When you run a virtual server in the cloud, you will typically pay for a minimum period, such as 10 minutes, and then pay per minute used thereafter. The unit cost per minute will vary depending on the characteristics of the server. Servers with more CPUs and memory will cost more than servers with fewer CPUs and less memory.

It is important for cloud engineers to understand the pricing model of their cloud provider. It is easy to run up a large bill for servers and storage if you are not monitoring your usage. In fact, some cloud customers find that running applications in the cloud can be more expensive than running them on-premise.

Elastic Resource Allocation

Another key differentiator between on-premise and public cloud computing is the ability to add and remove compute and storage resources on short notice. In the cloud, you could start 20 servers in a matter of minutes. In an on-premise data center, it could take days or weeks to do the same thing if additional hardware must be provisioned.

Cloud providers design their data centers with extensive compute, storage, and network resources. They optimize their investment by efficiently renting these resources to customers. With sufficient data about customer use patterns, they can predict the capacity they need to meet customer demand. Since they have many customers, the variation in demand of any one customer has little effect on the overall use of their resources.

Extensive resources and the ability to quickly shift resources between customers enables public cloud providers to offer elastic resource allocation more efficiently than can be done in smaller data centers.

Specialized Services

Specialized services are, by their nature, not widely understood. Many developers understand how to develop user interfaces or query a database, but fewer have been exposed to the details of natural language processing or machine learning. Large enterprises may have the financial resources to develop in-house expertise in areas such as data science and machine vision, but many others don't.

By offering specialized services, cloud providers are bringing advanced capabilities to a wider audience of developers. Like investing in large amounts of hardware, public cloud vendors can invest in specialized services and recover their costs and make a profit because the specialized services are used by a large number of customers.

Exam Essentials

Understand different ways of delivering cloud computing resources.   Computing resources can be allocated as individual VMs or clusters of VMs that you manage. You can also use managed kubernetes cluster (GKE) that relieve you of some of the operational overhead of managing a kubernetes cluster. Serverless computing options relieve users of any server management. Instead, developers run their code in a containerized environment managed by the cloud provider or in a compute platform designed for short-running code. Developers and DevOps professionals have the most control over resources when they manage their own servers and clusters. Managed services and serverless options are good choices when you do not need control over the computing environment and will get more value from not having to manage compute resources.

Understand the different forms of cloud storage and when to use them.   There are four main categories of storage: object, file, block, and in-memory caches. Object storage is designed for highly reliable and durable storage of objects, such as images or data sets. Object storage has more limited functionality than file system–based storage systems. File system–based storage provides hierarchical directory storage for files and supports common operating system and file system functions. File system services provide network-accessible file systems that can be accessed by multiple servers. Block storage is used for storing data on disks. File systems and databases make use of block storage systems. Block storage is used with persistent storage devices, such as SSDs and HDDs. Caches are in-memory data stores used to minimize the latency of retrieving data. They do not provide persistent storage and should never be considered a "system of truth."

Understand the differences between running an IT environment on-premise or in the cloud. Running an IT environment in the cloud has several advantages, including short-term rental of resources, pay-as-you-go model, elastic resource allocation, and the ability to use specialized services. The unit cost of cloud resources, such as the cost per minute of a mid-tier server, may be higher in the cloud than on-premise. It is important to understand the cost model of your cloud provider so you can make decisions about the most efficient distribution of workload between cloud and on-premise resources.

Review Questions

1. What is the fundamental unit of computing in cloud computing?

   A. Physical server

   B. VM

   C. Block

   D. Subnet

2. If you use a cluster that is managed by a cloud provider, which of these will be managed for you by the cloud provider?

   A. Monitoring

   B. Networking

   C. Some security management tasks

   D. All of the above

3. You need serverless computing for file processing and running the backend of a website; which two products can you choose from Google Cloud Platform?

   A. Kubernetes Engine and Compute Engine

   B. App Engine and Cloud Functions

   C. Cloud Functions and Compute Engine

   D. Cloud Functions and Kubernetes Engine

4. You have been asked to design a storage system for a web application that allows users to upload large data files to be analyzed by a business intelligence workflow. The files should be stored in a high-availability storage system. File system functionality is not required. Which storage system in Google Cloud Platform should be used?

   A. Block storage

   B. Object storage

   C. Cache

   D. Network File System

5. All block storage systems use what block size?

   A. 4KB

   B. 8KB

   C. 16KB

   D. Block size can vary.

6. You have been asked to set up network security in a virtual private cloud. Your company wants to have multiple subnetworks and limit traffic between the subnetworks. Which network security control would you use to control the flow of traffic between subnets?

    A. Identity access management

    B. Router

    C. Firewall

    D. IP address table

7. When you create a machine learning service to identify text in an image, what type of servers should you choose to manage compute resources?

    A. VMs

    B. Clusters of VMs

    C. No servers; specialized services are serverless

    D. VMs running Linux only

8. Investing in servers for extended periods of time, such as committing to use servers for three to five years, works well when?

    A. A company is just starting up

    B. A company can accurately predict server need for an extended period of time

    C. A company has a fixed IT budget

    D. A company has a variable IT budget

9. Your company is based in X and will be running a virtual server for Y. What factor determines the unit per minute cost?

    A. The time of day the VM is run

    B. The characteristics of the server

    C. The application you run

    D. None of the above

10. You plan to use Cloud Vision to analyze images and extract text seen in the image. You plan to process between 1,000 and 2,500 images per hour. How many VMs should you allocate to meet peak demand?

    A. 1

    B. 10

    C. 25

    D. None; Cloud Vision is a serverless service.

11. You have to run a number of services to support an application. Which of the following is a good deployment model?

    A. Run on a large, single VM

    B. Use containers in a managed cluster

    C. Use two large VMs, making one of them read only

    D. Use a small VM for all services and increase the size of the VM when CPU utilization exceeds 90 percent

12. You have created a VM. Which of the following system administration operations are you allowed to perform on it?

    A. Configure the file system

    B. Patch operating system software

    C. Change file and directory permissions

    D. All of the above

13. Cloud Filestore is based on what file system technology?

    A. Network File System (NFS)

    B. XFS

    C. EXT4

    D. ReiserFS

14. When setting up a network in GCP, your network the resources in it are treated as what?

    A. Virtual private cloud

    B. Subdomain

    C. Cluster

    D. None of the above

Not a sentence

15. You need to store data for X and therefore you are using a cache for Y. How will the cache affect data retrieval?

    A. A cache improves the execution of client-side JavaScript.

    B. A cache will continue to store data even if power is lost, improving availability.

    C. Caches can get out of sync with the system of truth.

    D. Using a cache will reduce latency, since retrieving from a cache is faster than retrieving from SSDs or HDDs.

16. Why can cloud providers offer elastic resource allocation?

    A. Cloud providers can take resources from lower-priority customers and give them to higher-priority customers.

    B. Extensive resources and the ability to quickly shift resources between customers enables public cloud providers to offer elastic resource allocation more efficiently than can be done in smaller data centers.

    C. They charge more the more resources you use.

    D. They don't.

17. What is not a characteristic of specialized services in Google Cloud Platform?

    A. They are serverless; you do not need to configure servers or clusters.

    B. They provide a specific function, such as translating text or analyzing images.

    C. They require monitoring by the user.

    D. They provide an API to access the functionality of the service.

18. Your client's transactions must access a drive attached to a VM that allows for random access to parts of files. What kind of storage does the attached drive provide?

    A. Object storage

    B. Block storage

    C. NoSQL storage

    D. Only SSD storage

19. You are deploying a new relational database to support a web application. Which type of storage system would you use to store data files of the database?

    A. Object storage

    B. Data storage

    C. Block storage

    D. Cache

20. A user prefers services that require minimal setup; why would you recommend Cloud Storage, App Engine, and Cloud Functions?

    A. They are charged only by time.

    B. They are serverless.

    C. They require a user to configure VMs.

    D. They can only run applications written in Go.

Chapter

2

Google Cloud Computing Services

THIS CHAPTER COVERS THE FOLLOWING OBJECTIVES OF THE GOOGLE ASSOCIATE CLOUD ENGINEER CERTIFICATION EXAM:

- ✓ 2.2 Planning and configuring compute resources, including selecting appropriate compute choices for a given workload

- ✓ 3.4 Deploying and implementing data solutions, including initializing data systems with products

Google Cloud Platform (GCP) is made up of almost 40 services that meet a variety of computing, storage, and networking needs. This chapter provides an overview of the most important GCP services and describes some important use cases for these services.

Computing Components of Google Cloud Platform

Google Cloud Platform is a suite of cloud computing services that includes compute, storage, and networking services designed to meet the needs of a wide range of cloud computing customers. Small businesses may be attracted to virtual machines (VMs) and storage services. Large businesses and other sizable organizations may be more interested in access to highly scalable clusters of VMs, a variety of relational and NoSQL databases, specialized networking services, and advanced artificial intelligence and machine learning capabilities.

This chapter provides an overview of many of GCP's services. The breadth of services available in the GCP continues to grow. By the time you read this, Google may be offering additional services. Most of the services can be grouped into several core categories.

- Computing resources
- Storage resources
- Databases
- Networking services
- Identity management and security
- Development tools
- Management tools
- Specialized services

A Google-certified Associate Cloud Engineer should be familiar with the services in each category, how they are used, and the advantages and disadvantages of the various services in each category.

Computing Resources

Public cloud services provide a range computing services options. At one end of the spectrum, customers can create and manage VMs themselves. This model gives the cloud user the greatest control of all the computing services. Users can choose the operating system to run, which packages to install, and when to back up and perform other maintenance operations. This type of computing service is typically referred to as infrastructure as a service (IaaS).

An alternative model is called platform as a service (PaaS), which provides a runtime environment to execute applications without the need to manage underlying servers, networks, and storage systems.

GCP's IaaS computing product is called Compute Engine, and the PaaS offerings are App Engine and Cloud Functions. In addition, Google offers Kubernetes Engine, which is a service for managing containers in a cluster; this type of service is an increasingly popular alternative to managing individual sets of VMs.

Compute Engine

Compute Engine is a service that allows users to create VMs, attach persistent storage to those VMs, and make use of other GCP services, such as Cloud Storage.

VMs are abstractions of physical servers. They are essentially programs that emulate physical servers and provide CPU, memory, storage, and other services that you would find if you ran your favorite operating system on a server under your desk or in a data center. VMs run within a low-level service called a *hypervisor*. GCP uses a security hardened version of the KVM hypervisor. KVM stands for Kernel Virtual Machine and provides virtualization on Linux systems running on x86 hardware.

Hypervisors run on an operating system like Linux or Windows Server. Hypervisors can run multiple operating systems, referred to as *guest operating systems*, while keeping the activities of each isolated from other guest operating systems. Each instance of an executing guest operating system is a VM instance. Figure 2.1 shows the logical organization of VM instances running on a physical server.

FIGURE 2.1   VM instances running within a hypervisor

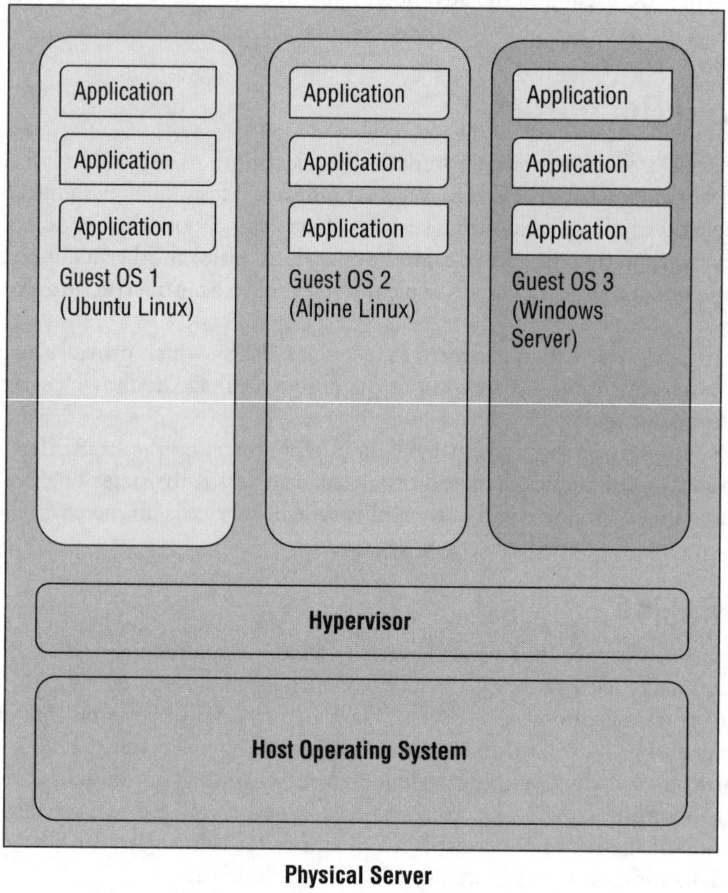

Physical Server

VMs come in a range of predefined sizes, but you can also create a customized configuration. When you create an instance, you can specify a number of parameters, including the following:

- The operating system
- Size of persistent storage
- Adding graphical processing units (GPUs) for compute-intensive operations like machine learning
- Making the VM preemptible

The last option, making a VM preemptible, means you may be charged significantly less for the VM than normal (around 80 percent less), but your VM could be shut down at any time by Google. It will frequently be shut down if the preemptible VM has run for at least 24 hours.

Chapter 4 will introduce the details of managing Compute Engine VMs. To explore Compute Engine, log into the Google Cloud Console, navigate to the main menu on the left, and select Compute Engine.

Kubernetes Engine

Kubernetes Engine is designed to allow users to easily run containerized applications on a cluster of servers. Containers are often compared to VMs because they are each used for isolating computing processing and resources. Containers take a different approach than VMs for isolating computing processes.

As mentioned, a VM runs a guest operating system on a physical server. The physical server runs an operating system as well, along with a hypervisor. Another approach to isolating computing resources is to use features of the host operating system to isolate processes and resources. With this approach, there is no need for a hypervisor; the host operating system maintains isolation. Instead, a container manager is used. That is, a single container manager coordinates containers running on the server. No additional, or guest, operating systems run on top of the container manager. Instead, containers make use of host operating system functionality, while the operating system and container manager ensure isolation between the running containers. Figure 2.2 shows the logical structure of containers.

FIGURE 2.2   Containers running on a physical server

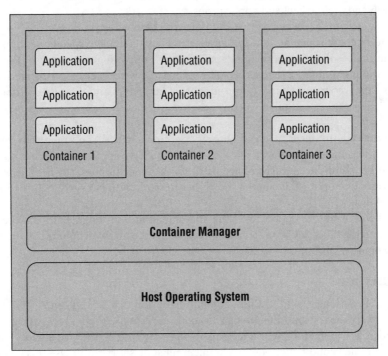

Kubernetes Engine is a GCP product that allows users to describe the compute, storage, and memory resources they'd like to run their services. Kubernetes Engine then provisions the underlying resources. It's easy to add and remove resources from a Kubernetes cluster using a command-line interface or a graphical user interface.

In addition, Kubernetes monitors the health of servers in the cluster and automatically repairs problems, such as failed servers. Kubernetes Engine also supports autoscaling, so if the load on your applications increases, Kubernetes Engine will allocate additional resources.

Chapter 7 will describe the details of planning and managing Kubernetes Engine. To explore Kubernetes Engine, log into the Google Cloud Console, navigate to the main menu on the left, and select Kubernetes Engine.

App Engine

App Engine is GCP's compute PaaS offering. With App Engine, developers and application administrators don't need to concern themselves with configuring VMs or specifying Kubernetes clusters. Instead, developers create applications in a popular programming language such as Java, Go, Python, or Node.js and deploy that code to a serverless application environment.

App Engine manages the underlying computing and network infrastructure. There is no need to configure VMs or harden networks to protect your application. App Engine is well suited for web and mobile backend applications.

App Engine is available in two types: standard and flexible.

In the standard environment, you run applications in a language-specific sandbox, so your application is isolated from the underlying server's operating system as well as from other applications running on that server. The standard environment is well suited to applications that are written in one of the supported languages and do not need operating system packages or other compiled software that would have to be installed along with the application code.

In the flexible environment, you run Docker containers in the App Engine environment. The flexible environment works well in cases where you have application code but also need libraries or other third-party software installed. As the name implies, the flexible environment gives you more options, including the ability to work with background processes and write to local disk.

Chapter 9 will introduce details for using and managing App Engine. To explore App Engine, log into the Google Cloud Console, navigate to the main menu on the left, and select App Engine.

Cloud Functions

Google Cloud Functions is a lightweight computing option that is well suited to event-driven processing. Cloud Functions runs code in response to an event, like a file being uploaded to Cloud Storage or a message being written to a message queue. The code that executes in the Cloud Functions environment must be short-running—this computing service is not designed to execute long-running code. If you need to support long-running applications or jobs, consider Compute Engine, Kubernetes Engine, or App Engine.

Cloud Functions is often used to call other services, such as third-party application programming interfaces (APIs) or other GCP services, like a natural language translation service.

Like App Engine, Cloud Functions is a serverless product. Users only need to supply code; they do not need to configure VMs or create containers. Cloud Functions will automatically scale as load increases.

In addition to the four main computing products, GCP offers a number of storage resources.

Chapter 10 will describe the details of using and managing Cloud Functions. To explore Cloud Functions, log into the Google Cloud Console, navigate to the main menu on the left, and select Cloud Functions.

Storage Components of Google Cloud Platform

Applications and services that run in the cloud have to meet a wide range of requirements when it comes to storage.

Storage Resources

Sometimes an application needs fast read and write times for moderate amounts of data. Other times, a business application may need access to petabytes of archival storage but can tolerate minutes and even hours to retrieve a document. GCP has several storage resources for storing objects and files.

Cloud Storage

Cloud Storage is GCP's object storage system. Objects can be any type of file or binary large object. Objects are organized into buckets, which are analogous to directories in a file system. It is important to remember that Cloud Storage is not a file system. It is a service that receives, stores, and retrieves files or objects from a distributed storage system. Cloud Storage is not part of a VM in the way an attached persistent disk is. Cloud Storage is accessible from VM (or any other network device with appropriate privileges) and so complements file systems on persistent disks.

Each stored object is uniquely addressable by a URL. For example, a .pdf version of this chapter, called chapter1.pdf, that is stored in a bucket named *ace-certification-exam-prep* would be addressable as follows:

```
https://storage.cloud.google.com/ace-certification-exam-prep/chapter1.pdf
```

GCP users and others can be granted permission to read and write objects to a bucket. Often, an application will be granted privileges through IAM roles to enable the application to read and write to buckets.

Cloud Storage is useful for storing objects that are treated as single units of data. For example, an image file is a good candidate for object storage. Images are generally read and written all at once. There is rarely a need to retrieve only a portion of the image. In general, if you write or retrieve an object all at once and you need to store it independently of servers that may or may not be running at any time, then Cloud Storage is a good option.

There are different classes of cloud storage. Regional storage keeps copies of objects in a single Google Cloud *region*. Regions are distinct geographic areas that can have multiple *zones*, or deployment areas. A zone is considered a single failure domain, which means that if all instances of your application are running in a zone and there is a failure, then all instances of your application will be inaccessible. Regional storage is well suited for applications that run in the same region and need low latency access to objects in Cloud Storage.

Cloud Storage has some useful advanced features, such as support for multiple regions. This provides for storing replicas of objects in multiple Google Cloud regions, which is important for high availability, durability, and low latency.

 Real World Scenario

Real-World Scenario

If there was an outage in region us-east1 and your objects were stored only in that region, then you would not be able to access those objects during the outage. However, if you enabled multiregion storage, then your objects stored in us-east1 would be stored in another region, such as us-west1, as well.

In addition to high availability and durability, multiregion storage allows for faster access to data when users or applications are distributed across regions.

Sometimes data needs to be kept for extended periods of time but is rarely accessed. In those cases, nearline storage is a good option because it costs less than regional or multiregional storage and is optimized for infrequent access.

The cold storage class is low-cost archival storage designed for high durability and infrequent access. This class of storage is suitable for data that is accessed less than once per year.

A useful feature of Cloud Storage is the set of lifecycle management policies that can automatically manage objects based on policies you define. For example, you could define a policy that moves all objects more than 60 days old in a bucket to nearline storage or deletes any object in a coldline storage bucket that is older than five years.

Persistent Disk

Persistent disks are storage service that are attached to VMs in Compute Engine or Kubernetes Engine. Persistent disks provide block storage on solid-state drives (SSDs) and hard disk drives (HDDs). SSDs are often used for low-latency applications where persistent disk performance is important. SSDs cost more than HDDs, so applications that require large amounts of persistent disk storage but can tolerate longer read and write times can use HDDs to meet their storage requirements.

An advantage of persistent disks on the Google Cloud Platform is that these disks support multiple readers without a degradation in performance. This allows for multiple instances to read a single copy of data. Disks can also be resized as needed while in use without the need to restart your VMs.

Persistent disks can be up to 64TB in size using either SSDs or HDDs.

Cloud Storage for Firebase

Mobile app developers may find Cloud Storage for Firebase to be the best combination of cloud object storage and the ability to support uploads and downloads from mobile devices with sometimes unreliable network connections.

The Cloud Storage for Firebase API is designed to provide secure transmission as well as robust recovery mechanisms to handle potentially problematic network quality. Once files, like photos or music recordings, are uploaded into Cloud Storage, you can access those files through the Cloud Storage command-line interface and software development kits (SDKs).

Cloud Filestore

Sometimes, developers need to have access to a file system housed on network-attached storage. For these use cases, the Cloud Filestore service provides a shared file system for use with Compute Engine and Kubernetes Engine.

Filestore can provide high numbers of input-output operations per second (IOPS) as well as variable storage capacity. File system administrators can configure Cloud Filestore to meet their specific IOPS and capacity requirements.

Filestore implements the Network File System (NFS) protocol so system administrators can easily mount shared file systems on virtual servers.

Storage systems like the ones just described are used to store coarse-grained objects, like files. When data is more finely structured and has to be retrieved using query languages that describe the subset of data to return, then it is best to use a database management system.

Chapter 11 describes details and guidance for planning storage services. To explore storage options, log into the Google Cloud Console, navigate to the main menu on the left, and select Storage or Filestore.

Databases

GCP provides several database options. Some are relational databases, and some are NoSQL databases. Some are serverless and others require users to manage clusters of servers. Some provide support for atomic transactions, and others are better suited for applications with less stringent consistency and transaction requirements. GCP users must understand their application requirements before choosing a service, and this is especially important when choosing a database, which often provides core storage services in the application stack.

Cloud SQL

Cloud SQL is GCP's managed relational database service that allows users to set up MySQL or PostgreSQL databases on VMs without having to attend to database administration tasks, such as backing up databases or patching database software. Cloud SQL is available in a number of configurations:

- First-generation MySQL databases use MySQL 5.5 or 5.6 and can have up to 16GB of RAM and 500GB of data storage.

- Second-generation MySQL databases use MySQL 5.6 or 5.7 and can have up to 416GB of RAM along with 10TB of data storage. Second-generation MySQL databases can be configured to automatically add storage as needed.

- PostgreSQL 9.6 runs on the second-generation platform and can be configured with up to 64 CPUs, 416GB of RAM, and up to 10TB of storage. Cloud SQL PostgreSQL also supports common extensions such as PostGIS, cubes for analytic processing, and hstore for storing key-value pairs in a single PostgreSQL value.

This database service includes management of replication and allows for automatic failover, providing for highly available databases.

Relational databases are well suited to applications with relatively consistent data structure requirements. For example, a banking database may track account numbers, customer names, addresses, and so on. Since virtually all records in the database will need the same information, this application is a good fit for a relational database.

Cloud Bigtable

Cloud Bigtable is designed for petabyte-scale applications that can manage up to billions of rows and thousands of columns. It is based on a NoSQL model known as a *wide-column data model*, and unlike Cloud SQL that supports relational databases. Bigtable is suited for applications that require low-latency write and read operations. It is designed to support millions of operations per second.

Bigtable integrates with other Google Cloud services, such as Cloud Storage, Cloud Pub/Sub, Cloud Dataflow, and Cloud Dataproc. It also supports the Hbase API, which is an API for data access in the Hadoop big data ecosystem. Bigtable also integrates with open source tools for data processing, graph analysis, and time-series analysis.

Cloud Spanner

Cloud Spanner is Google's globally distributed relational database that combines the key benefits of relational databases, such as strong consistency and transactions, with the ability to scale horizontally like a NoSQL database. Spanner is a high availability database with a 99.999 percent availability Service Level Agreements (SLA), making it a good option for enterprise applications that demand scalable, highly available relational database services.

Cloud Spanner also has enterprise-grade security with encryption at rest and encryption in transit, along with identity-based access controls.

Cloud Spanner supports ANSI 2011 standard SQL.

Cloud Datastore

Cloud Datastore is a NoSQL document database. This kind of database uses the concept of a document, or collection of key-value pairs, as the basic building block. Documents allow for flexible schemas. For example, a document about a book may have key-value pairs listing author, title, and date of publication. Some books may also have information about companion websites and translations into other languages. The set of keys that may be included does not have to be defined prior to use in document databases. This is especially helpful when applications must accommodate a range of attributes, some of which may not be known at design time.

Cloud Datastore is accessed via a REST API that can be used from applications running in Compute Engine, Kubernetes Engine, or App Engine. This database will scale automatically based on load. It will also *shard*, or partition, data as needed to maintain performance. Since Cloud Datastore is a managed service, it takes care of replication, backups, and other database administration tasks.

Although it is a NoSQL database, Cloud Datastore supports transactions, indexes, and SQL-like queries.

Cloud Datastore is well suited to applications that demand high scalability and structured data and do not always need strong consistency when reading data. Product catalogs, user profiles, and user navigation history are examples of the kinds of applications that use Cloud Datastore.

Cloud Memorystore

Cloud Memorystore is an in-memory cache service. Other databases offered in GCP are designed to store large volumes of data and support complex queries, but Cloud Memorystore is a managed Redis service for caching frequently used data in memory. Caches like this are used to reduce the time needed to read data into an application. Cloud Memorystore is designed to provide submillisecond access to data.

As a managed service, Cloud Memorystore allows users to specify the size of a cache while leaving administration tasks to Google. GCP ensures high availability, patching, and automatic failover so users don't have to.

Cloud Firestore

Cloud Firestore is another GCP-managed NoSQL database service designed as a backend for highly scalable web and mobile applications. A distinguishing feature of Cloud Firestore is its client libraries that provide offline support, synchronization, and other features for managing data across mobile devices, IoT devices, and backend data stores. For example, applications on mobile devices can be updated in real time as data in the backend changes.

Cloud Firebase includes a Datastore mode, which enables applications written for Datastore to work with Cloud Firebase as well. When running in Native mode, Cloud Firestore provides real-time data synchronization and offline support.

Cloud Firestore is currently in beta release.

Chapter 12 delves into details of how to create various types of databases, as well as how to load, delete, and query data. Each of the databases can be accessed from the main menu of the Google Cloud Console. From there you can begin to explore how each works and begin to see the differences.

Networking Components of Google Cloud Platform

In this section, we will review the major networking components. Details on setting up networks and managing them are described in Chapters 14 and 15.

Networking Services

Google Cloud Platform provides a number of networking services designed to allow users to configure virtual networks within Google's global network infrastructure, link on-premise data centers to Google's network, optimize content delivery, and protect your cloud resources using network security services.

Virtual Private Cloud

When an enterprise operates its own data center, it controls what is physically located in that data center and connected to its network. Its infrastructure is physically isolated from those of other organizations running in other data centers. When an organization moves to a public cloud, it shares infrastructure with other customers of that public cloud. Although multiple enterprises will use the same cloud infrastructure, each enterprise can logically isolate its cloud resources by creating a virtual private cloud (VPC).

A distinguishing feature of GPC is that a VPC can span the globe without relying on the public Internet. Traffic from any server on a VPC can be securely routed through the Google global network to any other point on that network. Another advantage of the Google network structure is that your backend servers can access Google services, such as machine learning or IoT services, without creating a public IP address for backend servers.

VPCs in the Google Cloud can be linked to on-premise virtual private networks using Internet Protocol Security (IPSec).

Although a VPC is global, enterprises can use separate projects and billing accounts to manage different departments or groups within the organization. Firewalls can be used to restrict access to resources on a VPC as well.

Cloud Load Balancing

Google provides global load balancing to distribute workloads across your cloud infrastructure. Using a single multicast IP address, Cloud Load Balancing can distribute the workload within and across regions, adapt to failed or degraded servers, and autoscale your compute resources to accommodate changes in workload. Cloud Load Balancing also supports internal load balancing, so no IP addresses need to be exposed to the Internet to get the advantages of load balancing.

Cloud Load Balancing is a software service that can load-balance HTTP, HTTPS, TCP/ SSL, and UDP traffic.

Cloud Armor

Services exposed to the Internet can become targets of distributed denial-of-service (DDoS) attacks. Cloud Armor is a Google network security service that builds on the Global HTTP(s) Load Balancing service. Cloud Armor features include the following:

- Ability to allow or restrict access based on IP address

- Predefined rules to counter cross-site scripting attacks

- Ability to counter SQL injection attacks

- Ability to define rules at both level 3 (network) and level 7 (application)

- Allows and restricts access based on the geolocation of incoming traffic

Cloud CDN

With content delivery networks (CDNs), users anywhere can request content from systems distributed in various regions. CDNs enable low-latency response to these requests by caching content on a set of endpoints across the globe. Google currently has more than 90 CDN endpoints that are managed as a global resource, so there is no need to maintain region-specific configurations.

CDNs are especially important for sites with large amounts of static content and a global audience. News sites, for example, could use the Cloud CDN service to ensure fast response to requests from any point in the world.

Cloud Interconnect

Cloud Interconnect is a set of GCP services for connecting your existing networks to the Google network. Cloud Interconnect offers two types of connections: interconnects and peering.

Interconnect with direct access to networks uses the Address Allocation for Private Internets standard (RFC 1918) to connect to devices in your VPC. A direct network connection is maintained between an on-premise or hosted data center and one of Google's colocation facilities, which are located in North America, South America, Europe, Asia, and Australia. Alternatively, if an organization cannot achieve a direct interconnect with a Google facility, it could use Partner Interconnect. This service depends on a third-party network provider to provide connectivity between the company's data center and a Google facility.

For organizations that do not require the bandwidth of a direct or peered interconnect, Google offers VPN services that enable traffic to transmit between data centers and Google facilities using the public Internet.

Cloud DNS

Cloud DNS is a domain name service provided in GCP. Cloud DNS is a high availability, low-latency service for mapping from domain names, such as example.com, to IP addresses, such as 74.120.28.18.

Cloud DNS is designed to automatically scale so customers can have thousands and millions of addresses without concern for scaling the underlying infrastructure. Cloud DNS also provides for private zones that allow you to create custom names for your VMs if you need those.

Identity Management

GCP's Cloud Identity and Access Management (IAM) service enables customers to define fine-grained access controls on resources in the cloud. IAM uses the concepts of users, roles, and privileges.

Identities are abstractions about users of services, such as a human user. After an identity is authenticated by logging in or some other mechanism, the authenticated user can access resources and perform operations based on the privileges granted to that identity. For example, a user may have the privilege to create a bucket in Cloud Storage or delete a VM running in Compute Engine.

Users often need similar sets of permissions. Someone who has the ability to create a VM will likely want to be able to modify or delete those VMs. Groups of related permissions can be bundled into roles. Roles are sets of permissions that can be assigned to an identity.

As a Google Certified Associate Cloud Engineer, you will become familiar with identities, roles, and permissions and how to administer them across organizations and projects.

You can find identity management tools under the IAM and admin menu in the Google Cloud Console. Chapter 17 provides details on identity, roles, and best practices for their management.

Development Tools

Google Cloud Platform is an excellent choice for developers and software engineers because of the easy access to infrastructure and data management services, but also for the tools it supports.

Cloud SDK is a command-line interface for managing GCP resources, including VMs, disk storage, network firewalls, and virtually any other resource you might deploy in GCP. In addition to a command-line interface, Cloud SDK has client libraries for Java, Python, Node.js, Ruby, GO, .NET, and PHP.

GCP also supports deploying applications to containers with Container Registry, Cloud Build, and Cloud Source Repositories.

Google has also developed plug-ins to make it easy to work with popular development tools. These include the following:

- Cloud Tools for IntelliJ
- Cloud Tools for PowerShell
- Cloud Tools for Visual Studio
- Cloud Tools for Eclipse
- App Engine Gradle Plugin
- App Engine Maven Plugin

Of course, applications move from development to production deployment, and GCP follows that flow with additional management tools to help monitor and maintain applications after they are deployed.

Additional Components of Google Cloud Platform

Management tools are designed for DevOps professionals who are responsible for ensuring the reliability, availability, and scalability of applications.

Management Tools

The following are some of the most important tools in the management tools category:

Stackdriver   This is a service that collects metrics, logs, and event data from applications and infrastructure and integrates the data so DevOps engineers can monitor, assess, and diagnose operational problems.

Monitoring   This extends the capabilities of Stackdriver by collecting performance data from GCP, AWS resources, and application instrumentation, including popular open source systems like NGINX, Cassandra, and Elasticsearch.

Logging   This service enables users to store and analyze and alert on log data from both GCP and AWS logs.

Error Reporting   This aggregates application crash information for display in a centralized interface.

Trace   This is a distributed tracing service that captures latency data about an application to help identify performance problem areas.

Debugger   This enables developers to inspect the state of executing code, inject commands, and view call stack variables.

Profiler   This is used to collect CPU and memory utilization information across the call hierarchy of an application. Profiler uses statistical sampling to minimize the impact of profiling on application performance.

The combination of management tools provides insights into applications as they run in production, enabling more effective monitoring and analysis of operational systems.

Specialized Services

In addition to IaaS and PaaS offerings, GCP has specialized services for APIs, data analytics, and machine learning.

Apigee API Platform

The Apigee API platform is a management service for GCP customers providing API access to their applications. The Apigee platform allows developers to deploy, monitor, and secure their APIs. It also generates API proxies based on the Open API Specification.

It is difficult to predict load on an API, and sometimes spikes in use can occur. For those times, the Apigee API platform provides routing and rate-limiting based on policies customers can define.

APIs can be authenticated using either OAuth 2.0 or SAML. Data is encrypted both in transit and at rest in the Apigee API platform.

Data Analytics

GCP has a number of services designed for analyzing big data in batch and streaming modes. Some of the most important tools in this set of services include the following:

- BigQuery, a petabyte-scale analytics database service for data warehousing
- Cloud Dataflow, a framework for defining batch and stream processing pipelines
- Cloud Dataproc, a managed Hadoop and Spark service
- Cloud Dataprep, a service that allows analysts to explore and prepare data for analysis

Often, data analytics and data warehousing projects use several of these services together.

AI and Machine Learning

Google is a leader in AI and machine learning, so it is no surprise that GCP includes several AI services. Specialized services in this area include the following:

Cloud AutoML   This is a tool that allows developers without machine learning experience to develop machine learning models.

Cloud Machine Learning Engine   This is a platform for building and deploying scalable machine learning systems to production.

Cloud Natural Language Processing   This tool is for analyzing human languages and extracting information from text.

Cloud Vision   This is an image analysis platform for annotating images with metadata, extracting text, or filtering content.

Exam Essentials

Understand the differences between Compute Engine, Kubernetes Engine, App Engine, and Cloud Functions.   Compute Engine is Google's VM service. Users can choose CPUs, memory, persistent disks, and operating systems. They can further customize a VM by adding graphics processing units for compute-intensive operations. VMs are managed individually or in groups of similar servers.

Kubernetes Engine manages groups of virtual servers and applications that run in containers. Containers are lighter weight than VMs. Kubernetes is called an *orchestration service* because it distributes containers across clusters, monitors cluster health, and scales as proscribed by configurations.

App Engine is Google's PaaS. Developers can run their code in a language-specific sandbox when using the standard environment or in a container when using the flexible environment. App Engine is a serverless service, so customers do not need to specify VM configurations or manage servers.

Cloud Functions is a serverless service that is designed to execute short-running code that responds to events, such as file uploads or messages being published to a message queue. Functions may be written in Node.js or Python.

Understand what is meant by serverless.   Serverless means customers using a service do not need to configure, monitor, or maintain the computing resources underlying the service. It does not mean there are no servers involved—there are always physical servers that run applications, functions, and other software. Serverless only refers to not needing to manage those underlying resources.

Understand the difference between object and file storage.   Object stores are used to store and access file-based resources. These objects are referenced by a unique identifier, such as a URL. Object stores do not provide block or file system services, so they are not suitable for database storage. Cloud Storage is GCP's object storage service.

File storage supports block-based access to files. Files are organized into directories and subdirectories. Google's Filestore is based on the NFS.

Know the different kinds of databases.   Databases are broadly divided into relational and NoSQL databases.

Relational databases support transactions, strong consistency, and the SQL query languages. Relational databases have been traditionally difficult to horizontally scale. Cloud Spanner is a global relational database that provides the advantages of relational databases with the scalability previously found only in NoSQL databases.

NoSQL databases are designed to be horizontally scalable. Other features, such as strong consistency and support for standard SQL, are often sacrificed to achieve scalability and low-latency query responses. NoSQL databases may be key-value stores like Cloud Memorystore, document databases like Cloud Datastore, or wide-column databases such as Cloud Bigtable.

Understand virtual private clouds.   A VPC is a logical isolation of an organization's cloud resources within a public cloud. In GCP, VPCs are global; they are not restricted to a single zone or region. All traffic between GCP services can be transmitted over the Google network without the need to send traffic over the public Internet.

Understand load balancing.   Load balancing is the process of distributing a workload across a group of servers. Load balancers can route workload based on network-level or application-level rules. GCP load balancers can distribute workloads globally.

Understand developer and management tools.   Developer tools support common workflows in software engineering, including using version control for software, building containers to run applications and services, and making containers available to other developers and orchestration systems, such as Kubernetes Engine.

Management tools, such as Stackdriver, Monitoring, and Logging, are designed to provide systems administration information to developers and operators who are responsible for ensuring applications are available and operating as expected.

Know the types of specialized services offered by Google Cloud Platform.   GCP includes a growing list of specialized services for data analytics, and AI and machine learning.

Know the main differences between on-premises and public cloud computing.   On-premise computing is computing, storage, networking, and related services that occur on infrastructure managed by a company or organization for its own use. Hardware may be located literally on the premises in a company building or in a third-party colocation facility. Colocation facilities provide power, cooling, and physical security, but the customers of the colocation facility are responsible for all the setup and management of the infrastructure.

Public cloud computing uses infrastructure and services provided by a cloud provider such as Google, AWS, or Microsoft. The cloud provider maintains all physical hardware and facilities. It provides a mix of services, such as VMs that are configured and maintained by customers and serverless offerings that enable customers to focus on application development-while the cloud provider takes on more responsibility for maintaining the underlying compute infrastructure.

Review Questions

You can find the answers in the Appendix.

1. You are planning to deploy a SaaS application for customers in North America, Europe, and Asia. To maintain scalability, you will need to distribute workload across servers in multiple regions. Which GCP service would you use to implement the workload distribution?

   A. Cloud DNS

   B. Cloud Spanner

   C. Cloud Load Balancing

   D. Cloud CDN

2. You have decided to deploy a set of microservices using containers. You could install and manage Docker on Compute Engine instances, but you'd rather have GCP provide some container management services. Which two GCP services allow you to run containers in a managed service?

   A. App Engine standard environment and App Engine flexible environment

   B. Kubernetes Engine and App Engine standard environment

   C. Kubernetes Engine and App Engine flexible environment

   D. App Engine standard environment and Cloud Functions

3. Why would an API developer want to use the Apigee API platform?

   A. To get the benefits of routing and rate-limiting

   B. Authentication services

   C. Version control of code

   D. A and B

   E. All of the above

4. You are deploying an API to the public Internet and are concerned that your service will be subject to DDoS attacks. Which GCP service should you consider to protect your API?

   A. Cloud Armor

   B. Cloud CDN

   C. Cloud IAM

   D. VPCs

5. You have an application that uses a Pub/Sub message queue to maintain a list of tasks that are to be processed by another application. The application that consumes messages from the Pub/Sub queue removes the message only after completing the task. It takes approximately 10 seconds to complete a task. It is not a problem if two or more VMs perform the same task. What is a cost-effective configuration for processing this workload?

   A. Use preemptible VMs

   B. Use standard VMs

   C. Use DataProc

   D. Use Spanner

6. Your department is deploying an application that has a database backend. You are concerned about the read load on the database server and want to have data available in memory to reduce the time to respond to queries and to reduce the load on the database server. Which GCP service would you use to keep data in memory?

   A. Cloud SQL

   B. Cloud Memorystore

   C. Cloud Spanner

   D. Cloud Datastore

7. The Cloud SDK can be used to configure and manage resources in which of the following services?

   A. Compute Engine

   B. Cloud Storage

   C. Network firewalls

   D. All of the above

8. What server configuration is required to use Cloud Functions?

   A. VM configuration

   B. Cluster configuration

   C. Pub/Sub configuration

   D. None

9. You have been assigned the task of consolidating log data generated by each instance of an application. Which of the Stackdriver management tools would you use?

   A. Monitoring

   B. Trace

   C. Debugger

   D. Logging

10. Which specialized services are most likely to be used to build a data warehousing platform that requires complex extraction, transformation, and loading operations on batch data as well as processing streaming data?

A. Apigee API platform

B. Data analytics

C. AI and machine learning

D. Cloud SDK

11. Your company has deployed 100,000 Internet of Things (IoT) sensors to collect data on the state of equipment in several factories. Each sensor will collect and send data to a data store every 5 seconds. Sensors will run continuously. Daily reports will produce data on the maximum, minimum, and average value for each metric collected on each sensor. There is no need to support transactions in this application. Which database product would you recommend?

A. Cloud Spanner

B. Cloud Bigtable

C. Cloud SQL MySQL

D. Cloud SQL PostgreSQL

12. You are the lead developer on a medical application that uses patients' smartphones to capture biometric data. The app is required to collect data and store it on the smartphone when data cannot be reliably transmitted to the backend application. You want to minimize the amount of development you have to do to keep data synchronized between smartphones and backend data stores. Which data store option should you recommend?

A. Cloud Firestore

B. Cloud Spanner

C. Cloud Datastore

D. Cloud SQL

13. A software engineer comes to you for a recommendation. She has implemented a machine learning algorithm to identify cancerous cells in medical images. The algorithm is computationally intensive, makes many mathematical calculations, requires immediate access to large amounts of data, and cannot be easily distributed over multiple servers. What kind of Compute Engine configuration would you recommend?

A. High memory, high CPU

B. High memory, high CPU, GPU

C. Mid-level memory, high CPU

D. High CPU, GPU

14. You are tasked with mapping the authentication and authorization policies of your on-premises applications to GPC's authentication and authorization mechanisms. The GCP documentation states that an identity must be authenticated in order to grant privileges to that identity. What does the term *identity* refer to?

A. VM ID

B. User

C. Role

D. Set of privileges

15. A client is developing an application that will need to analyze large volumes of text information. The client is not expert in text mining or working with language. What GCP service would you recommend they use?

A. Cloud Vision

B. Cloud ML

C. Cloud Natural Language Processing

D. Cloud Text Miner

16. Data scientists in your company want to use a machine learning library available only in Apache Spark. They want to minimize the amount of administration and DevOps work. How would you recommend they proceed?

A. Use Cloud Spark

B. Use Cloud Dataproc

C. Use Bigquery

D. Install Apache Spark on a cluster of VMs

17. Database designers at your company are debating the best way to move a database to GCP. The database supports an application with a global user base. Users expect support for transactions and the ability to query data using commonly used query tools. The database designers decide that any database service they choose will need to support ANSI 2011 and global transactions. Which database service would you recommend?

A. Cloud SQL

B. Cloud Spanner

C. Cloud Datastore

D. Cloud Bigtable

18. Which specialized service supports both batch and stream processing workflows?

A. Cloud Dataproc

B. Bigquery

C. Cloud Datastore

D. AutoML

19. You have a Python application you'd like to run in a scalable environment with the least amount of management overhead. Which GCP product would you select?

   A. App Engine flexible environment

   B. Cloud Engine

   C. App Engine standard environment

   D. Kubernetes Engine

20. A product manager at your company reports that customers are complaining about the reliability of one of your applications. The application is crashing periodically, but developers have not found a common pattern that triggers the crashes. They are concerned that they do not have good insight into the behavior of the application and want to perform a detailed review of all crash data. Which Stackdriver tool would you use to view consolidated crash information?

   A. DataProc

   B. Monitoring

   C. Logging

   D. Error Reporting

Chapter

3

Projects, Service Accounts, and Billing

THIS CHAPTER COVERS THE FOLLOWING OBJECTIVES OF THE GOOGLE ASSOCIATE CLOUD ENGINEER CERTIFICATION EXAM:

✓ **1.1 Setting up cloud projects and accounts**

✓ **1.2 Managing billing configuration**

Before delving into computing, storage, and networking services, we need to discuss how Google Cloud Platform (GCP) organizes resources and links the use of those resources to a billing system. This chapter introduces the GCP organizational hierarchy, which consists of organizations, folders, and projects. It also discusses service accounts, which are ways of assigning roles to compute resources so they can carry out functions on your behalf. Finally, the chapter briefly discusses billing.

How GCP Organizes Projects and Accounts

When you use GCP, you probably launch virtual machines or clusters, maybe create buckets to storage objects, and make use of serverless computing services such as App Engine and Cloud Functions. The list of resources you use can grow quickly. They can also change in dynamic, unpredicable ways as autoscaling services respond to workload.

If you run a single application or a few services for your department, you might be able to track all resources by viewing lists of resources in use. As the scope of your GCP use grows, you will probably have multiple departments, each with its own administrators who need different privileges. GCP provides a way to group resources and manage them as a single unit. This is called the *resource hierarchy*. The access to resources in the resource hierarchy is controlled by a set of policies that you can define.

GCP Resource Hierarchy

The central abstraction for managing GCP resources is the resource hierarchy. It consists of three levels:

- Organization
- Folder
- Project

Let's describe how these three components relate to each other.

Organization

An organization is the root of the resource hierarchy and typically corresponds to a company or organization. G-suite domains and a Cloud Identity accounts map to GCP organizations. G Suite is Google's office productivity suite, which includes Gmail, Docs, Drive, Calendar, and other services. If your company uses G Suite, you can create an organization in your GCP hierarchy. If your company does not use G Suite, you can use Cloud Identity, Google's identity as a service (IDaaS) offering (Figure 3.1).

FIGURE 3.1   You can create Cloud Identity accounts and manage G Suite users from the Identity & Organization form.

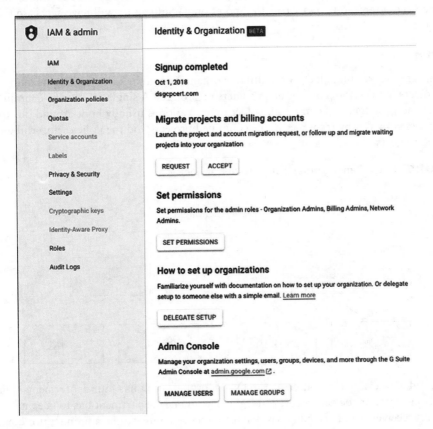

A single cloud identity is associated with at most one organization. Cloud identities have super admins, and those super admins assign the role of Organization Administrator Identity and Access Management (IAM) role to users who manage the organization. In addition, GCP will automatically grant Project Creator and Billing Account Creator IAM roles to all users in the domain. This allows any user to create projects and enable billing for the cost of resources used.

The users with the Organization Administrator IAM role are responsible for the following:

- Defining the structure of the resource hierarchy
- Defining identity access management policies over the resource hierarchy
- Delegating other management roles to other users

When a member of a G Suite organization / Cloud Identity account creates a billing account or project, GCP will automatically create an organization resource. All projects and billing accounts will be children of the organization resource. In addition, when the organization is created, all users in that organization are granted Project Creator and Billing Account Creator roles. From that point on, G Suite users will have access to GCP resources.

Folder

Folders are the building blocks of multilayer organizational hierarchies. Organizations contain folders. Folders can contain other folders or projects. A single folder may contain both folders and projects (see Figure 3.2). Folder organization is usually built around the kinds of services provided by resources in the contained projects and the policies governing folders and projects.

FIGURE 3.2   Generic organization folder project

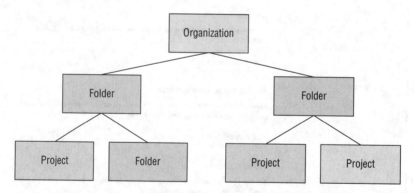

Consider an example resource hierarchy. An organization has four departments: finance, marketing, software development, and legal. The finance department has to keep its accounts receivable and accounts payable resources separate, so the administrator creates two folders within the Finance folder: Accounts Receivable and Accounts Payable. Software development uses multiple environments, including Dev, Test, Staging, and Production. Access to each of the environments is controlled by policies specific to that environment, so it makes sense to organize each environment into its own folder. Marketing and legal can have all of their resources shared across members of the department, so a single folder is sufficient for both of those departments. Figure 3.3 shows the organization hierarchy for this organization.

FIGURE 3.3   Example organization folder project

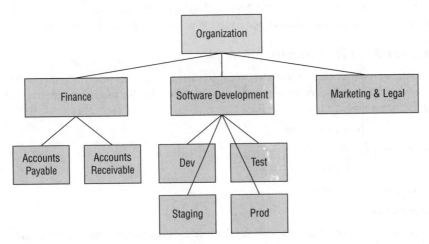

Now that we have an organization defined and have set up folders that correspond to our departments and how different groups of resources will be accessed, we can create projects.

Project

Projects are in some ways the most important part of the hierarchy. It is in projects that we create resources, use GCP services, manage permissions, and manage billing options.

The first step in working with a project is to create one. Anyone with the resourcemanager .projects.create IAM permission can create a project. By default, when an organization is created, every user in the domain is granted that permission.

Your organization will have a quota of projects it can create. The quota can vary between organizations. Google makes decisions about project quotas based on typical use, the customer's usage history, and other factors. If you reach your limit of projects and try to create another, you will be prompted to request an increase in the quota. You'll have to provide information such as the number of additional projects you need and what they will be used for.

After you have created your resource hierarchy, you can define policies that govern it.

Organization Policies

GCP provides an Organization Policy Service. This service controls access to an organization's resources. The Organization Policy Service complements the IAM service. The IAM lets you assign permissions so users or roles can perform specific operations in the cloud. The Organization Policy Service lets you specify limits on the ways resources can be used. One way to think of the difference is that IAM specifies who can do things, and the Organization Policy Service specifies what can be done with resources.

The organization policies are defined in terms of constraints on a resource.

Constraints on Resources

Constraints are restrictions on services. GCP has list constraints and Boolean constraints.

List constraints are lists of values that are allowed or disallowed for a resource. The following are some types of list constraints:

- Allow a specific set of values
- Deny a specific set of values
- Deny a value and all its child values
- Allow all allowed values
- Deny all values

Boolean constrains evaluate to true or false and determine whether the constraint is applied or not. For example, if you want to deny access to serial ports on VMs, you can set constraints/compute.disableSerialPortAccess to TRUE.

Policy Evaluation

Organizations may have standing policies to protect data and resources in the cloud. For example, there may be rules dictating who in the organization can enable a service API or create a service account. Your InfoSec department may require that all VMs disable serial port access. You could implement controls on each individual VM, but that is inefficient and prone to error. A better approach is to define a policy that constrains what can be done and attach that policy to an object in the resource hierarchy.

For example, since InfoSec wants all VMs to disable serial port access, you could specify a policy that constrains serial port access and then attach it to the organization. All folders and projects below the organization will inherit that policy. Since policies are inherited and cannot be disabled or overridden by objects lower in the hierarchy, this is an effective way to apply a policy across all organizational resources.

Policies are managed through the Organization Policies form in the IAM & admin form. Figure 3.4 shows an example set of policies.

Multiple policies can be in effect for a folder or project. For example, if the organization had a policy on serial port access and a folder containing a project had a policy limiting who can create service accounts, then the project would inherit both policies and both would constrain what could be done with resources in that project.

FIGURE 3.4   Organizational policies are managed in the IAM & admin console.

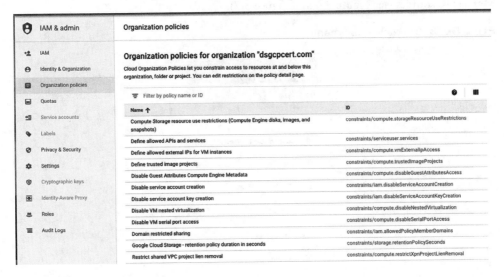

Managing Projects

One of the first tasks you will perform when starting a new cloud initiative is to set up a project. This can be done with the Google Cloud Console. Assuming you have created an account with GCP, navigate to the Google Cloud Console at `https://console.cloud.google.com` and log in. You will see the home page, which looks something like Figure 3.5.

FIGURE 3.5   Home page console

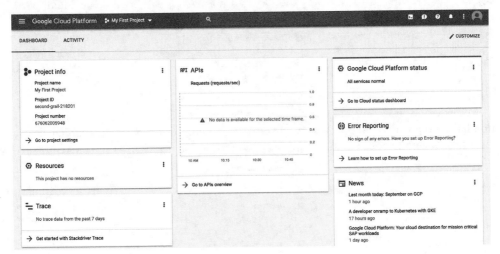

From the Navigation menu in the upper-left corner, select IAM & admin and then select Manage Resources (see Figure 3.6 and Figure 3.7).

FIGURE 3.6   Navigation menu

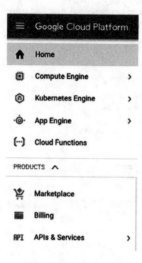

FIGURE 3.7   Select Manage Resources.

From there, you can click Create Project, which displays the Create Project dialog. You can enter the name of a project and select an organization in this dialog (Figure 3.8 and Figure 3.9).

FIGURE 3.8   Click Create Project.

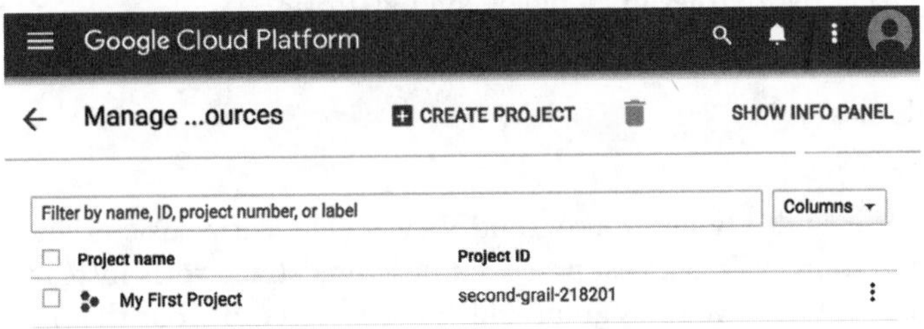

FIGURE 3.9   Create Project dialog

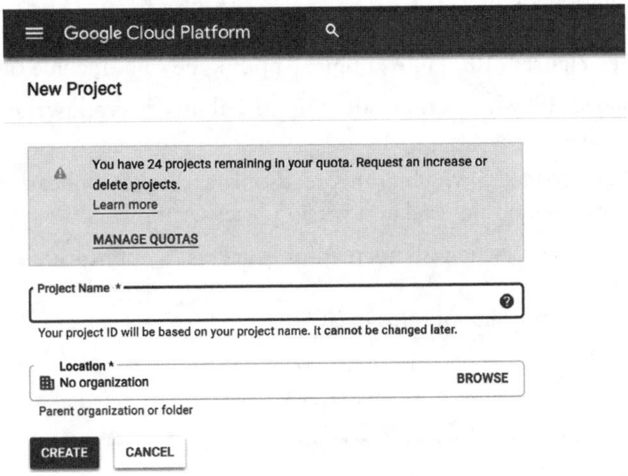

Note that when you create a project, your remaining quota of projects is displayed. If you need additional projects, click the Manage Quotas link to request an increase in your quota.

Roles and Identities

In addition to managing resources, as a cloud engineer you will have to manage access to those resources. This is done with the use of roles and identities.

Roles in GCP

A *role* is a collection of permissions. Roles are granted to users by binding a user to a role. When we talk of identities, we mean the record we use to represent a human user or service account in GCP. For example, Alice is a software engineer developing applications in the cloud (the human user), and she has an identity with a name such as alice@example.com. Roles are assigned to alice@example.com within GCP so that Alice can create, modify, delete, and use resources in GCP.

There are three types of roles in Google Cloud Platform:

- Primitive roles
- Predefined roles
- Custom roles

Primitive roles include Owner, Editor, and Viewer. These are basic privileges that can be applied to most resources. It is a best practice to use predefined roles instead of primitive roles when possible. Primitive roles grant wide ranges of permissions that may not always be needed by a user. By using predefined roles, you can grant only the permissions a user needs to perform their function. This practice of only assigning permissions that are needed and no more is known as the *principle of least privilege*. It is one of the fundamental best practices in information security.

Predefined roles provide granular access to resources in GCP, and they are specific to GCP products. (See Figure 3.10.) For example, App Engine roles include the following:

- appengine.appAdmin, which grants identities the ability to read, write, and modify all application settings
- appengine.ServiceAdmin, which grants read-only access to application settings and write-level access to module-level and version-level settings
- appengine.appViewer, which grants read-only access to applications.

FIGURE 3.10   A sample list of roles in GCP

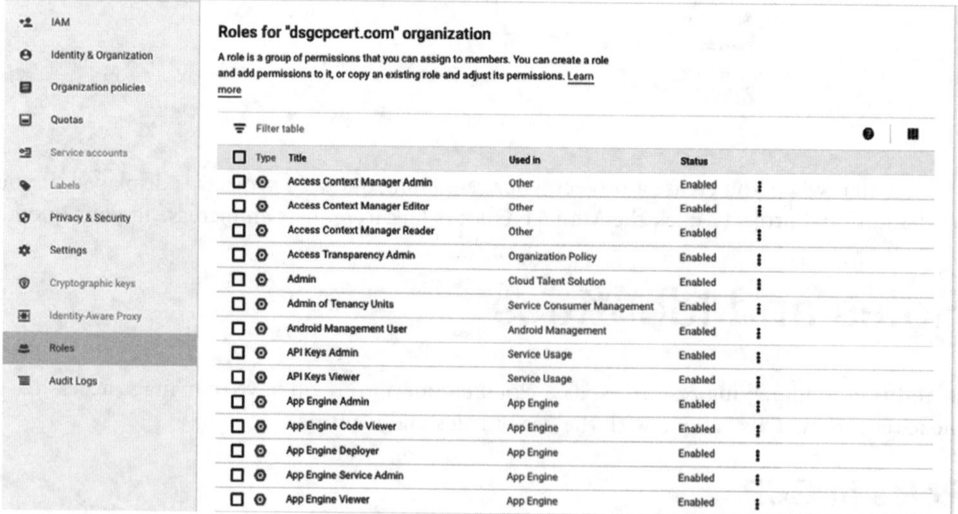

Custom roles allow cloud administrators to create and administer their own roles. Custom roles are assembled using permissions defined in IAM. While you can use most permissions in a custom role, some, such as `iam.ServiceAccounts.getAccessToken`, are not available in custom roles.

Granting Roles to Identities

Once you have determined which roles you want to provide to users, you can assign roles to users through the IAM console. It is important to know that permissions cannot be assigned to users. They can be assigned only to roles. Roles are then assigned to users.

From the IAM console, you can select a project that will display a permission interface, such as in Figure 3.11.

FIGURE 3.11   IAM permissions

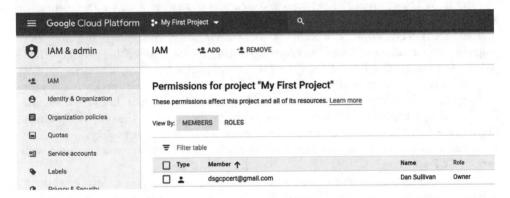

From there, select the Add option to display another dialog that prompts for usernames and roles (see Figure 3.12).

FIGURE 3.12   Adding a user

Add members to "My First Project"

Add members, roles to "My First Project" project

Enter one or more members below. Then select a role for these members to grant them access to your resources. Multiple roles allowed. Learn more

New members

Select a role

+ ADD ANOTHER ROLE

SAVE   CANCEL

Service Accounts

Identities are usually associated with individual users. Sometimes it is helpful to have applications or VMs act on behalf of a user or perform operations that the user does not have permission to perform.

For example, you may have an application that needs to access a database, but you do not want to allow users of the application to access the database directly. Instead, all user requests to the database should go through the application. A service account can be created that has access to the database. That service account can be assigned to the application so the application can execute queries on behalf of users without having to grant database access to those users.

Service accounts are somewhat unusual in that we sometimes treat them as resources and sometime as identities. When we assign a role to a service account, we are treating it as an identity. When we give users permission to access a service account, we are treating it as a resource.

There are two types of service accounts, user-managed service accounts and Google-managed service accounts. Users can create up to 100 service accounts per project. When you create a project that has the Compute Engine API enabled, a Compute Engine service account is created automatically. Similarly, if you have an App Engine application in your project, GCP will automatically create an App Engine service account. Both the Compute Engine and App Engine service accounts are granted editor roles on the projects in which they are created. You can also create custom service accounts in your projects.

Google may also create service accounts that it manages. These accounts are used with various GCP services.

Service accounts can be managed as a group of accounts at the project level or at the individual service account level. For example, if you grant iam.serviceAccountUser to a user for a specific project, then that user can manage all service accounts in the project. If you prefer to limit users to manage only specific service accounts, you could grant iam.serviceAccountUser for a specific service account.

Service accounts are created automatically when resources are created. For example, a service account will be created for a VM when the VM is created. There may be situations in which you would like to create a service account for one of your applications. In that case, you can navigate to the IAM & admin console and select Service Accounts. From there you can click Create Service Account at the top, as shown in Figure 3.13.

FIGURE 3.13 Service accounts listing in the IAM & admin console

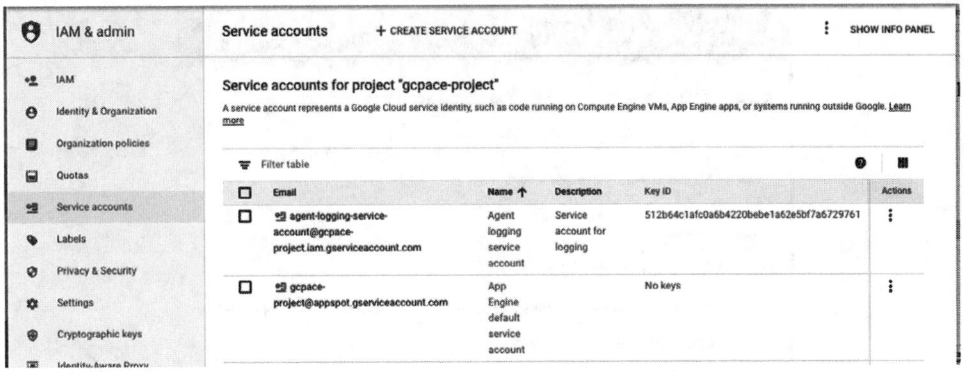

This brings up a form that prompts for the information needed to create a service account.

Billing

Using resources such as VMs, object storage, and specialized services usually incurs charges. The GCP Billing API provides a way for you to manage how you pay for resources used.

Billing Accounts

Billing accounts store information about how to pay charges for resources used. A billing account is associated with one or more projects. All projects must have a billing account unless they use only free services.

Billing accounts can follow a similar structure to the resource hierarchy. If you are working with a small company, you may have only a single billing account. In that case, all resource costs are charged to that one account. If your company is similar to the example from earlier in the chapter, with finance, marketing, legal, and software development departments, then you may want to have multiple billing accounts. You could have one billing account for each department, but that may not be necessary. If finance, marketing, and legal all pay for their cloud services from the same part of your company's budget, then they could use a single billing account. If software development services are paid from a different part of your company's budget, then it could use a different billing account.

From the main Google Cloud Console, you can navigate to the Billing console (see Figure 3.14), which lists existing billing accounts.

FIGURE 3.14   The main Billing form listing existing billing accounts

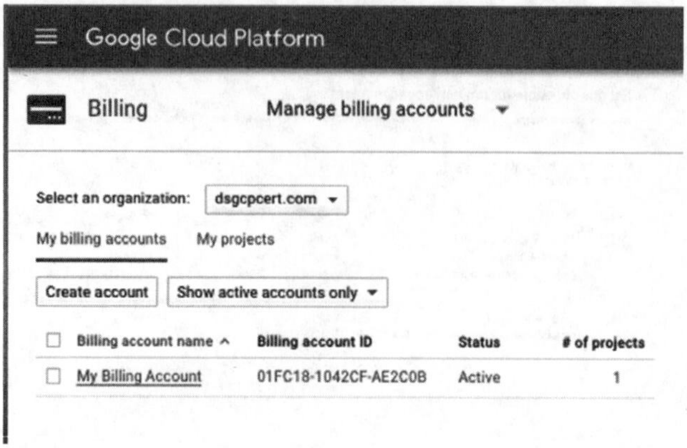

From here, you can create a new billing account, as shown in Figure 3.15.

FIGURE 3.15   The form to create a new billing account

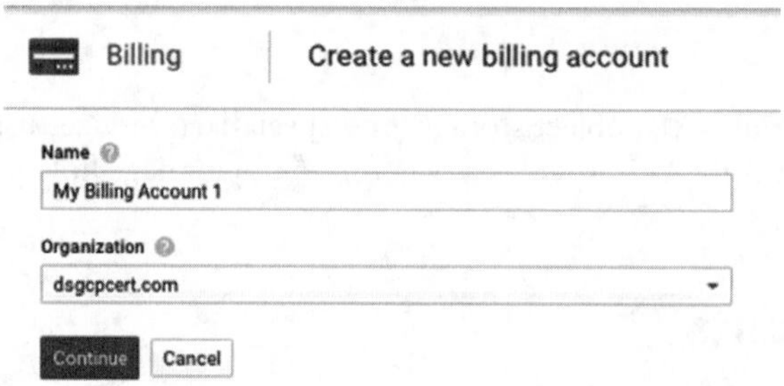

From the Billing overview page, you can view and modify projects linked to billing accounts.

There are two types of billing accounts: self-serve and invoiced. Self-serve accounts are paid by credit card or direct debit from a bank account. The costs are charged automatically. The other type is an invoiced billing account, in which bills or invoices are sent to customers. This type of account is commonly used by enterprises and other large customers.

Several roles are associated with billing. It is important to know them for the exam. The billing roles are as follows:

- Billing Account Creator, which can create new self-service billing accounts
- Billing Account Administrator, which manages billing accounts but cannot create them
- Billing Account User, which enables a user to link projects to billing accounts
- Billing Account Viewer, which enables a user to view billing account cost and transactions

Few users will likely have Billing Account Creator, and those who do will likely have a financial role in the organization. Cloud admins may have Billing Account Administrator to manage the accounts. Any user who can create a project should have Billing Account User so new projects can be linked to the appropriate billing account. Billing Account

Viewer is useful for some, like an auditor who needs to be able to read billing account information but not change it.

Billing Budgets and Alerts

The GCP Billing service includes an option for defining a budget and setting billing alerts. You can navigate to the budget form from the main console menu, selecting Billing and then Budgets & alerts (see Figure 3.16).

FIGURE 3.16   The budget form enables you to have notices sent to you when certain percentages of your budget have been spent in a particular month.

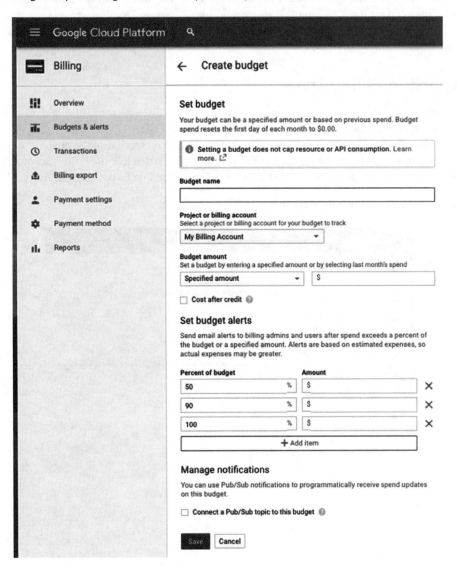

In the budget form, you can name your budget and specify a billing account to monitor. Note that a budget is associated with a billing account, not a project. One or more projects can be linked to a billing account, so the budget and alerts you specify should be based on what you expect to spend for all projects linked to the billing account.

You can specify a particular amount or specify that your budget is the amount spent in the previous month.

With a budget, you can set three alert percentages. By default, three percentages are set: 50 percent, 90 percent, and 100 percent. You can change those to percentages that work best for you. If you'd like more than three alerts, you can click Add Item in the Set Budget Alerts section to add additional alert thresholds.

When that percentage of a budget has been spent, it will notify billing administrators and billing account users by email. If you would like to respond to alerts programmatically, you can have notifications sent to a Pub/Sub topic by checking the appropriate box in the Manage Notification sections.

Exporting Billing Data

You can export billing data for later analysis or for compliance reasons. Billing data can be exported to either a BigQuery database or a Cloud Storage file.

To export billing data to BigQuery, navigate to the Billing section of the console and select Billing export from the menu. In the form that appears, select the billing account you would like to export and choose either BigQuery Export or File Export (see Figure 3.17).

FIGURE 3.17   Billing export form

For BigQuery, click Edit Setting. Select the projects you want to include. You will need to create a BigQuery data set to hold the data. Click Go To BigQuery to open a BigQuery form. This will create a Billing export data set, which will be used to hold exported data. (See Figure 3.18.) For additional information on using BigQuery, see Chapter 12.

FIGURE 3.18   Exporting to BigQuery

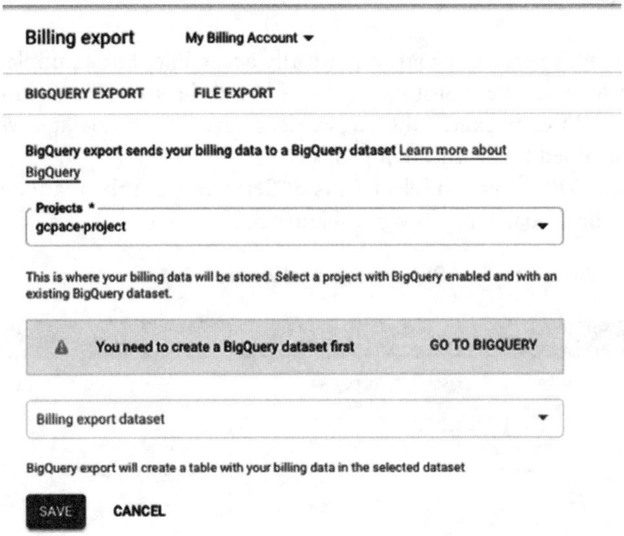

Alternatively, you can export billing data to a file stored in Cloud Storage. From the Billing Export form, select the File Export tab to display a form as shown in Figure 3.19.

FIGURE 3.19   Exporting billing data to a file

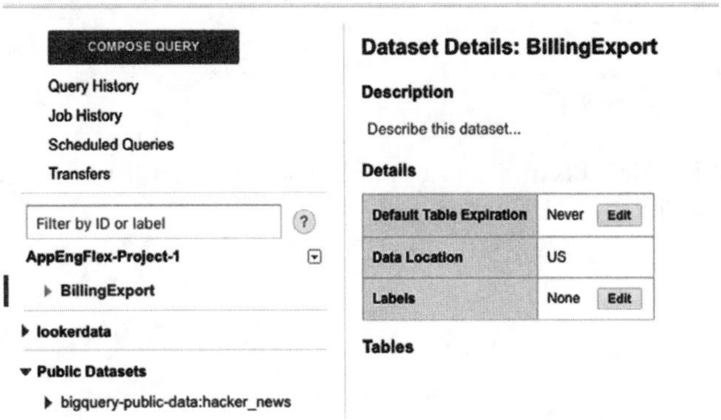

When exporting to a file, you will need to specify a bucket name and a report prefix. You have the option of choosing either the CSV or JSON file format. There may be questions about available file format options, so remember these two options.

Enabling APIs

GCP uses APIs to make services programmatically accessible. For example, when you use a form to create a VM or a Cloud Storage bucket, behind the scenes, API functions are executed to create the VM or bucket. All GCP services have APIs associated with them. Most, however, are not enabled by default in a project.

To enable service APIs, you can select APIs & Services from the main console menu. This will display a dashboard, as shown in Figure 3.20.

FIGURE 3.20   An example API services dashboard

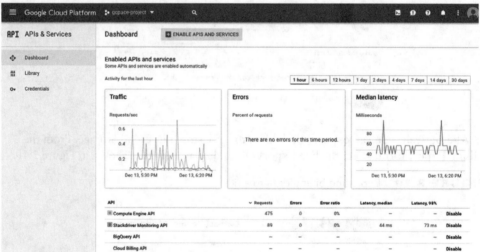

If you click the Enable APIs and Services link, you will see a list of services that you can enable, as shown in Figure 3.21.

FIGURE 3.21   Services that can have their APIs enabled

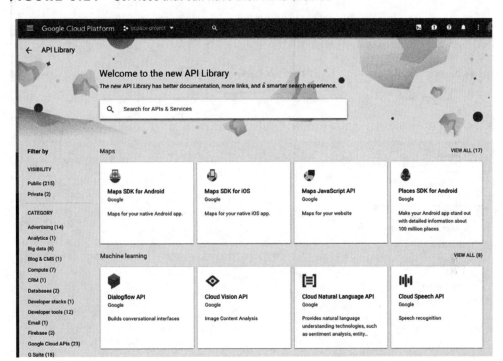

This form is a convenient way to enable APIs you know you will need. If you attempt an operation that requires an API that is not enabled, you may be prompted to decide if you want to enable the API.

Also, note in Figure 3.20 the list of APIs and their status. Enabled APIs will have a Disable option. You can click that to disable the API. You can also click the name of an API in the list to drill down into details about API usage, as shown in Figure 3.22.

FIGURE 3.22   Details about API usage

Provisioning Stackdriver Workspaces

When you are setting up organizations and projects, you will spend time on the tasks outlined in this chapter, such as creating identities, assigning roles, and setting up billing accounts. Another thing you should do is create a Stackdriver Workspaces. (These were formerly called Stackdriver accounts, so you may see that term sometimes.)

Stackdriver is a set of services for monitoring, logging, tracing, and debugging applications and resources (see Figure 3.23). For monitoring and logging data to be saved into Stackdriver, you need to create a workspace to save it. You can do this by selecting Stackdriver from the main console menu.

FIGURE 3.23   The main Stackdriver dashboard

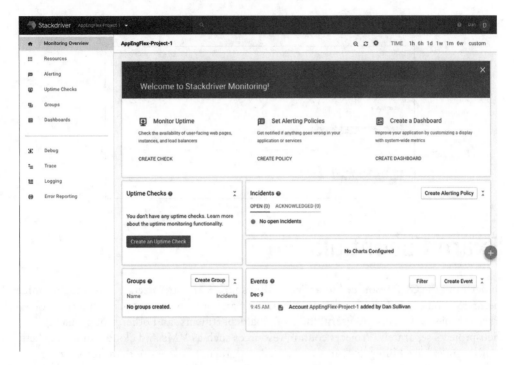

At the top of the dashboard, the name of the current project is displayed. Click the drop-down icon next to the name of the project to display a list of administrative options. One of them is Create Workspace (See Figure 3.24).

FIGURE 3.24   Administrative functions for managing Stackdriver workspaces

If you click Create Workspace, you will see a form like that in Figure 3.25. Select a project from the list that appears when you click in the Google Cloud Platform project box and then click Create Workspace. This will create a workspace and associate it with the project. You will now be able to use monitoring, logging, and other Stackdriver services with your project.

You can find more details on Stackdriver in Chapter 18.

FIGURE 3.25 Create Workspace dialog

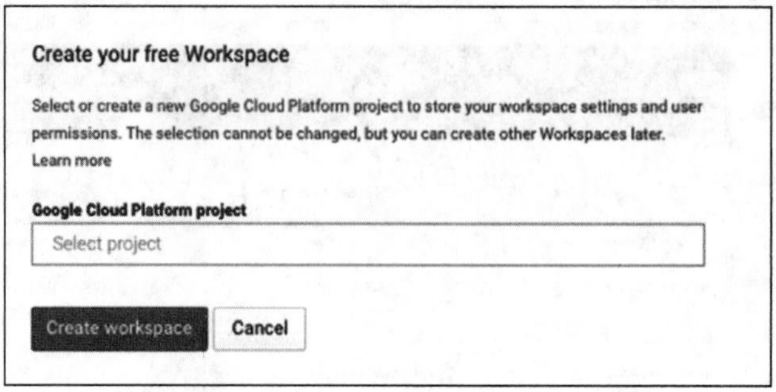

Create your free Workspace

Select or create a new Google Cloud Platform project to store your workspace settings and user
permissions. The selection cannot be changed, but you can create other Workspaces later.
Learn more

Google Cloud Platform project

Select project

Create workspace   Cancel

Exam Essentials

Understand the GCP resource hierarchy. All resources are organized within your resource
hierarchy. You can define the resource hierarchy using one organization and multiple folders and projects. Folders are useful for grouping departments, and other groups manage
their projects separately. Projects contain resources such as VMs and cloud storage buckets.
Projects must have billing accounts associated with them to use more than free services.

Understand organization policies. Organization policies restrict resources in the resource
hierarchy. Policies include constraints, which are rules that define what can or cannot be
done with a resource. For example, a constraint can be set to block access to the serial port
on all VMs in a project. Also, understand the policy evaluation process and how to override inherited policies.

Understand service accounts and how they are used. Service accounts are identities that are
not associated with a specific user but can be assigned to a resource, like a VM. Resources
that are assigned a service account can perform operations that the service account has permission to perform. Understand service accounts and how to create them.

Understand GCP Billing. GCP Billing must be enabled to use services and resources
beyond free services. Billing associates a billing method, such as a credit card or invoicing
information, with a project. All costs associated with resources in a project are billed to the
project's billing account. A billing account can be associated with more than one project.
You manage your billing through the Billing API.

Know how to enable APIs and create Stackdriver Workspaces. A convenient form lets
you enable APIs you know you will need. You can also show a list of APIs and their status.
Stackdriver is a set of services for monitoring, logging, tracing, and debugging applications and resources. To monitor and log data to save into Stackdriver, you need to create a
workspace.

Review Questions   *80%*

You can find the answers in the Appendix.

1. You are designing cloud applications for a healthcare provider. The records management application will manage medical information for patients. Access to this data is limited to a small number of employees. The billing department application will have insurance and payment information. Another group of employees will have access billing information. In addition, the billing system will have two components: a private insurance billing system and a government payer billing system. Government regulations require that software used to bill the government must be isolated from other software systems. Which of the following resource hierarchies would meet these requirements and provide the most flexibility to adapt to changing requirements?

    A. One organization, with folders for records management and billing. The billing folder would have private insurer and government payer folders within it. Common constraints would be specified in organization-level policies. Other policies would be defined at the appropriate folder.

    B. One folder for records management, one for billing, and no organization. Policies defined at the folder level.

    C. One organization, with folders for records management, private insurer, and government payer below the organization. All constraints would be specified in organization-level policies. All folders would have the same policy constraints.

    D. None of the above.

2. When you create a hierarchy, you can have more than one of which structure?

    A. Organization only

    B. Folder only

    C. Folder and project

    D. Project only

3. You are designing an application that uses a series of services to transform data from its original form into a format suitable for use in a data warehouse. Your transformation application will write to the message queue as it processes each input file. You don't want to give users permission to write to the message queue. You could allow the application to write to the message queue by using which of the following?

    A. Billing account

    B. Service account

    C. Messaging account

    D. Folder

4. Your company has a number of policies that need to be enforced for all projects. You decide to apply policies to the resource hierarchy. Not long after you apply the policies, an engineer finds that an application that had worked prior to implementing policies is no longer working. The engineer would like you to create an exception for the application. How can you override a policy inherited from another entity in the resource hierarchy?

    A. Inherited policies can be overridden by defining a policy at a folder or project level.

    B. Inherited policies cannot be overridden.

    C. Policies can be overridden by linking them to service accounts.

    D. Policies can be overridden by linking them to billing accounts.

5. Constraints are used in resource hierarchy policies. Which of the following are types of constraints allowed?

    A. Allow a specific set of values

    B. Deny a specific set of values

    C. Deny a value and all its child values

    D. Allow all allowed values

    E. All of the above

6. A team with four members needs you to set up a project that needs only general permissions for all resources. You are granting each person a primitive role for different levels of access, depending on their responsibilities in the project. Which of the following are not included as primitive roles in Google Cloud Platform?

    A. Owner

    B. Publisher

    C. Editor

    D. Viewer

7. You are deploying a new custom application and want to delegate some administration tasks to DevOps engineers. They do not need all the privileges of a full application administrator, but they do need a subset of those privileges. What kind of role should you use to grant those privileges?

    A. Primitive

    B. Predefined

    C. Advanced

    D. Custom

8. An app for a finance company needs access to a database and a Cloud Storage bucket. There is no predefined role that grants all the needed permissions without granting some permissions that are not needed. You decide to create a custom role. When defining custom roles, you should follow which of the following principles?

    A. Rotation of duties

    B. Least principle

C. Defense in depth

D. Least privilege

9. How many organizations can you create in a resource hierarchy?

A. 1

B. 2

C. 3

D. Unlimited

10. You are contacted by the finance department of your company for advice on how to automate payments for GCP services. What kind of account would you recommend setting up?

A. Service account

B. Billing account

C. Resource account

D. Credit account

11. You are experimenting with GCP for your company. You do not have permission to incur costs. How can you experiment with GCP without incurring charges?

A. You can't; all services incur charges.

B. You can use a personal credit card to pay for charges.

C. You can use only free services in GCP.

D. You can use only serverless products, which are free to use.

12. Your DevOps team has decided to use Stackdriver monitoring and logging. You have been asked to set up Stackdriver workspaces. When you set up a Stackdriver workspace, what kind of resource is it associated with?

A. A Compute Engine instance only

B. A Compute Engine instance or Kubernetes Engine cluster only

C. A Compute Engine instance, Kubernetes Engine cluster, or App Engine app

D. A project

13. A large enterprise is planning to use GCP across a number of subdivisions. Each subdivision is managed independently and has its own budget. Most subdivisions plan to spend tens of thousands of dollars per month. How would you recommend they set up their billing account(s)?

A. Use a single self-service billing account.

B. Use multiple self-service billing accounts.

C. Use a single invoiced billing account.

D. Use multiple invoiced billing accounts.

14. An application administrator is responsible for managing all resources in a project. She wants to delegate responsibility for several service accounts to another administrator. If additional service accounts are created, the other administrator should manage those as well. What is the best way to delegate privileges needed to manage the service accounts?

- **A.** Grant `iam.serviceAccountUser` to the administrator at the project level.
- **B.** Grant `iam.serviceAccountUser` to the administrator at the service account level.
- **C.** Grant `iam.serviceProjectAccountUser` to the administrator at the project level.
- **D.** Grant `iam.serviceProjectAccountUser` to the administrator at the service account level.

15. You work for a retailer with a large number of brick and mortar stores. Every night the stores upload daily sales data. You have been tasked with creating a service that verifies the uploads every night. You decide to use a service account. Your manager questions the security of your proposed solution, particularly about authenticating the service account. You explain the authentication mechanism used by service accounts. What authentication mechanism is used?

- **A.** Username and password
- **B.** Two-factor authentication
- **C.** Encrypted keys
- **D.** Biometrics

16. What objects in GCP are sometimes treated as resources and sometimes as identities?

- **A.** Billing accounts
- **B.** Service accounts
- **C.** Projects
- **D.** Roles

17. You plan to develop a web application using products from the GCP that already include established roles for managing permissions such as read-only access or the ability to delete old versions. Which of the following roles offers these capabilities?

- **A.** Primitive roles
- **B.** Predefined roles
- **C.** Custom roles
- **D.** Application roles

18. You are reviewing a new GCP account created for use by the finance department. An auditor has questions about who can create projects by default. You explain who has privileges to create projects by default. Who is included?

- **A.** Only project administrators
- **B.** All users
- **C.** Only users without the role `resourcemanager.projects.create`
- **D.** Only billing account users

19. How many projects can be created in an account?

- **A.** 10
- **B.** 25
- **C.** There is no limit.
- **D.** Each account has a limit determined by Google.

20. You are planning how to grant privileges to users of your company's GCP account. You need to document what each user will be able to do. Auditors are most concerned about a role called Organization IAM roles. You explain that users with that role can perform a number of tasks, which include all of the following except which one?

- **A.** Defining the structure of the resource hierarchy
- **B.** Determining what privileges a user should be assigned
- **C.** Defining IAM policies over the resource hierarchy
- **D.** Delegating other management roles to other users

Chapter

4

Introduction to Computing in Google Cloud

THIS CHAPTER COVERS THE FOLLOWING OBJECTIVES OF THE GOOGLE ASSOCIATE CLOUD ENGINEER CERTIFICATION EXAM:

✓ **2.2 Planning and configuring compute resources**

In this chapter, you will learn about each of the compute options available in Google Cloud Platform (GCP) and when to use them. We will also discuss preemptible virtual machines and when they can help reduce your overall computing costs.

Compute Engine

Compute Engine is a service that provides VMs that run on GCP. We usually refer to a running VM as an *instance*. When you use Compute Engine, you create and manage one or more instances.

Virtual Machine Images

Instances run images, which contain operating systems, libraries, and other code. You may choose to run a public image provided by Google (Figure 4.1). Both Linux and Windows images are available. In addition to the images maintained by Google, there are other public images provided by open source projects or third-party vendors.

FIGURE 4.1   A subset of operating system images available in Compute Engine

Boot disk

Select an image or snapshot to create a boot disk; or attach an existing disk

OS images   Application images   Custom images   Snapshots   Existing disks

○ SUSE Linux Enterprise Server 12 SP2 For SAP x86_64
built on 2018-08-16
○ SUSE Linux Enterprise Server 12 SP3 For SAP x86_64
built on 2018-08-14
○ SUSE Linux Enterprise Server 12 SP4 For SAP x86_64
built on 2018-12-12
○ SUSE Linux Enterprise Server 15 For SAP x86_64
built on 2018-08-16
○ Windows Server version 1709 Datacenter Core for Containers
Server Core, x64 built on 20181113
○ Windows Server version 1709 Datacenter Core
Server Core, x64 built on 20181113
○ Windows Server version 1803 Datacenter Core for Containers
Server Core, x64 built on 20181113
○ Windows Server version 1803 Datacenter Core
Server Core, x64 built on 20181113
○ Windows Server 2008 R2 Datacenter
Server with Desktop Experience, x64 built on 20181113
○ Windows Server 2012 R2 Datacenter Core
Server Core, x64 built on 20181113
○ Windows Server 2012 R2 Datacenter
Server with Desktop Experience, x64 built on 20181113
○ Windows Server 2016 Datacenter Core
Server Core, x64 built on 20181113
○ Windows Server 2016 Datacenter

The public images include a range of operating systems, such as CentOS, Container Optimized OS from Google, Debian, Red Hat Enterprise Linux, SUSE Enterprise Linux Server, Ubuntu, and Windows Server.

If there is no public image that meets your needs, you can create a custom image from a boot disk or by starting with another image. To create a VM from the console, navigate to Compute Engine and then to VM Instances. You will see a screen similar to Figure 4.2.

FIGURE 4.2 Creating a VM in Compute Engine

From there, click Create Instance to create a VM. Choose an image that is close to what you need and create the VM. Then make any changes you need to the image, such as installing libraries or other software packages. Once you have created the VM and made any changes you'd like, navigate to the Compute Engine menu in Google Cloud Console and select Snapshots, as shown in Figure 4.3.

FIGURE 4.3 The first step in creating a snapshot

Click Create Snapshot. In the form that appears, you can specify a name for your snapshot, a description, and, most importantly, the disk that is the source for the snapshot. In Figure 4.4, the boot disk from a VM called myvm is selected. After selecting options, click the Create button to save the snapshot, which can then be used as the image for other VMs.

FIGURE 4.4   Creating a snapshot in Compute Engine

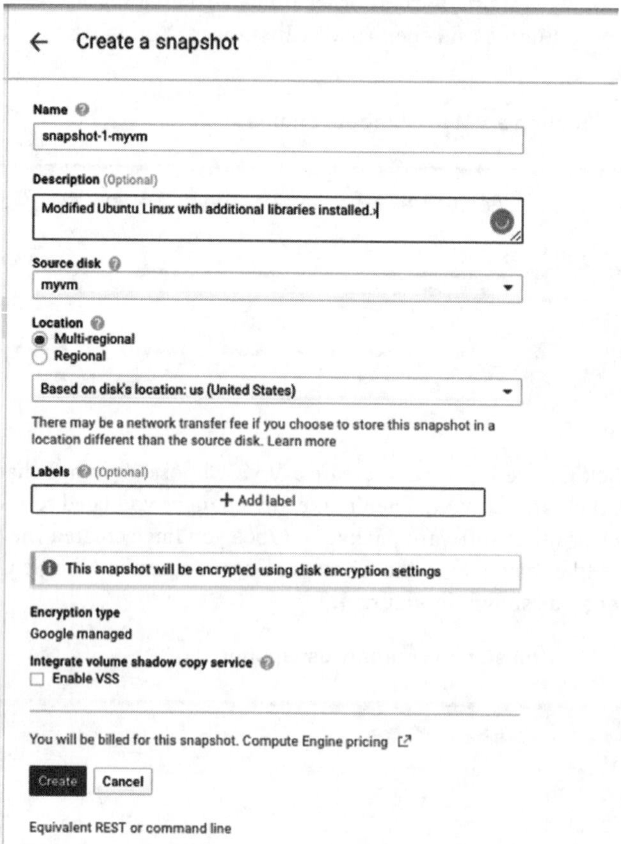

Custom images are especially useful if you have to configure an operating system and install additional software on each instance of a VM that you run. Instead of repeatedly configuring and installing software for each instance, you could configure and install once and then create a custom image from the boot disk of the instance. You then specify that custom image when you start other instances, which will have the configuration and software available without any additional steps.

There may be cases where you have a custom image in your local environment or data center. You can import such an image using the virtual disk import tool provided by Google. This utility is part of the gcloud command-line tool, which will be described in more detail in the next chapter.

Custom images must be compatible with GCP. At the time of writing, the following base operating systems are available to build custom images that will run in Compute Engine:

- Linux operating systems
  - CentOS 6
  - CentOS 7
  - Debian 8
  - Debian 9
  - Red Hat Enterprise Linux 6
  - Red Hat Enterprise Linux 7
  - Ubuntu 14.04 LTS
  - Ubuntu 15.04 LTS
- Windows operating systems
  - Windows Server 2008 R2
  - Windows Server 2012 R2
  - Windows Server 2012 R2 Core
  - Windows Server 2016
  - Windows Server 2016 Core

Virtual Machines Are Contained in Projects

When you create an instance, you specify a project to contain the instance. As you may recall, projects are part of the GCP resource hierarchy. Projects are the lowest-level structure in the hierarchy. Projects allow you to manage related resources with common policies.

When you open Google Cloud Console, you will notice at the top of the form either the name of a project or the phrase Select A Project, as shown in Figure 4.5.

FIGURE 4.5   The current project name or the option to select one is displayed in Google Cloud Console.

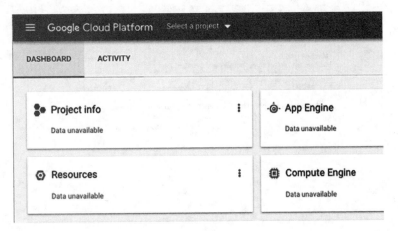

When you choose Select a Project, a form like that in Figure 4.6 appears. From there, you can select the project you want to store your resources, including VMs.

FIGURE 4.6   Choosing a project from existing projects in an account

Virtual Machines Run in a Zone and Region

In addition to having a project, VM instances have a zone assigned. Zones are data center–like resources, but they may be comprised of one or more closely coupled data centers. They are located within regions. A *region* is a geographical location, such as asia-east1, europe-west2, and us-east4. The zones within a region are linked by low-latency, high-bandwidth network connections.

You specify a region and a zone when you create a VM. As you can see in Figure 4.7, the Create VM form includes drop-down lists from which you can select the region and zone.

FIGURE 4.7   Selecting a region and zone in the Create VM form

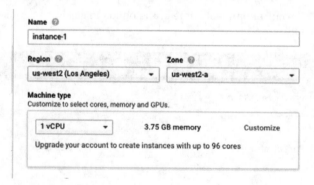

You may want to consider several factors when choosing where to run your VM, including the following:

- Cost, which can vary between regions.

- Data locality regulations, such as keeping data about European Union citizens in the European Union.

- High availability. If you are running multiple instances, you may want them in different zones and possibly different regions. If one of the zones or regions become inaccessible, the instances in other zones and regions can still provide services.

- Latency, which is important if you have users in different parts of the world. Keeping instances and data geographically close to application users can help reduce latency.

- Need for specific hardware platforms, which can vary by region. For example, at the time of writing europe-west1 has Intel Xeon E5, also known as Sandy Bridge, platforms, but Europe-west2 does not.

Users Need Privileges to Create Virtual Machines

To create Compute Engine resources in a project, users must be team members on the project or a specific resource and have appropriate permissions to perform specific tasks. Users can be associated with projects as follows:

- Individual users

- A Google group

- A G Suite domain

- A service account

Once a user or set of users is added to a project, you can assign permissions by granting roles to the user or set of users. This process is explained in detail in Chapter 17. Predefined roles are especially useful because they group permissions that are often needed together for a user to carry out a set of tasks. Here are some examples of predefined roles:

Compute Engine Admin   Users with this role have full control over Compute Engine instances.

Compute Engine Network Admin   Users with this role can create, modify, and delete most networking resources, and it provides read-only access to firewall rules and SSL certifications. This role does not give the user permission to create or alter instances.

Compute Engine Security Admin   Users with this role can create, modify, and delete SSL certificates and firewall rules.

Compute Engine Viewer   Users with this role can get and list Compute Engine resources but cannot read data from those resources.

When privileges are granted to users at the project level, then those permissions apply to all resources within a project. For example, if a user is granted the Compute Engine Admin role at the project level, then that person can administer all Compute Engine instances in the project. Figure 4.8 shows an example listing of users and roles.

FIGURE 4.8   An example listing of users and roles

An alternative way to grant permissions is to attach IAM policies directly to resources. In this way, privileges can be tailored to specific resources instead of for all resources in a project. For example, you could specify that user Alice has the Compute Engine Admin role on one instance and Bob has the same role on another instance. Alice and Bob would be able to administer their own VM instances, but they could not administer other instances.

Preemptible Virtual Machines

Consider if you have a workload that is the opposite of needing high availability. Preemptible VMs are short-lived compute instances suitable for running certain types of workloads—particularly for applications that perform financial modeling, rendering, big data, continuous integration, and web crawling operations. These VMs offer the same configuration options as regular compute instances and persist for up to 24 hours. If an application is fault-tolerant and can withstand possible instance interruptions (with a 30 second warning), then using preemptible VM instances can reduce Google Compute Engine costs significantly.

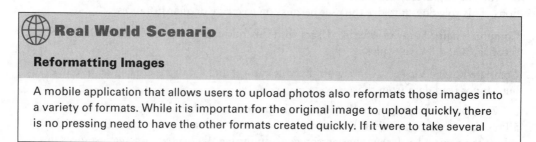

Real World Scenario

Reformatting Images

A mobile application that allows users to upload photos also reformats those images into a variety of formats. While it is important for the original image to upload quickly, there is no pressing need to have the other formats created quickly. If it were to take several minutes, that would still meet the application requirements. This is a good use case for preemptible machines.

When a file is uploaded, it triggers a cloud function (described in detail in Chapter 10), which starts the reformatting process on a preemptible VM. When the reformatting is complete, the reformatted image is written to storage. If the machine shuts down while reformatting an image, that image could be reformatted again when another VM starts up. When the reformatting application starts, it checks for any images that do not have all reformatted versions. If some images are missing some reformatted options, it can start reformatting those. This process can run at regular intervals to check whether any images have not been reformatted. In this way, we can use preemptible VMs and still meet the service-level objectives.

Some big data analysis jobs run on clusters of servers running software like Hadoop and Spark. The platforms are designed to be resilient to failure. If a node goes down in the middle of a job, the platform detects the failure and moves workload to other nodes in the server. You may have analytic jobs that are well served by a combination of reliable VMs and preemptible VMs. With some percentage of reliable VMs, you know you can get your jobs processed within your time constraints, but if you add low-cost, preemptible VMs, you can often finish your jobs faster and at lower overall cost.

Limitations of Preemptible Virtual Machines

As you decide where to use preemptible VMs, keep in mind their limitations and differences compared to conventional VM instances in GCP. Preemptible VMs have the following characteristics:

- May terminate at any time. If they terminate within 10 minutes of starting, you will not be charged for that time.
- Will be terminated within 24 hours.
- May not always be available. Availability may vary across zones and regions.
- Cannot migrate to a regular VM.
- Cannot be set to automatically restart.
- Are not covered by any service level agreement (SLA).

Custom Machine Types

Compute Engine has more than 25 predefined machine types grouped into standard types, high-memory machines, high-CPU machines, shared core type, and memory-optimized machines. These predefined machine types vary in the number of virtual CPUs (vCPUs) and amount of memory. Here are some examples:

- n1-standard-1 has 1 vCPU and 3.75GB of memory.

- n1-standard-32 has 32 vCPUs and 120GB of memory.

- n1-highmem-32 has 32 vCPUs and 208GB of memory.

- n1-highcpu-32 has 32 vCPUs and 28.8GB of memory.

The predefined options for VMs will meet the needs of many use cases, but there may be times where your workload could run more cost effectively and faster on a configuration that is not already defined. In that case, you may want to use a custom machine type.

To create a custom image, select the Create VM option in the console. Click the Customize link in the Machine Type section. This expands the Machine Type section, as shown in Figure 4.9. From there you can adjust the sliders to increase or decrease the number of CPUs and the amount of memory you require.

FIGURE 4.9 Customizing a VM by adjusting the number of CPUs and the amount of memory

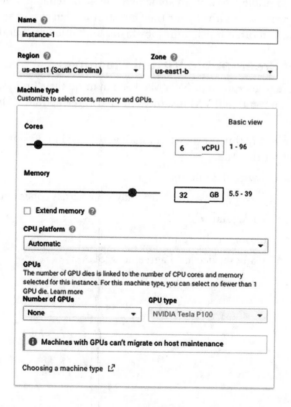

Custom machine types can have between 1 and 64 vCPUs and up to 6.5GB of memory per vCPU. The price of a custom configuration is based on the number of vCPUs and the memory allocated.

Use Cases for Compute Engine Virtual Machines

Compute Engine is a good option when you need maximum control over VM instances. With Compute Engine, you can do the following:

- Choose the specific image to run on the instance.

- Install software packages or custom libraries.

- Have fine-grained control over which users have permissions on the instance.

- Have control over SSL certificates and firewall rules for the instance.

Relative to other computing services in GCP, Google Compute Engine provides the least amount of management. Google does provide public images and a set of VM configurations, but you as an administrator must make choices about which image to use, the number of CPUs, the amount of memory to allocate, how to configure persistent storage, and how to configure network configurations.

In general, the more control over a resource you have in GCP, the more responsibility you have to configure and manage the resource.

App Engine

App Engine is a PaaS compute service that provides a managed platform for running applications. When you use App Engine, your focus is on your application and not on the VMs that run the application. Instead of configuring VMs, you specify some basic resource requirements along with your application code, and Google will manage the resources needed to run the code. This means that App Engine users have less to manage, but they also have less control over the compute resources that are used to execute the application.

Like VM instances, applications in App Engine are created within a project.

Structure of an App Engine Application

App Engine applications have a common structure, and they consist of services. Services provide a specific function, like computing sales tax in a retail web application or updating inventory as products are sold on a site. Services have versions, and this allows multiple versions to run at one time. Each version of a service runs on an instance that is managed by App Engine (see Figure 4.10).

FIGURE 4.10   The structure of an App Engine application

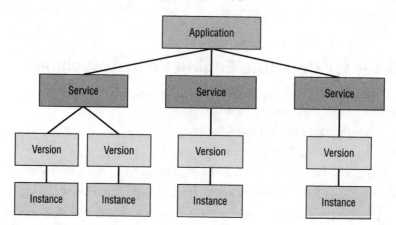

The number of instances used to provide an application depends on your configuration for the application and the current load on the application. As the load increases, Google can add more instances to meet the need. Similarly, if the load lessens, instances can be shut down to save on the cost of unutilized instances. This kind of autoscaling is available with dynamic instances.

In addition to dynamic instances, App Engine also provides resident instances. These instances run continually. You can add or remove resident instances manually.

When the number of deployed instances changes frequently, it can be difficult to estimate the costs of running instances. Fortunately, GCP allows users to set up daily spending limits as well as create budgets and set alarms.

App Engine Standard and Flexible Environments

App Engine provides two types of runtime environments: standard and flexible. The standard environment provides language runtimes, while the flexible environment is a more generalized container execution platform.

App Engine Standard Environment

The standard environment is the original App Engine environment. It consists of a preconfigured, language-specific runtime. There are currently two generations of the standard environment. The second generation improves on the performance of the first generation and has fewer limitations.

Currently, App Engine standard environment users can choose from the following supported languages:

First Generation

- Python 2.7
- PHP 5.5
- Go 1.9

Second Generation

- Java 8
- Python 3.7 (beta)
- PHP 7.2 (beta)
- Node.js 8 (beta) and 10 (beta)
- Go 1.11 (beta)

With the second-generation standard environment, developers can use any language extension, but in the first generation only a select set of whitelisted extensions and libraries are allowed. Network access is restricted in the first generation, but users have full network access in the second generation.

App Engine Flexible Environment

The App Engine flexible environment provides more options and control to developers who would like the benefits of a platform as a service (PaaS) like App Engine, but without the language and customization constraints of the App Engine standard environment (Figure 4.11).

The App Engine flexible environment uses containers as the basic building block abstraction. Users can customize their runtime environments by configuring a container. The flexible environment uses Docker containers, so developers familiar with Docker files can specify base operating system images, additional libraries and tools, and custom tools. It also has native support for Java 8, Eclipse Jetty 9, Python 2.7 and Python 3.6, Node.js, Ruby, PHP, .NET core, and Go.

In some ways, the App Engine flexible environment is similar to the Kubernetes Engine, which will be discussed in the next section. Both of these Google products can run customized Docker containers. The App Engine flexible environment provides a fully managed PaaS and is a good option when you can package your application and services into a small set of containers. These containers can then be autoscaled according to load. Kubernetes Engine, as we will see shortly, is designed to manage containers executing in a cluster that you control. With Kubernetes Engine you have control over your cluster but must monitor and manage that cluster using tools such as Stackdriver monitoring and autoscaling. With the App Engine flexible environment, the health of App Engine servers is monitored by Google and corrected as needed without any intervention on your part.

FIGURE 4.11   Interface to create a Kubernetes cluster in Kubernetes Engine

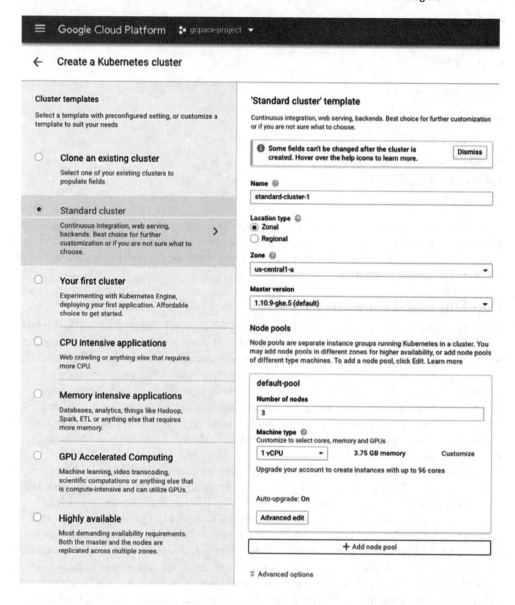

Use Cases for App Engine

The App Engine product is a good choice for a computing platform when you have little need to configure and control the underlying operating system or storage system. App Engine manages underlying VMs and containers and relieves developers and DevOps professionals of some common system administration tasks, like patching and monitoring servers.

When to Use App Engine Standard Environment

The App Engine standard environment is designed for applications written in one of the supported languages. The standard environment provides a language-specific runtime that comes with its own constraints. The constraints are fewer in the second-generation App Engine standard environment.

If you are starting a new development effort and plan to use the App Engine standard environment, then it is best to choose second-generation instances. First-generation instances will continue to be supported, but that kind of instance should be used only for applications that already exist and were designed for that platform.

When to Use App Engine Flexible Environment

The App Engine flexible environment is well suited for applications that can be decomposed into services and where each service can be containerized. For example, one service could use a Django application to provide an application user interface, another could embed business logic for data storage, and another service could schedule batch processing of data uploaded through the application. If you need to install additional software or run commands during startup, you can specify those in the Dockerfile. For example, you could add a run command to a Dockerfile to run `apt-get` update to get the latest version of installed packages. Docker files are text files with commands for configuring a container, such as specifying a base image to start with and specifying package manager commands, like `apt-get` and yum, for installing packages.

The App Engine standard environment scales down to no running instances if there is no load, but this is not the case with the flexible environment. There will always be at least one container running with your service, and you will be charged for that time even if there is no load on the system.

Kubernetes Engine

Compute Engine allows you to create and manage VMs either individually or in groups called *instances groups*. Instance groups let you manage similar VMs as a single unit. This is helpful if you have a fleet of servers that all run the same software and have the same operational lifecycle. Modern software, however, is often built as a collection of services, sometimes referred to as *microservices*. Different services may require different configurations of VMs, but you still may want to manage the various instances as a single resource, or cluster. You can use Kubernetes Engine for that.

Kubernetes is an open source tool created by Google for administering clusters of virtual and bare-metal machines. (Kubernetes is sometimes abbreviated K8s.) Kubernetes is a container orchestration service that helps you. It allows you to do the following:

- Create clusters of VMs that run the Kubernetes orchestration software for containers
- Deploy containerized applications to the cluster
- Administer the cluster
- Specify policies, such as autoscaling
- Monitor cluster health

Kubernetes Engine is GCP's managed Kubernetes service. If you wanted, you could deploy a set of VMs, install Kubernetes on your VMs, and manage the Kubernetes platform yourself. With Kubernetes Engine you get the benefits of Kubernetes without the administrative overhead.

Kubernetes Functionality

Kubernetes is designed to support clusters that run a variety of applications. This is different from other cluster management platforms that provide a way to run one application over multiple servers. Spark, for example, is a big data analytics platform that runs Spark services on a cluster of servers. Spark is not a general-purpose cluster management platform like Kubernetes.

Kubernetes Engine provides the following functions:

- Load balancing across Compute Engine VMs that are deployed in a Kubernetes cluster
- Automatic scaling of nodes (VMs) in the cluster
- Automatic upgrading of cluster software as needed
- Node monitoring and health repair
- Logging
- Support for node pools, which are collections of nodes all with the same configuration

Kubernetes Cluster Architecture

A Kubernetes cluster includes a cluster master node and one or more worker nodes. These are referred to as the *master* and *nodes*, respectively.

The master node manages the cluster. Cluster services, such as the Kubernetes API server, resource controllers, and schedulers, run on the master. The Kubernetes API Server is the coordinator for all communications to the cluster. The master determines what containers and workloads are run on each node.

When a Kubernetes cluster is created from either Google Cloud Console or a command line, a number of nodes are created as well. These are Compute Engine VMs. The default

VM type is n1-standard-1 (1 vCPU and 3.75GB memory), but you can specify a different machine type when creating the cluster.

Kubernetes deploys containers in groups called *pods*. Containers within a single pod share storage and network resources. Containers within a pod share an IP address and port space. A pod is a logically single unit for providing a service. Containers are deployed and scaled as a unit.

 It is important to note that some overhead is dedicated to running Kubernetes software on nodes. Some amount of CPU and memory is allocated for Kubernetes and therefore is not available for workload processing. Kubernetes Engine reserves memory resources as follows:

- 25 percent of the first 4GB of memory

- 20 percent of the next 4GB of memory, up to 8GB

- 10 percent of the next 8GB of memory, up to 16GB

- 6 percent of the next 112GB of memory, up to 128GB

- 2 percent of any memory above 128GB

CPU resources are reserved as follows:

- 6 percent of the first core

- 1 percent of the next core (up to two cores)

- 0.5 percent of the next two cores (up to four cores)

- 0.25 percent of any cores above four cores

Kubernetes High Availability

One way Kubernetes maintains cluster health is by shutting down pods that become starved for resources. Kubernetes supports something called *eviction policies* that set thresholds for resources. When a resource is consumed beyond the threshold, then Kubernetes will start shutting down pods.

Another way Kubernetes provides for high reliability is by running multiple identical pods. A group of running identical pods is called a *deployment*. The identical pods are referred to as *replicas*.

When deployments are rolled out, they can be in one of three states.

- Progressing, which means the deployment is in the process of performing a task

- Completed, which means the rollout of containers is complete and all pods are running the latest version of containers

- Failed, which indicates the deployment process encountered a problem it could not recover from

There are additional considerations when running stateful applications versus stateless applications. Those issues will be addressed in Chapter 7.

Kubernetes Engine Use Cases

Kubernetes Engine is a good choice for large-scale applications that require high availability and high reliability. Kubernetes Engine supports the concept of pods and deployment sets, which allow application developers and administrators to manage services as a logical unit. This can help if you have a set of services that support a user interface, another set that implements business logic, and a third set that provides backend services. Each of these different groups of services can have different lifecycles and scalability requirements. Kubernetes helps to manage these at levels of abstraction that make sense for users, developers, and DevOps professionals.

Cloud Functions

Cloud Functions is a serverless computing platform designed to run single-purpose pieces of code in response to events in the GCP environment. There is no need to provision or manage VMs, containers, or clusters when using Cloud Functions. Code that is written in Node.js 6, Node.js 8, or Python 3.7 can run in Cloud Functions.

Cloud Functions is not a general-purpose computing platform like Compute Engine or App Engine. Cloud Functions provides the "glue" between services that are otherwise independent.

For example, one service may create a file and upload it to Cloud Storage, and another service has to pick up those files and perform some processing on the file. Both of these services can be developed independently. There is no need for either to know about the other. However, you will need some way to detect that a new file has been written to Cloud Storage, and then the other application can begin processing it. We don't want to write applications in ways that make assumptions about other processes that may provide input or consume output. Services can change independently of each other. We should not have to keep track of dependencies between services if we can avoid it. Cloud Functions helps us avoid that situation.

Cloud Functions Execution Environment

GCP manages everything that is needed to execute your code in a secure, isolated environment. Of course, below the serverless abstraction, there are virtual and physical servers running your code, but you as a cloud engineer do not have to administer any of that infrastructure. Three key things to remember about Cloud Functions are the following:

- The functions execute in a secure, isolated execution environment.
- Compute resources scale as needed to run as many instances of Cloud Functions as needed without you having to do anything to control scaling.
- The execution of one function is independent of all others. The lifecycles of Cloud Functions are not dependent on each other.

There is an important corollary to these key points. That is, Cloud Functions may be running in multiple instances at one time. If two mobile app users uploaded an image file for processing at the same time, two different instances of Cloud Functions would execute at roughly the same time. You do not have to do anything to prevent conflicts between the two instances; they are independent.

Since each invocation of a Cloud Function runs in a separate instance, functions do not share memory or variables. In general, this means that Cloud Functions should be stateless. That means the function does not depend on the state of memory to compute its output. This is a reasonable constraint in many cases, but sometimes you can optimize processing if you can save state between invocations. Cloud Functions does offer some ways of doing this, which will be described in Chapter 11.

Cloud Functions Use Cases

Cloud Functions is well suited to short-running, event-based processing. If your workflows upload, modify, or otherwise alter files in Cloud Storage or use message queues to send work between services, then the Cloud Functions service is a good option for running code that starts the next step in processing. Some application areas that fit this pattern include the following:

- Internet of Things (IoT), in which a sensor or other device can send information about the state of a sensor. Depending on the values sent, Cloud Functions could trigger an alert or start processing data that was uploaded from the sensor.

- Mobile applications that, like IoT apps, send data to the cloud for processing

- Asynchronous workflows in which each step starts at some time after the previous steps completes, but there are no assumptions about when the processing steps will complete

Summary

GCP offers several computing options. The options vary in the level of control that you, as a user of GCP, have over the computing platform. Generally, with more control comes more responsibility and management overhead. Your objective when choosing a computing platform is to choose one that meets your requirements while minimizing DevOps overhead and cost.

Compute Engine is the GCP service that lets you provision VMs. You can choose from predefined configurations, or you can create a custom configuration with the best combination of virtual CPUs and memory for your needs. If you can tolerate some disruption in VM functioning, you can save a significant amount of money by using preemptible VMs.

App Engine is Google's PaaS offering. This is one of the serverless options. You provide application code and, in the case of the App Engine flexible environment, a specification for a

Docker container to run your application. The App Engine standard environment is appropriate for applications that can run in language-specific sandboxes.

Modern software applications are built on multiple services that may have different computing requirements and change on different lifecycles. Kubernetes Engine runs clusters of servers that can be used to run a variety of services while efficiently allocating work to servers as needed. Kubernetes Engine also provides monitoring, scaling, and remediation when something goes wrong with a VM in the cluster.

Loosely coupled applications may be strung together to implement complex workflows. Often, we want each component to be independent of others. In such cases, we often need to execute "glue" code that moves workload from one stage to another. Cloud Functions is the serverless computing option designed to meet this need.

Exam Essentials

Understand how images are used to create instances of VMs and how VMs are organized in projects.   Instances run images, which contain operating systems, libraries, and other code. When you create an instance, you specify a project to contain the instance.

Know that GCP has multiple geographic regions and regions have one or more zones.   VMs run in zones. A region is a geographical location, such as asia-east1, europe-west2, and us-east4. The zones within a region are linked by low-latency, high-bandwidth network connections.

Understand what preemptible VMs are and when they are appropriate to use.   Also understand when not to use them. GCP offers an option called a preemptible VM for workloads that can be disrupted without creating problems.

Understand the difference between the App Engine standard and flexible environments.   The standard environment runs a language-specific platform, and the App Engine flexible environment allows you to run custom containers.

Know that Kubernetes is a container orchestration platform.   It also runs containers in a cluster.

Understand Kubernetes.   It provides load balancing, automatic scaling, logging, and node health checks and repair.

Understand Cloud Functions.   This service is used to run programs in response to events, such as file upload or a message being added to a queue.

Review Questions   *90 %*

You can find the answers in the Appendix.

1. You are deploying a Python web application to GCP. The application uses only custom code and basic Python libraries. You expect to have sporadic use of the application for the foreseeable future and want to minimize both the cost of running the application and the DevOps overhead of managing the application. Which computing service is the best option for running the application?

    A. Compute Engine

    B. App Engine standard environment

    C. App Engine flexible environment

    D. Kubernetes Engine

2. Your manager is concerned about the rate at which the department is spending on cloud services. You suggest that your team use preemptible VMs for all of the following except which one?

    A. Database server

    B. Batch processing with no fixed time requirement to complete

    C. High-performance computing cluster

    D. None of the above

3. What parameters need to be specified when creating a VM in Compute Engine?

    A. Project and zone

    B. Username and admin role

    C. Billing account

    D. Cloud Storage bucket

4. Your company has licensed a third-party software package that runs on Linux. You will run multiple instances of the software in a Docker container. Which of the following GCP services could you use to deploy this software package?

    A. Compute Engine only

    B. Kubernetes Engine only

    C. Compute Engine, Kubernetes Engine, and the App Engine flexible environment only

    D. Compute Engine, Kubernetes Engine, the App Engine flexible environment, or the App Engine standard environment

5. You can specify packages to install into a Docker container by including commands in which file?

    A. `Docker.cfg`

    B. `Dockerfile`

    C. `Config.dck`

    D. `install.cfg`

6. How much memory of a node does Kubernetes require as overhead?

    A. 10GB to 20GB

    B. 1GB to 2GB

    C. 1.5GB

    D. A scaled amount starting at 25 percent of memory and decreasing to 2 percent of marginal memory as the total amount of memory increases.

7. Your manager is making a presentation to executives in your company advocating that you start using Kubernetes Engine. You suggest that the manager highlight all the features Kubernetes provides to reduce the workload on DevOps engineers. You describe several features, including all of the following except which one?

    A. Load balancing across Compute Engine VMs that are deployed in a Kubernetes cluster

    B. Security scanning for vulnerabilities

    C. Automatic scaling of nodes in the cluster

    D. Automatic upgrading of cluster software as needed

8. Your company is about to release a new online service that builds on a new user interface experience driven by a set of services that will run on your servers. There is a separate set of services that manage authentication and authorization. A data store set of services keeps track of account information. All three sets of services must be highly reliable and scale to meet demand. Which of the GCP services is the best option for deploying this?

    A. App Engine standard environment

    B. Compute Engine

    C. Cloud Functions

    D. Kubernetes Engine

9. A mobile application uploads images for analysis, including identifying objects in the image and extracting text that may be embedded in the image. A third party has created the mobile application, and you have developed the image analysis service. You both agree to use Cloud Storage to store images. You want to keep the two services completely decoupled, but you need a way to invoke the image analysis as soon as an image is uploaded. How should this be done?

    A. Change the mobile app to start a VM running the image analysis service and have that VM copy the file from storage into local storage on the VM. Have the image service run on the VM.

    B. Write a function in Python that is invoked by Cloud Functions when a new image file is written to the Cloud Storage bucket that receives new images. The function should submit the URL of the uploaded file to the image analysis service. The image analysis service will then load the image from Cloud Storage, perform analysis, and generate results, which can be saved to Cloud Storage.

    C. Have a Kubernetes cluster running continuously, with one pod dedicated to listing the contents of the upload bucket and detecting new files in Cloud Storage and another pod dedicated to running the image analysis software.

    D. Have a Compute Engine VM running and continuously listing the contents of the upload bucket in Cloud Storage to detect new files. Another VM should be continually running the image analysis software.

10. Your team is developing a new pipeline to analyze a stream of data from sensors on manufacturing devices. The old pipeline occasionally corrupted data because parallel threads overwrote data written by other threads. You decide to use Cloud Functions as part of the pipeline. As a developer of a Cloud Function, what do you have to do to prevent multiple invocations of the function from interfering with each other?

    A. Include a check in the code to ensure another invocation is not running at the same time.

    B. Schedule each invocation to run in a separate process.

    C. Schedule each invocation to run in a separate thread.

    D. Nothing. GCP ensures that function invocations do not interfere with each other.

11. A client of yours processes personal and health information for hospitals. All health information needs to be protected according to government regulations. Your client wants to move their application to Google Cloud but wants to use the encryption library that they have used in the past. You suggest that all VMs running the application have the encryption library installed. Which kind of image would you use for that?

    A. Custom image

    B. Public image

    C. CentOS 6 or 7

12. What is the lowest level of the resource hierarchy?

    A. Folder

    B. Project

    C. File

    D. VM instance

13. Your company is seeing a marked increase in the rate of customer growth in Europe. Latency is becoming an issue because your application is running in us-central1. You suggest deploying your services to a region in Europe. You have several choices. You should consider all of the following factors except which one?

    A. Cost

    B. Latency

    C. Regulations

    D. Reliability

14. What role gives users full control over Compute Engine instances?

    A. Compute Manager role

    B. Compute Admin role

    C. Compute Manager role

    D. Compute Security Admin

15. Which of the following are limitations of a preemptible VM?

    A. Will be terminated within 24 hours.

    B. May not always be available. Availability may vary across zones and regions.

    C. Cannot migrate to a regular VM.

    D. All of the above

16. Custom VMs can have up to how many vCPUs?

    A. 16

    B. 32

    C. 64

    D. 128

17. When using the App Engine standard environment, which of the following language's runtime is not supported?

    A. Java

    B. Python

    C. C

    D. Go

18. Kubernetes reserves CPU resources in percentage of cores available. The percentage is what range?

    A. 1 percent to 10 percent

    B. 0.25 percent to 6 percent

    C. 0.25 percent to 2 percent

    D. 10 percent to 12 percent

19. Kubernetes deployments can be in what states?

    A. Progressing, stalled, completed

    B. Progressing, completed, failed

    C. Progressing, stalled, failed, completed

    D. Progressing, stalled, running, failed, completed

20. A client has brought you in to help reduce their DevOps overhead. Engineers are spending too much time patching servers and optimizing server utilization. They want to move to serverless platforms as much as possible. Your client has heard of Cloud Functions and wants to use them as much as possible. You recommend all of the following types of applications except which one?

    A. Long-running data warehouse data load procedures

    B. IoT backend processing

    C. Mobile application event processing

    D. Asynchronous workflows

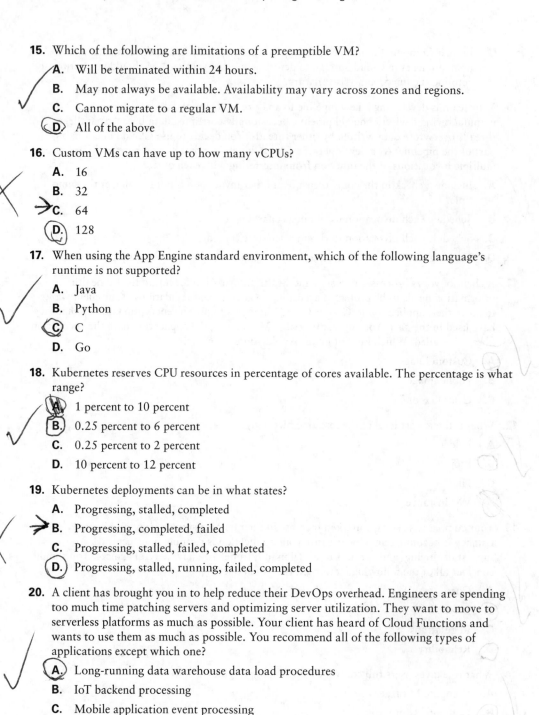

Chapter

5

Computing with Compute Engine Virtual Machines

THIS CHAPTER COVERS THE FOLLOWING OBJECTIVES OF THE GOOGLE ASSOCIATE CLOUD ENGINEER EXAM:

✓ **1.3   Installing and configuring the command line interface (CLI), specifically Cloud SDK (e.g., setting the default project)**

✓ **2.2   Planning and configuring compute resources. Considerations include:**

- Selecting appropriate compute choices for a given workload (e.g., Compute Engine, Kubernetes Engine, App Engine)

- Using preemptible VMs and custom machine types as appropriate

In this chapter, you will learn about Google Cloud Console, a graphical user interface for working with Google Cloud Platform (GCP). You will learn how to install Google Cloud SDK and use it to create virtual machine instances and how to use Cloud Shell as an alternative to installing Google Cloud SDK locally.

Creating and Configuring Virtual Machines with the Console

Let's create a VM in Compute Engine. We have three options for doing this: we can use Google Cloud Console, Google Cloud SDK, or Google Cloud Shell. Let's start with the console.

Google Cloud Console is a web-based graphical user interface for creating, configuring, and managing resources in Google Cloud. In this chapter, we will use it to create a VM.

To open the console, navigate in your browser to `https://console.cloud.google.com` and log in. Figure 5.1 shows an example of the main form in the console.

FIGURE 5.1 The main starting form of Google Cloud Console

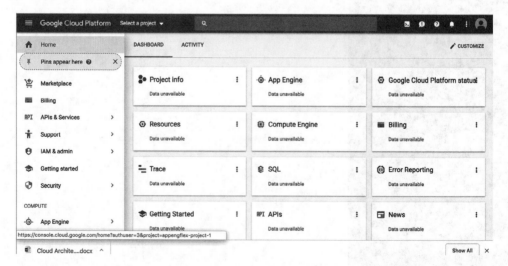

In the upper-left section of the form, click the Select A Project option to display the existing projects. You can also create a new project from this form, which is shown in Figure 5.2.

FIGURE 5.2   The Project form lets you choose the project to work with when creating VMs. You can also create a new project here.

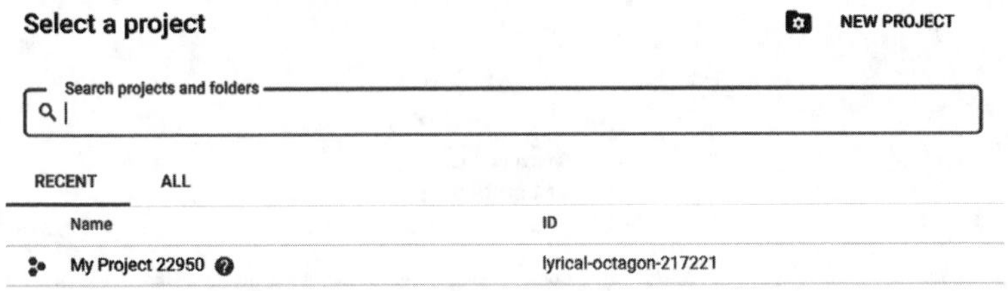

Select a project   ⬚   NEW PROJECT

┌─ Search projects and folders ─────────────────────────────────────┐
│ Q | │
└───┘

RECENT   ALL

Name   ID

⁘ **My Project 22950** ❓   lyrical-octagon-217221

After you select an existing project or create a new project, you can return to the main console panel. The first time you try to work a VM you will have to create a billing account if one has not already been created. Figure 5.3 shows a message and button on the main panel for creating a billing account.

FIGURE 5.3   When a billing account does not exist for a project, you will be given the option to create a billing account when you try to create a VM.

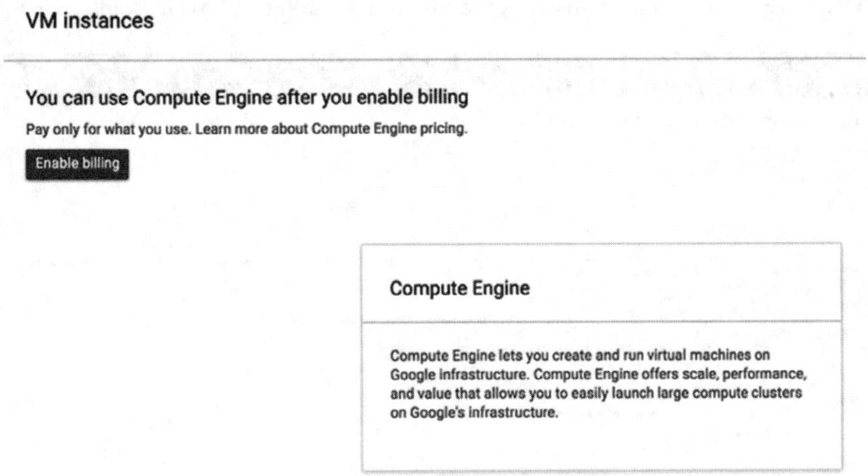

VM instances

───

You can use Compute Engine after you enable billing

Pay only for what you use. Learn more about Compute Engine pricing.

Enable billing

┌──┐
│ **Compute Engine**   │
│   │
│ Compute Engine lets you create and run virtual machines on │
│ Google infrastructure. Compute Engine offers scale, performance, │
│ and value that allows you to easily launch large compute clusters │
│ on Google's infrastructure.   │
└──┘

Click Enable Billing and fill in the billing information, such as name, address, and credit card. Once billing is enabled, you will return to the main panel (see Figure 5.4).

FIGURE 5.4   The starting panel for creating a VM

Click the Create button in the dialog box to bring up a VM configuration, as shown in Figure 5.5.

FIGURE 5.5   Part of the main configuration form for creating VMs in Compute Engine

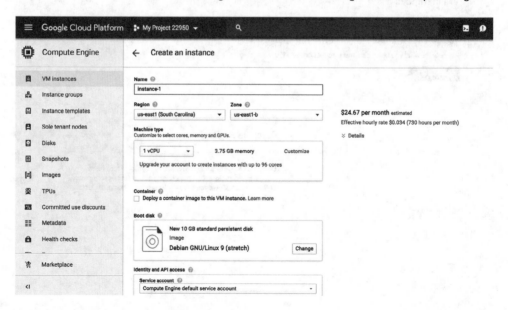

Main Virtual Machine Configuration Details

Within the console, you can specify all the needed details about the configuration of the VM that you are creating, including the following:

- Name of the VM
- Region and zone where the VM will run
- Machine type, which determines the number of CPUs and the amount of memory in the VM
- Boot disk, which includes the operating system the VM will run

You can choose the name of your VM. This is primarily for your use. Google Cloud uses other identifiers internally to manage VMs.

You will need to specify a region. Regions are major geographical areas. A partial list of regions is shown in Figure 5.6.

FIGURE 5.6 A partial list of regions providing Compute Engine services

```
asia-east1 (Taiwan)
asia-east2 (Hong Kong)
asia-northeast1 (Tokyo)
asia-south1 (Mumbai)
asia-southeast1 (Singapore)
australia-southeast1 (Sydney)
europe-north1 (Finland)
europe-west1 (Belgium)
europe-west2 (London)
europe-west3 (Frankfurt)
europe-west4 (Netherlands)
northamerica-northeast1 (Montréal)
southamerica-east1 (São Paulo)
us-central1 (Iowa)
us-east1 (South Carolina)
us-east4 (Northern Virginia)
us-west1 (Oregon)
us-west2 (Los Angeles)
```

After you select a region, you can select a zone. Remember, a zone is a data center–like facility within a region. Figure 5.7 shows an example list of zones available in the us-east-1 region.

FIGURE 5.7 A list of zones within the us-east-1 region

After you specify a region and zone, Google Cloud can determine the VMs available in that zone. Not all zones have the same availability. Figure 5.8 shows an example listing of machine types available in the us-east1-b zone.

FIGURE 5.8   A list of machine types available in the us-east1-b zone

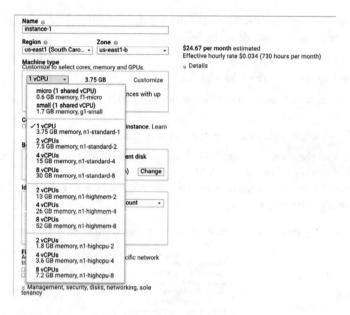

The Boot Disk Option section lists a default configuration. Clicking the Change button brings up the Boot Disk Option dialog, as shown in Figure 5.9.

FIGURE 5.9   Dialog for configuring the boot disk of the VM

Boot disk

Select an image or snapshot to create a boot disk; or attach an existing disk

OS images   Application images   Custom images   Snapshots   Existing disks

ℹ️ Shielded VM is in Beta. Learn more   Dismiss

☐ Show images with Shielded VM features ❓

○ Debian GNU/Linux 9 (stretch)
  amd64 built on 20181011
○ CentOS 6
  x86_64 built on 20181011
○ CentOS 7
  x86_64 built on 20181011
◉ CoreOS alpha 1925.0.0
  amd64-usr published on 2018-10-11
○ CoreOS beta 1911.1.1
  amd64-usr published on 2018-10-11
○ CoreOS stable 1855.4.0
  amd64-usr published on 2018-09-11
○ Ubuntu 14.04 LTS
  amd64 trusty image built on 2018-10-04
○ Ubuntu 16.04 LTS
  amd64 xenial image built on 2018-10-04
○ Ubuntu 18.04 LTS

Can't find what you're looking for? Explore hundreds of VM solutions in Marketplace

Boot disk type ❓   Size (GB) ❓

Standard persistent disk   ▼   9

Here you can choose the operating system you want to use. You can also choose the boot disk type, which can be either Standard Persistent Disk or SSD Persistent Disk. You can also specify the size of the disk.

Following the Boot Disk section is the Identity and API Access section. Here you can specify a service account for the VM and set the scope of API access. If you want the processes running on this VM to use only some APIs, you can use these options to limit the VM's access to specific APIs.

FIGURE 5.10 Identity and API Access and Firewall configurations

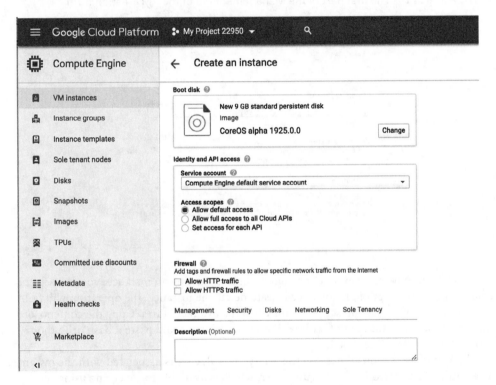

In the next section, you can select if you want the VM to accept HTTP or HTTPS traffic.

Additional Configuration Details

Click Management, Security, Disks, Networking, and Sole Tenancy to expose additional configuration options.

Management Tab

The Management tab of the form (Figure 5.11) provides a space where you can describe the VM and its use. You can also create labels, which are key-value pairs. You can assign any label you like. Labels and a general description are often used to help manage your VMs and understand how they are being used. Labels are particularly important when your number of servers grows. It is a best practice to include a description and labels for all VMs.

FIGURE 5.11   The first part of the Management tab of the VM creation form

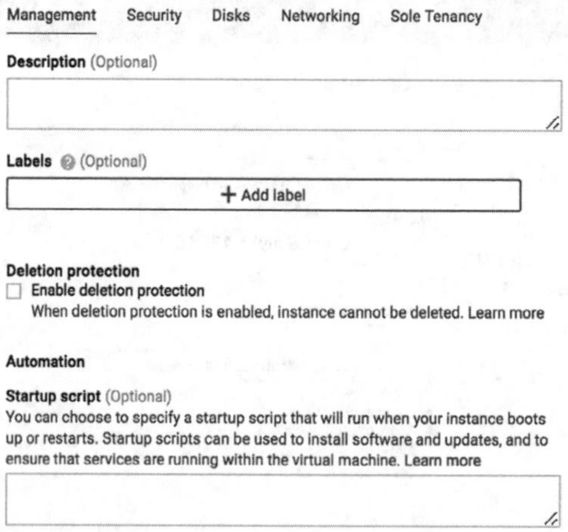

If you want to force an extra confirmation before deleting an instance, you can select the deletion protection option. If someone tries to delete the instance, the operation will fail.

You can specify a startup script to run when the instance starts. Copy the contents of the startup script to the script text box. For example, you could paste a bash or Python script directly into the text box.

The Metadata section allows you to specify key-value pairs associated with the instance. These values are stored in a metadata server, which is available for querying using the Compute Engine API. Metadata tags are especially useful if you have a common script you want to run on startup or shutdown but want the behavior of the script to vary according to some metadata values.

The Availability Policy sets three parameters.

- Preemptibility, which when enabled allows Google to shut down the server with a 30-second notice. In return, the cost of a preemptible server is much lower than that of a nonpreemptible server.

- Automatic restart, which indicates if the server stops because of a hardware failure, maintenance event, or some other non-user–controlled event
- On host maintenance, which indicates whether the virtual server should be migrated to another physical server when a maintenance event occurs

FIGURE 5.12   The second part of the Management tab of the VM creation form

Metadata (Optional)
You can set custom metadata for an instance or project outside of the server-defined metadata. This is useful for passing in arbitrary values to your project or instance that can be queried by your code on the instance. Learn more

Key	Value	✕

＋ Add item

Availability policy

Preemptibility
A preemptible VM costs much less, but lasts only 24 hours. It can be terminated sooner due to system demands. Learn more

Off (recommended) ▾

Automatic restart
Compute Engine can automatically restart VM instances if they are terminated for non-user-initiated reasons (maintenance event, hardware failure, software failure, etc.)

On (recommended) ▾

On host maintenance
When Compute Engine performs periodic infrastructure maintenance it can migrate your VM instances to other hardware without downtime

Migrate VM instance (recommended) ▾

In the Security section, you can specify if you want to use Shielded VMs and Secure Shell (SSH) keys.

Shielded VMs are configured to have additional security mechanisms that you can choose to run. These include the following:

- Secure Boot, which ensures that only authenticated operating system software runs on the VM. It does this by checking the digital signatures of the software. If a signature check fails, the boot process will halt.

- Virtual Trusted Platform Module (vTPM), which is a virtualized version of a trusted platform module (TPM). A TPM is a specialized computer chip designed to protect security resources, like keys and certificates.

- Integrity Monitoring, which uses a known good baseline of boot measurements to compare to recent boot measurements. If the check fails, then there is some difference between the baseline measurement and the current measurements.

FIGURE 5.13   Additional security controls can be placed on VMs.

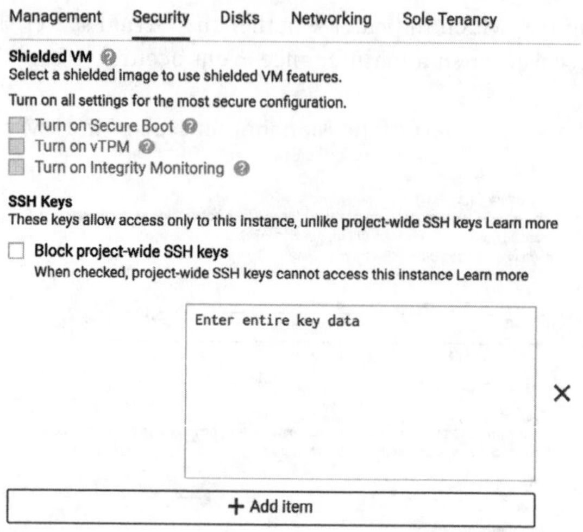

GCP supports the concept of project-wide SSH keys, which are used to give users project-wide access to VMs. You can block that behavior at the VM if you use project-wide SSH keys and do not want all project users to have access to this machine.

The next advanced tab is the Boot Disk tab. Here you can specify whether the boot disk should be deleted when the instance is deleted. You can also select how you would like to manage encryption keys for the boot disk. By default, Google manages those keys.

Within the Boot Disk configuration tab, you also have the option of adding a new disk or attaching an existing disk. Figure 5.14 shows the tab for adding a new disk.

FIGURE 5.14   Boot disk advanced configuration

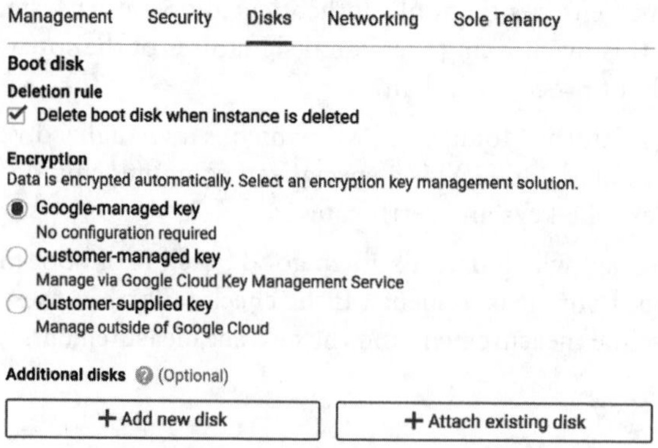

When adding an existing disk, the dialog form appears, as in Figure 5.15. Note that the Disk drop-down has a list of existing disks you can choose from. You can make the disk read-only or read/write. You can also indicate if you want the disk deleted when the instance is deleted. Using an existing disk in read-only mode is a good way of replicating reference data across multiple instances of VMs.

FIGURE 5.15   Dialog for adding an existing disk to a VM

You can also add a new disk using the dialog shown in Figure 5.16. When adding a new disk, you need to provide the following information:

- Name of the disk
- Disk type, either standard or SSD Persistent disk
- Source image, if this is not a blank disk
- Indication of whether to delete the disk when the instance is deleted
- Size in gigabytes
- How the encryption keys will be managed

FIGURE 5.16   Dialog for adding a new disk to a VM

On the Networking tab, you can see the network interface information, including the IP address of the VM. If you have multiple networks, you have the option of adding another network interface to that other network. This use of dual network interfaces can be useful if you are running some type of proxy or server that acts as a control for flow of some traffic between the networks. In addition, you can also add network tags in this dialog (see Figure 5.17).

FIGURE 5.17   Dialog for network configuration of a VM

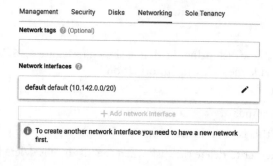

If you need to ensure that your VMs run on a server only with your other VMs, then you can specify sole tenancy. The Sole Tenancy tab allows you to specify labels regarding sole tenancy for the server (see Figure 5.18).

FIGURE 5.18   Sole Tenancy configuration form

Compute Engine		← Create a node group
VM instances		**Name** ⊘
Instance groups		node-group-1
Instance templates		**Region** ⊘ **Zone** ⊘
Sole tenant nodes		us-east1 (South Carolina) ▼ us-east1-b ▼
Disks		**Node template**
Snapshots		▼
Images		**Number of nodes**
TPUs		nodes 0 - 100

You will be billed for nodes in this group. Compute Engine pricing ↗

Create   Cancel

Creating and Configuring Virtual Machines with Cloud SDK

A second way to create and configure VMs is with Google Cloud SDK, which provides a command-line interface. To use Cloud SDK, you will first need to install it on your local device.

Installing Cloud SDK

You have three options for interacting with Google Cloud resources:

- Using a command-line interface
- Using a RESTful interface
- Using the Cloud Shell

Before using either of the first two options from your local system, you will need to install Cloud SDK on your machine. Cloud Console is a graphical user interface you can access through a browser at https://console.cloud.google.com.

Cloud SDK can be installed on Linux, Windows, or Mac computers.

Installing Cloud SDK on Linux

If you are using Linux, you can install Cloud SDK using your operating system's package manager. Ubuntu and other Debian distributions use apt-get to install packages. Red Hat Enterprise, CentOS, and other Linux distributions use yum. For instructions on using apt-get, see https://cloud.google.com/sdk/docs/quickstart-debian-ubuntu. For instructions on installing on Red Hat Enterprise or CentOS, see https://cloud.google .com/sdk/docs/quickstart-redhat-centos.Installing.

Cloud SDK on Mac OS

Instructions for installing on a Mac and the installation file for Cloud SDK are available at https://cloud.google.com/sdk/docs/quickstart-macos. The first step is to verify that you have Python 2.7 installed. There are two versions of Cloud SDK, one for 32-bit macOS and one for 64-bit macOS.

Installing Cloud SDK on Windows

To install Cloud SDK on a Windows platform, you will need to download the appropriate installer. You can find instructions at https://cloud.google.com/sdk/docs/quickstart-windows.

Example Installation on Ubuntu Linux

The first step in installing Cloud SDK is to get the appropriate version of the package for your operating system. The following commands are for installing Cloud SDK on Ubuntu. See https://cloud.google.com/sdk/docs/quickstart-debian-ubuntu for any updates to this procedure.

You need to identify which version of the operating system you are using because the Google naming convention for Cloud SDK references the operating system name. The following command creates an environment variable with the name of the Cloud SDK package for the current operating system:

```
export CLOUD_SDK_REPO="cloud-sdk-$(lsb_release -c -s)"
```

Note that if you receive an error message that the lsb_release command is not found, you can install it with the following commands:

```
sudo apt-get update
sudo apt-get install lsb-core
```

You can see the value of the variable CLOUD_SDK_REPO using the following command:

```
echo $CLOUD_SDK_REPO
```

This will display a value such as cloud-sdk-bionic. Bionic is the code name for Ubuntu 18.04.

Next, you need to specify where to find Cloud SDK. We do this by adding the URL of the Cloud SDK package to the /etc/apt/sources.list.d/google-cloud-sdk.list file. Now apt-get will know where to find the package.

```
echo "deb http://packages.cloud.google.com/apt $CLOUD_SDK_REPO main" | sudo tee
-a /etc/apt/sources.list.d/google-cloud-sdk.list
```

You also need to import the GCP public key, which you do with this command:

```
curl https://packages.cloud.google.com/apt/doc/apt-key.gpg | sudo apt-key add -
```

Finally, you need to update the apt-get package list and then use apt-get to install Cloud SDK.

```
sudo apt-get update && sudo apt-get install google-cloud-sdk
```

Now Cloud SDK is installed and you can execute commands using it. The first step is to initialize Cloud SDK using the gcloud init command, as shown here:

```
gcloud init
```

When you receive an authentication link, copy it into your browser. You are prompted to authenticate with Google when you go to that URL. Next, a response code appears in your browser. Copy that to your terminal window and paste it in response to the prompt that should appear.

Next, you are prompted to enter a project. If projects already exist in your account, they will be listed. You also have the option of creating a new project at this point. The project you select or create will be the default project used when issuing commands through Cloud SDK.

Creating a Virtual Machine with Cloud SDK

To create a VM from the command line, you will use the gcloud command. You use this command for many cloud management tasks, including the following:

- Compute Engine
- Cloud SQL instances
- Kubernetes Engine
- Cloud Dataproc
- Cloud DNS
- Cloud Deployment

The gcloud command is organized into a hierarchy of groups, such as the compute group for Compute Engine commands. We'll discuss other groups in later chapters; the focus here is on Compute Engine.

A typical gcloud command starts with the group, as shown here:

```
gcloud compute
```

A subgroup is used in Compute Engine commands to indicate what type of compute resource you are working with. To create an instance, you use this command:

```
gcloud compute instances
```

And the action you want to take is to create an instance, so you would use this:

```
gcloud compute instances create ace-instance-1, ace-instance-2
```

If you do not specify additional parameters, such as a zone, Google Cloud will use your information from your default project. You can view your project information using the following gcloud command:

```
gcloud compute project-info describe
```

To create a VM in the us-central1-a zone, add the zone parameter like this:

```
gcloud compute instances create ace-instance-1 ace-instance-2 --zone
us-central1-a
```

You can list the VMs you've create using this:

```
gcloud compute instances list
```

Here are commonly used parameters with the create instance command:

- --boot-disk-size is the size of the boot disk for a new disk. Disk size may be between 10GB and 2TB.
- --boot-disk-type is the type of disk. Use gcloud compute disk-types list for a list of disk types available in the zone the VM is created in.
- --labels is the list of key-value pairs in the format of KEY=VALUE.
- --machine-type is the type of machine to use. If not specified, it uses n1-standard-1. Use gcloud compute machine-types list to view a list of machine types available in the zone you are using.
- --preemptible, if included, specifies that the VM will be preemptible.

For additional parameters, see the glcoud compute instance create documentation at https://cloud.google.com/sdk/gcloud/reference/compute/instances/create.

To create a standard VM with 8 CPUs and 30GB of memory, you can specify n1-standard-8 as the machine type.

```
gcloud compute instances create ace-instance-n1s8 --machine-type=n1-standard-8
```

If you want to make this instance preemptible, you add the preemptible parameter:

```
gcloud compute instances create --machine-type=n1-standard-8 --preemptible ace-
instance-1
```

Creating a Virtual Machine with Cloud Shell

An alternative to running gcloud commands locally is to run them in a cloud instance. Cloud Shell provides this capability. To use Cloud Shell, start it from Cloud

Console by clicking the shell icon in the upper-right corner of the browser, as shown in Figure 5.19.

FIGURE 5.19   Cloud Shell is activated through Cloud Console.

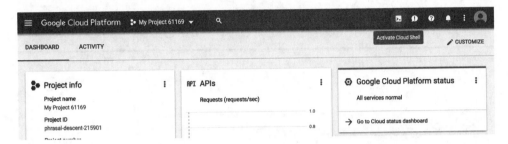

Cloud Shell provides a Linux command line, as shown in Figure 5.20, and Cloud SDK is already installed. All gcloud commands that you can enter on your local device with Cloud SDK installed can be used in Cloud Shell.

FIGURE 5.20   Cloud Shell opens a command-line window in the browser.

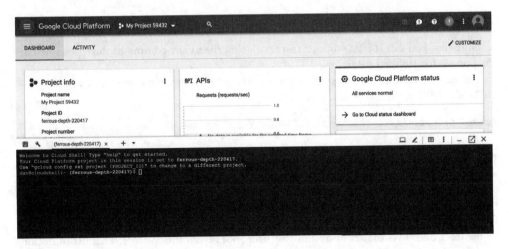

Basic Virtual Machine Management

When VMs are running, you can perform basic management tasks by using the console or using gcloud commands.

Starting and Stopping Instances

In the console you view a list of instances by selecting Compute Engine and then VM Instances from the left-side panel of the console. You can then select a VM to operate on and list command options by clicking the three dot icons on the right. Figure 5.21 shows an example.

FIGURE 5.21 Basic operations on VMs can be performed using a pop-up menu in the console.

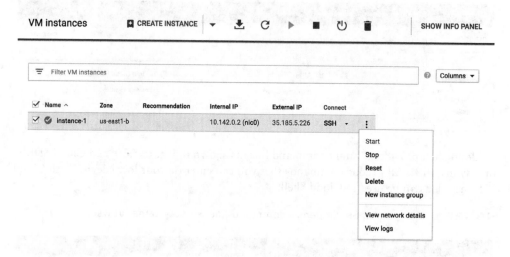

Note that you can start a stopped instance using the start command that is enabled in the pop-up for stopped instances.

You can also use gcloud to stop an instance with the following command, where INSTANCE-NAME is the name of the instance:

```
gcloud compute instances stop INSTANCE-NAME
```

Network Access to Virtual Machines

As a cloud engineer, you will sometimes need to log into a VM to perform some administration tasks. The most common way is to use SSH when logging into a Linux server or Remote Desktop Protocol (RDP) when logging into a Windows server.

Figure 5.22 shows the set of options for using SSH from the console. This list of options appears when you click the SSH button associated with a VM.

FIGURE 5.22 From the console, you can start an SSH session to log into a Linux server.

Choosing the Open In Browser Window option will open a new browser window and display a terminal window for accessing the command line on the server.

FIGURE 5.23   A terminal window opens in a new browser window when using Cloud Shell.

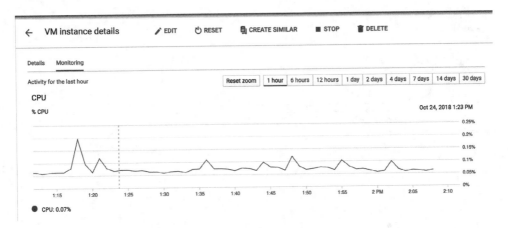

Monitoring a Virtual Machine

While your VM is running you can monitor CPU, disk, and network load by viewing the Monitoring page in the VM Instance Details page.

To access monitoring information in the console, select a VM instance from the VM Instance page by clicking the name of the VM you want to monitor. This will show the Details page of the VM. Select the Monitoring option near the top of the page to view monitoring details.

Figures 5.24, 5.25, and 5.26 show the information displayed about CPU, network utilization, and disk operations.

FIGURE 5.24   The Monitoring tab of the VM Instance Details page shows CPU utilization.

FIGURE 5.25   The Monitoring tab of the VM Instance Details page also shows network utilization.

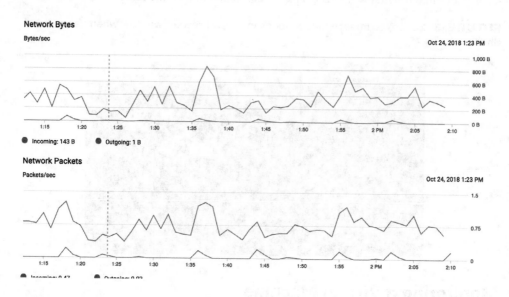

FIGURE 5.26   Disk utilization is included in the Monitoring tab of the VM Instance Details page.

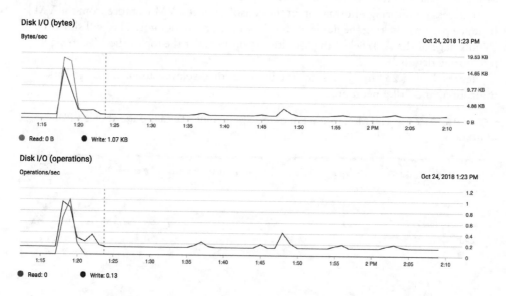

Cost of Virtual Machines

Part of the basic management of a VM is tracking the costs of the instances you are running. If you want to track costs automatically, you can enable Cloud Platform billing and setup Billing Export. This will produce daily reports on the usage and cost of VMs.

The following are the most important things to remember about VM costs:

- VMs are billed in 1-second increments.
- The cost is based on machine type. The more CPUs and memory used, the higher the cost.
- Google offers discounts for sustained usage.
- VMs are charged for a minimum of 1 minute of use.
- Preemptible VMs can save you up to 80 percent of the cost of a VM.

Guidelines for Planning, Deploying, and Managing Virtual Machines

Consider the following guidelines to help with streamlining your work with VMs. These guidelines apply to working with a small number of VMs. Later chapters will provide additional guidelines for working with clusters and instance groups, which are sets of similarly configured VMs.

- Choose a machine type with the fewest CPUs and the smallest amount of memory that still meets your requirements, including peak capacity. This will minimize the cost of the VM.
- Use the console for ad hoc administration of VMs. Use scripts with gcloud commands for tasks that will be repeated.
- Use startup scripts to perform software updates and other tasks that should be performed on startup.
- If you make many modifications to a machine image, consider saving it and using it with new instances rather than running the same set of modifications on every new instance.
- If you can tolerate unplanned disruptions, use preemptible VMs to reduce cost.
- Use SSH or RDP to access a VM to perform operating system–level tasks.
- Use Cloud Console, Cloud Shell, or Cloud SDK to perform VM-level tasks.

Summary

Google Cloud Console is a web-based graphical user interface for managing GCP resources. Cloud SDK is a command-line package that allows engineers to manage cloud resources from the command line of their local device. Cloud Shell is a web-based terminal interface to VMs. Cloud SDK is installed in Cloud Shell.

When creating a VM, you have to specify a number of parameters, including a name for the VM, a region and zone where the VM will run, a machine type that specifies the number of vCPUs and the amount of memory, and a boot disk that includes an operating system.

gcloud is the top-level command of the hierarchical command structure in Cloud SDK.

Common tasks when managing VMs are starting and stopping instances, using SSH to access a terminal on the VM, monitoring, and tracking the cost of the VM.

Exam Essentials

Understand how to use Cloud Console and Cloud SDK to create, start, and stop VMs. Parameters that you will need to provide when creating a VM include name, machine type, region, zone, and boot disk. Understand the need to create a VM in a project.

Know how to configure a preemptible VM using Cloud Console and the `gcloud` commands. Know when to use a preemptible VM and when not to. Know that preemptible VMs cost up to 80 percent less than nonpreemptible VMs.

Know the purpose of advanced options, including Shielded VMs and advanced boot disk configurations. Know that advanced options provide additional security. Understand the kinds of protections provided.

Know how to use `gcloud` compute instance commands to list, start, and stop VMs. Know the structure of gcloud commands. gcloud commands start with gcloud followed by a service, such as compute, followed by a resource type, such as instances, followed by a command or verb, like create, list, or describe.

Understand how to monitor a VM. Know where to find CPU utilization, network monitoring, and disk monitoring in the VM Instances pages of the console. Know the difference between listing and describing instances with a gcloud command.

Know the factors that determine the cost of a VM. Know that Google charges by the second with a 1-minute minimum. Understand that the costs of a machine type may be different in different locations. Know that cost is based on the number of vCPUs and memory.

Review Questions *90%.*

You can find the answers in the Appendix.

1. You have just opened the GCP console at console.google.com. You have authenticated with the user you want to use. What is one of the first things you should do before performing tasks on VMs?

    A. Open Cloud Shell.

    B. Verify you can SSH into a VM.

    C. Verify that the selected project is the one you want to work with.

    D. Review the list of running VMs.

2. What is a one-time task you will need to complete before using the console?

    A. Set up billing

    B. Create a project

    C. Create a storage bucket

    D. Specify a default zone

3. A colleague has asked for your assistance setting up a test environment in Google Cloud. They have never worked in GCP. You suggest starting with a single VM. Which of the following is the minimal set of information you will need?

    A. A name for the VM and a machine type

    B. A name for the VM, a machine type, a region, and a zone

    C. A name for the VM, a machine type, a region, a zone, and a CIDR block

    D. A name for the VM, a machine type, a region, a zone, and an IP address

4. An architect has suggested a particular machine type for your workload. You are in the console creating a VM and you don't see the machine type in the list of available machine types. What could be the reason for this?

    A. You have selected the incorrect subnet.

    B. That machine type is not available in the zone you specified.

    C. You have chosen an incompatible operating system.

    D. You have not specified a correct memory configuration.

5. Your manager asks for your help with understanding cloud computing costs. Your team runs dozens of VMs for three different applications. Two of the applications are for use by the marketing department and one is use by the finance department. Your manager wants a way to bill each department for the cost of the VMs used for their applications. What would you suggest to help solve this problem?

    A. Access controls

    B. Persistent disks

    C. Labels and descriptions

    D. Descriptions only

6. If you wanted to set the preemptible property using Cloud Console, in which section of the Create An Instance page would you find the option?

    A. Availability Policy

    B. Identity And API Access

    C. Sole Tenancy

    D. Networking

7. You need to set up a server with a high level of security. You want to be prepared in case of attacks on your server by someone trying to inject a rootkit (a kind of malware that can alter the operating system). Which option should you select when creating a VM?

    A. Firewall

    B. Shield VM

    C. Project-wide SSH keys

    D. Boot disk integrity check

8. All of the following parameters can be set when adding an additional disk through Google Cloud Console, except one. Which one?

    A. Disk type

    B. Encryption key management

    C. Block size

    D. Source image for the disk

9. You lead a team of cloud engineers who maintain cloud resources for several departments in your company. You've noticed a problem with configuration drift. Some machine configurations are no longer in the same state as they were when created. You can't find notes or documentation on how the changes were made or why. What practice would you implement to solve this problem?

    A. Have all cloud engineers use only command-line interface in Cloud Shell.

    B. Write scripts using gcloud commands to change configuration and store those scripts in a version control system.

    C. Take notes when making changes to configuration and store them in Google Drive.

    D. Limit privileges so only you can make changes so you will always know when and why configurations were changed.

10. When using the Cloud SDK command-line interface, which of the following is part of commands for administering resources in Compute Engine?

    A. `gcloud compute instances`

    B. `gcloud instances`

    C. `gcloud instances compute`

    D. None of the above

11. A newly hired cloud engineer is trying to understand what VMs are running in a particular project. How could the engineer get summary information on each VM running in a project?

   A. Execute the command gcloud compute list

   B. Execute the command gcloud compute instances list

   C. Execute the command gcloud instances list

   D. Execute the command gcloud list instances

12. When creating a VM using the command line, how should you specify labels for the VM?

   A. Use the --labels option with labels in the format of KEYS:VALUES.

   B. Use the --labels option with labels in the format of KEYS=VALUE.

   C. Use the --labels option with labels in the format of KEYS,VALUES.

   D. This is not possible in the command line.

13. In the boot disk advanced configuration, which operations can you specify when creating a new VM?

   A. Add a new disk, reformat an existing disk, attach an existing disk

   B. Add a new disk and reformat an existing disk

   C. Add a new disk and attach an existing disk

   D. Reformat an existing disk and attach an existing disk

14. You have acquired a 10 GB data set from a third-party research firm. A group of data scientists would like to access this data from their statistics programs written in R. R works well with Linux and Windows file systems, and the data scientists are familiar with file operations in R. The data scientists would each like to have their own dedicated VM with the data available in the VM's file system. What is a way to make this data readily available on a VM and minimize the steps the data scientists will have to take?

   A. Store the data in Cloud Storage.

   B. Create VMs using a source image created from a disk with the data on it.

   C. Store the data in Google Drive.

   D. Load the data into BigQuery.

15. The Network tab of the create VM form is where you would perform which of the following operations?

   A. Set the IP address of the VM

   B. Add a network interface to the VM

   C. Specify a default router

   D. Change firewall configuration rules

16. You want to create a VM using the gcloud command. What parameter would you include to specify the type of boot disk?

    A. boot-disk-type

    B. boot-disk

    C. disk-type

    D. type-boot-disk

17. Which of the following commands will create a VM with four CPUs that is named web-server-1?

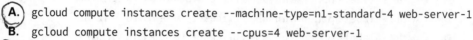

    A. gcloud compute instances create --machine-type=n1-standard-4 web-server-1

    B. gcloud compute instances create --cpus=4 web-server-1

    C. gcloud compute instances create --machine-type=n1-standard-4 –instance-name web-server-1

    D. gcloud compute instances create --machine-type=n1-4-cpu web-server-1

18. Which of the following commands will stop a VM named web-server-1?

    A. gcloud compute instances halt web-server-1

    B. gcloud compute instances --terminate web-server1

    C. gcloud compute instances stop web-server-1

    D. gcloud compute stop web-server-1

19. You have just created an Ubuntu VM and want to log into the VM to install some software packages. Which network service would you use to access the VM?

    A. FTP

    B. SSH

    C. RDP

    D. ipconfig

20. Your management team is considering three different cloud providers. You have been asked to summarize billing and cost information to help the management team compare cost structures between clouds. Which of the following would you mention about the cost of VMs in GCP?

    A. VMs are billed in 1-second increments, cost varies with the number of CPUs and amount of memory in a machine type, you can create custom machine types, preemptible VMs cost up to 80 percent less than standard VMs, and Google offers discounts for sustained usage.

    B. VMs are billed in 1-second increments and VMs can run up to 24 hours before they will be be shut down.

    C. Google offers discounts for sustained usage in only some regions, cost varies with the number of CPUs and amount of memory in a machine type, you can create custom machine types, preemptible VMs cost up to 80 percent less than standard VMs.

    D. VMs are charged for a minimum of 1 hour of use and cost varies with the number of CPUs and amount of memory in a machine type.

Chapter

6

Managing Virtual Machines

**THIS CHAPTER COVERS THE FOLLOWING
OBJECTIVES OF THE GOOGLE ASSOCIATE
CLOUD ENGINEER CERTIFICATION EXAM:**

✓ **4.1 Managing Compute Engine resources**

After creating virtual machines, a cloud engineer will need to work with both single instances of virtual machines (VMs) and groups of VMs that run the same configuration. The latter are called *instance groups* and are introduced in this chapter.

This chapter begins with a description of common management tasks and how to complete them in the console, followed by a description of how to complete them in Cloud Shell or with the Cloud SDK command line. Next, you will learn how to configure and manage instance groups. The chapter concludes with a discussion of guidelines for managing VMs.

Managing Single Virtual Machine Instances

We begin by discussing how to manage a single instance of a VM. By single instance, we mean one created by itself and not in an instance group or other type of cluster. Recall from previous chapters that there are three ways to work with instances: in Cloud Console, in Cloud Shell, and with the Cloud SDK command line. Both Cloud Shell and the Cloud SDK command lines make use of gcloud commands, so we will describe Cloud Shell and Cloud SDK together in this section.

Managing Single Virtual Machine Instances in the Console

The basic VM management tasks that a cloud engineer should be familiar with are creating, stopping, and deleting instances. We covered creating instances in the previous chapter, so we'll focus on the other tasks here. You should also be familiar with listing VMs, attaching graphics processing units (GPUs) to VMs, and working with snapshots and images.

Starting, Stopping, and Deleting Instances

To start working, open the console and select Compute Engine. Then select VM instances. This will display a window such as in Figure 6.1, but with different VMs listed. In this example, there are three VMs.

FIGURE 6.1   The VM Instance panel in the Compute Engine section of Cloud Console

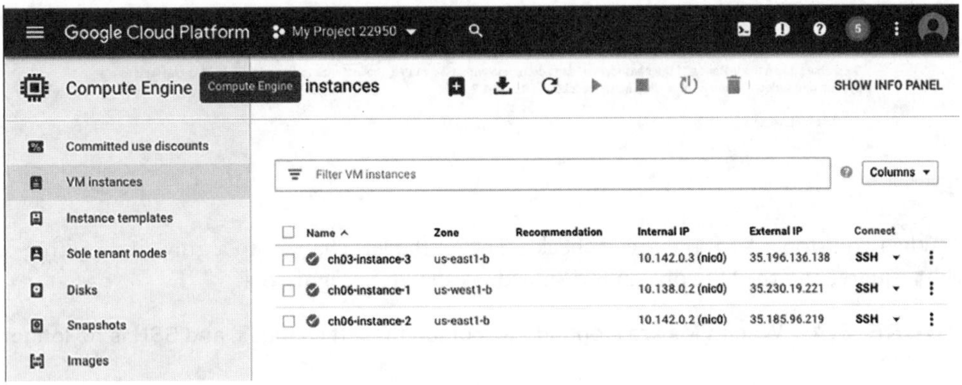

The three instances in Figure 6.1 are all running. You can stop the instances by clicking the three-dot icon on the right side of the line listing the VM attributes. This action displays a list of commands. Figure 6.2 shows the list of commands available for `instancech06-instance-1`.

FIGURE 6.2   The list of commands available from the console for changing the state of a VM

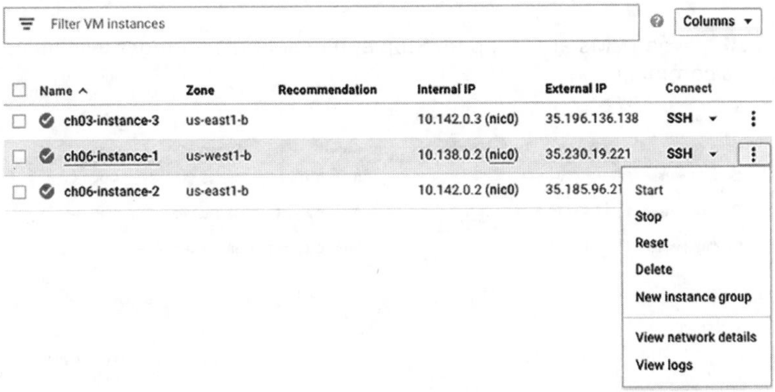

If you select Stop from the command menu, the instance will be stopped. When an instance is stopped, it is not consuming compute resources, so you will not be charged. The instance still exists and can be started again when you need it. Figure 6.3 shows a warning form that indicates you are about to stop a VM. You can click the dialog box in the lower left to suppress this message.

FIGURE 6.3   A warning message that may appear about stopping a VM

Stop VM instance

Stop shuts down the instance. If the shutdown doesn't complete within 2 minutes, the instance is forced to halt. This can lead to file-system corruption. Do you want to stop instance "ch06-instance-1"?

☐ Do not show again

CANCEL   STOP

When you stop a VM, the green check mark on the left changes to a gray circle with a white square, and the SSH option is disabled, as shown in Figure 6.4.

FIGURE 6.4   When VMs are stopped the icon on the left changes, and SSH is no longer available.

	Name ∧	Zone	Recommendation	Internal IP	External IP	Connect	
☐ ✅	ch03-instance-3	us-east1-b		10.142.0.3 (nic0)	35.196.136.138	SSH ▾	⋮
☐ ◯	ch06-instance-1	us-west1-b		10.138.0.2 (nic0)	35.230.19.221	SSH ▾	⋮
☐ ✅	ch06-instance-2	us-east1-b		10.142.0.2 (nic0)	35.185.96.219	SSH ▾	⋮

To start a stopped VM, click the three-dot icon on the right to display the menu of available commands. Notice in Figure 6.5 that Start is now available, but Stop and Reset are not.

FIGURE 6.5   When VMs are stopped, Stop and Reset are no longer available, but Start is available as a command.

	Name ∧	Zone	Recommendation	Internal IP	External IP	Connect	
☐ ✅	ch03-instance-3	us-east1-b		10.142.0.3 (nic0)	35.196.136.138	SSH ▾	⋮
☐ ◯	ch06-instance-1	us-west1-b		10.138.0.2 (nic0)	35.230.19.221	SSH ▾	⋮
☐ ✅	ch06-instance-2	us-east1-b		10.142.0.2 (nic0)	35.185.96.21		

Start
Stop
Reset
Delete
New instance group

View network details
View logs

The Reset command restarts a VM. The properties of the VM will not change, but data in memory will be lost.

> **NOTE**   When a VM is restarted, the contents of memory are lost. If you need to preserve data between reboots or for use on other VMs, save the data to a persistent disk or Cloud Storage.

When you are done with an instance and no longer need it, you can delete it. Deleting a VM removes it from Cloud Console and releases resources, like the storage used to keep the VM image when stopped. Deleting an instance from Cloud Console will display a message such as in Figure 6.6.

FIGURE 6.6   Deleting an instance from the console will display a warning message such as this.

Delete an instance

Are you sure you want to delete instance "ch03-instance-3"? (This will also delete boot disk "ch03-instance-3")

CANCEL   DELETE

Viewing Virtual Machine Inventory

The VM Instances page of Cloud Console will show a list of VMs, if any exist in the current project. If you have a large number of instances, it can help to filter the list to see only instances of interest. Do this using the Filter VM Instances box above the list of VMs, as shown in Figure 6.7.

FIGURE 6.7   List of instances filtered by search criteria

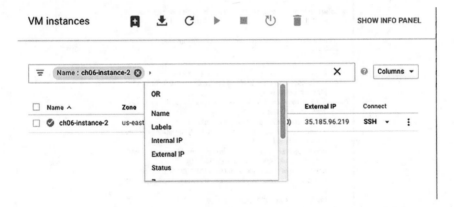

In this example, we have specified that we want to see only the instance named ch06-instance-2. In addition to specifying instance names, you can also filter by the following:

- Labels
- Internal IP
- External IP
- Status
- Zone
- Network

- Deletion protection
- Member of managed instance group
- Member of unmanaged instance group

If you set multiple filter conditions, then all must be true for a VM to be listed unless you explicitly state the OR operator.

Attaching GPUs to an Instance

GPUs are used for math-intensive applications such as visualizations and machine learning. GPUs perform math calculations and allow some work to be off-loaded from the CPU to the GPU.

To add a GPU to an instance, you must start an instance in which GPU libraries have been installed or will be installed. For example, you can use one of the Google Cloud Platform (GCP) images that has GPU libraries installed, including the Deep Learning images, as shown in Figure 6.8. You must also verify that the instance will run in a zone that has GPUs available.

FIGURE 6.8   When attaching GPUs, it is best to use an image that has the necessary libraries installed. You can use a GCP-provided image or a custom image with the necessary libraries.

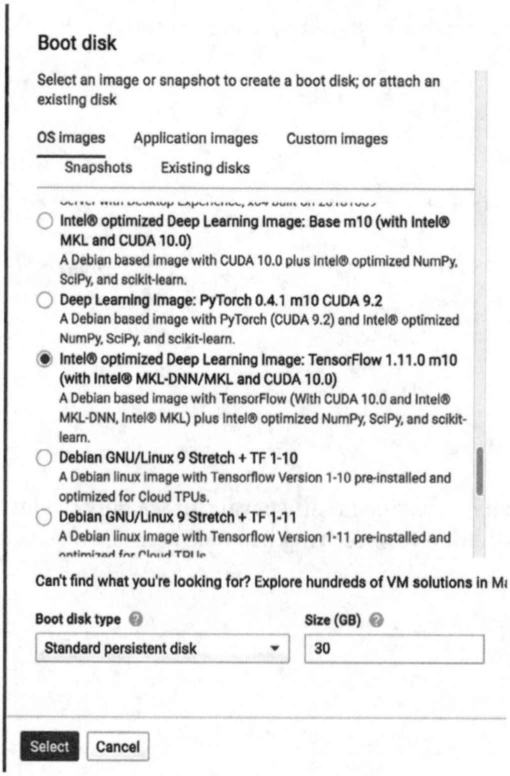

You will also need to customize the configuration for the machine type; Figure 6.9 shows the form.

FIGURE 6.9   The Cloud Console form for configuring machine type

Machine type
Customize to select cores, memory and GPUs.

4 vCPUs ▼	15 GB memory	Customize

Upgrade your account to create instances with up to 96 cores

Click Customize. This will expand the set of machine type parameters, as shown in Figure 6.10.

FIGURE 6.10   This form is used when creating a customized machine type.

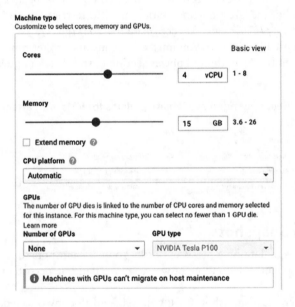

Select the number of GPUs to attach. The options are None, 1, 2, or 4 (see Figure 6.11). Then select the GPU type, as shown in Figure 6.12.

FIGURE 6.11   Selecting the number of GPUs to attach to the VM

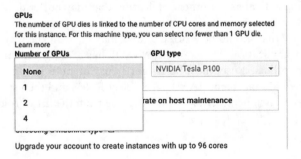

FIGURE 6.12   Selecting the type of GPUs to attach to the VM

GPUs
The number of GPU dies is linked to the number of CPU cores and memory selected for this instance. For this machine type, you can select no fewer than 1 GPU die.
Learn more

Number of GPUs	GPU type
1 ▼	NVIDIA Tesla P100
	NVIDIA Tesla P100 Virtual Workstation
ⓘ Machines with GPUs can't migrat	NVIDIA Tesla V100

There are some restrictions on the use of GPUs. The CPU must be compatible with the GPU selected. For example, if you are running a VM on a server with an Intel Skylake or later CPU, then you cannot use the Tesla K80 GPU. GPUs cannot be attached to shared memory machines. For the latest documentation on GPU restrictions and a list of zones with GPUs, see https://cloud.google.com/compute/docs/gpus/.

Also, if you add a GPU to a VM, you must set the instance to terminate during maintenance. This is set in the Availability Policies section of the VM configuration form (see Figure 6.13).

FIGURE 6.13   Recommended availability policies for VMs with attached GPUs

Availability policies

Preemptibility	Off (recommended)
Automatic restart	On (recommended)
On host maintenance	Terminate VM instance

Working with Snapshots

Snapshots are copies of data on a persistent disk. You use snapshots to save data on a disk so you can restore it. This is a convenient way to make multiple persistent disks with the same data.

When you first create a snapshot, GCP will make a full copy of the data on the persistent disk. The next time you create a snapshot from that disk, GCP will copy only the data that has changed since the last snapshot. This optimizes storage while keeping the snapshot up to date with the data that was on the disk the last time a snapshot operation occurred.

If you are running a database or other application that may buffer data in memory before writing to disk, be sure to flush disk buffers before you create the snapshot; otherwise, data in memory that should be written to disk may be lost. The way to flush the disk buffers will vary by application. For example, MySQL has a FLUSH statement.

To work with snapshots, a user must be assigned the Compute Storage Admin role. Go to the Identity Access Management (IAM) page, select Roles, and then specify the email address of a user to be assigned the role. Select the role from the list of roles, as shown in Figure 6.14.

FIGURE 6.14   To work with snapshots, a user needs to have the Cloud Storage Admin role.

To create a snapshot from Cloud Console, display the Compute Engine options and select Snapshots from the left panel, as shown in Figure 6.15.

FIGURE 6.15   Creating a snapshot using Cloud Console

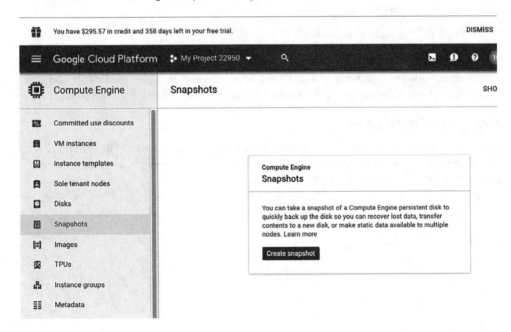

Then, click Create Snapshot to display the form in Figure 6.16. Specify and name and, optionally, a description. You can add labels to the snapshot as well. It is a good practice to label all resources with a consistent labeling convention. In the case of snapshots, the labels may indicate the type of data on the disk and the application that uses the data.

FIGURE 6.16   Form for creating a snapshot

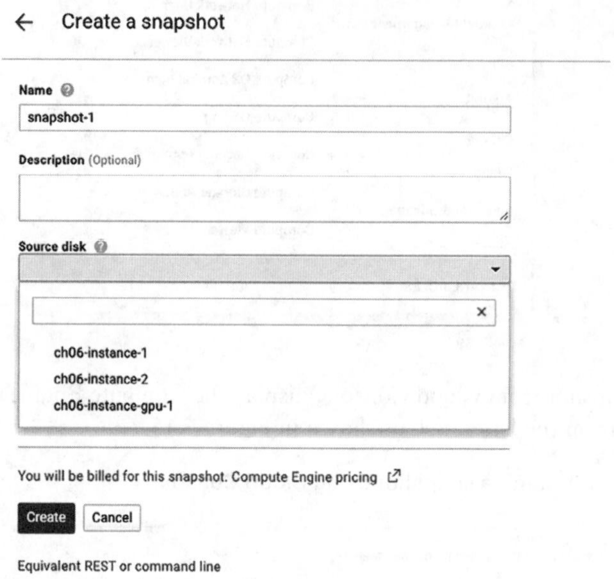

←   Create a snapshot

Name
snapshot-1

Description (Optional)

Source disk

ch06-instance-1
ch06-instance-2
ch06-instance-gpu-1

You will be billed for this snapshot. Compute Engine pricing ↗

Create   Cancel

Equivalent REST or command line

If you are making a snapshot of a disk on a Windows server, check the Enable VSS box to create an application-consistent snapshot without having to shut down the instance.

Working with Images

Images are similar to snapshots in that they are copies of disk contents. The difference is that snapshots are used to make data available on a disk, while images are used to create VMs. Images can be created from the following:

- Disk
- Snapshot
- Cloud storage file
- Another image

To create an image, choose the Image option from the Compute Engine page in Cloud Console, as shown in Figure 6.17. This lists available images.

FIGURE 6.17   Images available. From here, you can create additional images.

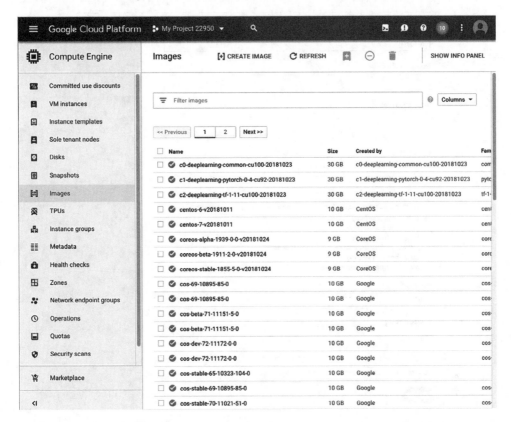

Select Create Image to show the form in Figure 6.18. This allows you to create a new image by specifying name, description, and labels. Images have an optional attribute called Family, which allows you to group images. When a family is specified, the latest, nondeprecated image in the family is used.

FIGURE 6.18   Cloud Console form for creating an image

← Create an image

Name ⍰

image-1|

Family (Optional) ⍰

Description (Optional)

Labels ⍰ (Optional)

+ Add label

Encryption
Data is encrypted automatically. Select an encryption key management solution.
◉ **Google-managed key**
   No configuration required
○ **Customer-managed key**
   Manage via Google Cloud Key Management Service
○ **Customer-supplied key**
   Manage outside of Google Cloud

Source ⍰

Disk   ▾

Source disk ⍰

                                                                              ▾

You will be billed for this image. Compute Engine pricing ↗

Create   Cancel

The form provides a drop-down list of options for the source of the image, as shown in Figure 6.19.

FIGURE 6.19   Options for the source of an image

Source ⍰

Disk
Snapshot
Image
Cloud Storage file

When Disk is selected as the source, you can choose from disks on VMs, as shown in Figure 6.20.

FIGURE 6.20   Options when using a disk as the source of an image

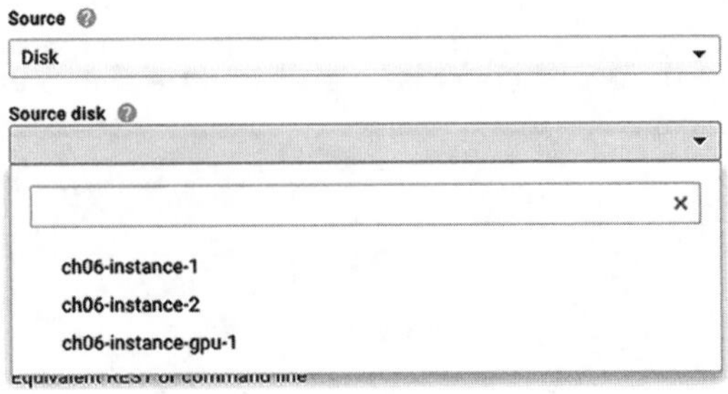

When you choose Image as the source type, you can choose an image from the current project or other projects (see Figure 6.21).

FIGURE 6.21   When using an image as a source, you can choose a source image from another project.

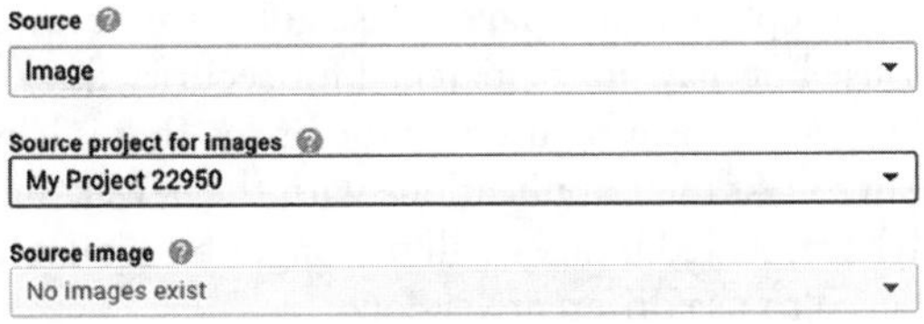

If you choose a Cloud Storage file as a source, you can browse your Cloud Storage bucket to find a file to use as the source (see Figure 6.22).

FIGURE 6.22   When using a Cloud Storage file as a source, you browse your storage buckets for a file.

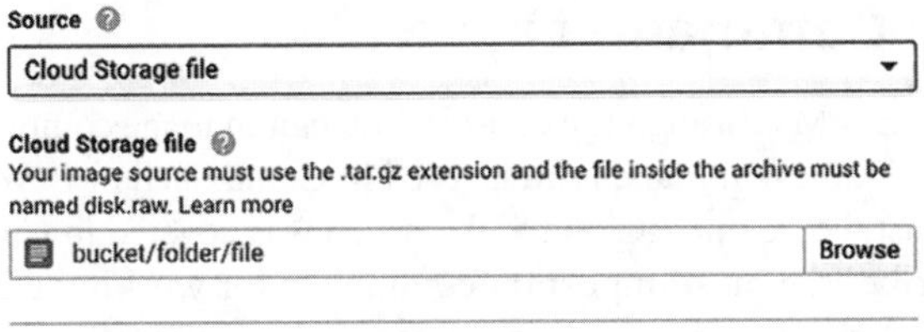

After you have created an image, you can delete it or deprecate it by checking the box next to the image name and selecting Delete or Deprecate from the line of commands above the list, as shown in Figure 6.23. You can delete and deprecate only custom images, not GCP-supplied images.

FIGURE 6.23 The Delete and Deprecate commands are available when one of your custom images is selected.

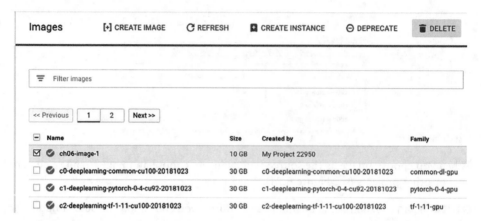

Delete removes the image, while Deprecated marks the image as no longer supported and allows you to specify a replacement image to use going forward. Google's deprecated images are available for use but may not be patched for security flaws or other updates. Deprecation is a useful way of informing users of the image that it is no longer supported and that they should plan to test their applications with the newer, supported versions of the image. Eventually, deprecated images will no longer be available, and users of the deprecated images will need to use different versions.

After you have created an image, you can create an instance using that image by selecting the Create Instance option in the line of commands above the image listing.

In addition to managing VMs through the console, you can manage compute resources using the command line.

Managing a Single Virtual Machine Instance with Cloud Shell and the Command Line

In addition to managing VMs through the console, you can manage compute resources using the command line. The same commands can be used in Cloud Shell or in your local environment after you have installed Google Cloud SDK, which was covered in Chapter 5.

This section describes the most important commands for working with instances. Commands have their own specific sets of parameters; however, all gcloud commands support sets of flags. These are referred to as gcloud-wide flags, also known as gcloud global flags, and include the following:

- --account specifies a GCP account to use overriding the default account.

- --configuration uses a named configuration file that contains key-value pairs.

- --flatten generates separate key-value records when a key has multiple values.

- `--format` specifies an output format, such as a default (human readable) CSV, JSON, YAML, text, or other possible options.
- `--help` displays a detailed help message.
- `--project` specifies a GCP project to use, overriding the default project.
- `--quiet` disables interactive prompts and uses defaults.
- `--verbosity` specifies the level of detailed output messages. Options are debug, `info`, `warning`, and `error`.

Throughout this section, commands can take an optional `--zone` parameter. We assume a default zone was set when you ran `gcloud init`.

Starting Instances

To start an instance, use the `gcloud` command, specifying that you are working with a compute service and instances specifically. You also need to indicate that you will be starting an instance by specifying `start`, followed by the name of one or more instances.

The command syntax is as follows:

```
gcloud compute instances start  INSTANCE_NAMES
```

An example is as follows:

```
gcloud compute instances start  ch06-instance-1 ch06-instance-2
```

The `instance start` command also takes optional parameters. The `--async` parameter displays information about the `start` operation. The `--verbose` option in many Linux commands provides similar functionality. An example is as follows:

```
gcloud compute instances start  ch06-instance-1 ch06-instance-2 --async
```

GCP needs to know in which zone to create an instance. This can be specified with the `--zone` parameter as follows:

```
gcloud compute instances start  ch06-instance-1 ch06-instance-2 --zone us-central1-c
```

You can get a list of zones with the following command:

```
gcloud compute zones list
```

If no zone is specified, the command will prompt for one.

Stopping Instances

To stop an instance, use `gcloud compute instances` and specify `stop` followed by the name of one or more instances.

The command syntax is as follows:

```
gcloud compute instances stop  INSTANCE_NAMES
```

An example is as follows:

```
gcloud compute instances stop  ch06-instance-3 ch06-instance-4
```

Like the instance start command, the stop command takes optional parameters. The --async parameter causes information about the start operation to be displayed:

```
gcloud compute instances stop  ch06-instance-1 ch06-instance-2 -async
```

GCP needs to know which zone contains the instance to stop. This can be specified with the --zone parameter as follows:

```
gcloud compute instances stop ch06-instance-1 ch06-instance-2 --zone us-central1-c
```

You can get a list of zones with the following command:

```
gcloud compute zones list
```

Deleting Instances

When you are finished working with a VM, you can delete it with the delete command. Here's an example:

```
gcloud compute instances delete ch06-instance-1
```

The delete command takes the --zone parameter to specify where the VM to delete is located. Here's an example:

```
gcloud compute instances delete ch06-instance-1 --zone us-central2-b
```

When an instance is deleted, the disks on the VM may be deleted or saved by using the --delete-disks and --keep-disks parameters, respectively. You can specify all to keep all disks, boot to specify the partition of the root file system, and data to specify nonboot disks.

For example, the following command keeps all disks:

```
gcloud compute instances delete ch06-instance-1 --zone us-central2-b --keep-
disks=all
```

while the following deletes all nonboot disks:

```
gcloud compute instances delete ch06-instance-1 --zone us-central2-b --delete-
disks=data
```

Viewing VM Inventory

The command to view the set of VMs in your inventory is as follows:

```
gcloud compute instances list
```

This command takes an optional name of an instance. To list VMs in a particular zone, you can use the following:

```
gcloud compute instances list --filter="zone:ZONE"
```

where *ZONE* is the name of a zone. You can list multiple zones using a comma-separated list.

The --limit parameter is used to limit the number of VMs listed, and the --sort-by parameter is used to reorder the list of VMs by specifying a resource field. You can see the resource fields for a VM by running the following:

```
gcloud compute instances describe
```

Working with Snapshots

You can create a snapshot of a disk using the following command:

```
gcloud compute disks snapshot DISK_NAME --snapshot-names=NAME
```

where *DISK_NAME* is the name of a disk and *NAME* is the name of the snapshot. To view a list of snapshots, use the following:

```
gcloud compute snapshots list
```

For detailed information about a snapshot, use the following:

```
gcloud compute snapshots describe SNAPSHOT_NAME
```

where SNAPSHOT_NAME is the name of the snapshot to describe. To create a disk, use this:

```
gcloud compute disks create DISK_NAME --source-snapshot=SNAPSHOT_NAME
```

You can also specify the size of the disk and disk type using the --size and --parameters. Here's an example:

```
gcloud compute disks create ch06-disk-1 --source-snapshot=ch06-snapshot
--size=100 --type=pd-standard
```

This will create a 100GB disk using the ch06-snapshot using a standard persistent disk.

Working with Images

GCP provides a wide range of images to use when creating a VM; however, you may need to create a specialized image of your own. This can be done with the following command:

```
gcloud compute images create IMAGE_NAME
```

where *IMAGE_NAME* is the name given to the images. The source for the images is specified using one of the source parameters, which are as follows:

- --source-disk
- --source-image
- --source-image-family
- --source-snapshot
- --source-uri

The source-disk, source-image, and source-snapshot parameters are used to create an image using a disk, image, and snapshot, respectively. The source-image-family parameter uses the latest version of an image in the family. Families are groups of related images, which are usually different versions of the same underlying image. The source-uri parameter allows you to specify an image using a web address.

An image can have a description and a set of labels. These are assigned using the --description and --labels parameters.

Here is an example of creating a new image from a disk:

```
gcloud compute images create ch06-image-1 --source-disk ch06-disk-1
```

You can also delete images when they are no longer needed using this:

```
gcloud compute images delete IMAGE_NAME
```

It is often helpful to store images on Cloud Storage. You can export an image to Cloud Storage with the following command:

```
gcloud compute images export --destination-uri DESTINATION_URI --image IMAGE_NAME
```

where DESTINATION_URI is the address of a Cloud Storage bucket to store the image.

Introduction to Instance Groups

Instance groups are sets of VMs that are managed as a single entity. Any gcloud or console command applied to an instance group is applied to all members of the instance group. Google provides two types of instance groups: managed and unmanaged.

Managed groups consist of groups of identical VMs. They are created using an instance template, which is a specification of a VM configuration, including machine type, boot disk image, zone, labels, and other properties of an instance. Managed instance groups can automatically scale the number of instances in a group and be used with load balancing to distribute workloads across the instance group. If an instance in a group crashes, it will be recreated automatically. Managed groups are the preferred type of instance group.

Unmanaged groups should be used only when you need to work with different configurations within different VMs within the group.

Creating and Removing Instance Groups and Templates

To create an instance group, you must first create an instance group template. To create an instance template, use the following command:

```
gcloud compute instance-templates create INSTANCE
```

You can specify an existing VM as the source of the instance template by using the --source-instance parameter (GCP will use a n1-standard1 image by default). Here's an example:

```
gcloud compute instance-templates create ch06-instance-template-1 --source-
instance=ch06-instance-1
```

Instance group templates can also be created in the console using the Instance Groups Template page, as shown in Figure 6.24.

FIGURE 6.24   Instance group templates can be created in the console using a form similar to the create instance form.

← **Create an instance template**

Describe a VM instance once and then use that template to create groups of identical instances Learn more

Name ②

| instance-template-1| |

Machine type
Customize to select cores, memory and GPUs.

| 1 vCPU ▾ | 3.75 GB memory | Customize |

Container ②
☐ Deploy a container image to this VM instance. Learn more

Boot disk ②

New 10 GB standard persistent disk
Image
Debian GNU/Linux 9 (stretch) | Change |

Identity and API access ②

Service account ②
| Compute Engine default service account ▾ |

Access scopes ②
⦿ Allow default access
○ Allow full access to all Cloud APIs
○ Set access for each API

Firewall ②
Add tags and firewall rules to allow specific network traffic from the Internet
☐ Allow HTTP traffic
☐ Allow HTTPS traffic

⩒ Management, security, disks, networking, sole tenancy

| Create | | Cancel |

Equivalent REST or command line

Instance groups can contain instances in a single zone or across a region. The first is called a *zonal* managed instance group, and the second is called a *regional* managed instance group. Regional managed instance groups are recommended because that configuration spreads the workload across zones, increasing resiliency.

You can remove instance templates by deleting them from the Instance Group Template page in the console. Select the instance group template by checking the box in the list of templates and then delete it by clicking the delete icon, as shown in Figure 6.25.

FIGURE 6.25   Instance group templates can be deleted in the console.

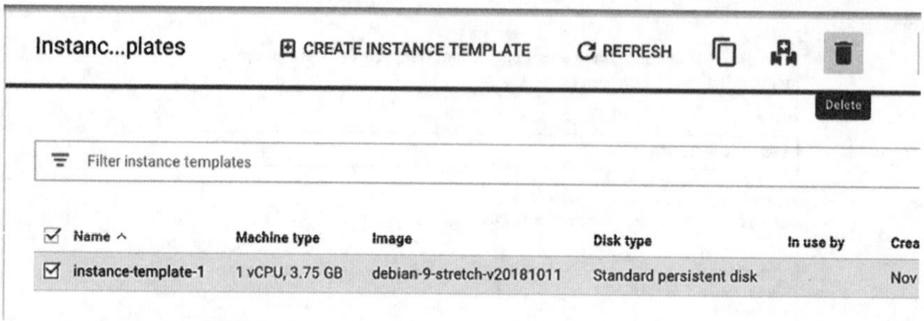

You can also delete an instance group template using the following command:

```
gcloud compute instance-templates delete NAME
```

where *INSTANCE-TEMPLATE-NAME* is the name of the template to delete.

To delete instance groups in the console, select the instance group to delete from the list of instance groups and click the delete icon, as shown in Figure 6.26.

FIGURE 6.26   The instance group can be deleted in the console.

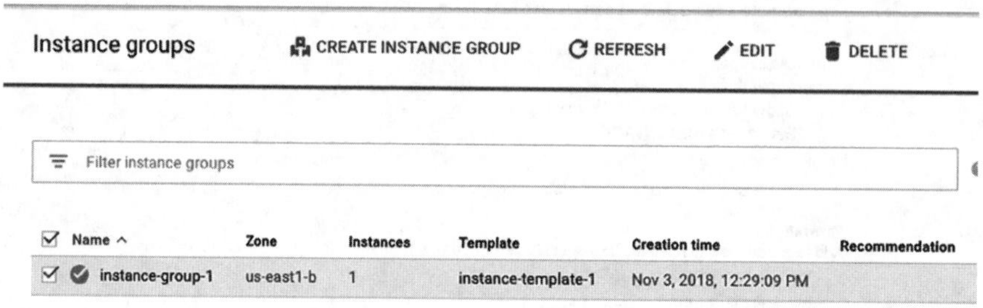

Delete instance groups from the command line using the following:

```
gcloud compute instance-groups managed delete-instances NAME
```

where *INSTANCE-GROUP-NAME* is the name of the instance group to delete.

To list templates and instance groups, use the following:

```
gcloud compute instance-templates list
gcloud compute instance-groups managed list-instances
```

To list the instances in an instance group, use the following:

```
gcloud compute instance-groups managed list-instances INSTANCE-GROUP-NAME
```

Instance Groups Load Balancing and Autoscaling

To deploy a scalable, highly available application, you can run that application on a load-balanced set of instances. GCP offers a number of types of load balancing, and they all require use of an instance group.

In addition to load balancing, managed instance groups can be configured to autoscale. You can configure an autoscaling policy to trigger adding or removing instances based on CPU utilization, monitoring metric, load-balancing capacity, or queue-based workloads.

 Real World Scenario

No More Peak Capacity Planning

Prior to the advent of the cloud, IT organizations often had to plan their hardware purchases around the maximum expected load. This is called *peak capacity planning*. If there is little variation in load, peak capacity planning is a sound approach. Businesses with highly variable workloads, such as retailers in the United States that have high demand during the last two months of the year, would have to support idle capacity for months out of the year. Cloud computing and autoscaling have eliminated the need for peak capacity planning. Additional servers are acquired in minutes, not weeks or months. When capacity is not needed, it is dropped. Instance groups automate the process of adding and removing VMs, allowing cloud engineers to finely tune when to add and when to remove VMs.

 When autoscaling, ensure you leave enough time for VMs to boot up or shut down before triggering another change in the cluster configuration. If the time between checks is too small, you may find that a recently added VM is not fully started before another is added. This can lead to more VMs being added than are actually needed.

Guidelines for Managing Virtual Machines

Here are some guidelines for managing VMs:

- Use labels and descriptions. This will help you identify the purpose of an instance and also help when filtering lists of instances.

- Use managed instance groups to enable autoscaling and load balancing. These are key to deploying scalable and highly available services.

- Use GPUs for numeric-intensive processing, such as machine learning and high-performance computing. For some applications, GPUs can give greater performance benefit than adding another CPU.

- Use snapshots to save the state of a disk or to make copies. These can be saved in Cloud Storage and act as backups.

- Use preemptible instances for workloads that can tolerate disruption. This will reduce the cost of the instance by up to 80 percent.

Summary

In this chapter, you learned how to a managed single VM instances and instance groups. Single VM instances can be created, configured, stopped, started, and deleted using Cloud Console or using gcloud commands from Cloud Shell or your local machine if you have SDK installed.

Snapshots are copies of disks and are useful as backups and for copying data to other instances. Images are copies of disks that are in a format suitable for creating VMs.

The main command used to manage VMs is the gcloud compute instances command. gcloud uses a hierarchical structure to order the command elements. The command begins with gcloud, followed by a GCP resource, such as compute for Compute Engine, followed by an entity type such as instances or snapshots. An action is then specified, such as create, delete, list, or describe.

GPUs can be attached to instances that have GPU libraries installed in the operating system. GPUs are used for compute-intensive tasks, such as building machine learning models.

Instance groups are groups of instances that are managed together. Managed instance groups have instances that are the same. These groups support load balancing and autoscaling.

Exam Essentials

Understand how to navigate Cloud Console.   Cloud Console is the graphical interface for working with GCP. You can create, configure, delete, and list VM instances from the Compute Engine area of the console.

Understand how to install Cloud SDK.   Cloud SDK allows you to configure default environment variables, such as a preferred zone, and issue commands from the command line. If you use Cloud Shell, Cloud SDK is already installed.

Know how to create a VM in the console and at the command line. You can specify machine type, choose an image, and configure disks with the console. You can use commands at the command line to list and describe, and you can find the same information in the console. Understand when to use customized images and how to deprecate them. Images are copies of contents of a disk, and they are used to create VMs. Deprecated marks an image as no longer supported.

Understand why GPUs are used and how to attach them to a VM. GPUs are used for compute-intensive operations; a common use case for using GPUs is machine learning. It is best to use an image that has GPU libraries installed. Understand how to determine which locations have GPUs available, because there are some restrictions. The CPU must be compatible with the GPU selected, and GPUs cannot be attached to shared memory machines. Know how GPU costs are charged.

Understand images and snapshots. Snapshots save the contents of disks for backup and data-sharing purposes. Images save the operating system and related configurations so you can create identical copies of the instance.

Understand instance groups and instance group templates. Instance groups are sets of instances managed as a single entity. Instance group templates specify the configuration of an instance group and the instances in it. Managed instance groups support autoscaling and load balancing.

Review Questions   60 %.

You can find the answers in the Appendix.

1. Which page in Google Cloud Console would you use to create a single instance of a VM?

    A. Compute Engine

    B. App Engine

    C. Kubernetes Engine

    D. Cloud Functions

2. You view a list of Linux VM instances in the console. All have public IP addresses assigned. You notice that the SSH option is disabled for one of the instances. Why might that be the case?

    A. The instance is preemptible and therefore does not support SSH.

    B. The instance is stopped.

    C. The instance was configured with the No SSH option.

    D. The SSH option is never disabled.

3. You have noticed unusually slow response time when issuing commands to a Linux server, and you decide to reboot the machine. Which command would you use in the console to reboot?

    A. Reboot

    B. Reset

    C. Restart

    D. Shutdown followed by Startup

4. In the console, you can filter the list of VM instances by which of the following?

    A. Labels only

    B. Member of managed instance group only

    C. Labels, status, or members of managed instance group

    D. Labels and status only

5. You will be building a number of machine learning models on an instance and attaching GPU to the instance. When you run your machine learning models they take an unusually long time to run. It appears that GPU is not being used. What could be the cause of this?

    A. GPU libraries are not installed.

    B. The operating system is based on Ubuntu.

    C. You do not have at least eight CPUs in the instance.

    D. There isn't enough persistent disk space available.

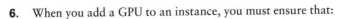

6. When you add a GPU to an instance, you must ensure that:

   A. The instance is set to terminate during maintenance.

   B. The instance is preemptible.

   C. The instance does not have nonboot disks attached.

   D. The instance is running Ubuntu 14.02 or later.

7. You are using snapshots to save copies of a 100GB disk. You make a snapshot and then add 10GB of data. You create a second snapshot. How much storage is used in total for the two snapshots (assume no compression)?

   A. 210 GB, with 100GB for the first and 110GB for the second

   B. 110 GB, with 100GB for the first and 10GB for the second

   C. 110 GB, with 110 for the second (the first snapshot is deleted automatically)

   D. 221 GB, with 100GB for the first, 110GB for the second, plus 10 percent of the second snapshot (11 GB) for metadata overhead

8. You have decided to delegate the task of making backup snapshots to a member of your team. What role would you need to grant to your team member to create snapshots?

   A. Compute Image Admin

   B. Storage Admin

   C. Compute Snapshot Admin

   D. Compute Storage Admin

9. The source of an image may be:

   A. Only disks

   B. Snapshots or disks only

   C. Disks, snapshots, or another image

   D. Disks, snapshots, or any database export file

10. You have built images using Ubuntu 14.04 and now want users to start using Ubuntu 16.04. You don't want to just delete images based on Ubuntu 14.04, but you want users to know they should start using Ubuntu 16.04. What feature of images would you use to accomplish this?

    A. Redirection

    B. Deprecated

    C. Unsupported

    D. Migration

11. You want to generate a list of VMs in your inventory and have the results in JSON format. What command would you use?

    A. `gcloud compute instances list`

    B. `gcloud compute instances describe`

    C. `gcloud compute instances list --format json`

    D. `gcloud compute instances list --output json`

12. You would like to understand details of how GCP starts a virtual instance. Which optional parameter would you use when starting an instance to display those details?

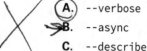

   A. `--verbose`

   B. `--async`

   C. `--describe`

   D. `--details`

13. Which command will delete an instance named ch06-instance-3?

   A. `gcloud compute instances delete instance=ch06-instance-3`

   B. `gcloud compute instance stop ch06-instance-3`

   C. `gcloud compute instances delete ch06-instance-3`

   D. `gcloud compute delete ch06-instance-3`

14. You are about to delete an instance named ch06-instance-1 but want to keep its boot disk. You do not want to keep other attached disks. What gcloud command would you use?

   A. `gcloud compute instances delete ch06-instance-1 --keep-disks=boot`

   B. `gcloud compute instances delete ch06-instance-1 --save-disks=boot`

   C. `gcloud compute instances delete ch06-instance-1 --keep-disks=filesystem`

   D. `gcloud compute delete ch06-instance-1 --keep-disks=filesystem`

15. You want to view a list of fields you can use to sort a list of instances. What command would you use to see the field names?

   A. `gcloud compute instances list`

   B. `gcloud compute instances describe`

   C. `gcloud compute instances list --detailed`

   D. `gcloud compute instances describe --detailed`

16. You are deploying an application that will need to scale and be highly available. Which of these Compute Engine components will help achieve scalability and high availability?

   A. Preemptible instances

   B. Instance groups

   C. Cloud Storage

   D. GPUs

17. Before creating an instance group, you need to create what?

   A. Instances in the instance group

   B. Instance group template

   C. Boot disk image

   D. Source snapshot

18. How would you delete an instance group template using the command line?

   A. `gcloud compute instances instance-template delete`

   B. `glcoud compute instance-templates delete`

   C. `gcloud compute delete instance-template`

   D. `gcloud compute delete instance-templates`

19. What can be the basis for scaling up an instance group?

   A. CPU utilization and operating system updates

   B. Disk usage and CPU utilization only

   C. Network latency, load balancing capacity, and CPU utilization

   D. Disk usage and operating system updates only

20. An architect is moving a legacy application to Google Cloud and wants to minimize the changes to the existing architecture while administering the cluster as a single entity. The legacy application runs on a load-balanced cluster that runs nodes with two different configurations. The two configurations are required because of design decisions made several years ago. The load on the application is fairly consistent, so there is rarely a need to scale up or down. What GCP Compute Engine resource would you recommended using?

   A. Preemptible instances

   B. Unmanaged instance groups

   C. Managed instance groups

   D. GPUs

Chapter

7

Computing with Kubernetes

THIS CHAPTER COVERS THE FOLLOWING
OBJECTIVES OF THE GOOGLE ASSOCIATE
CLOUD ENGINEER CERTIFICATION EXAM:

✓ 3.2   Deploying and implementing Kubernetes
Engine resources

This chapter introduces Kubernetes, a container orchestration system created and open sourced by Google. You will learn about the architecture of Kubernetes and the ways it manages workloads across nodes in a cluster. You will also learn how to manage Kubernetes resources with Cloud Console, Cloud Shell, and Cloud SDK. The chapter also covers how to deploy application pods (a Kubernetes structure) and monitor and log Kubernetes resources.

Introduction to Kubernetes Engine

Kubernetes Engine is Google Cloud Platform's (GCP's) managed Kubernetes service. With this service, GCP customers can create and maintain their own Kubernetes clusters without having to manage the Kubernetes platform.

Kubernetes runs containers on a cluster of virtual machines (VMs). It determines where to run containers, monitors the health of containers, and manages the full lifecycle of VM instances. This collection of tasks is known as *container orchestration*.

It may sound as if a Kubernetes cluster is similar to an instance group, which was discussed in Chapter 6. There are some similarities. Both are sets of VMs that can be managed as a group. Instance groups, however, are much more restricted. All VMs generally run the same image in an instance group. That is not the case with Kubernetes. Also, instance groups have no mechanism to support the deployment of containers. Containers offer a highly-portable, light-weight means of distributing and scaling your applications or work-loads, like VMs, without replicating the guest OS. They can start and stop much faster (usually in seconds) and use fewer resources. You can think of a container as similar to shipping containers for applications and workloads. Like shipping containers that can ride on ships, trains, and trucks without reconfiguration, application containers can be moved from development laptops, to testing and production servers without reconfiguration. That would have to be done manually. Instance groups have some monitoring and can restart instances that fail, but Kubernetes has much more flexibility with regard to maintaining a cluster of servers.

Let's take a look at Kubernetes architecture, which consists of several objects and a set of controllers.

Keep in mind: when you use Kubernetes Engine, you will manage Kubernetes and your applications and workloads running in containers on the Kubernetes platform.

Kubernetes Cluster Architecture

A Kubernetes cluster consists of a cluster master and one or more nodes, which are the workers of the cluster. The cluster master controls the cluster and can be replicated and distributed for high-availability and fault tolerance.

The cluster master manages services provided by Kubernetes, such as the Kubernetes API, controllers, and schedulers. All interactions with the cluster are done through the master using the Kubernetes API. The cluster master issues the command that performs an action on a node. Users can also interact with a cluster using the kubectl command.

Nodes execute the workloads run on the cluster. Nodes are VMs that run containers configured to run an application. Nodes are primarily controlled by the cluster master, but some commands can be run manually. The nodes run an agent called *kubelet,* which is the service that communicates with the cluster master.

When you create a cluster, you can specify a machine type, which defaults to n1-standard-1 with 1 vCPU and 3.75GB of memory. These VMs run specialized operating systems optimized to run containers. Some of the memory and CPU is reserved for Kubernetes and so is not available to applications running on the node.

Kubernetes organizes processing into workloads. There are several organizing objects that make up the core functionality of how Kubernetes processes workloads.

Kubernetes Objects

Workloads are distributed across nodes in a Kubernetes cluster. To understand how work is distributed, it is important to understand some basic concepts, in particular the following:

- Pods
- Services
- Volumes
- Namespaces

Each of these objects contributes to the logical organization of workloads.

Pods

Pods are single instances of a running process in a cluster. Pods contain at least one container. They usually run a single container, but can run multiple containers. Multiple containers are used when two or more containers must share resources. Pods also use shared networking and storage across containers. Each pod gets a unique IP address and a set of ports. Containers connect to a port. Multiple containers in a pod connect to different ports and can talk to each other on localhost. This structure is designed to support running one instance of an application within the cluster as a pod. A pod allows its containers to behave as if they are running on an isolated VM, sharing common storage, one IP address, and a set of ports. By doing this, you can deploy multiple instance of the same application, or different instances of different applications on the same node or different nodes, without having to change their configuration.

Pods treat the multiple containers as a single entity for management purposes.

Pods are generally created in groups. Replicas are copies of pods and constitute a group of pods that are managed as a unit. Pods support autoscaling as well. Pods are considered ephemeral; that is, they are expected to terminate. If a pod is unhealthy—for example, if it is stuck in a waiting mode or crashing repeatedly—it is terminated. The mechanism that manages scaling and health monitoring is known as a *controller.*

You may notice that pods are similar to Compute Engine managed instance groups. A key difference is that pods are for executing applications in containers and may be placed on various nodes in the cluster, while managed instance groups all execute the same application code on each of the nodes. Also, you typically manage instance groups yourself by executing commands in Cloud Console or through the command line. Pods are usually managed by a controller.

Services

Since pods are ephemeral and can be terminated by a controller, other services that depend on pods should not be tightly coupled to particular pods. For example, even though pods have unique IP addresses, applications should not depend on that IP address to reach an application. If the pod with that address is terminated and another is created, it may have another IP address. The IP address may be re-assigned to another pod running a different container.

Kubernetes provides a level of indirection between applications running in pods and other applications that call them: it is called a *service*. A service, in Kubernetes terminology, is an object that provides API endpoints with a stable IP address that allow applications to discover pods running a particular application. Services update when changes are made to pods, so they maintain an up-to-date list of pods running an application.

ReplicaSet

A ReplicaSet is a controller used by a deployment that ensures the correct number identical of pods are running. For example, if a pod is determined to be unhealthy, a controller will terminate that pod. The ReplicaSet will detect that not enough pods for that application or workload are running and will create another. ReplicaSets are also used to update and delete pods.

Deployment

Another important concept in Kubernetes is the deployment. Deployments are sets of identical pods. The members of the set may change as some pods are terminated and others are started, but they are all running the same application. The pods all run the same application because they are created using the same pod template.

A pod template is a definition of how to run a pod. The description of how to define the pod is called a *pod specification*. Kubernetes uses this definition to keep a pod in the state specified in the template. That is, if the specification has a minimum number of pods that should be in the deployment and the number falls below that, then additional pods will be added to the deployment by calling on a ReplicaSet.

StatefulSet

Deployments are well suited to stateless applications. Those are applications that do not need to keep track of their state. For example, an application that calls an API to perform a calculation on the input values does not need to keep track of previous calls or calculations. An application that calls that API may reach a different pod each time it makes a call. There are times, however, when it is advantageous to have a single pod respond to all calls for a client during a single session.

StatefulSets are like deployments, but they assign unique identifiers to pods. This enables Kubernetes to track which pod is used by which client and keep them together. StatefulSets are used when an application needs a unique network identifier or stable persistent storage.

Job

A job is an abstraction about a workload. Jobs create pods and run them until the application completes a workload. Job specifications are specified in a configuration file and include specifications about the container to use and what command to run.

Now that you're familiar with how Kubernetes is organized and how workloads are run, we'll cover how to deploy a Kubernetes cluster using Kubernetes Engine.

Deploying Kubernetes Clusters

Kubernetes clusters can be deployed using either Cloud Console or the command line in Cloud Shell, or your local environment if Cloud SDK is installed.

Deploying Kubernetes Clusters Using Cloud Console

To use Kubernetes Engine, you will need to enable the Kubernetes Engine API. Once you have enabled the API, you can navigate to the Kubernetes Engine page in Cloud Console. Figure 7.1 shows an example of the Overview page.

FIGURE 7.1 The Overview page of the Kubernetes Engine section of Cloud Console

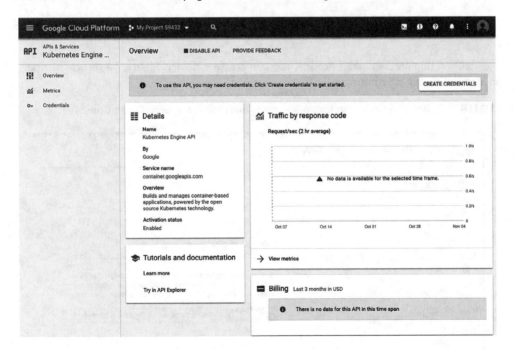

The first time you use Kubernetes Engine, you may need to create credentials. You can do this by clicking the Create Credentials button near the top of the Overview page. A form such as the one shown in Figure 7.2 will appear. You can specify which API you are using and then generate your credentials.

FIGURE 7.2   The form for creating credentials needed to use Kubernetes Engine

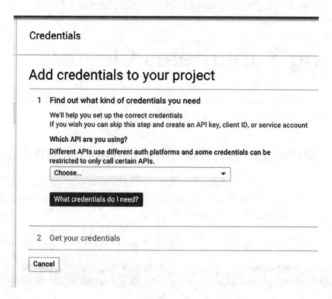

After creating credentials, if needed, you can create a cluster. Figure 7.3 shows the first page in the cluster creation step.

FIGURE 7.3   The first form for creating a Kubernetes cluster in Cloud Console

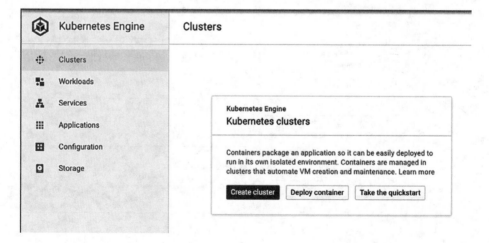

When you click Create Cluster, you will be presented with the option to choose from several templates, as shown in Figure 7.4. The templates vary in the number of vCPUs, memory, and use of GPUs. For example, the Standard Cluster template uses three nodes with one vCPU and 3.75 GB of memory, while the CPU Intensive template uses four vCPUs and 3.6GB of memory.

FIGURE 7.4   Templates for creating a Kubernetes cluster

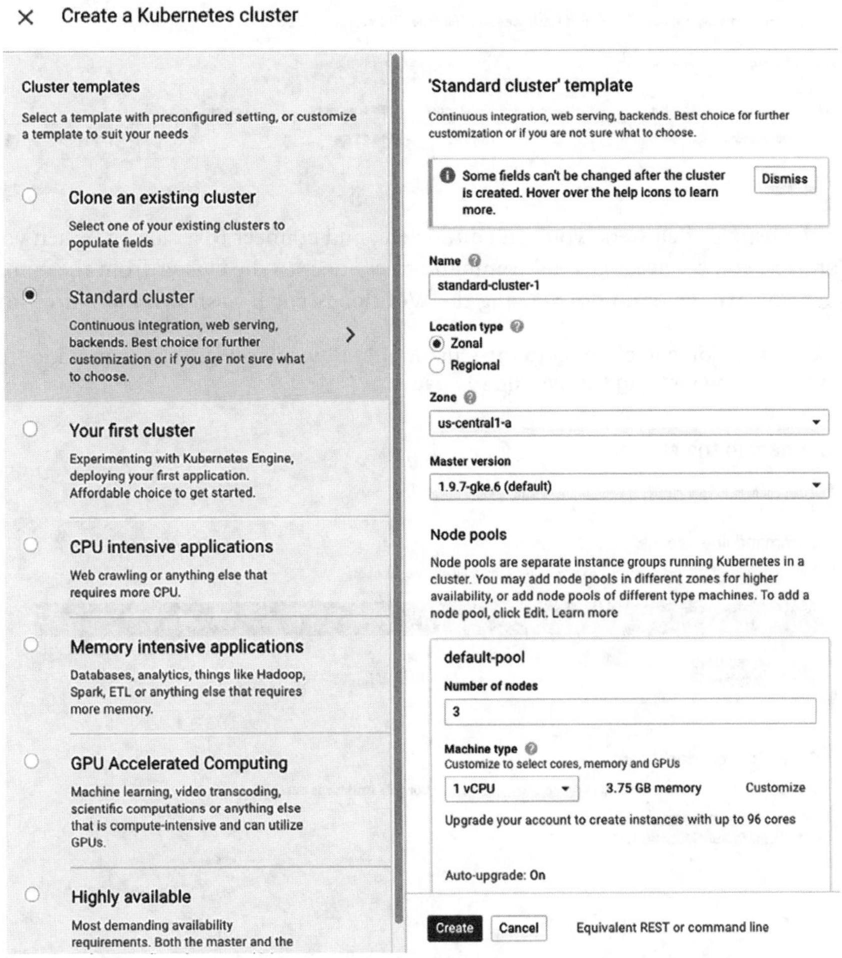

You can modify the parameters provided in the template. For example, if you want to run VMs in different zones to improve availability, you can specify multiple node pools. Node pools are instance groups in a Kubernetes cluster. They're much like a Managed Instance Group but not the same.

It can take a few minutes to create a cluster. When the cluster is created, it will appear in the list of clusters, as in Figure 7.5.

FIGURE 7.5   The cluster listing shows the number of instances, total cores, and total memory.

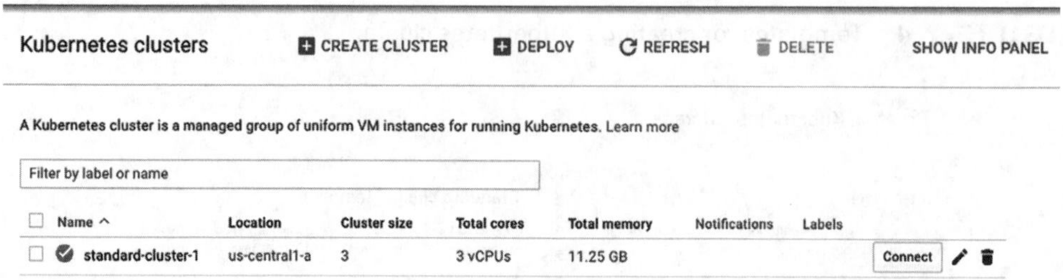

From the listing of clusters, you can edit, delete, and connect to a cluster. When you click Connect, you receive a gcloud command to connect to the cluster from the command line. You also have the option of viewing the Workloads page, as shown in Figure 7.6.

FIGURE 7.6   You can connect to the cluster either by using a gcloud command from the command line or by viewing the Workloads page.

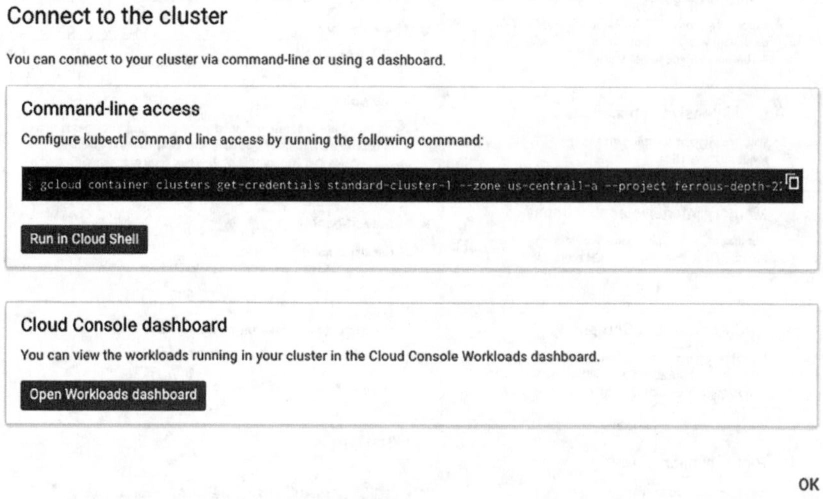

Kubernetes runs a number of workloads to manage the cluster. You can view the currently running workloads in the Workloads page of the Kubernetes Engine section of Cloud Console. Figure 7.7 shows a subset of the workloads running on a newly started cluster.

FIGURE 7.7   The Workloads page lists currently running workloads.

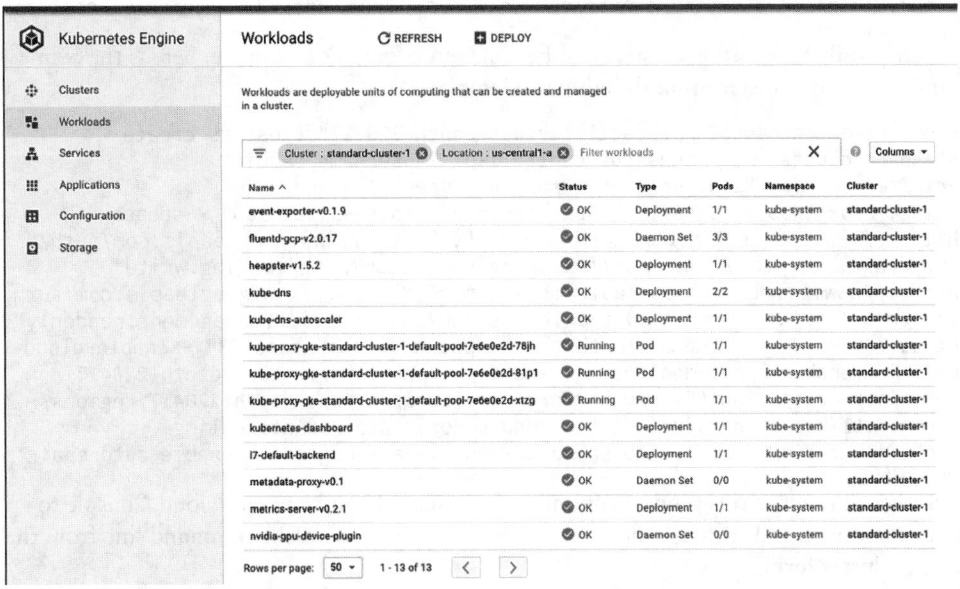

Deploying Kubernetes Clusters Using Cloud Shell and Cloud SDK

Like other GCP services, Kubernetes Engine can be managed using the command line. The basic command for working with Kubernetes Engine is the following gcloud command:

```
gcloud beta container
```

Notice that Kubernetes Engine commands include the word *beta*. Google indicates a service that is not yet in general availability by including the word *alpha* or *beta* in the gcloud command. By the time you read this, Kubernetes Engine may be generally available, in which case the *beta* term will no longer be used.

This gcloud command has many parameters, including the following:

- Project
- Zone
- Machine type
- Image type
- Disk type
- Disk size
- Number of nodes

A basic command for creating a cluster looks like this:

```
gcloud container clusters create ch07-cluster --num-nodes=3 --region=us-central1
```

Commands for creating clusters can become quite long. For example, here is the command to create a cluster using the standard template:

```
gcloud beta container --project "ferrous-depth-220417" clusters create
"standard-cluster-2" --zone "us-central1-a" --username "admin"
--cluster-version "1.9.7-gke.6" --machine-type "n1-standard-1"
--image-type "COS" --disk-type "pd-standard" --disk-size "100" --scopes
"https://www.googleapis.com/auth/compute","https://www.googleapis.com/auth/
devstorage.read_only","https://www.googleapis.com/auth/logging.write",
"https://www.googleapis.com/auth/monitoring","https://www.googleapis.com/auth/
servicecontrol","https://www.googleapis.com/auth/service.management.readonly",
"https://www.googleapis.com/auth/trace.append" --num-nodes "3" --enable-cloud-
logging --enable-cloud-monitoring --network "projects/ferrous-depth-220417/
global/networks/default" --subnetwork "projects/ferrous-depth-220417/regions/
us-central1/subnetworks/default" --addons HorizontalPodAutoscaling,
HttpLoadBalancing,KubernetesDashboard --enable-autoupgrade --enable-autorepair
```

Rather than write this kind of command from scratch, you can use Cloud Console to select a template and then use the option to generate the equivalent command line from the Create Cluster form.

Deploying Application Pods

Now that you have created a cluster, let's deploy an application.

From the Cluster page of the Kubernetes Engine on Cloud Console, select Create Deployment. A form such as the one in Figure 7.8 appears. Within this form you can specify the following:

- Container image
- Environment variables
- Initial command
- Application name
- Labels
- Namespace
- Cluster to deploy to

FIGURE 7.8 The Create Deployment option provides a form to specify a container to run and an initial command to start the application running.

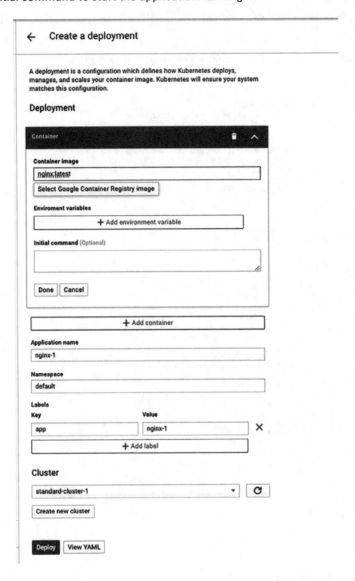

Once you have specified a deployment, you can display the corresponding YAML specification, which can be saved and used to create deployments from the command line. Figure 7.9 shows an example deployment YAML file. The output is always displayed in YAML format.

FIGURE 7.9   YAML specification for a Kubernetes deployment

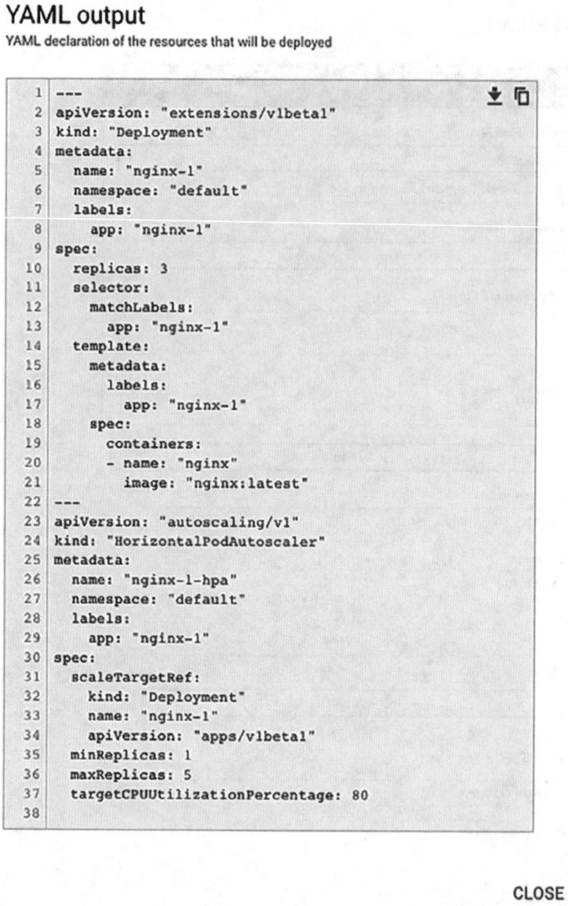

YAML output
YAML declaration of the resources that will be deployed

```
 1  ---
 2  apiVersion: "extensions/v1beta1"
 3  kind: "Deployment"
 4  metadata:
 5    name: "nginx-1"
 6    namespace: "default"
 7    labels:
 8      app: "nginx-1"
 9  spec:
10    replicas: 3
11    selector:
12      matchLabels:
13        app: "nginx-1"
14    template:
15      metadata:
16        labels:
17          app: "nginx-1"
18      spec:
19        containers:
20        - name: "nginx"
21          image: "nginx:latest"
22  ---
23  apiVersion: "autoscaling/v1"
24  kind: "HorizontalPodAutoscaler"
25  metadata:
26    name: "nginx-1-hpa"
27    namespace: "default"
28    labels:
29      app: "nginx-1"
30  spec:
31    scaleTargetRef:
32      kind: "Deployment"
33      name: "nginx-1"
34      apiVersion: "apps/v1beta1"
35    minReplicas: 1
36    maxReplicas: 5
37    targetCPUUtilizationPercentage: 80
38
```

CLOSE

In addition to installing Cloud SDK, you will need to install the Kubernetes command-line tool kubectl to work with clusters from the command line. You can do this with the following command:

```
gcloud components install kubectl
```

If the Cloud SDK Manager is disabled, you may receive an error when running gcloud components install kubectl. If that occurs, you can use the component manager, following the instructions at https://cloud.google.com/sdk/install.

The Cloud SDK component manager works only if you don't install SDK through another package manager. If you want to use the component manager, you can install it using one of these methods:

https://cloud.google.com/sdk/downloads#versioned

https://cloud.google.com/sdk/downloads#interactive

Additional packages are available in our deb and yum repos; all the same components are available, and you just need to use your existing package manager to install them.

https://cloud.google.com/sdk/downloads#apt-get
https://cloud.google.com/sdk/downloads#yum

You can then use kubectl to run a Docker image on a cluster by using the kubectl run command. Here's an example:

```
kubectl run ch07-app-deploy --image=ch07-app --port=8080
```

This will run a Docker image called ch07-app and make its network accessible on port 8080. If after some time you'd like to scale up the number of replicas in the deployment, you can use the kubectl scale command:

```
kubectl scale deployment ch07-app-deploy --replicas=5
```

This example would create five replicas.

Monitoring Kubernetes

Stackdriver is GCP's comprehensive monitoring, logging, and alerting product. It can be used to monitor Kubernetes clusters.

When creating a cluster, be sure to enable Stackdriver monitoring and logging by selecting Advanced Options in the Create Cluster form in Cloud Console. Under Additional Features, choose Enable Logging Service and Enable Monitoring Service, as shown in Figure 7.10.

FIGURE 7.10 Expanding the Advanced Options in the Create Cluster dialog will show two check boxes for enabling Stackdriver logging and monitoring.

To set up Stackdriver from Cloud Console, select Stackdriver from the top-level menu on the left. Initially, you will need to create a workspace in your project by selecting a new workspace and launching monitoring when prompted (see Figure 7.11). Once a workspace is created, you can monitor your GCP resources, including Kubernetes clusters.

Workspaces are resources for monitoring and can support up to 100 monitored projects. Workspaces contain dashboards, alerting policies, group definitions, and notification checks.

FIGURE 7.11 An initial dialog box to create a workspace in Stackdriver

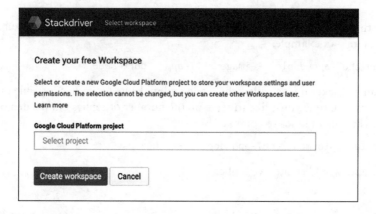

After you create a workspace, open Stackdriver, and it displays the Monitoring Overview page, shown in Figure 7.12.

FIGURE 7.12   The Stackdriver Monitoring Overview page

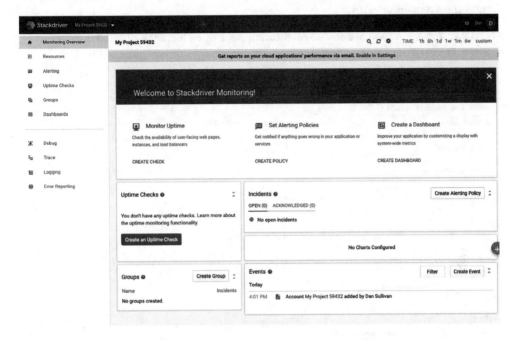

From the Overview Page, click Resources and select Instances to list the instances in your cluster. This displays a list such as in Figure 7.13.

FIGURE 7.13   List of instances in a Kubernetes cluster

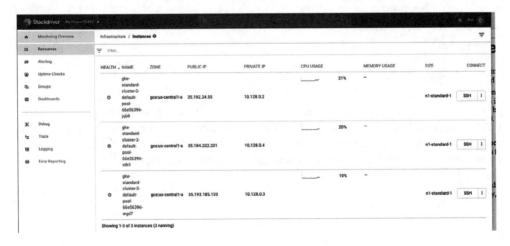

Click the names of any of the instances to show a detailed page of monitoring information, as shown in Figure 7.14.

FIGURE 7.14   A typical detailed monitoring page of an instance running in a Kubernetes cluster

From the Details page, you can view an overview of details about the instance and view CPU usage, disk IO, and network traffic. You can also create alerting policies to notify you if some condition, such as high CPU utilization, occurs on the instance. When you create alerts, they can be applied to an individual instance in the cluster or to all instances in the cluster.

In the detail Stackdriver page, create an alert by clicking the Create Alerting Policy button. This displays a dialog such as in Figure 7.15, from which you can create conditions, notifications, and documentation. You can also name the policy.

FIGURE 7.15   When creating an alerting policy, this form allows you to specify components of the policy.

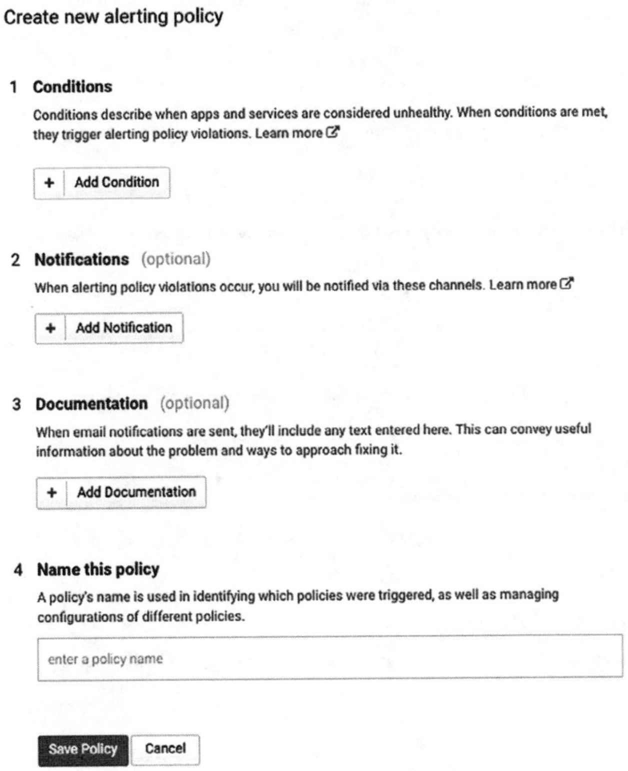

Create new alerting policy

1   **Conditions**

Conditions describe when apps and services are considered unhealthy. When conditions are met, they trigger alerting policy violations. Learn more ☐

+   Add Condition

2   **Notifications** (optional)

When alerting policy violations occur, you will be notified via these channels. Learn more ☐

+   Add Notification

3   **Documentation** (optional)

When email notifications are sent, they'll include any text entered here. This can convey useful information about the problem and ways to approach fixing it.

+   Add Documentation

4   **Name this policy**

A policy's name is used in identifying which policies were triggered, as well as managing configurations of different policies.

enter a policy name

Save Policy   Cancel

When you add a condition, a form such as the one shown in Figure 7.16 appears.

FIGURE 7.16   Stackdriver supports a number of condition types.

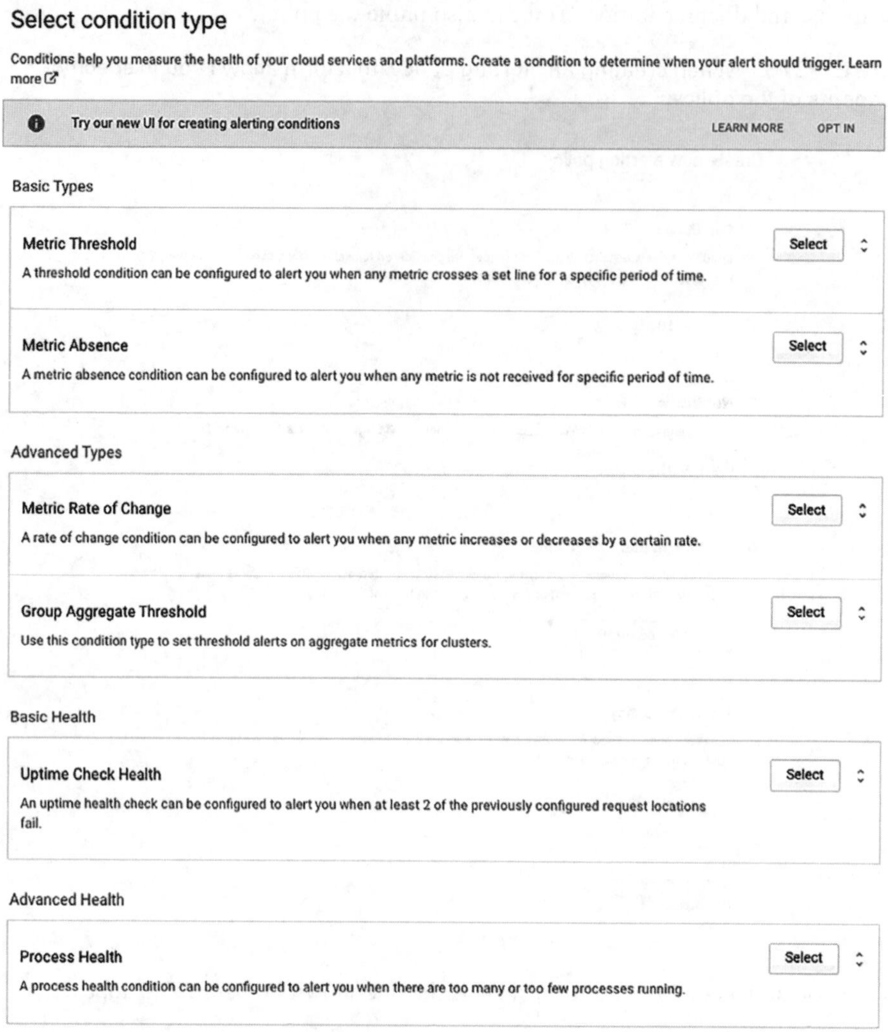

Select condition type

Conditions help you measure the health of your cloud services and platforms. Create a condition to determine when your alert should trigger. Learn more ☐

ⓘ   Try our new UI for creating alerting conditions   LEARN MORE   OPT IN

Basic Types

| Metric Threshold | Select | ↕ |
| A threshold condition can be configured to alert you when any metric crosses a set line for a specific period of time. | | |

| Metric Absence | Select | ↕ |
| A metric absence condition can be configured to alert you when any metric is not received for specific period of time. | | |

Advanced Types

| Metric Rate of Change | Select | ↕ |
| A rate of change condition can be configured to alert you when any metric increases or decreases by a certain rate. | | |

| Group Aggregate Threshold | Select | ↕ |
| Use this condition type to set threshold alerts on aggregate metrics for clusters. | | |

Basic Health

| Uptime Check Health | Select | ↕ |
| An uptime health check can be configured to alert you when at least 2 of the previously configured request locations fail. | | |

Advanced Health

| Process Health | Select | ↕ |
| A process health condition can be configured to alert you when there are too many or too few processes running. | | |

Select Metric Threshold to display a form like Figure 7.17, which shows how to specify an alert on CPU utilization over 80 percent for 5 minutes.

FIGURE 7.17 Stackdriver metric threshold conditions are based on a set of monitored resources, such as CPU utilization.

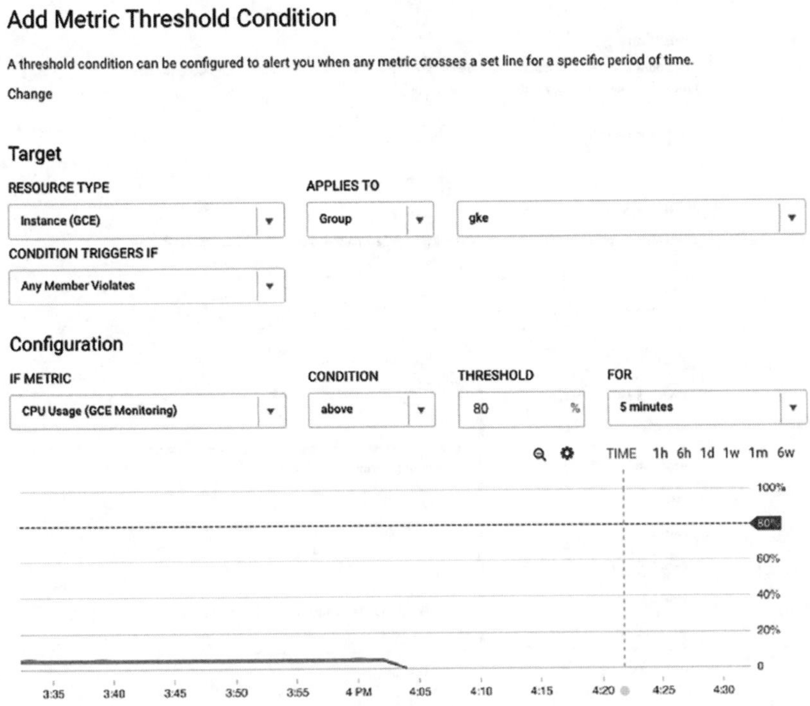

Add Metric Threshold Condition

A threshold condition can be configured to alert you when any metric crosses a set line for a specific period of time.

Change

Target

RESOURCE TYPE	APPLIES TO	
Instance (GCE) ▾	Group ▾	gke ▾

CONDITION TRIGGERS IF

Any Member Violates ▾

Configuration

IF METRIC	CONDITION	THRESHOLD	FOR
CPU Usage (GCE Monitoring) ▾	above ▾	80 %	5 minutes ▾

Stackdriver will need to know how to notify you if an alert is triggered. You can specify your choice of notification channels in the Create New Alerting Policy form, as shown in Figure 7.18. Channels include email, webhooks, and SMS text messaging as well as third-party tools such as PagerDuty, Campfire, and Slack.

Stackdriver supports more advanced alerting as well, including process health, uptime checks, group aggregate thresholds, and metric rates of change.

Let's walk through an example of creating a policy to monitor CPU utilization.

FIGURE 7.18 Stackdriver supports a number of condition types.

Create new alerting policy

1 **Conditions**

Conditions describe when apps and services are considered unhealthy. When conditions are met, they trigger alerting policy violations. Learn more ⟳

  ┌─────────────────────┐
  │ **+**   Add Condition │
  └─────────────────────┘

2 **Notifications** (optional)

When alerting policy violations occur, you will be notified via these channels. Learn more ⟳

| Email ▼ | you@domain.com | ✕ |

| |

| **Email** |
| **Cloud Console mobile app** |

3 | **Advanced** | 'll include any text entered here. This can convey useful
                                                          ys to approach fixing it.
  | **PagerDuty** |

  | **SMS** |

  | **Hipchat** |

  | **Campfire** |

4 | **Webhook** | which policies were triggered, as well as managing

  | **Slack Channel** |

| enter a policy name |

┌────────────┐ ┌────────┐
│ Save Policy │ │ Cancel │
└────────────┘ └────────┘

NOTE For more details on monitoring, see Chapter 18. To create a policy to monitor CPU utilization, navigate to the monitoring page in Stackdriver and click Create Policy. This will display the form to create a policy, which is a four-step process: create a condition, specify a notification channel, add a description, and name the policy. (See Figure 7.19.)

FIGURE 7.19   Creating a policy to monitor CPU utilization

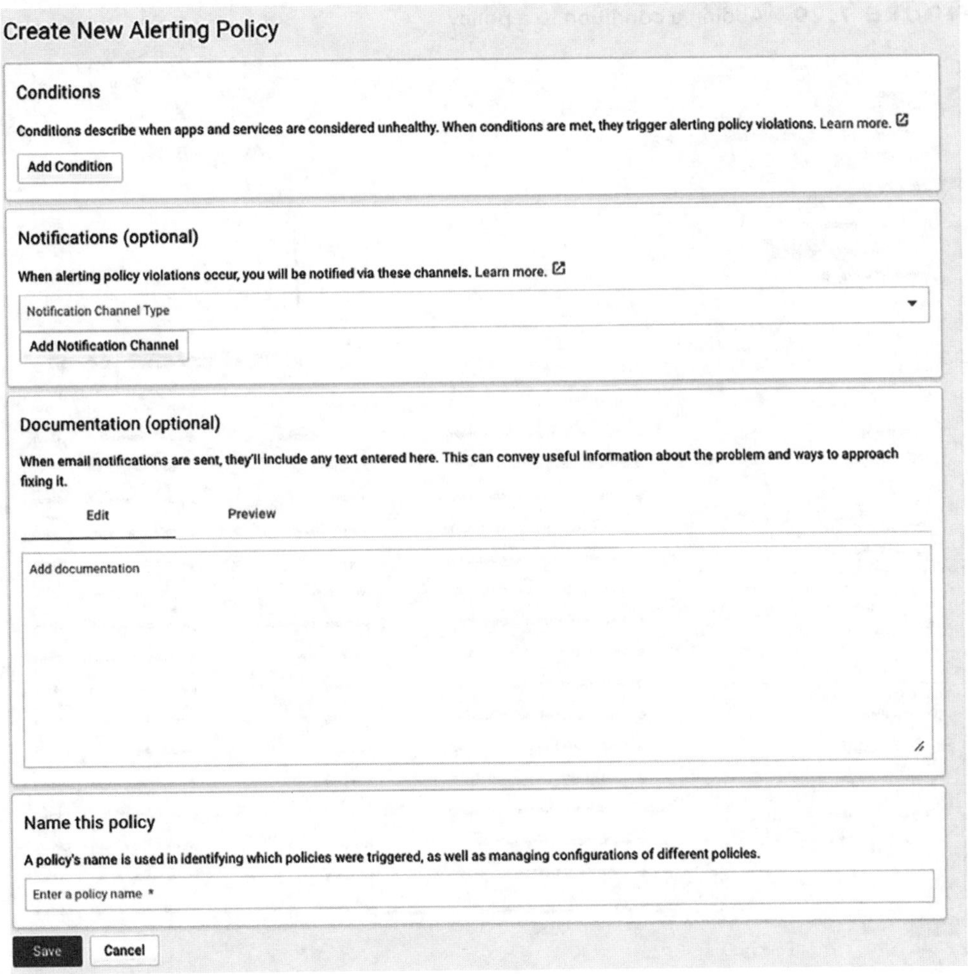

Create New Alerting Policy

Conditions

Conditions describe when apps and services are considered unhealthy. When conditions are met, they trigger alerting policy violations. Learn more. ☒

[Add Condition]

Notifications (optional)

When alerting policy violations occur, you will be notified via these channels. Learn more. ☒

| Notification Channel Type | ▼ |

[Add Notification Channel]

Documentation (optional)

When email notifications are sent, they'll include any text entered here. This can convey useful information about the problem and ways to approach fixing it.

| Edit | Preview |

Add documentation

Name this policy

A policy's name is used in identifying which policies were triggered, as well as managing configurations of different policies.

Enter a policy name *

[Save]   [Cancel]

Click Add Condition to display a form like that shown in Figure 7.20.

FIGURE 7.20   Adding a condition to a policy

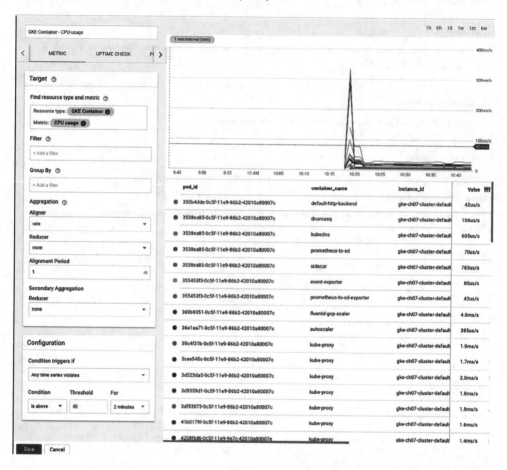

In the Filter parameter, enter **GKE Container** and **CPU Usage**. In the Configuration section, specify 80 percent as the threshold and 2 minutes as the time period. Save the condition. This will return to the Create Policy form. In the Notification parameter, select Email from the drop-down list, as shown in Figure 7.21.

FIGURE 7.21   Choosing a notification channel

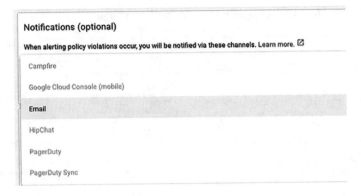

Add a description and policy name, as shown in Figure 7.22.

FIGURE 7.22   A completed policy creation form

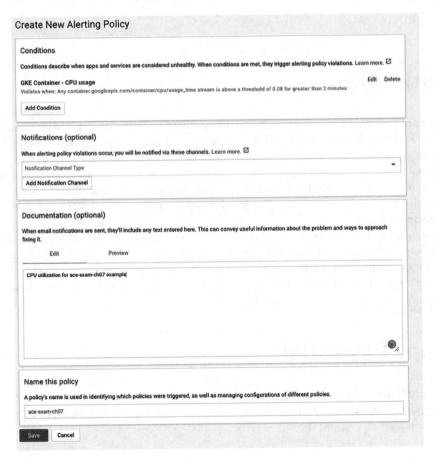

Save the policy specification to display a monitoring summary, as shown in Figure 7.23.

FIGURE 7.23 Monitoring results of policy on CPU usage

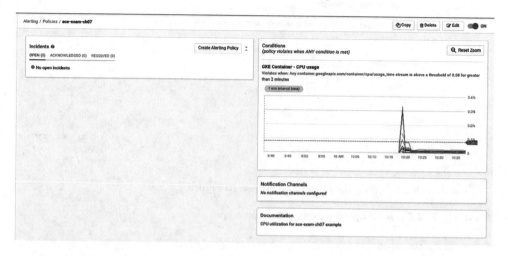

Summary

Kubernetes Engine is a container orchestration system for deploying applications to run in clusters. Kubernetes is architected with a single cluster manager and worker nodes.

Kubernetes uses the concept of pods are instances running a container. It is possible to run multiple containers in a pod, but that occurs less frequently than single-container pods. ReplicaSets are controllers for ensuring that the correct number of pods are running. Deployments are sets of identical pods. StatefulSets are a type of deployment used for stateful applications.

Kubernetes clusters can be deployed through Cloud Console or by using gcloud commands. You deploy applications by bundling the application in a container and using the console or the kubectl command to create a deployment that runs the application on the cluster.

Stackdriver is used to monitor instances in clusters. You can create alerts and have notifications delivered to a variety of channels.

Exam Essentials

Understand that Kubernetes is a container orchestration system. Kubernetes Engine is a GCP product that provides Kubernetes to GCP customers. Kubernetes manages containers that run in a set of VM instances.

Understand that Kubernetes uses a single cluster master that controls nodes that execute workloads.   Kubernetes uses the master to coordinate execution and monitor the health of pods. If there is a problem with a pod, the master can correct the problem and reschedule the disrupted job.

Be able to describe pods.   Pods are single instances of a running process, services provide a level of indirection between pods and clients calling services in the pods, a ReplicaSet is a kind of controller that ensures that the right number of pods are running, and a deployment is a set of identical pods.

Kubernetes can be deployed using Cloud Console or using `gcloud` commands.   gcloud commands manipulate the Kubernetes Engine service, while kubectl commands are used to manage the internal state of clusters from the command line. The base command for working with Kubernetes Engine is gcloud container. Note that gcloud and kubectl have different command syntaxes. kubectl commands specify a verb and then a resource, as in kubectl scale deployment ..., while gcloud specifies a resource before the verb, as in gcloud container clusters create. Deployments are created using Cloud Console or at the command line using a YAML specification.

Deployments are sets of identical pods. StatefulSets are a type of deployment used for stateful applications. Kubernetes is monitored using Stackdriver.   Stackdriver can be configured to generate alerts and notify you on a variety of channels. To monitor the state of a cluster, you can create a policy that monitors a metric, like CPU utilization, and have notifications sent to email or other channels.

Review Questions 80%

You can find the answers in the Appendix.

1. A new engineer is asking for clarification about when it is best to use Kubernetes and when to use instance groups. You point out that Kubernetes uses instance groups. What purpose do instance groups play in a Kubernetes cluster?

   A. They monitor the health of instances.

   B. They create pods and deployments.

   C. They create sets of VMs that can be managed as a unit.

   D. They create alerts and notification channels.

2. What kinds of instances are required to have a Kubernetes cluster?

   A. A cluster master and nodes to execute workloads.

   B. A cluster master, nodes to execute workloads, and Stackdriver nodes to monitor node health.

   C. Kubernetes nodes; all instances are the same.

   D. Instances with at least four vCPUs.

3. What is a pod in Kubernetes?

   A. A set of containers

   B. Application code deployed in a Kubernetes cluster

   C. A single instance of a running process in a cluster

   D. A controller that manages communication between clients and Kubernetes services

4. You have developed an application that calls a service running in a Kubernetes cluster. The service runs in pods that can be terminated if they are unhealthy and replaced with other pods that might have a different IP address. How should you code your application to ensure it functions properly in this situation?

   A. Query Kubernetes for a list of IP addresses of pods running the service you use.

   B. Communicate with Kubernetes services so applications do not have to be coupled to specific pods.

   C. Query Kubernetes for a list of pods running the service you use.

   D. Use a gcloud command to get the IP addresses needed.

5. You have noticed that an application's performance has degraded significantly. You have recently made some configuration changes to resources in your Kubernetes cluster and suspect that those changes have alerted the number of pods running in the cluster. Where would you look for details on the number of pods that should be running?

   A. Deployments

   B. Stackdriver

   C. ReplicaSet

   D. Jobs

6. You are deploying a high availability application in Kubernetes Engine. You want to maintain availability even if there is a major network outage in a data center. What feature of Kubernetes Engine would you employ?

   A. Multiple instance groups

   B. Multizone/region cluster

   C. Regional deployments

   D. Load balancing

7. You want to write a script to deploy a Kubernetes cluster with GPUs. You have deployed clusters before, but you are not sure about all the required parameters. You need to deploy this script as quickly as possible. What is one way to develop this script quickly?

   A. Use the GPU template in the Kubernetes Engine cloud console to generate the `gcloud` command to create the cluster

   B. Search the Web for a script

   C. Review the documentation on gcloud parameters for adding GPUs

   D. Use an existing script and add parameters for attaching GPUs

8. What gcloud command will create a cluster named `ch07-cluster-1` with four nodes?

   A. `gcloud beta container clusters create ch07-cluster-1 --num-nodes=4`

   B. `gcloud container beta clusters create ch07-cluster-1 --num-nodes=4`

   C. `gcloud container clusters create ch07-cluster-1 --num-nodes=4`

   D. `gcloud beta container clusters create ch07-cluster-1 4`

9. When using Create Deployment from Cloud Console, which of the following cannot be specified for a deployment?

   A. Container image

   B. Application name

   C. Time to live (TTL)

   D. Initial command

10. Deployment configuration files created in Cloud Console use what type of file format?

   A. CSV

   B. YAML

   C. TSV

   D. JSON

11. What command is used to run a Docker image on a cluster?

   A. `gcloud container run`

   B. `gcloud beta container run`

   C. `kubectl run`

   D. `kubectl beta run`

12. What command would you use to have 10 replicas of a deployment named ch07-app-deploy?

   A. `kubectl upgrade deployment ch07-app-deploy --replicas=5`

   B. `gcloud containers deployment ch07-app-deploy --replicas=5`

   C. `kubectl scale deployment ch07-app-deploy --replicas=10`

   D. `kubectl scale deployment ch07-app-deploy --pods=5`

13. Stackdriver is used for what operations on Kubernetes clusters?

   A. Notifications only

   B. Monitoring and notifications only

   C. Logging only

   D. Notifications, monitoring, and logging

14. Before monitoring a Kubernetes cluster, what must you create with Stackdriver?

   A. Log

   B. Workspace

   C. Pod

   D. ReplicaSet

15. What kind of information is provided in the Details page about an instance in Stackdriver?

   A. CPU usage only

   B. Network traffic only

   C. Disk I/O, CPU usage, and network traffic

   D. CPU usage and disk I/O

16. When creating an alerting policy, what can be specified?

   A. Conditions, notifications, and time to live

   B. Conditions, notifications, and documentation

   C. Conditions only

   D. Conditions, documentation, and time to live

17. Your development team needs to be notified if there is a problem with applications running on several Kubernetes clusters. Different team members prefer different notification methods in addition to Stackdriver alerting. What is the most efficient way to send notifications and meet your team's requests?

   A. Set up SMS text messaging, Slack, and email notifications on an alert.

   B. Create a separate alert for each notification channel.

   C. Create alerts with email notifications and have those notification emails forwarded to other notification systems.

   D. Use a single third-party notification mechanism.

18. A new engineer is trying to set up alerts for a Kubernetes cluster. The engineer seems to be creating a large number of alerts and you are concerned this is not the most efficient way and will lead to more maintenance work than required. You explain that a more efficient way is to create alerts and apply them to what?

    A. One instance only

    B. An instance or entire group

    C. A group only

    D. A pod

19. You are attempting to execute commands to initiate a deployment on a Kubernetes cluster. The commands are not having any effect. You suspect that a Kubernetes component is not functioning correctly. What component could be the problem?

    A. The Kubernetes API

    B. A StatefulSet

    C. Cloud SDK gcloud commands

    D. ReplicaSet

20. You have deployed an application to a Kubernetes cluster. You have noticed that several pods are starved for resources for a period of time and the pods are shut down. When resources are available, new instantiations of those pods are created. Clients are still able to connect to pods even though the new pods have different IP addresses from the pods that were terminated. What Kubernetes component makes this possible?

    A. Services

    B. ReplicaSet

    C. Alerts

    D. StatefulSet

Chapter

8

Managing Kubernetes Clusters

THIS CHAPTER COVERS THE FOLLOWING OBJECTIVE OF THE GOOGLE ASSOCIATE CLOUD ENGINEER CERTIFICATION EXAM:

✓ 4.2 Managing Kubernetes Engine resources

This chapter describes how to perform basic Kubernetes management tasks, including the following:

- Viewing the status of Kubernetes clusters
- Viewing image repositories and image details
- Adding, modifying, and removing nodes
- Adding, modifying, and removing pods
- Adding, modifying, and removing services

You'll see how to perform each of these tasks using Google Cloud Console and Cloud SDK, which you can use locally on your development machines, on GCP virtual machines, and by using Cloud Shell.

Viewing the Status of a Kubernetes Cluster

Assuming you have created a cluster using the steps outlined in Chapter 7, you can view the status of a Kubernetes cluster using either Google Cloud Console or the gcloud commands.

Viewing the Status of Kubernetes Clusters Using Cloud Console

Starting from the Cloud Console home page, open the navigation menu by clicking the three stacked lines icon in the upper-left corner. This displays the list of GCP services, as shown in Figure 8.1.

FIGURE 8.1   Navigation menu in Google Cloud Console

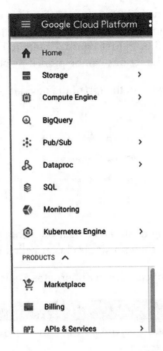

Select Kubernetes Engine from the lists of services, as shown in Figure 8.2.

FIGURE 8.2   Selecting Kubernetes Engine from the navigation menu

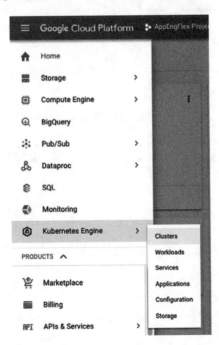

Pinning Services to the Top of the Navigation Menu

In Figure 8.2, Kubernetes Engine has been *"pinned"* so it is displayed at the top. You can pin any service in the navigation menu by mousing over the product and clicking the pin icon that appears, as in Figure 8.3. In that figure, Compute Engine and Kubernetes Engine are already pinned, and Cloud Functions can be pinned by clicking the gray pin icon.

FIGURE 8.3   Pinning a service to the top of the navigation menu

After clicking Kubernetes Engine in the navigation menu, you will see a list of running clusters, as in Figure 8.4, which shows a single cluster called `standard-cluster-1`.

FIGURE 8.4   Example list of clusters in Kubernetes Engine

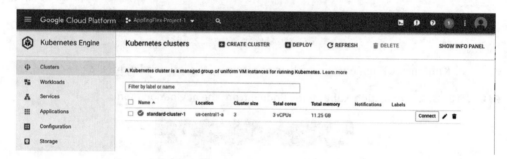

Mouse over the name of the cluster to highlight it, as in Figure 8.5, and click the name to display details of the cluster, as in Figure 8.6.

FIGURE 8.5   Click the name of a cluster to display its details.

Name ∧	Location	Cluster size	Total cores	Total mem
☑ standard-cluster-1	us-central1-a	3	3 vCPUs	11.25 GB

FIGURE 8.6 The first part of the cluster Details page describes the configuration of the cluster.

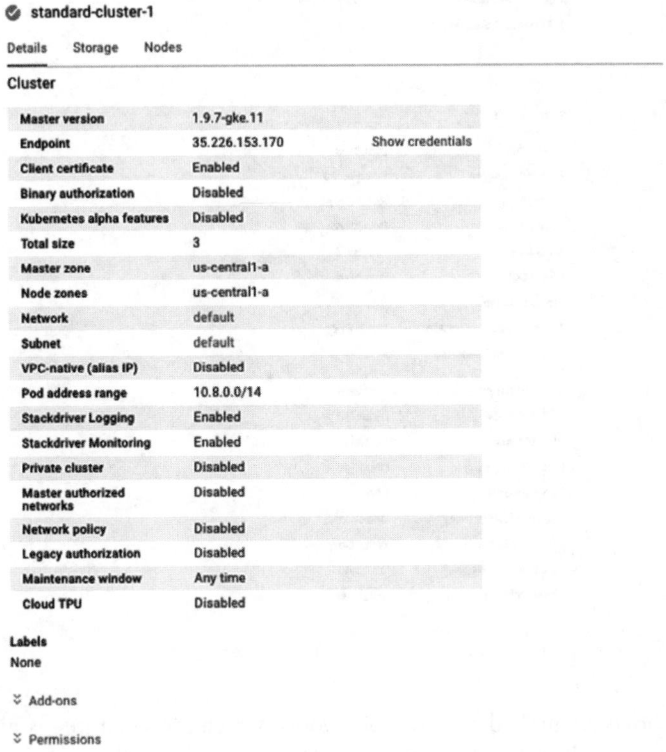

✓ standard-cluster-1

Details   Storage   Nodes

Cluster

Master version	1.9.7-gke.11	
Endpoint	35.226.153.170	Show credentials
Client certificate	Enabled	
Binary authorization	Disabled	
Kubernetes alpha features	Disabled	
Total size	3	
Master zone	us-central1-a	
Node zones	us-central1-a	
Network	default	
Subnet	default	
VPC-native (alias IP)	Disabled	
Pod address range	10.8.0.0/14	
Stackdriver Logging	Enabled	
Stackdriver Monitoring	Enabled	
Private cluster	Disabled	
Master authorized networks	Disabled	
Network policy	Disabled	
Legacy authorization	Disabled	
Maintenance window	Any time	
Cloud TPU	Disabled	

Labels
None

⌄ Add-ons

⌄ Permissions

Clicking the Add-ons and Permissions links displays information like that shown in Figure 8.7. The Add-ons section displays the status of optional add-on features of a cluster. The Permissions section shows which GCP service APIs are enabled for the cluster.

FIGURE 8.7   Add-on and permission details for a cluster

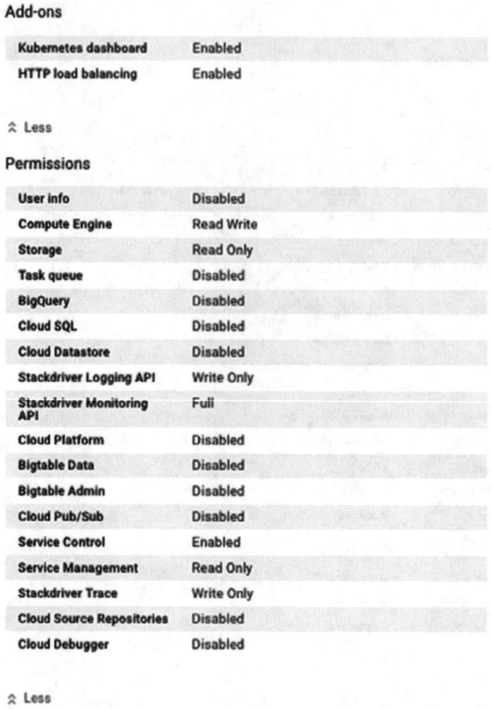

Add-ons

Kubernetes dashboard	Enabled
HTTP load balancing	Enabled

⌃ Less

Permissions

User info	Disabled
Compute Engine	Read Write
Storage	Read Only
Task queue	Disabled
BigQuery	Disabled
Cloud SQL	Disabled
Cloud Datastore	Disabled
Stackdriver Logging API	Write Only
Stackdriver Monitoring API	Full
Cloud Platform	Disabled
Bigtable Data	Disabled
Bigtable Admin	Disabled
Cloud Pub/Sub	Disabled
Service Control	Enabled
Service Management	Read Only
Stackdriver Trace	Write Only
Cloud Source Repositories	Disabled
Cloud Debugger	Disabled

⌃ Less

Figure 8.8 shows example details of node pools, which are separate instance groups running in a Kubernetes clusters. The details in this section include the node image running on the nodes, the machine type, the total number of vCPUs (listed as Total Cores), the disk type, and whether the nodes are preemptible.

Below the name of the cluster is a horizontal list of three options: Details, Storage, and Nodes. So far, we have described the contents of the Details page. Click Storage to display information such as in Figure 8.9, which displays persistent volumes and the storage classes used by the cluster.

This cluster does not have persistent volumes but uses standard storage. Persistent volumes are durable disks that are managed by Kubernetes and implemented using Compute Engine persistent disks. A storage class is a type of storage with a set of policies specifying quality of service, backup policy, and a provisioner (which is a service that implements the storage).

FIGURE 8.8   Details about node pools in the cluster

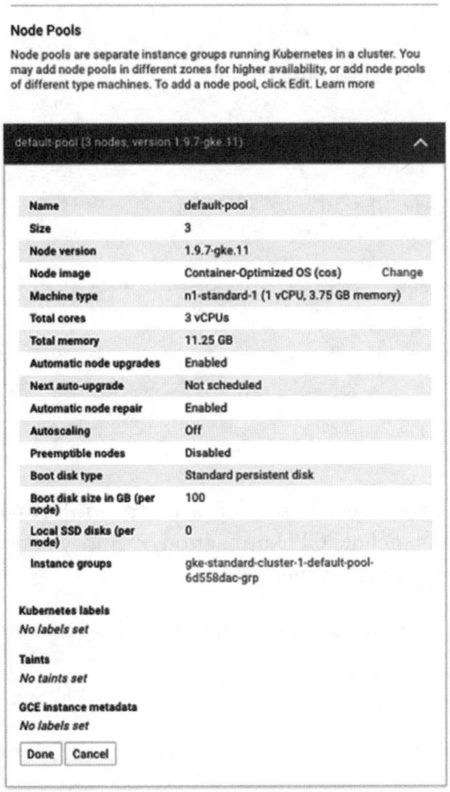

Node Pools

Node pools are separate instance groups running Kubernetes in a cluster. You may add node pools in different zones for higher availability, or add node pools of different type machines. To add a node pool, click Edit. Learn more

default-pool (3 nodes, version 1.9.7-gke.11)

Name	default-pool
Size	3
Node version	1.9.7-gke.11
Node image	Container-Optimized OS (cos) Change
Machine type	n1-standard-1 (1 vCPU, 3.75 GB memory)
Total cores	3 vCPUs
Total memory	11.25 GB
Automatic node upgrades	Enabled
Next auto-upgrade	Not scheduled
Automatic node repair	Enabled
Autoscaling	Off
Preemptible nodes	Disabled
Boot disk type	Standard persistent disk
Boot disk size in GB (per node)	100
Local SSD disks (per node)	0
Instance groups	gke-standard-cluster-1-default-pool-6d558dac-grp

Kubernetes labels
No labels set

Taints
No taints set

GCE instance metadata
No labels set

Done   Cancel

FIGURE 8.9   Storage information about a cluster

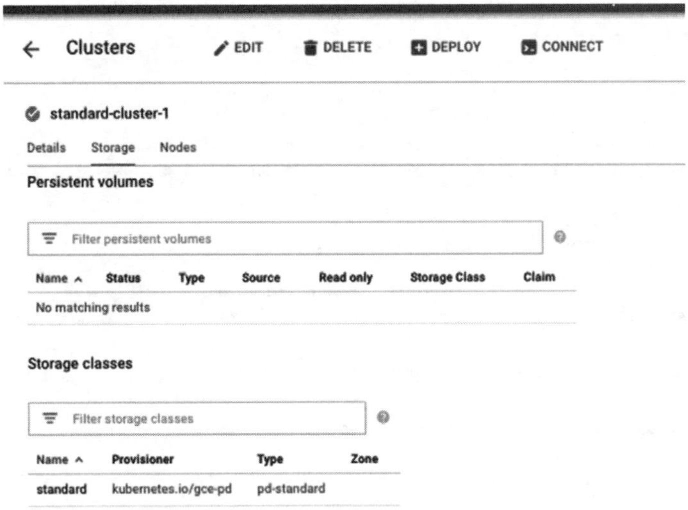

← Clusters   ✏ EDIT   🗑 DELETE   ➕ DEPLOY   ▶ CONNECT

✔ standard-cluster-1

Details   Storage   Nodes

Persistent volumes

Filter persistent volumes

Name ∧	Status	Type	Source	Read only	Storage Class	Claim

No matching results

Storage classes

Filter storage classes

Name ∧	Provisioner	Type	Zone
standard	kubernetes.io/gce-pd	pd-standard	

Under the Nodes option of the cluster status menu, you can see a list of nodes or VMs running in the cluster, as shown in Figure 8.10. The nodes list shows basic configuration information.

FIGURE 8.10 Listing of nodes in the cluster

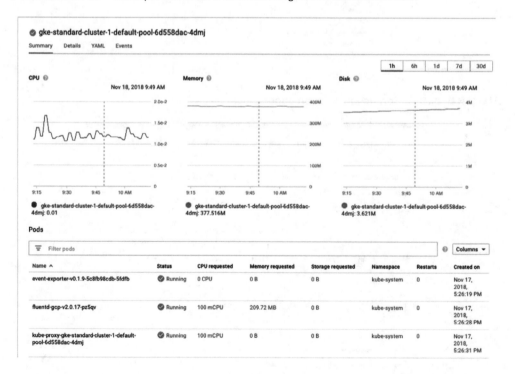

Click the name of one of the nodes to see detailed status information such as in Figure 8.11. The node details include CPU utilization, memory consumption, and disk IO. There is also a list of pods running on the node.

FIGURE 8.11 Example details of a node running in a Kubernetes cluster

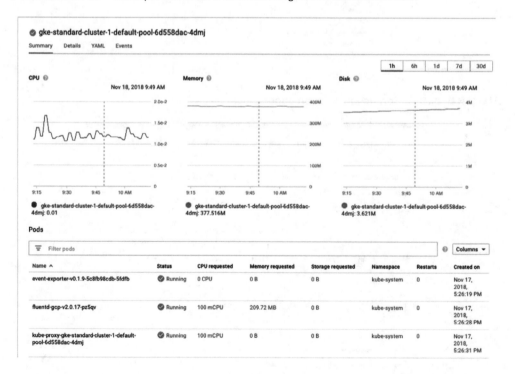

Click the name of a pod to see its details. The pod display is similar to the node display with CPU, memory, and disk statistics. Configuration details include when the pod was created, labels assigned, links to logs, and status (which is shown as Running in Figure 8.12).

Other possible statuses are Pending, which indicates the pod is downloading images; Succeeded, which indicates the pod terminated successfully; Failed, which indicates at least one container failed; and Unknown, which means the master cannot reach the node and status cannot be determined.

FIGURE 8.12 Pod status display, with status as Running

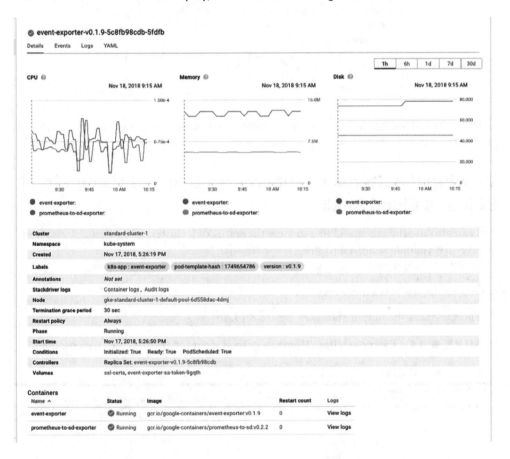

At the bottom of the pod display is a list of containers running. Click the name of a container to see its details. Figure 8.13 shows the details of the container named event-exporter. Information includes the status, the start time, the command that is running, and the volumes mounted.

FIGURE 8.13   Details of a container running in a pod

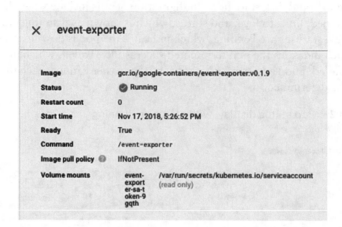

Using Cloud Console, you can list all clusters and view details of their configuration and status. You can then drill down into each node, pod, and container to view their details.

Viewing the Status of Kubernetes Clusters Using Cloud SDK and Cloud Shell

You can also use the command line to view the status of a cluster. The gcloud container cluster list command is used to show those details.

To list the names and basic information of all clusters, use this command:

```
gcloud container clusters list
```

This produces the output shown in Figure 8.14.

FIGURE 8.14   Example output from the gcloud container clusters list command

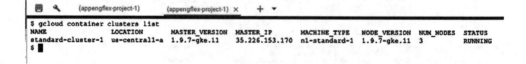

Why Don't Commands Start with `gcloud kubernetes`?

`gcloud` commands start with the word `gcloud` followed by the name of the service, for example, `gcloud compute` for Compute Engine commands and `gcloud sql` for Cloud SQL commands. You might expect the Kubernetes Engine commands to start with `gcloud kubernetes`, but the service was originally called Google Container Engine. In November 2017, Google renamed the service Kubernetes Engine, but the `gcloud` commands remained the same.

To view the details of a cluster, use the `gcloud container clusters describe` command. You will need to pass in the name of a zone or region using the `--zone` or `--region` parameter. For example, to describe a cluster named `standard-cluster-1` located in the us-central1-a zone, you would use this command:

`gcloud container clusters describe --zone us-central1-a standard-cluster-1`

This will display details like those shown in Figure 8.15 and Figure 8.16. Note that the describe command also displays authentication information such as client certificate, username, and password. That information is not shown in the figures.

FIGURE 8.15   Part 1 of the information displayed by the `gcloud container clusters describe` command

FIGURE 8.16   Part 2 of the information displayed by the gcloud container clusters describe command

```
masterAuthorizedNetworksConfig: {}
monitoringService: monitoring.googleapis.com
name: standard-cluster-1
network: default
networkConfig:
  network: projects/appengflex-project-1/global/networks/default
  subnetwork: projects/appengflex-project-1/regions/us-central1/subnetworks/default
networkPolicy: {}
nodeConfig:
  diskSizeGb: 100
  diskType: pd-standard
  imageType: COS
  machineType: n1-standard-1
  oauthScopes:
  - https://www.googleapis.com/auth/compute
  - https://www.googleapis.com/auth/devstorage.read_only
  - https://www.googleapis.com/auth/logging.write
  - https://www.googleapis.com/auth/monitoring
  - https://www.googleapis.com/auth/servicecontrol
  - https://www.googleapis.com/auth/service.management.readonly
  - https://www.googleapis.com/auth/trace.append
  serviceAccount: default
nodeIpv4CidrSize: 24
nodePools:
- autoscaling: {}
  config:
    diskSizeGb: 100
    diskType: pd-standard
    imageType: COS
    machineType: n1-standard-1
    oauthScopes:
    - https://www.googleapis.com/auth/compute
    - https://www.googleapis.com/auth/devstorage.read_only
    - https://www.googleapis.com/auth/logging.write
    - https://www.googleapis.com/auth/monitoring
    - https://www.googleapis.com/auth/servicecontrol
    - https://www.googleapis.com/auth/service.management.readonly
    - https://www.googleapis.com/auth/trace.append
    serviceAccount: default
  initialNodeCount: 3
  instanceGroupUrls:
  - https://www.googleapis.com/compute/v1/projects/appengflex-project-1/zones/us-central1-a/instanceGroupManagers/gke-standard-cluster-1-default-
pool-6d558dac-grp
  management:
    autoRepair: true
    autoUpgrade: true
  name: default-pool
  selfLink: https://container.googleapis.com/v1/projects/appengflex-project-1/zones/us-central1-a/clusters/standard-cluster-1/nodePools/default-p
ool
  status: RUNNING
  version: 1.9.7-gke.11
selfLink: https://container.googleapis.com/v1/projects/appengflex-project-1/zones/us-central1-a/clusters/standard-cluster-1
servicesIpv4Cidr: 10.11.240.0/20
status: RUNNING
subnetwork: default
zone: us-central1-a
```

To list information about nodes and pods, use the kubectl command.

First, you need to ensure you have a properly configured kubeconfig file, which contains information on how to communicate with the cluster API. Run the command gcloud container clusters get-credentials with the name of a zone or region and the name of a cluster. Here's an example:

```
gcloud container clusters get-credentials --zone us-central1-a standard-cluster-1
```

This will configure the kubeconfig file on a cluster named standard-cluster-1 in the use-central1-a zone. Figure 8.17 shows an example output of that command, which includes the status of fetching and setting authentication data.

FIGURE 8.17 Example output of the get-credentials command

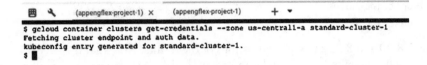

```
       ⊞  ⚒     (appengflex-project-1) ×      (appengflex-project-1)        +  ▾
$ gcloud container clusters get-credentials --zone us-central1-a standard-cluster-1
Fetching cluster endpoint and auth data.
kubeconfig entry generated for standard-cluster-1.
$ ▊
```

You can list the nodes in a cluster using the following:

kubectl get nodes

This produces output such as in Figure 8.18, which shows the status of three nodes.

FIGURE 8.18 Example output of the kubectl get nodes command

```
    ⊞  ⚒     (appengflex-project-1) ×      (appengflex-project-1)        +  ▾
$ kubectl get nodes
NAME                                             STATUS    ROLES     AGE     VERSION
gke-standard-cluster-1-default-pool-6d558dac-4dmj Ready    <none>    18h     v1.9.7-gke.11
gke-standard-cluster-1-default-pool-6d558dac-jj15 Ready    <none>    18h     v1.9.7-gke.11
gke-standard-cluster-1-default-pool-6d558dac-q95d Ready    <none>    18h     v1.9.7-gke.11
$ ▊
```

Similarly, to list pods, use the following command:

kubectl get pods

This produces output such as in Figure 8.19, which lists pods and their status.

FIGURE 8.19 Example output of the kubectl get pods command

```
    ⊞  ⚒     (appengflex-project-1) ×      (appengflex-project-1)        +  ▾
$ kubectl get pods
NAME                                             READY    STATUS      RESTARTS   AGE
nginx-1-7cb5b65464-qthgr                         1/1      Running     0          17h
nginx-2-6bd764c757-7z99w                         1/1      Running     0          17h
seldon-core-1-deployer-wzt9v                     0/1      Completed   0          17h
seldon-core-1-redis-585647f8bf-7cbbr             1/1      Running     0          17h
seldon-core-1-seldon-apiserver-69df56d98d-vqtxr  1/1      Running     0          17h
seldon-core-1-seldon-cluster-manager-65d8b4b4b8-zd6ns 1/1 Running     0          17h
$ ▊
```

For more details about nodes and pods, use these commands:

```
kubectl describe nodes
kubectl describe pods
```

Figures 8.20 and 8.21 show partial listings of the results. Note that the kubectl describe pods command also includes information about containers, such as name, labels, conditions, network addresses, and system information.

FIGURE 8.20   Partial listing of the details shown by the kubectl describe nodes command

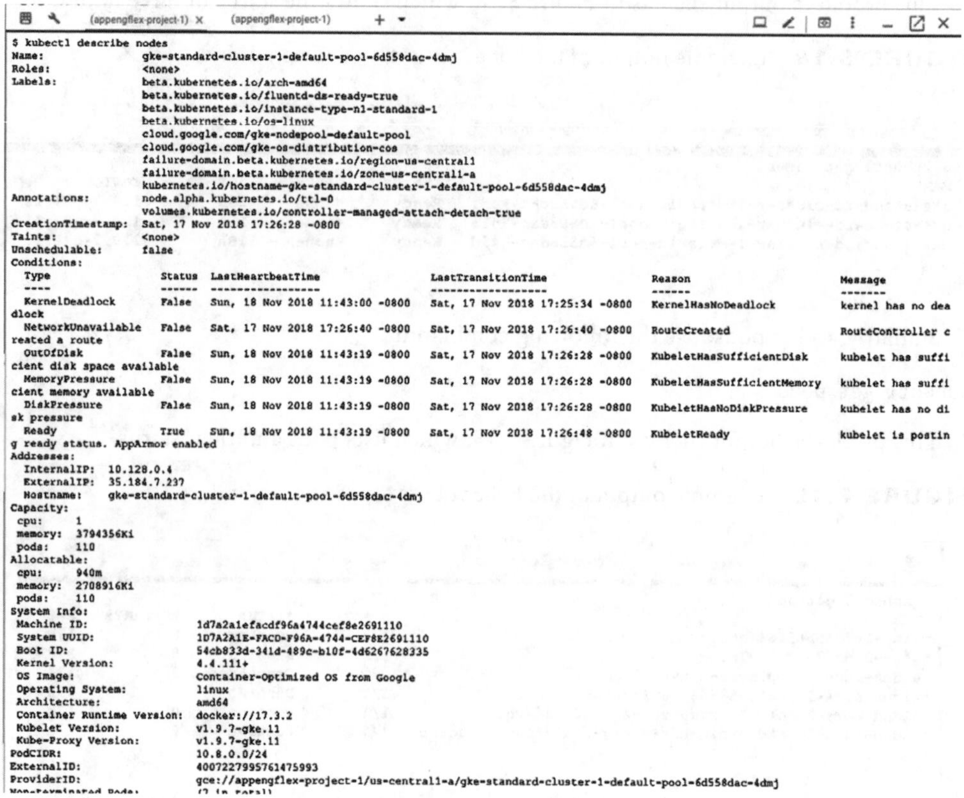

FIGURE 8.21   Partial listing of the details shown by the kubectl describe pods command

```
$ kubectl describe pods
Name:               nginx-1-7cb5b65464-qthgr
Namespace:          default
Node:               gke-standard-cluster-1-default-pool-6d558dac-4dmj/10.128.0.4
Start Time:         Sat, 17 Nov 2018 18:11:46 -0800
Labels:             app-nginx-1
                    pod-template-hash-3761621020
Annotations:        kubernetes.io/limit-ranger-LimitRanger plugin set: cpu request for container nginx
Status:             Running
IP:                 10.8.0.8
Controlled By:      ReplicaSet/nginx-1-7cb5b65464
Containers:
  nginx:
    Container ID:   docker://f0182edbfb3b290bd1842f764544d30fa1f45b4dd8bcfe7fbf4aa7dc9dfd9f76
    Image:          nginx:latest
    Image ID:       docker-pullable://nginx@sha256:05db58c525db34c3fea90585ff7900282bb1bec2dfeb04d4489a72113613f533
    Port:           <none>
    Host Port:      <none>
    State:          Running
      Started:      Sat, 17 Nov 2018 18:11:51 -0800
    Ready:          True
    Restart Count:  0
    Requests:
      cpu:          100m
    Environment:    <none>
    Mounts:
      /var/run/secrets/kubernetes.io/serviceaccount from default-token-412q4 (ro)
Conditions:
  Type              Status
  Initialized       True
  Ready             True
  PodScheduled      True
Volumes:
  default-token-412q4:
    Type:           Secret (a volume populated by a Secret)
    SecretName:     default-token-412q4
    Optional:       false
QoS Class:          Burstable
Node-Selectors:     <none>
Tolerations:        node.kubernetes.io/not-ready:NoExecute for 300s
                    node.kubernetes.io/unreachable:NoExecute for 300s
Events:             <none>


Name:               nginx-2-6bd764c757-7z99w
Namespace:          default
Node:               gke-standard-cluster-1-default-pool-6d558dac-jj15/10.128.0.2
Start Time:         Sat, 17 Nov 2018 18:32:33 -0800
Labels:             app-nginx-2
                    pod-template-hash-2683207313
Annotations:        kubernetes.io/limit-ranger-LimitRanger plugin set: cpu request for container nginx
Status:             Running
IP:                 10.8.2.10
Controlled By:      ReplicaSet/nginx-2-6bd764c757
Containers:
  nginx:
    Container ID:   docker://ba2585651e9d131e5a522d0ef0541c4182f49fb15af87953e7d42e1b24e5af07
    Image:          nginx:latest
    Image ID:       docker-pullable://nginx@sha256:05db58c525db34c3fea90585ff7900282bb1bec2dfeb04d4489a72113613f533
    Port:           <none>
    Host Port:      <none>
    State:          Running
      Started:      Sat, 17 Nov 2018 18:32:34 -0800
    Ready:          True
    Restart Count:  0
    Requests:
      cpu:          100m
```

To view the status of clusters from the command line, use the gcloud container commands, but to get information about Kubernetes managed objects, like nodes, pods, and containers, use the kubectl command.

Adding, Modifying, and Removing Nodes

You can add, modify, and remove nodes from a cluster using either Cloud Console or Cloud SDK in your local environment, on a GCP virtual machine, or in Cloud Shell.

Adding, Modifying, and Removing Nodes with Cloud Console

From Cloud Console, navigate to the Kubernetes Engine page and display a list of clusters. Click the name of a cluster to display its details, as in Figure 8.22. Note the Edit option near the top of the screen. Click that to open an Edit form.

FIGURE 8.22   Details of a cluster in Cloud Console

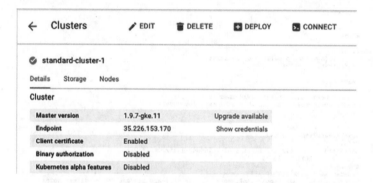

Scroll down to the Node Pools section, which lists the name, size, node image, machine type, and other information about the cluster. The size parameter is optional. In the example shown in Figure 8.23, the cluster has three nodes.

FIGURE 8.23   Details of a node pool in Cloud Console

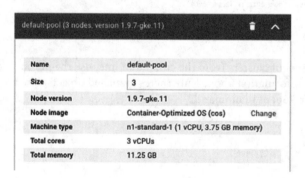

To add nodes, increase the size to the number of nodes you would like. To remove nodes, decrease the size to the number of nodes you'd like to have.

Adding, Modifying, and Removing with Cloud SDK and Cloud Shell

The command to add or modify nodes is gcloud container clusters resize. The command takes three parameters, as shown here:

- cluster name
- node pool name
- cluster size

For example, assume you have a cluster named standard-cluster-1 running a node pool called default-pool. To increase the size of the cluster from 3 to 5, use this command:

```
gcloud container clusters resize standard-cluster-1 --node-pool default-pool
--size 5 --region=us-central1
```

Once a cluster has been created, you can modify it using the gcloud container clusters update command. For example, to enable autoscaling, use the update command to specify the maximum and minimum number of nodes. The command to update a cluster named standard-cluster-1 running in a node pool called default-pool is as follows:

```
gcloud container clusters update standard-cluster-1 --enable-autoscaling
--min-nodes 1 \
--max-nodes 5 --zone us-central1-a --node-pool default-pool
```

 Real World Scenario

Keeping Up with Demand with Autoscaling

Often it is difficult to predict demand on a service. Even if there are regular patterns, such as large batch jobs run during nonbusiness hours, there can be variation in when those peak loads run. Rather than keep manually changing the number of vCPUs in a cluster, enable autoscaling to automatically add or remove nodes as needed based on demand. Autoscaling can be enabled when creating clusters with either Cloud Console or gcloud. This approach is more resilient to unexpected spikes and shifts in long-term patterns of peak use. It will also help optimize the cost of your cluster by not running too many servers when not needed. It will also help maintain performance by having sufficient nodes to meet demand.

Adding, Modifying, and Removing Pods

You can add, modify, and remove pods from a cluster using either Cloud Console or Cloud SDK in your local environment, on a GCP VM, or in Cloud Shell.

It is considered a best practice to not manipulate pods directly. Kubernetes will maintain the number of pods specified for a deployment. If you would like to change the number of pods, you should change the deployment configuration.

Adding, Modifying, and Removing Pods with Cloud Console

Pods are managed through deployments. A deployment includes a configuration parameter called *replicas*, which are the number of pods running the application specified in the deployment. This section describes how to use Cloud Console to change the number of replicas, which will in turn change the number of pods.

From Cloud Console, select the Workloads options from the navigation menu on the left. This displays a list of deployments, as in Figure 8.24.

FIGURE 8.24   List of deployments in a cluster

Click the name of the deployment you want to modify; a form is displayed with details such as in Figure 8.25. Note the Actions option in the top horizontal menu.

FIGURE 8.25   Multiple forms contain details of a deployment and include a menu of actions you can perform on the deployment.

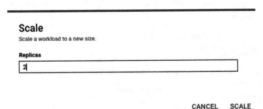

Click Actions to list the options, which are Autoscale, Expose, Rolling Update, and Scale, as shown in Figure 8.26.

FIGURE 8.26   List of actions available for deployments

Select Scale to display a dialog that allows you to set a new size for the workload, as shown in Figure 8.27. In this example, the number of replicas has been changed to 2.

FIGURE 8.27   Set the number of replicas for a deployment.

Scale

Scale a workload to a new size.

Replicas

```
2
```

CANCEL   SCALE

You can also have Kubernetes automatically add and remove replicas (and pods) depending on need by specifying autoscaling. Choose Autoscaling from the menu to display the form shown in Figure 8.28. You can specify a minimum and maximum number of replicas to run here.

FIGURE 8.28   Enable autoscaling to automatically add and remove replicas as needed depending on load.

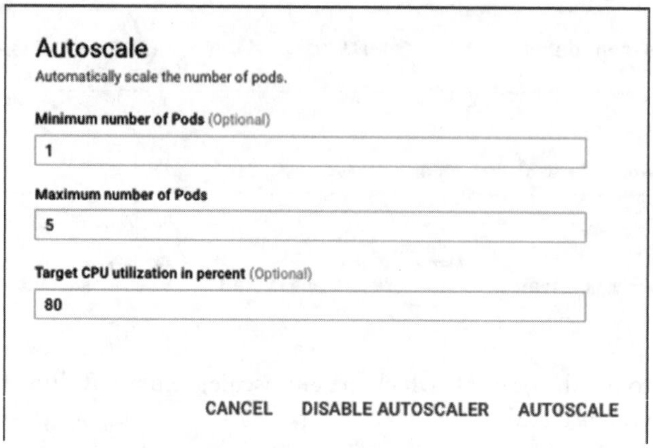

Autoscale

Automatically scale the number of pods.

Minimum number of Pods (Optional)

1

Maximum number of Pods

5

Target CPU utilization in percent (Optional)

80

CANCEL   DISABLE AUTOSCALER   AUTOSCALE

The Action menu also provides options to expose a service on a port, as shown in Figure 8.29, and to specify parameters to control rolling updates to deployed code, as shown in Figure 8.30. The parameters include the minimum seconds to wait before considering the pod updated, the maximum number of pods above target size allowed, and the maximum number of unavailable pods.

FIGURE 8.29   Form to expose services running on pods

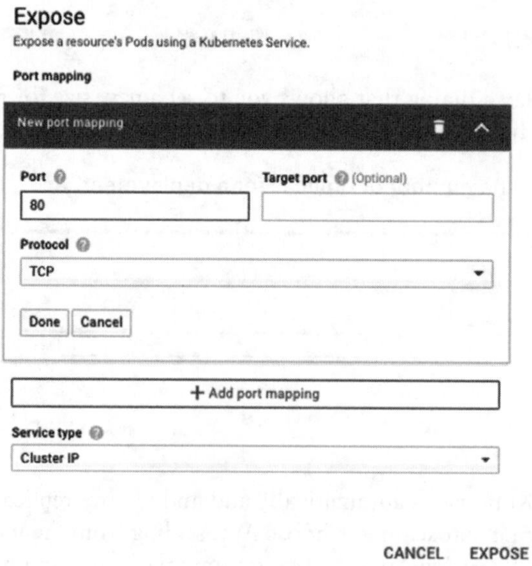

Expose

Expose a resource's Pods using a Kubernetes Service.

Port mapping

New port mapping

Port 🔵

80

Target port 🔵 (Optional)

Protocol 🔵

TCP

Done   Cancel

+ Add port mapping

Service type 🔵

Cluster IP

CANCEL   EXPOSE

FIGURE 8.30   Form to specify parameters for rolling updates of code running in pods

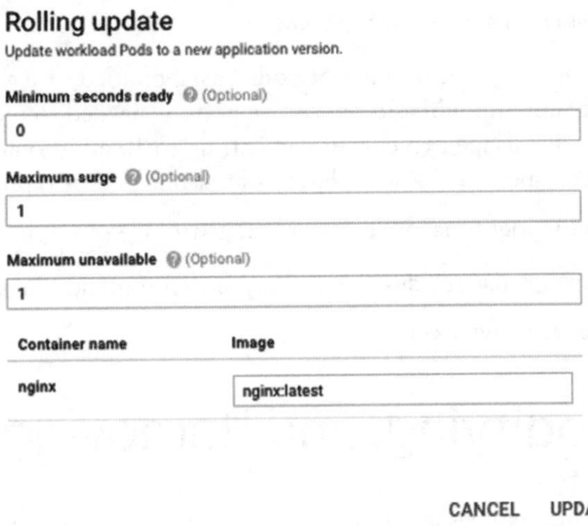

Rolling update
Update workload Pods to a new application version.

Minimum seconds ready @ (Optional)

```
0
```

Maximum surge @ (Optional)

```
1
```

Maximum unavailable @ (Optional)

```
1
```

Container name	Image
nginx	nginx:latest

CANCEL   UPDATE

Adding, Modifying, and Removing Pods with Cloud SDK and Cloud Shell

Working with pods in Cloud SDK and Cloud Shell is done by working with deployments; deployments were explained earlier in the section "Adding, Modifying, and Removing Pods with Cloud Console." You can use the kubectl command to work with deployments.

To list deployments, use the following command:

```
kubectl get deployments
```

This will produce a list of deployments such as in Figure 8.31.

FIGURE 8.31   A list of deployments on the command line

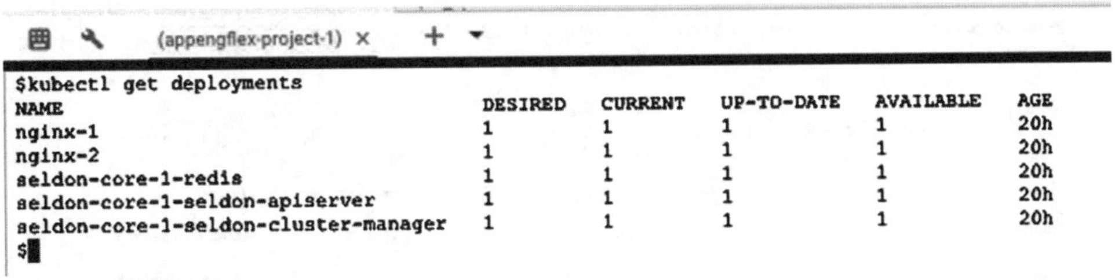

```
          (appengflex-project-1)  ×    +   ▼

$kubectl get deployments
NAME                                    DESIRED   CURRENT   UP-TO-DATE   AVAILABLE   AGE
nginx-1                                 1         1         1            1           20h
nginx-2                                 1         1         1            1           20h
seldon-core-1-redis                     1         1         1            1           20h
seldon-core-1-seldon-apiserver          1         1         1            1           20h
seldon-core-1-seldon-cluster-manager    1         1         1            1           20h
$
```

To add and remove pods, change the configuration of deployments using the kubectl scale deployment command. For this command, you have to specify the deployment name and number of replicas. For example, to set the number of replicas to 5 for a deployment named nginx-1, use this:

```
kubectl scale deployment nginx-1 --replicas 5
```

To have Kubernetes manage the number of pods based on load, use the autoscale command. The following command will add or remove pods as needed to meet demand based on CPU utilization. If CPU usage exceeds 80 percent, up to 10 additional pods or replicas will be added. The deployment will always have at least one pod or replica.

```
kubectl autoscale deployment nginx-1 --max 10 --min 1 --cpu-percent 80
```

To remove a deployment, use the delete deployment command like so:

```
kubectl delete deployment nginx-1
```

Adding, Modifying, and Removing Services

You can add, modify, and remove services from a cluster using either Cloud Console or Cloud SDK in your local environment, on a GCP VM, or in Cloud Shell.

A service is an abstraction that groups a set of pods as a single resource.

Adding, Modifying, and Removing Services with Cloud Console

Services are added through deployments. In Cloud Console, select the Workloads option from the navigation menu to display a list of deployments, as in Figure 8.32. Note the Deploy option in the horizontal menu at the top of the page.

FIGURE 8.32   List of deployments along with a Deploy command to create new services

Workloads   C REFRESH   ✚ DEPLOY

Workloads are deployable units of computing that can be created and managed in a cluster.

| ⇥ | Is system object : False ⊗ Filter workloads | | | ✕ | ❓ | Columns ▾ |

Name ∧	Status	Type	Pods	Namespace	Cluster
nginx-1	✅ OK	Deployment	1/1	default	standard-cluster-1
nginx-2	✅ OK	Deployment	1/1	default	standard-cluster-1
seldon-core-1-deployer	✅ OK	Job	0/0	default	standard-cluster-1
seldon-core-1-redis	✅ OK	Deployment	1/1	default	standard-cluster-1
seldon-core-1-seldon-apiserver	✅ OK	Deployment	1/1	default	standard-cluster-1
seldon-core-1-seldon-cluster-manager	✅ OK	Deployment	1/1	default	standard-cluster-1

Click Deploy to show the deployment form, as in Figure 8.33.

FIGURE 8.33 Form to specify a new deployment for a service

A deployment is a configuration which defines how Kubernetes deploys, manages, and scales your container image. Kubernetes will ensure your system matches this configuration.

Deployment

Container

Container image

nginx:latest

Select Google Container Registry image

Enviroment variables

+ Add environment variable

Initial command (Optional)

Done   Cancel

+ Add container

Application name

nginx-3

Namespace

default

Labels

Key   Value

app   nginx-3   ×

+ Add label

Cluster

standard-cluster-1

Create new cluster

Deploy   View YAML

In the Container Image parameter, you can specify the name of an image or select one from the Google Container Repository. To specify a name directly, specify a path to the image using a URL such as this:

```
gcr.io/google-samples/hello-app:2.0
```

You can specify labels, the initial command to run, and a name for your application.
When you click the name of a deployment, like those listed earlier in Figure 8.32, you will see details of that deployment, including a list of services, like that shown in Figure 8.34.

FIGURE 8.34   Details of a service running in a deployment

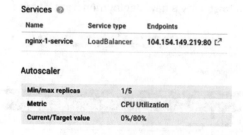

Clicking the name of a service opens the Detail form of the service, which includes a Delete option in the horizontal menu, as shown in Figure 8.35.

FIGURE 8.35   Navigate to the Service Details page to delete a service using the Delete option in the horizontal menu.

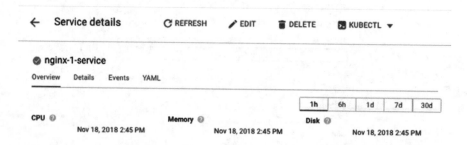

Adding, Modifying, and Removing Services with Cloud SDK and Cloud Shell

Use the kubectl get services command to list services. Figure 8.36 shows an example listing.

FIGURE 8.36   A list of services displayed by a kubectl get services command

```
$kubectl get services
NAME                             TYPE           CLUSTER-IP     EXTERNAL-IP       PORT(S)                          AGE
kubernetes                       ClusterIP      10.11.240.1    <none>            443/TCP                          21h
nginx-1-service                  LoadBalancer   10.11.246.160  104.154.149.219   80:32519/TCP                     20h
nginx-2-service                  LoadBalancer   10.11.254.216  35.239.143.176    80:30657/TCP                     20h
seldon-core-1-redis              ClusterIP      10.11.244.219  <none>            6379/TCP                         20h
seldon-core-1-seldon-apiserver   NodePort       10.11.250.14   <none>            8080:31721/TCP,5000:31530/TCP    20h
$
```

To add a service, use the kubectl run command to start a service. For example, to add a service called hello-server using the sample application by the same name provided by Google, use the following command:

```
kubectl run hello-server --image=gcr.io/google/samples/hello-app:1.0 --port 8080
```

This command will download and start running the image found at the path gcr.io/google-samples/ called hello-app, version 1. It will be accessible on port 8080. Services need to be exposed to be accessible to resources outside the cluster. This can be set using the expose command, as shown here:

```
kubectl expose deployment hello-server --type="LoadBalancer"
```

This command exposes the services by having a load balancer act as the endpoint for outside resources to contact the service.

To remove a service, use the delete service command, as shown here:

```
kubectl delete service hello-server
```

Viewing the Image Repository and Image Details

Container Registry is a GCP service for storing container images. Once you have created a registry and pushed images to it, you can view the contents of the registry and image details using Cloud Console and Cloud SDK and Cloud Shell.

Viewing the Image Repository and Image Details with Cloud Console

In Cloud Console, select Container Registry from the navigation menu to display the contents of a registry. Figure 8.37 shows an example listing with three images for Nginx, Redis, and WordPress.

FIGURE 8.37   A listing of images in a Container Registry

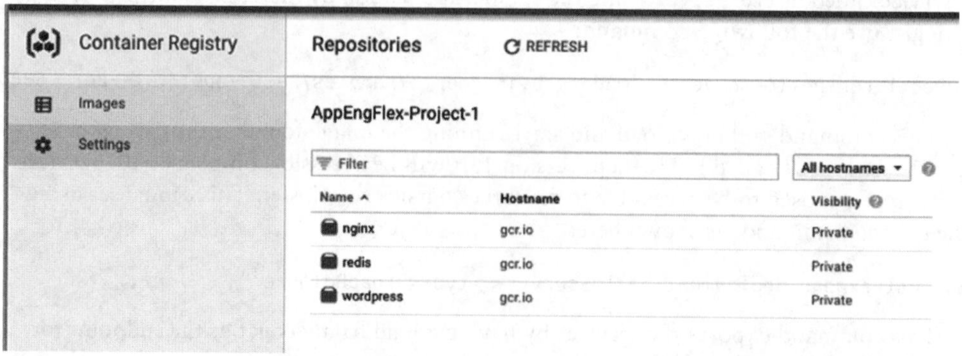

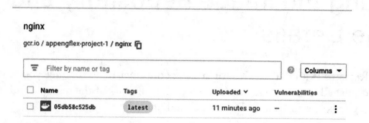

To see the details of an image, click the image name. For example, Figure 8.38 shows a listing for the Nginx image. This listing will list one entry for each version of the image. Since there is only one version of the image, there is only one listed.

FIGURE 8.38   A list of versions for an image

To see the details of that version, click the version name. This displays a listing such as in Figure 8.39, which includes the image type, size, and time created.

FIGURE 8.39 Details of a version of an image

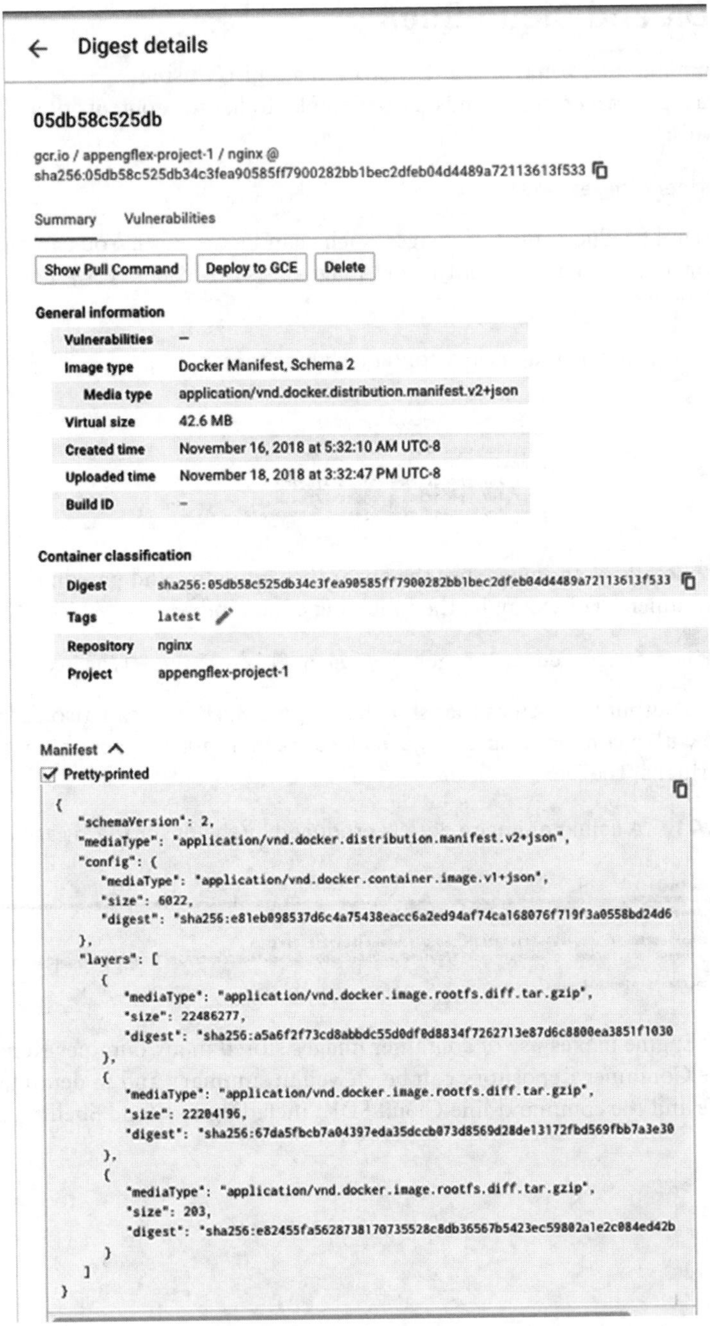

Viewing the Image Repository and Image Details with Cloud SDK and Cloud Shell

From the command line, you work with images in a registry using `gcloud container images` commands. For example, to list the contents of a registry, use this:

```
gcloud container images list
```

This command produces a list of images, such as in Figure 8.40. You can also list Google containers using `gcloud container images list --repository gcr.io/google-containers`.

FIGURE 8.40   List of images in a container repository

To view the details of an image, use the `describe` command and pass in the name of the image as an argument. For example, the following command:

```
gcloud container images describe gcr.io/appengflex-project-1/nginx
```

will produce an output list such as that shown in Figure 8.41. You can also describe a Google image with a command such as `gcloud container images describe gcr.io/google-containers/toolbox`.

FIGURE 8.41   A listing of image details produced by the `describe` image command

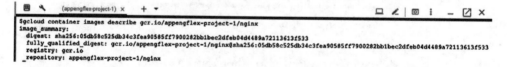

Kubernetes Engine makes use of container images stored in a Container Repository. The contents of the Container Repository can be viewed in summary and in detail using both Cloud Console and the command-line Cloud SDK, including in Cloud Shell.

Summary

In this chapter, you learned how to perform basic management tasks for working with Kubernetes clusters, nodes, pods, and services. The chapter also described how to list the contents of container image repositories. You learned how to pin services in the Cloud Console menu, view the status of Kubernetes clusters, and view image repository and image details using gcloud commands. This chapter also described how to modify and remove nodes and pods. You also saw the benefits of autoscaling in a real-world scenario.

Both Cloud Console and Cloud SDK, including Cloud Shell, can be used to add, remove, and modify nodes, pods, and services. They both can be used to review the contents of an image repository. Some of the most useful commands include gcloud container clusters create and gcloud container clusters resize. The kubectl command is used to modify Kubernetes resources such as deployments and pods.

Exam Essentials

Know how to view the status of a Kubernetes cluster.   Use Cloud Console to list clusters and drill down into clusters to see details of the cluster, including node, pod, and container details. Know the gcloud container clusters command and its options.

Understand how to add, modify, and remove nodes.   Use Cloud Console to modify nodes and know how to add and remove nodes by changing deployments. Use the gcloud container clusters resize command to add and remove nodes.

Understand how to add, modify, and remove pods.   Use Cloud Console to modify pods and to add and remove pods by changing deployments. Use kubectl get deployments to list deployments, kubectl scale deployment to modify the number of deployments, and kubectl autoscale deployment to enable autoscaling.

Understand how to add, modify, and remove services.   Use Cloud Console to modify services and add and remove services by changing deployments. Use kubectl run to start services and kubectl expose deployment to make a service accessible outside the cluster. Delete a service using the kubectl delete service command.

Know how to view Container Registry images and their details.   Navigate the Container Registry pages in Cloud Console. Know the gcloud container images list and gcloud container images describe commands.

Review Questions

90%

You can find the answers in the Appendix.

1. You are running several microservices in a Kubernetes cluster. You've noticed some performance degradation. After reviewing some logs, you begin to think the cluster may be improperly configured, and you open Cloud Console to investigate. How do you see the details of a specific cluster?

    A.   Type the cluster name into the search bar.

    B.   Click the cluster name.

    C.   Use the gcloud cluster details command.

    D.   None of the above.

2. You are viewing the details of a cluster in Cloud Console and want to see how many vCPUs are available in the cluster. Where would you look for that information?

    A.   Node Pools section of the Cluster Details page

    B.   Labels section of the Cluster Details page

    C.   Summary line of the Cluster Listing page

    D.   A and C

3. You have been assigned to help diagnose performance problems with applications running on several Kubernetes clusters. The first thing you want to do is understand, at a high level, the characteristics of the clusters. Which command should you use?

    A.   gcloud container list

    B.   gcloud container clusters list

    C.   gcloud clusters list

    D.   None of the above

4. When you first try to use the kubectl command, you get an error message indicating that the resource cannot be found or you cannot connect to the cluster. What command would you use to try to eliminate the error?

    A.   gcloud container clusters access

    B.   gdcloud container clusters get-credentials

    C.   gcloud auth container

    D.   gcloud auth container clusters

5. An engineer recently joined your team and is not aware of your team's standards for creating clusters and other Kubernetes objects. In particular, the engineer has not properly labeled several clusters. You want to modify the labels on the cluster from Cloud Console. How would you do it?

    A.   Click the Connect button.

    B.   Click the Deploy menu option.

    C.   Click the Edit menu option.

    D.   Type the new labels in the Labels section.

6. You receive a page in the middle of the night informing you that several services running on a Kubernetes cluster have high latency when responding to API requests. You review monitoring data and determine that there are not enough resources in the cluster to keep up with the load. You decide to add six more VMs to the cluster. What parameters will you need to specify when you issue the `cluster resize` command?

   A. Cluster size

   B. Cluster name

   C. Node pool name

   D. All of the above

7. You want to modify the number of pods in a cluster. What is the best way to do that?

   A. Modify pods directly

   B. Modify deployments

   C. Modify node pools directly

   D. Modify nodes

8. You want to see a list of deployments. Which option from the Kubernetes Engine navigation menu would you select?

   A. Clusters

   B. Storage

   C. Workloads

   D. Deployments

9. What actions are available from the Actions menu when viewing deployment details?

   A. Scale and Autoscale only

   B. Autoscale, Expose, and Rolling Update

   C. Add, Modify, and Delete

   D. None of the above

10. What is the command to list deployments from the command line?

   A. `gcloud container clusters list-deployments`

   B. `gcloud container clusters list`

   C. `kubectl get deployments`

   D. `kubectl deployments list`

11. What parameters of a deployment can be set in the Create Deployment page in Cloud Console?

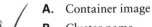

   A. Container image

   B. Cluster name

   C. Application name

   D. All of the above

12. Where can you view a list of services when using Cloud Console?

   A. In the Deployment Details page

   B. In the Container Details page

   C. In the Cluster Details page

   D. None of the above

13. What kubectl command is used to add a service?

   A. run

   B. start

   C. initiate

   D. deploy

14. You are supporting machine learning engineers who are testing a series of classifiers. They have five classifiers, called ml-classifier-1, ml-classifier-2, etc. They have found that ml-classifier-3 is not functioning as expected and they would like it removed from the cluster. What would you do to delete a service called ml-classifier-3?

   A. Run the command kubectl delete service ml-classifier-3.

   B. Run the command kubectl delete ml-classifier-3.

   C. Run the command gcloud service delete ml-classifier-3.

   D. Run the command gcloud container service delete ml-classifier-3.

15. What service is responsible for managing container images?

   A. Kubernetes Engine

   B. Compute Engine

   C. Container Registry

   D. Container Engine

16. What command is used to list container images in the command line?

   A. gcloud container images list

   B. gcloud container list images

   C. kubectl list container images

   D. kubectl container list images

17. A data warehouse designer wants to deploy an extraction, transformation, and load process to Kubernetes. The designer provided you with a list of libraries that should be installed, including drivers for GPUs. You have a number of container images that you think may meet the requirements. How could you get a detailed description of each of those containers?

   A. Run the command gcloud container images list details.

   B. Run the command gcloud container images describe.

   C. Run the command gcloud image describe.

   D. Run the command gcloud container describe.

18. You have just created a deployment and want applications outside the cluster to have access to the services provided by the deployment. What do you need to do to the service?

    A. Give it a public IP address.

    B. Issue a `kubectl expose deployment` command.

    C. Issue a `gcloud expose deployment` command.

    D. Nothing, making it accessible must be done at the cluster level.

19. You have deployed an application to a Kubernetes cluster that processes sensor data from a fleet of delivery vehicles. The volume of incoming data depends on the number of vehicles making deliveries. The number of vehicles making deliveries is dependent on the number of customer orders. Customer orders are high during daytime hours, holiday seasons, and when major advertising campaigns are run. You want to make sure you have enough nodes running to handle the load, but you want to keep your costs down. How should you configure your Kubernetes cluster?

    A. Deploy as many nodes as your budget allows.

    B. Enable autoscaling.

    C. Monitor CPU, disk, and network utilization and add nodes as necessary.

    D. Write a script to run `gcloud` commands to add and remove nodes when peaks usually start and end, respectively.

20. When using Kubernetes Engine, which of the following might a cloud engineer need to configure?

    A. Nodes, pods, services, and clusters only

    B. Nodes, pods, services, clusters, and container images

    C. Nodes, pods, clusters, and container images only

    D. Pods, services, clusters, and container images only

Chapter

9

Computing with App Engine

THIS CHAPTER COVERS THE FOLLOWING OBJECTIVE OF THE GOOGLE ASSOCIATE CLOUD ENGINEER CERTIFICATION EXAM:

✓ **3.3** Deploying and implementing App Engine and Cloud Functions resources

This chapter describes how to deploy App Engine Standard applications. We begin by reviewing the structure of an App Engine application and then examine how to specify an application configuration. Then, we will turn our attention to tuning App Engine applications through scaling and traffic splitting. We also discuss App Engine application versions along the way.

Google App Engine was originally designed to run applications in language-specific environments. Since the introduction of App Engine, Google has introduced App Engine Flexible, which can be used to deploy custom runtimes in containers. This chapter describes how to deploy applications to the original App Engine environment, known as App Engine Standard.

App Engine Components

App Engine Standard applications consist of four components:

- Application
- Service
- Version
- Instance

An App Engine application is a high-level resource created in a project; that is, each project can have one App Engine application. All resources associated with an App Engine app are created in the region specified when the app is created.

Apps have at least one service, which is the code executed in the App Engine environment. Because multiple versions of an application's code base can exist, App Engine supports versioning of apps. A service can have multiple versions, and these are usually slightly different, with newer versions incorporating new features, bug fixes, and other changes relative to earlier versions. When a version executes, it creates an instance of the app.

Services are typically structured to perform a single function with complex applications made up of multiple services, known as *microservices*. One microservice may handle API requests for data access, while another microservice performs authentication and a third records data for billing purposes.

FIGURE 9.1   The component hierarchy of App Engine applications

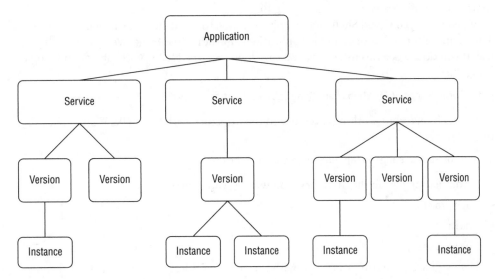

Services are defined by their source code and their configuration file. The combination of those files constitutes a version of the app. If you slightly change the source code or configuration file, it creates another version. In this way, you can maintain multiple versions of your application at one time, which is especially helpful for testing new features on a small number of users before rolling the change out to all users. If bugs or other problems occur with a version, you can easily roll back to an early version. Another advantage of keeping multiple versions is that they allow you to migrate and split traffic, which we'll describe in more detail later in the chapter.

Deploying an App Engine Application

The Google Associate Cloud Engineer certification exam does not require engineers to write an application, but we are expected to know how to deploy one. In this section, you will download a Hello World example from Google and use it as a sample application that you will deploy. The app is written in Python, so you'll use the Python runtime in App Engine.

Deploying an App Using Cloud Shell and SDK

First, you will work in a terminal window using Cloud Shell, which you can start from the console by clicking the Cloud Shell icon. Make sure gcloud is configured to work with App Engine by using the following command:

```
gcloud components install app-engine-python
```

This will install or update the App Engine Python library as needed. If the library is up to date, you will receive a message saying that.

When you open Cloud Shell, you may have a directory named python-docs-samples. This contains a number of example applications, including the Hello World app we'll use. If you do not see this directory, you can download the Hello World app from Google using this:

```
git clone https://github.com/GoogleCloudPlatform/python-docs-samples
```

Next, change your working directory to the directory with the Hello World app, using the following:

```
cd python-docs-samples/appengine/standard/hello_world
```

If you list the files in the directory, you will see three files.

- app.yaml
- main.py
- main_test.py

Here you are primarily concerned with the app.yaml file. List the contents of this file using the following command:

```
cat app.yaml
```

This will show the configuration details, as shown in Figure 9.2.

FIGURE 9.2   The contents of an app.yaml file for a Python application

The app configuration file specifies the version of Python to use, the API version you are deploying, and a Python parameter called threadsafe, which is set to true. The last three lines specify the script to run, which in this case is main.py.

To deploy your app, you can use the following command:

```
gcloud app deploy app.yml
```

However, app.yml is the default, so if you are using that for the filename, you do not have to specify app.yml in the deploy command.

This command must be executed from the directory with the app.yaml file. The gcloud app deploy command has some optional parameters:

- --version to specify a custom version ID
- --project to specify the project ID to use for this app
- --no-promote to deploy the app without routing traffic to it

When you issue the `gcloud app deploy` command, you will see output such as in Figure 9.3.

FIGURE 9.3　The output of the `gcloud app deploy` command

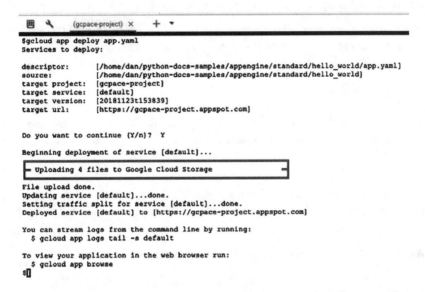

You can see the output of the Hello World program by navigating in a browser to your project URL, such as `https://gcpace-project.appspot.com`. The project URL is the project name followed by `.appspot.com`. For example, Figure 9.4 shows the output.

FIGURE 9.4　The output of the Hello World app when running in App Engine Standard

You can also assign a custom domain if you would rather not use an `appspot.com` URL. You can do this from the Add New Custom domain function on the App Engine Settings page.

From the App Engine console, select Services from the left panel menu to see a listing of services, as in Figure 9.5.

FIGURE 9.5　A listing of services in the App Engine console

Services	DELETE			SHOW INFO PANEL
Service	Versions	Dispatch routes	Last version deployed	Diagnose
default	1		Nov 23, 2018, 3:38:58 PM by dan@dsgcpcert.com	Tools

Figure 9.6 shows a list of versions. You can display this by selecting Versions from the left-panel menu.

FIGURE 9.6   A listing of versions in the App Engine console

Figure 9.7 shows the instance performance details. You can display these details by selecting Instances from the left-panel menu. This information is useful for understanding the load on your application.

FIGURE 9.7   A listing of services in the App Engine console

You can stop serving versions using the `gcloud app versions stop` command and passing a list of versions to stop. For example, to stop serving versions named v1 and v2, use the following:

```
gcloud app versions stop v1 v2
```

You can also disable an entire application in the App Engine console, under Settings, by clicking the Disable App button.

Scaling App Engine Applications

Instances are created to execute an application on an App Engine managed server. App Engine can automatically add or remove instances as needed based on load. When instances are scaled based on load, they are called *dynamic* instances. These dynamic instances help optimize your costs by shutting down when demand is low.

Alternatively, you can configure your instances to be resident or running all the time. These are optimized for performance so users will wait less while an instance is started.

Your configuration determines whether an instance is resident or dynamic. If you configure autoscaling or basic scaling, then instances will be dynamic. If you configure manual scaling, then your instances will be resident.

To specify automatic scaling, add a section to `app.yaml` that includes the term `automatic_scaling` followed by key-value pairs of configuration options. These include the following:

- `target_cpu_utilization`
- `target_throughput_utilization`
- `max_concurrent_requests`
- `max_instances`
- `min_instances`
- `max_pending_latency`
- `min_pending_latency`

Target CPU Utilization   Specifies the maximum CPU utilization that occurs before additional instances are started.

Target Throughput Utilization   Specifies the maximum number of concurrent requests before additional instances are started. This is specified as a number between 0.5 and 0.95.

Maximum Concurrent Requests   Specifies the max concurrent requests an instance can accept before starting a new instance. The default is 10; the max is 80.

Maximum and Minimum Instances   Indicates the range of number of instances that can run for this application.

Maximum and Minimum Latency   Indicates the maximum and minimum time a request will wait in the queue to be processed.

FIGURE 9.8   An example app.yaml for the Hello World app with autoscaling parameters

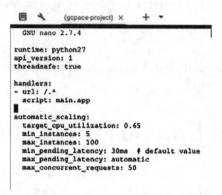

```
GNU nano 2.7.4

runtime: python27
api_version: 1
threadsafe: true

handlers:
- url: /.*
  script: main.app

automatic_scaling:
  target_cpu_utilization: 0.65
  min_instances: 5
  max_instances: 100
  min_pending_latency: 30ms  # default value
  max_pending_latency: automatic
  max_concurrent_requests: 50
```

You can also use basic scaling to enable automatic scaling. The only parameters for basic scaling are idle_timeout and max_instances.

Figure 9.9 shows an example Hello World app.yaml file configured for basic scaling with a maximum of 10 instances and an idle_timeout of 20 minutes.

FIGURE 9.9   Example app.yaml using basic scaling

```
runtime: python27
api_version: 1
threadsafe: true

handlers:
- url: /.*
  script: main.app

basic_scaling:
  max_instances: 10
  idle_timeout: 20m
```

If you prefer to use manual scaling because you need to control scaling, then specify the manual_scaling parameter and the number of instances to run. In the example in Figure 9.10, the Hello World app is configured to run with seven instances.

FIGURE 9.10   Example app.yaml using manual scaling

```
runtime: python27
api_version: 1
threadsafe: true

handlers:
- url: /.*
  script: main.app

manual_scaling:
  instances: 7
```

⊕ **Real World Scenario**

Microservices vs. Monolithic Applications

Scalable applications are often written as collections of microservices. This has not always been the case. In the past, many applications were monolithic, or designed to include all functionality in a single compiled program or script. This may sound like a simpler, easy way to manage applications, but in practice it creates more problems than it solves.

- Any changes to the application require redeploying the entire application, which can take longer than deploying microservices. Developers tended to bundle changes before releasing them.

- If a bundled release had a bug in a feature change, then all feature changes would be rolled back when the monolithic application was rolled back.

- It was difficult to coordinate changes when teams of developers had to work with a single file or a small number of files of source code.

Microservices divide application code into single-function applications, allowing developers to change one service and roll it out without impacting other services. Source code management tools, like Git, make it easy for multiple developers to contribute components of a larger system by coordinating changes to source code files. This single-function code and the easy integration with other code promote more frequent updates and the ability to test new versions before rolling them out to all users at once.

Splitting Traffic between App Engine Versions

If you have more than one version of an application running, you can split traffic between the versions. App Engine provides three ways to split traffic: by IP address, by HTTP cookie, and by random selection. IP address splitting provides some stickiness, so a client is always routed to the same split, at least as long as the IP address does not change. HTTP cookies are useful when you want to assign users to versions. Random selection is useful when you want to evenly distribute workload.

When using IP address splitting, App Engine creates a hash, that is, a number generated based on an input string between 0 and 999, using the IP address of each version. This can create problems if users change IP address, such as if they start working with the app in the office and then switch to a network in a coffee shop. If state information is maintained in a version, it may not be available after an IP address change.

The preferred way to split traffic is with a cookie. When you use a cookie, the HTTP request header for a cookie named GOOGAPPUID contains a hash value between

0 and 999. With cookie splitting, a user will access the same version of the app even if the user's IP address changes. If there is no GOOGAPPUID cookie, then the traffic is routed randomly.

The command to split traffic is gcloud app services set-traffic. Here's an example:

```
gcloud app services set-traffic serv1 --splits v1=.4,v2=.6
```

This will split traffic with 40 percent going to version 1 of the service named serv1 and 60 percent going to version 2. If no service name is specified, then all services are split.

The gcloud app services set-traffic command takes the following parameters:

- --migrate indicates that App Engine should migrate traffic from the previous version to the new version.
- --split-by specifies how to split traffic using either IP or cookies. Possible values are ip, cookie, and random.

You can also migrate traffic from the console. Navigate to the Versions page and select the Migrate command.

Summary

App Engine Standard is a serverless platform for running applications in language-specific environments. As a cloud engineer, you are expected to know how to deploy and scale App Engine applications. App Engine applications consist of services, versions, and instances. You can have multiple versions running at one time. You can split traffic between versions and have all traffic automatically migrate to a new version. App Engine applications are configured through app.yaml configuration files. You can specify the language environment, scaling parameters, and other parameters to customize your deployment.

Exam Essentials

Know the structure of App Engine Standard applications.   These consist of services, versions, and instances. Services usually provide a single function. Versions are different versions of code running in the App Engine environment. Instances are managed instances running the service.

Know how to deploy an App Engine app.   This includes configuring the App Engine environment using the app.yaml file. Know that a project can have only one App Engine app at a time. Know how to use the gcloud app deploy command.

Know how to view the status of an application in the App Engine Console.   This includes viewing a list of services, versions, and instances.

Understand the different scaling options.   Three scaling options are autoscaling, basic scaling, and manual scaling. Only autoscaling and basic scaling are dynamic. Manual scaling creates resident instances. Autoscaling allows for more configuration options than basic scaling.

Know how to split traffic.   Use the `gcloud app services set-traffic` command to split traffic. It takes a `--splits` parameter, which specifies the percent of traffic to route to each version.

Understand how to migrate traffic to a new version.   You can migrate from the Versions page of the App Engine console or using the `--migrate` parameter with the `gcloud app services set-traffic` command.

Review Questions

You can find the answers in the Appendix.

1. You have designed a microservice that you want to deploy to production. Before it can be deployed, you have to review how you will manage the service lifecycle. The architect is particularly concerned about how you will deploy updates to the service with minimal disruption. What aspect of App Engine components would you use to minimize disruptions during updates to the service?

   A. Services

   B. Versions

   C. Instance groups

   D. Instances

2. You've just released an application running in App Engine Standard. You notice that there are peak demand periods in which you need up to 12 instances, but most of the time 5 instances are sufficient. What is the best way to ensure that you have enough instances to meet demand without spending more than you have to?

   A. Configure your app for autoscaling and specify max instances of 12 and min instances of 5.

   B. Configure your app for basic scaling and specify max instances of 12 and min instances of 5.

   C. Create a cron job to add instances just prior to peak periods and remove instances after the peak period is over.

   D. Configure your app for instance detection and do not specify a max or minimum number of instances.

3. In the hierarchy of App Engine components, what is the lowest-level component?

   A. Application

   B. Instance

   C. Version

   D. Service

4. What command should you use to deploy an App Engine app from the command line?

   A. gcloud components app deploy

   B. gcloud app deploy

   C. gcloud components instances deploy

   D. gcloud app instance deploy

5. You have deployed a Django 1.5 Python application to App Engine. This version of Django requires Python 3. For some reason, App Engine is trying to run the application using Python 2. What file would you check and possibly modify to ensure that Python 3 is used with this application?

   A. `app.config`

   B. `app.yaml`

   C. `services.yaml`

   D. `deploy.yaml`

6. You have several App Engine apps you plan to deploy from your project. What have you failed to account for in this design?

   A. App Engine only supports one app per project.

   B. App Engine only supports two apps per project.

   C. App Engine apps exist outside of projects.

   D. Nothing, this is a common pattern.

7. The latest version of your microservice code has been approved by your manager, but the product owner does not want the new features released until a press release is published. You'd like to get the code out but not expose it to customers. What is the best way to get the code out as soon as possible without exposing it to customers?

   A. Deploy with `gcloud app deploy --no-traffic`.

   B. Write a cron job to deploy after the press release is published.

   C. Deploy with `gcloud app deploy --no-promote`.

   D. Deploy as normal after the press release is published.

8. You have just deployed an app that hosts services that provide the current time in any time zone. The project containing the code is called `current-time-zone`, the service providing the user interface is called `time-zone-ui`, and the service performing the calculation is called `time-zone-calculate`. What is the URL where a user could find your service?

   A. `current-time-zone.appengine.com`

   B. `current-time-zone.appspot.com`

   C. `time-zone-ui.appspot.com`

   D. `time-zone-calculate.appspot.com`

9. You are concerned that as users make connections to your application, the performance will degrade. You want to make sure that more instances are added to your App Engine application when there are more than 20 concurrent requests. What parameter would you specify in `app.yaml`?

   A. `max_concurrent_requests`

   B. `target_throughput_utilization`

   C. `max_instances`

   D. `max_pending_latency`

10. What parameters can be configured with basic scaling?

   A. `max_instances` and `min_instances`

   B. `idle_timeout` and `min_instances`

   C. `idle_timeout` and `max_instances`

   D. `idle_timeout` and `target_throughput_utilization`

11. The `runtime` parameter in `app.yaml` is used to specify what?

   A. The script to execute

   B. The URL to access the application

   C. The language runtime environment

   D. The maximum time an application can run

12. What are the two kinds of instances available in App Engine Standard?

   A. Resident and dynamic

   B. Persistent and dynamic

   C. Stable and dynamic

   D. Resident and nonresident

13. You work for a startup, and costs are a major concern. You are willing to take a slight performance hit if it will save you money. How should you configure the scaling for your apps running in App Engine?

   A. Use dynamic instances by specifying autoscaling or basic scaling.

   B. Use resident instances by specifying autoscaling or basic scaling.

   C. Use dynamic instances by specifying manual scaling.

   D. Use resident instances by specifying manual scaling.

14. A team of developers has created an optimized version of a service. This should run 30 percent faster in most cases. They want to roll it out to all users immediately, but you are concerned that the substantial changes need to be released slowly in case there are significant bugs. What can you do to allocate some users to the new version without exposing all users to it?

   A. Issue the command `gcloud app services set-traffic`.

   B. Issue the command `gcloud instances services set-traffic`.

   C. Issue the command `gcloud app set-traffic`.

   D. Change the target IP address of the service for some clients.

15. What parameter to `gcloud app services set-traffic` is used to specify the method to use when splitting traffic?

   A. `--split-traffic`

   B. `--split-by`

   C. `--traffic-split`

   D. `--split-method`

16. What parameter to `gcloud app services set-traffic` is used to specify the percentage of traffic that should go to each instance?

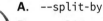

   A. `--split-by`

   B. `--splits`

   C. `--split-percent`

   D. `--percent-split`

17. You have released a new version of a service. You have been waiting for approval from the product manager to start sending traffic to the new version. You get approval to route traffic to the new version. What parameter to `gcloud app services set-traffic` is used to specify that traffic should be moved to a newer version of the app?

   A. `--move-to-new`

   B. `--migrate-to-new`

   C. `--migrate`

   D. `--move`

18. The status of what components can be viewed in the App Engine console?

   A. Services only

   B. Versions only

   C. Instances and versions

   D. Services, versions, and instances

19. What are valid methods for splitting traffic?

   A. By IP address only

   B. By HTTP cookie only

   C. Randomly and by IP address only

   D. By IP address, HTTP cookies, and randomly

20. What is the name of the cookie used by App Engine when cookie-based splitting is used?

   A. GOOGID

   B. GOOGAPPUID

   C. APPUID

   D. UIDAPP

Chapter

10

Computing with Cloud Functions

THIS CHAPTER COVERS THE FOLLOWING OBJECTIVES OF THE GOOGLE ASSOCIATE CLOUD ENGINEER CERTIFICATION EXAM:

✓ **3.3 Deploying and implementing App Engine and Cloud Functions resources**

In this chapter, we describe the purpose of Cloud Functions as well as how to implement and deploy the functions. We will use examples of the functions written in Python. If you are unfamiliar with Python, that should not dissuade you from following along. The important details of Python functions will be explained. You will learn how to use the Cloud Console and gcloud commands to create and manage Cloud Functions.

This chapter covers Cloud Functions only. App Engine is covered in Chapter 9.

Introduction to Cloud Functions

Cloud Functions is a serverless compute service provided by Google Cloud Platform (GCP). Cloud Functions is similar to App Engine in that they are both serverless. A primary difference, though, is that App Engine supports multiple services organized into a single application, while Cloud Functions supports individual services that are managed and operate independently of other services.

App Engine is a good serverless option for web applications that have a front-end user interface running in one service, a set of APIs running in one or more other services, and business logic running in another service. The services together make up the application, so it makes sense to treat them as a single managed unit.

Not all computing requirements need multiple services. For example, your department may upload a daily data extract from a database, which is then loaded into an enterprise data warehouse. If the data extract files are loaded into Cloud Storage, then you could use a function to perform preprocessing, such as verifying the file is the right format and meets other business rules. If the file passes checks, a message is written to a Pub/Sub topic, a messaging service in GCP, which is read by the data warehouse load process. Cloud Functions allows developers to decouple the initial data quality check from the rest of the extraction, transformation, and load process.

There are limits to Cloud Functions. By default, the functions will time out after one minute, although you can set the timeout for as long as nine minutes.

Events, Triggers, and Functions

There are some terms you need to know before going any further into Cloud Functions:

- Events
- Triggers
- Functions

Events are a particular action that happens in Google Cloud, such as a file is uploaded to Cloud Storage or a message (called a *topic*) is written to a Pub/Sub message queue. There are different kinds of actions associated with each of the events. Currently, GCP supports events in five categories:

- Cloud Storage
- Cloud Pub/Sub
- HTTP
- Firebase
- Stackdriver Logging

Events in Cloud Storage include uploading, deleting, and archiving a file. Cloud Pub/Sub has an event for publishing a message. The HTTP type of event allows developers to invoke a function by making an HTTP request using POST, GET, PUT, DELETE, and OPTIONS calls. Firebase events are actions taken in the Firebase database, such as database triggers, remote configuration triggers, and authentication triggers. You can set up a function to respond to a change in Stackdriver Logging by forwarding log entries to a Pub/Sub topic and triggering a response from there.

For each of the Cloud Functions–enabled events that can occur, you can define a trigger. A *trigger* is a way of responding to an event.

Triggers have an associated *function*. The function is passed arguments with data about the event. The function executes in response to the event.

Runtime Environments

Functions run in their own environment. Each time a function is invoked, it is run in a separate instance from all other invocations. There is no way to share information between invocations of functions using only Cloud Functions. If you need to coordinate the updating of data, such as keeping a global count, or need to keep information about the state of functions, such as the name of the last event processed, then you should use a database, such as Cloud Datastore, or a file in Cloud Storage.

Google currently supports three runtime environments:

- Python 3
- Node.js 6
- Node.js 8

Let's walk through an example function. You want to record information about file uploads to a particular bucket in Cloud Storage. You can do this by writing a Python function that receives information about an event and then issues print commands to send a description of that data to a log file. Here is the Python code:

```python
def cloud_storage_function_test(event_data, event_context):
print('Event ID: {}'.format(event_context.event_id))
    print('Event type: {}'.format(event_context.event_type))
    print('File: {}'.format(event_data['name']))
```

The first line begins the creation of a function called `cloud_storage_function_test`. It takes two arguments, `event_data` and `event_context`. These are Python data structures with information about the object of the event and about the event itself. The next three lines print the values of the `event_id`, `event_type`, and name of the file. Since this code will be run as a function, and not interactively, the output of a print statement will go to the function's log file.

Python functions should be saved in a file called `main.py`.

 Real World Scenario

Making Documents Searchable

Litigation, or lawsuits, between businesses often involve reviewing a large volume of documents. Electronic documents may be in readily searchable formats, such as Microsoft Word documents or PDF files. Others may be scanned images of paper documents. In that case, the file needs to be preprocessed using an optical character recognition (OCR) program.

Functions can be used to automate the OCR process. When a file is uploaded, a Cloud Storage trigger fires and invokes a function. The function determines whether the file is in a searchable format or needs to be preprocessed by the OCR program. If the file does require OCR processing, the function writes the location of the file into a Pub/Sub topic.

A second function is bound to a new message event. When a file location is written in a message, the function calls the OCR program to scan the document and produce a searchable version of the file. That searchable version is written to a Cloud Storage bucket, where it can be indexed by the search tool along with other searchable files.

Cloud Functions Receiving Events from Cloud Storage

Cloud Storage is GCP's object storage. This service allows you to store files in containers known as *buckets*. We will go into more detail about Cloud Storage in Chapter 11, but for this chapter you just need to understand that Cloud Storage uses buckets to store files. When files are created, deleted, or archived, or their metadata changes, an event can invoke a function. Let's go through an example of deploying a function for Cloud Storage Events using Cloud Console and gcloud commands in Cloud SDK and Cloud Shell.

Deploying a Cloud Function for Cloud Storage Events Using Cloud Console

To create a function using Cloud Console, select the Cloud Function options from the vertical menu in the console, as in Figure 10.1.

FIGURE 10.1   Opening the Cloud Functions console

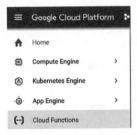

In the Cloud Functions console, you may be prompted to enable the Cloud Functions API if it is not already enabled. After the Cloud Functions API is enabled, you will have the option to create a new function, as shown in Figure 10.2.

FIGURE 10.2   The prompt to create a new function in Cloud Console

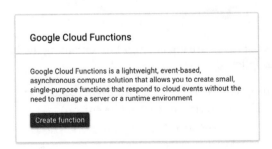

When you create a new function in the console, a form such as in Figure 10.3 appears. In Figure 10.3, the options, which have been filled in, include:

- Function name
- Memory allocated for the function
- Trigger
- Event type
- Source of the function code
- Runtime
- Source code
- Python, Go or Node.js function to execute

FIGURE 10.3   Creating a function in the console

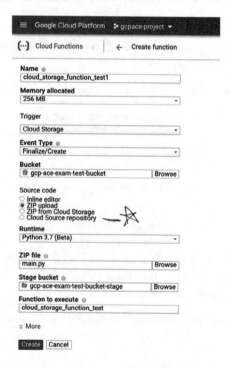

In the following example, we are uploading a file containing the function code. The contents of that file are as follows:

```
def cloud_storage_function_test(event_data, event_context):
  print('Event ID: {}'.format(event_context.event_id))
  print('Event type: {}'.format(event_context.event_type))
  print('File: {}'.format(event_data['name']))
```

The function name is the name GCP will use to refer to this function. Memory Allocated is the amount of memory that will be available to the function. Memory options range from 128MB to 2GB. Trigger is one of the defined triggers, such as HTTP, Cloud Pub/Sub, and Cloud Storage. There are several options for specifying where to find the source code, including uploading it, getting it from Cloud Storage or a Cloud Source repository, or entering the code in an editor. Runtime indicates which runtime to use to execute the code. The editor is where you can enter function code. Finally, the function to execute is the name of the function in the code that should run when the event occurs.

After a function is created, you will see a list of functions in the Cloud Functions console, such as in Figure 10.4.

FIGURE 10.4   List of functions in the console

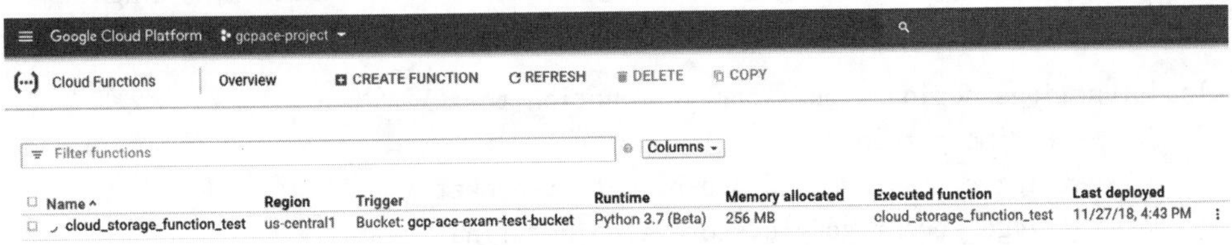

Note that at the top of the list of functions there is the option to delete a function.

Deploying a Cloud Function for Cloud Storage Events Using gcloud Commands

The first step to using `gcloud` commands for Cloud Functions is to make sure you have the latest version of the commands installed. You can update standard `gcloud` commands using this:

```
gcloud components update
```

The Python commands are in beta at the time of writing, so you can ensure that they are installed with the following command:

```
gcloud components install beta
```

Let's assume you have created a Cloud Storage bucket called `gcp-ace-exam-test-bucket`. You can deploy a function using the `gcloud functions deploy` command. This command takes the name of a function as its argument. There are also three parameters you will need to pass in:

- `runtime`
- `trigger-resource`
- `trigger-event`

runtime indicates whether you are using Python 3.7 Node.js 6, or Node.js 8. trigger-resources indicates the bucket name associated with the trigger. trigger-event is the kind of event that will trigger the execution of the function. The possible options are as follows:

- google.storage.object.finalize

- google.storage.object.delete

- google.storage.object.archive

- google.storage.object.metadataUpdate

finalize is the term used to describe when a file is fully uploaded.

Whenever a new file is uploaded to the bucket called gcp-ace-exam-test-bucket, we want to execute the cloud_storage_function_test. We accomplish this by issuing the following command:

```
gcloud functions deploy cloud_storage_function_test \
        --runtime python37 \
        --trigger-resource gcp-ace-exam-test-bucket \
        --trigger-event google.storage.object.finalize
```

When you upload a file to the bucket, the function will execute and create a log message similar to what is shown in Figure 10.5.

FIGURE 10.5 Example log message generated by the cloud_storage_function_test function

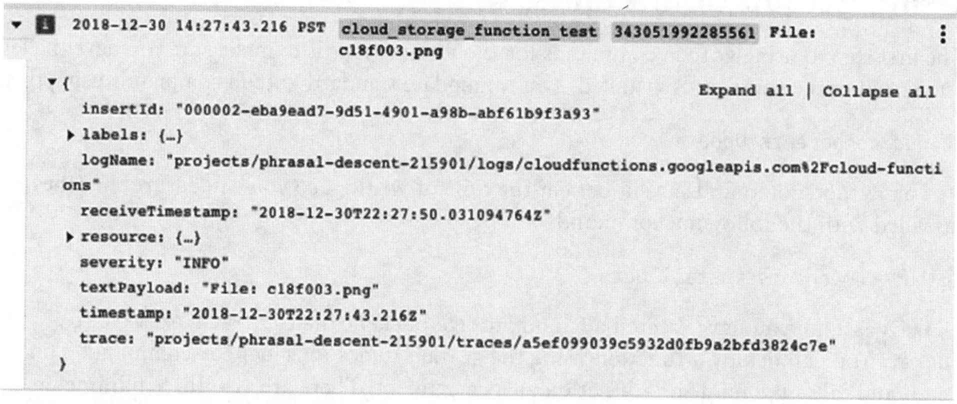

When you are done with the function and want to delete it, you can use the gcloud function's delete command, like so:

```
gcloud functions delete cloud_storage_function_test
```

Cloud Functions Receiving Events from Pub/Sub

A function can be executed each time a message is written to a Pub/Sub topic. You can use Cloud Console or gcloud commands to deploy functions triggered by a Cloud Pub/Sub event.

Deploying a Cloud Function for Cloud Pub/Sub Events Using Cloud Console

Assume you are using a function similar to one used in the previous Cloud Storage example. This time we'll call the function pub_sub_function_test.

To create a function using Cloud Console, select the Cloud Function options from the vertical menu in the console. In the Cloud Functions console, you may be prompted to enable the Cloud Functions API if it is not already enabled. After the Cloud Functions API is enabled, you will have the option to create a new function. When creating a function, you will need to specify several parameters, including the cloud function name, memory allocated, event type, and source code. Here is the source code for pub_sub_function_test:

```
def pub_sub_function_test(event_data, event_context):
    import base64
print('Event ID: {}'.format(event_context.event_id))
    print('Event type: {}'.format(event_context.event_type))
    if 'name' in event_data:
    name = base64.b64decode(event_data['name']).decode('utf-8')
    print('Message name: {}'.format(event_data['name']))
```

This function prints the event ID and event type associated with the message. If the event data has a key-value pair with the key of name, then the function will also print the name in the message. Note that this function has an import statement and uses a function called base64.b64decode. This is because messages in Pub/Sub are encoded to allow for binary data in a place where text data is expected, and the base64.b64decode function is used to convert it to a more common text encoding called UTF-8.

The code is deployed in the same way as the previous Cloud Storage example with two exceptions. Instead of selecting a Cloud Storage trigger, choose Cloud Pub/Sub from the list of triggers, as shown in Figure 10.6. You can also specify the name of the Cloud Pub/Sub topic after specifying this is a Cloud Pub/Sub trigger. If the topic does not exist, it will be created.

FIGURE 10.6   Selecting a trigger from options in Cloud Console

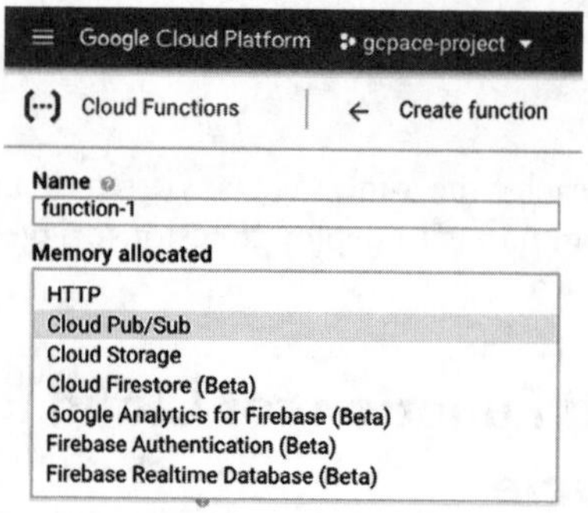

Deploying a Cloud Function for Cloud Pub/Sub Events Using gcloud Commands

As with functions for Cloud Storage, if you are deploying Cloud Functions, it's a good idea to use the latest gcloud commands by issuing this:

```
gcloud components update
```

If you are using Python, you will want to install beta gcloud components as well:

```
gcloud components install beta
```

To deploy this function, you use the gcloud functions deploy command. When deploying a Cloud Pub/Sub function, you specify the name of the topic that will contain messages that will trigger the function. Like deploying for Cloud Storage, you have to specify the runtime environment you want to use. Here's an example:

```
gcloud functions deploy pub_sub_function_test --runtime python37 --trigger-topic
gcp-ace-exam-test-topic
```

You can delete this function using the gcloud functions delete command. Here's an example:

```
gcloud functions delete pub_sub_function_test
```

Summary

In this chapter, we worked with Cloud Functions and saw how to implement and deploy functions. We used examples of functions written in Python, but they could have been written in Node.js as well. Functions can be created using either the Google Cloud Console or the command line. To use Cloud Functions, it is important to understand the relationship between events, triggers, and functions. Events are actions that happen in the cloud. Different services have different types of events. Triggers are how you indicate you want to execute a function when an event occurs. Functions refer to the code that is executed when an event occurs that has a trigger defined for it.

Exam Essentials

Know the relationship between events, triggers, and functions.   Events are actions that happen, such as when a file is uploaded to Cloud Storage or a message is written to a Cloud Pub/Sub topic. Triggers are declarations that an action should be taken when an event occurs. Functions associated with triggers define what actions are taken when an event occurs.

Know when to use Cloud Functions versus App Engine applications.   Cloud Functions is a service that supports single-purpose functions that respond to events in the cloud. App Engine is also a serverless computing option, but it is used to deploy multifunction applications, including those that users interact with directly.

Know the runtimes supported in Cloud Functions.   Cloud Functions supports the following runtimes: Node.js 6, Node.js 8, and Python 3.

Know the parameters for defining a cloud function on a Cloud Storage event.   Parameters for Cloud Storage include the following:

Cloud function name

Memory allocated for the function

Trigger

Event type

Source of the function code

Runtime

Source code

Name of the Python or Node.js function to execute

Know the parameters for defining a Cloud Function on a Cloud Pub/Sub event. Parameters for Pub/Sub include the following:

Cloud function name

Memory allocated for the function

Trigger

Topic

Source of the function code

Runtime

Source code

Name of the Python or Node.js function to execute

Know the gcloud **commands for working with Cloud Functions.**   These include the following:

gcloud functions deploy

gcloud functions delete

Review Questions

You can find the answers in the Appendix.

1. A product manager is proposing a new application that will require several backend services, three business logic services, and access to relational databases. Each service will provide a single function, and it will require several of these services to complete a business task. Service execution time is dependent on the size of input and is expected to take up to 30 minutes in some cases. Which GCP product is a good serverless option for running this related service?

   A. Cloud Functions

   B. Compute Engine

   C. App Engine

   D. Cloud Storage

2. You have been asked to deploy a cloud function to reformat image files as soon as they are uploaded to Cloud Storage. You notice after a few hours that about 10 percent of the files are not processed correctly. After reviewing the files that failed, you realize they are all substantially larger than average. What could be the cause of the failures?

   A. There is a syntax error in the function code.

   B. The wrong runtime was selected.

   C. The timeout is too low to allow enough time to process large files.

   D. There is a permissions error on the Cloud Storage bucket containing the files.

3. When an action occurs in GCP, such as a file being written to Cloud Storage or a message being added to a Cloud Pub/Sub topic, that action is called what?

   A. An incident

   B. An event

   C. A trigger

   D. A log entry

4. All of the following generate events that can be triggered using Cloud Functions, except which one?

   A. Cloud Storage

   B. Cloud Pub/Sub

   C. SSL

   D. Firebase

5. Which runtimes are supported in Cloud Functions?

    A. Node.js 5, Node.js 6, and Node.js 8

    B. Node.js 8, Python, and Go

    C. Node.js 6, Node.js 8, and Python

    D. Node.js 8, Python, and Go

6. An HTTP trigger can be invoked by making a request using which of the following?

    A. GET only

    B. POST and GET only

    C. DELETE, POST, and GET

    D. DELETE, POST, REVISE, and GET

7. What types of events are available to Cloud Functions working with Cloud Storage?

    A. Upload or finalize and delete only

    B. Upload or finalize, delete, and list only

    C. Upload or finalize, delete, and metadata update only

    D. Upload or finalize, delete, metadata update, and archive

8. You are tasked with designing a function to execute in Cloud Functions. The function will need more than the default amount of memory and should be applied only when a finalize event occurs after a file is uploaded to Cloud Storage. The function should only apply its logic to files with a standard image file type. Which of the following required features cannot be specified in a parameter and must be implemented in the function code?

    A. Cloud function name

    B. Memory allocated for the function

    C. File type to apply the function to

    D. Event type

9. How much memory can be allocated to a Cloud Function?

    A. 128MB to 256MB

    B. 128MB to 512MB

    C. 128MB to 1GB

    D. 128MB to 2GB

10. How long can a cloud function run by default before timing out?

    A. 30 seconds

    B. 1 minute

    C. 9 minutes

    D. 20 minutes

11. You want to use the command line to manage Cloud Functions that will be written in Python. In addition to running the gcloud components update command, what command should you run to ensure you can work with Python functions?

   A. gcloud component install

   B. gcloud components install beta

   C. gcloud components install python

   D. gcloud functions install beta

12. You want to create a cloud function to transform audio files into different formats. The audio files will be uploaded into Cloud Storage. You want to start transformations as soon as the files finish uploading. Which trigger would you specify in the cloud function to cause it to execute after the file is uploaded?

   A. google.storage.object.finalize

   B. google.storage.object.upload

   C. google.storage.object.archive

   D. google.storage.object.metadataUpdate

13. You are defining a cloud function to write a record to a database when a file in Cloud Storage is archived. What parameters will you have to set when creating that function?

   A. runtime only

   B. trigger-resource only

   C. runtime, trigger-resource, trigger-event only

   D. runtime, trigger-resource, trigger-event, file-type

14. You'd like to stop using a cloud function and delete it from your project. Which command would you use from the command line to delete a cloud function?

   A. gcloud functions delete

   B. gcloud components function delete

   C. gcloud components delete

   D. gcloud delete functions

15. You have been asked to deploy a cloud function to work with Cloud Pub/Sub. As you review the Python code, you notice a reference to a Python function called base64.b64decode. Why would a decode function be required in a Pub/Sub cloud function?

   A. It's not required and should not be there.

   B. Messages in Pub/Sub topics are encoded to allow binary data to be used in places where text data is expected. Messages need to be decoded to access the data in the message.

   C. It is required to add padding characters to the end of the message to make all messages the same length.

   D. The decode function maps data from a dictionary data structure to a list data structure.

16. Which of these commands will deploy a Python cloud function called pub_sub_function_test?

    A. `gcloud functions deploy pub_sub_function_test`

    B. `gcloud functions deploy pub_sub_function_test --runtime python37`

    C. `gcloud functions deploy pub_sub_function_test --runtime python37 --trigger-topic gcp-ace-exam-test-topic`

    D. `gcloud functions deploy pub_sub_function_test --runtime python --trigger-topic gcp-ace-exam-test-topic`

17. When specifying a Cloud Storage cloud function, you have to specify an event type, such as finalize, delete, or archive. When specifying a Cloud Pub/Sub cloud function, you do not have to specify an event type. Why is this the case?

    A. Cloud Pub/Sub does not have triggers for event types.

    B. Cloud Pub/Sub has triggers on only one event type, when a message is published.

    C. Cloud Pub/Sub determines the correct event type by analyzing the function code.

    D. The statement in the question is incorrect; you do have to specify an event type with Cloud Pub/Sub functions.

18. Your company has a web application that allows job seekers to upload résumé files. Some files are in Microsoft Word, some are PDFs, and others are text files. You would like to store all résumés as PDFs. How could you do this in a way that minimizes the time between upload and conversion and with minimal amounts of coding?

    A. Write an App Engine application with multiple services to convert all documents to PDF.

    B. Implement a Cloud Function on Cloud Storage to execute on a finalize event. The function checks the file type, and if it is not PDF, the function calls a PDF converter function and writes the PDF version to the bucket that has the original.

    C. Add the names of all files to a Cloud Pub/Sub topic and have a batch job run at regular intervals to convert the original files to PDF.

    D. Implement a Cloud Function on Cloud Pub/Sub to execute on a finalize event. The function checks the file type, and if it is not PDF, the function calls a PDF converter function and writes the PDF version to the bucket that has the original.

19. What are options for uploading code to a cloud function?

    A. Inline editor

    B. Zip upload

    C. Cloud source repository

    D. All of the above

20. What type of trigger allows developers to use HTTP POST, GET, and PUT calls to invoke a cloud function?

    A. HTTP

    B. Webhook

    C. Cloud HTTP

    D. None of the above

Chapter

11

Planning Storage in the Cloud

THIS CHAPTER COVERS THE FOLLOWING OBJECTIVES OF THE GOOGLE ASSOCIATE CLOUD ENGINEER CERTIFICATION EXAM:

✓ **2.3 Planning and configuring data storage options**

As a cloud engineer, you will have to understand the various storage options provided in Google Cloud Platform (GCP). You will be expected to choose the appropriate option for a given use case while knowing the relative trade-offs, such as having access to SQL for a query language versus the ability to store and query petabytes of data streaming into your database.

Unlike most other chapters in the book, this chapter focuses more on storage concepts than on performing specific tasks in GCP. The material here will help you answer questions about choosing the best storage solution. Chapter 12 will provide details on deploying and implementing data solutions.

To choose between storage options, it helps to understand how storage solutions vary by:

- Time to access data

- Data model

- Other features, such as consistency, availability, and support for transactions

This chapter includes guidelines for choosing storage solutions for different kinds of requirements.

Types of Storage Systems

A main consideration when you choose a storage solution is the time in which the data must be accessed. At one extreme, data in an L1 cache on a CPU chip can be accessed in 0.5 nanoseconds (ns). At the other end of the spectrum some services can require hours to return data files. Most storage requirements fall between these extremes.

Nanoseconds, Milliseconds and Microseconds

Some storage systems operate at speeds as unfamiliar to us as what happens under an electron microscope. One second is an extremely long time when talking about the time it takes to access data in-memory or on disk. We measure time to access, or "latency," with three units of measure.

- Nanosecond (ns), which is 10^{-9} second

- Microsecond (μs), which is 10^{-6} second

- Millisecond (ms), which is 10^{-3} second

Note, the number 10^{-3} is in scientific notation and means 0.001 second. Similarly, 10^{-6} is the same as 0.000001, and 10^{-9} is the same as 0.000000001 second.

Another consideration is persistence. How durable is the data stored in a particular system? Caches offer the lowest latency for accessing data, but this type of volatile data exists only as long as power is supplied to memory. Shut down the server and away goes your data. Disk drives have higher durability rates, but they can fail. Redundancy helps here. By making copies of data and storing them on different servers, in different racks, in different zones, and in different regions, you reduce the risk of losing data due to hardware failures.

GCP has several storage services, including the following:

- A managed Redis cache service for caching
- Persistent disk storage for use with VMs
- Object storage for shared access to files across resources
- Archival storage for long-term, infrequent access requirements

Cache

A cache is an in-memory data store designed to provide applications with sub millisecond access to data. Its primary advantage over other storage systems is its low latency. Caches are limited in size by the amount of memory available, and if the machine hosting the cache shuts down, then the contents of the cache are lost. These are significant limitations, but in some use cases, the benefits of fast access to data outweigh the disadvantages.

MemoryStore

GCP offers Memorystore, a managed Redis service. Redis is a widely used open source cache. Since Memorystore is protocol-compatible with Redis, tools and applications written to work with Redis should work with Memorystore.

Caches are usually used with an application that cannot tolerate long latencies when retrieving data. For example, an application that has to read from a hard disk drive might have to wait 80 times longer than if the data were read from an in-memory cache. Application developers can use caches to store data that is retrieved from a database and then retrieved from the cache instead of the disk the next time that data is needed.

When you use Memorystore, you create instances that run Redis. The instance is configured with 1GB to 300GB of memory. It can also be configured for high availability, in which case Memorystore creates failover replicas.

Configuring Memorystore

Memorystore caches can be used with applications running in Compute Engine, App Engine, and Kubernetes Engine. Figure 11.1 shows the parameters used to configure Memorystore. You can navigate to this form by choosing Memorystore from the main console menu and then selecting the option to create a Redis instance.

FIGURE 11.1 Configuration parameters for a Memorystore cache

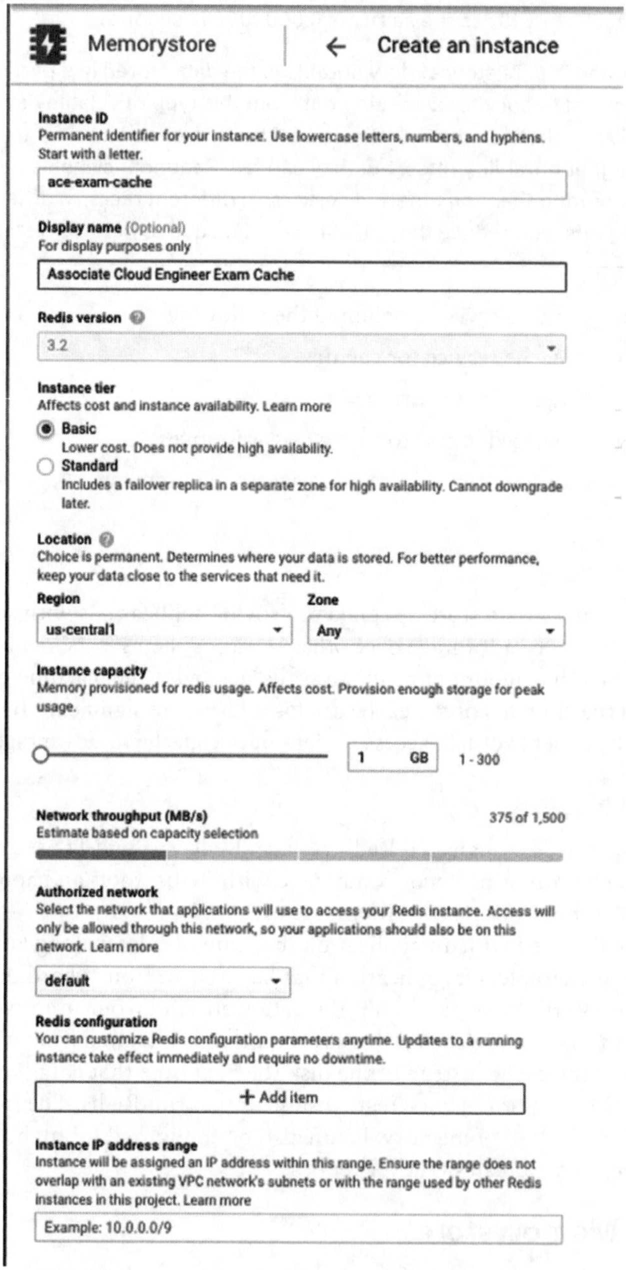

To configure a Redis cache in Memorystore, you will need to specify an instance ID, a display name, and a Redis version. Currently only Redis 3.2 is supported. You can choose to have a replica in a different zone for high availability by selecting the Standard instance tier. The Basic instance tier does not include a replica but costs less.

You will need to specify a region and zone along with the amount of memory to dedicate to your cache. The cache can be 1GB to 300GB in size. The Redis instance will be accessible from the default network unless you specify a different network. (See Chapters 14 and 15 for more on networks in GCP). The advanced options for Memorystore allow you to assign labels and define an IP range from which the IP address will be assigned.

Persistent Storage

In GCP, persistent disks provide durable block storage. Persistent disks can be attached to VMs in Google Compute Engine (GCE) and Google Kubernetes Engine (GKE). Since persistent disks are block storage devices, you can create file systems on these devices. Persistent disks are not directly attached to physical servers hosting your VMs but are network accessible. VMs can have locally attached solid-state drives (SSDs), but the data on those drives is lost when the VM is terminated. The data on persistent disks continues to exist after VMs are shut down and terminated. Persistent disks exist independently of virtual machines; local attached SSDs do not.

Features of Persistent Disks

Persistent disks are available in SSD and hard disk drive (HDD) configurations. SSDs are used when high throughput is important. SSDs provide consistent performance for both random access and sequential access patterns. HDDs have longer latencies but cost less, so HDDs are a good option when storing large amounts of data and performing batch operations that are less sensitive to disk latency than interactive applications. Hard drive–backed persistent disks can perform 0.75 read input output operations per second (IOPS) per gigabyte and 1.5 write IOPS per gigabyte, while network-attached SSDs can perform 30 read and write IOPS per gigabyte. Locally attached SSDs can achieve read IOPS rates between 266 and 453 per gigabyte and write IOPS rates between 186 and 240 per gigabyte.

Persistent disks can be mounted on multiple VMs to provide multireader storage. Snapshots of disks can be created in minutes, so additional copies of data on a disk can be distributed for use by other VMs. If a disk created from a snapshot is mounted to a single VM, it can support both read and write operations.

The size of persistent disks can be increased while mounted to a VM. If you do resize a disk, you may need to perform operating system commands to make that additional space accessible to the file system. Both SSD and HDD disks can be up to 64TB.

Persistent disks automatically encrypt data on the disk.

When planning your storage options, you should also consider whether you want your disks to be zonal or regional. Zonal disks store data across multiple physical drives in a single zone. If the zone becomes inaccessible, you will lose access to your disks. Alternatively, you could use regional persistent disks, which replicate data blocks across two zones within a region but is more expensive than zonal storage.

Configuring Persistent Disks

You can create and configure persistent disks from the console by navigating to Compute Engine and selecting Disks. From the Disk page, click Create a Disk to display a form like that in Figure 11.2.

FIGURE 11.2   Form to create a persistent disk

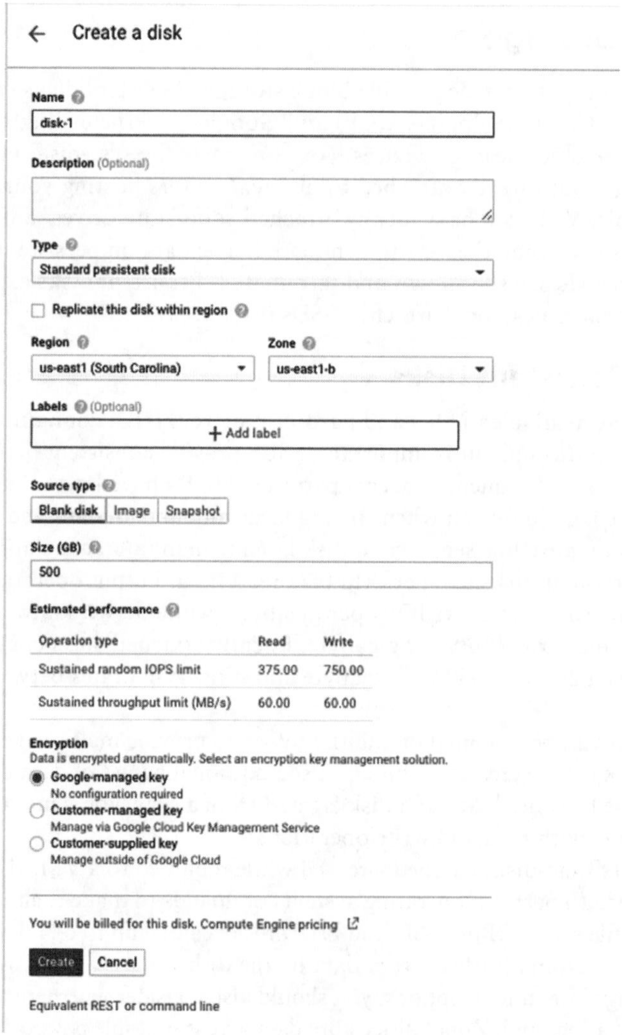

You will need to provide a name for the disk, but the description is optional. There are two types of disk: standard, and SSD persistent disk. For higher availability, you can have a replica created within the region. You will need to specify a region and zone. Labels are optional, but recommended to help keep track of each disk's purpose.

Persistent disks can be created blank or from an image or snapshot. Use the image option if you want to create a persistent boot disk. Use a snapshot if you want to create a replica of another disk.

When you store data at rest in GCP, it is encrypted by default. When creating a disk, you can choose to have Google manage encryption keys, in which case no additional configuration is required. You could use GCP's Cloud Key Management Service to manage keys yourself and store them in GCP's key repository. Choose the customer-managed MKey option for this. You will need to specify the name of a key you have created in Cloud Key Management Service. If you create and manage keys using another key management system, then select customer-supplied SKey. You will have to enter the key into the form if you choose the customer-supplied key option.

Object Storage

Caches are used for storing relatively small amounts of data that must be accessible with submillisecond latency. Persistent storage devices can store up to 64TB on a single disk and provide up to hundreds of IOPS for read and write operations. When you need to store large volumes of data, that is, up to exabytes, and share it widely, object storage is a good option. GCP's object storage is Cloud Storage.

Features of Cloud Storage

Cloud Storage is an object storage system, which means files that are stored in the system are treated as atomic units—that is, you cannot operate on part of the file, such as reading only a section of the file. You can perform operations on an object, like creating or deleting it, but Cloud Storage does not provide functionality to manipulate subcomponents of a file. For example, there is no Cloud Storage command for overwriting a section of the file. Also, Cloud Storage does not support concurrency and locking. If multiple clients are writing to a file, then the last data written to the file is stored and persisted.

Cloud Storage is well suited for storing large volumes of data without requiring any consistent data structure. You can store different types of data in a bucket, which is the logical unit of organization in Cloud Storage. Buckets are resources within a project. It is important to remember that buckets share a global namespace, so each bucket name must be globally unique. We shouldn't be surprised if we can't name a bucket "mytestbucket" but it's not too difficult to find a unique filename, especially if you follow a bucket and object naming convention.

It is important to remember that object storage does not provide a file system. Buckets are analogous to directories in that they help organize objects into groups, but buckets are not true directories that support features such as subdirectories. Google does support an open source project called Cloud Storage Fuse, which provides a way to mount a bucket as a file system on Linux and Mac operating systems. Using Cloud Storage Fuse, you can download and upload files to buckets using file system commands, but it does not provide full file system functionality. Cloud Storage Fuse has the same limitations as Cloud Storage. Its purpose is to make it more convenient to move data in and out of buckets when working in a Linux or Mac file system.

Cloud Storage provides four different classes of object storage: mult-regional, regional, nearline, and coldline.

Multiregional and Regional Storage

When you create a bucket, you specify a location to create the bucket. The bucket and its contents are stored in this location. You can store your data in a single region, known as a regional bucket, or multiple regions, not surprisingly known as multiregional buckets. Multiregional buckets provide more than 99.99 percent typical monthly availability with a 99.95 percent availability service level agreement (SLA). Data is replicated in multiple regions. Regional buckets have a 99.99 percent typical monthly availability and a 99.9 percent availability SLA. Regional buckets are redundant across zones.

Multiregional buckets are used when content needs to be stored in multiple regions to ensure acceptable times to access content. It also provides redundancy in case of zone-level failures. These benefits come with a higher cost, however. At the time of writing, multi-regional storage in the United States costs $0.26/GB/month, while regional storage costs $0.20/GB/month. (You are not likely to be asked about specific prices on the Associate Cloud Engineer exam, but you should know the relative costs so that you can identify the lowest-cost solution that meets a set of requirements.)

Both regional and multiregional storage are used for frequently used data. If you have an application where users download and access files often, such as more than once per month, then it is most cost-effective to choose regional or multiregional. You choose between regional and multiregional based on the location of your users. If users are globally dispersed and require access to synchronized data, then multi-regional may provide better performance and availability.

What if your data is not actively used? For example, if you have files you need to store for seven years for compliance but don't expect to access, then you may want archival storage. Similarly, if you are storing files you need only for disaster recovery, then you may want a storage class designed for highly infrequent access, such as less than once per year. For these kinds of use cases, Google designed nearline and coldline storage classes.

 A note on terminology: Google sometimes uses the term *georedundant*. Georedundant data is stored in at least two locations that are at least 100 miles apart. If your data is in multiregional locations, then it is georedundant.

Nearline and Coldline Storage

For infrequently accessed data, the nearline and coldline storage classes are good options. Nearline storage is designed for use cases in which you expect to access files less than once per month. Coldline storage is designed, and priced, for files expected to be accessed once per year or less.

Nearline storage has a 99.95 percent typical monthly availability in multiregional locations and a 99.9 percent typical availability in regional locations. The SLAs for nearline are 99.9 percent in multiregional locations and 99.0 percent in regional locations. These lower SLAs come with a significantly lower cost: $0.10/GB/month. Before you start moving all your regional and multiregional data to nearline to save on costs, you should know that Google adds a data retrieval charge to nearline and coldline storage. The retrieval price for nearline storage is $0.01/GB. There is also a minimum 30-day storage duration for nearline storage.

Coldline storage has a 99.95 percent typical monthly availability in multiregional locations and a 99.9 percent typical availability in regional locations. The SLAs are 99.9 percent for multiregional locations and 99.0 percent for regional locations. Coldline also has the lowest cost per gigabyte at $0.07/GB/month. Remember, that is only the storage charge. Like nearline storage, coldline storage has access charges. Google expects data in coldline storage to be accessed once per year or less and have at least a 90-day minimum storage. The retrieval price for coldline storage is $0.05/GB.

It is more important to understand the relative cost relationships than the current prices. Prices can change, but the costs of each class relative to other classes of storage are more likely to stay the same. See Table 11.1 for a summary of features, costs and use cases for different storage types.

TABLE 11.1   Storage Services—Summary of Features

: :	Regional	Multiregional	Nearline	Coldline
Features	Object storage replicated across multiple zones	Object storage replicated across multiple regions	Object storage for access less than once per month	Object storage for access less than once per year
Storage cost	$0.20/GB/month	$0.26/GB/month	$0.10/GB/month	$0.07/GB/month
Access cost			$0.01/GB	$0.05/GB
Use case	Object storage shared across applications	Global access to shared objects	Older data in data lakes, backups	Document retention, compliance

Versioning and Object Lifecycle Management

Buckets in Cloud Storage can be configured to retain versions of objects when they are changed. When versioning is enabled on a bucket, a copy of an object is archived each time the object is overwritten or when it is deleted. The latest version of the object is known as the live version. Versioning is useful when you need to keep a history of changes to an object or want to mitigate the risk of accidentally deleting an object.

Cloud Storage also provides lifecycle management policies to automatically change an object's storage class or delete the object after a specified period. A lifecycle policy, sometimes called a configuration, is a set of rules. The rules include a condition and an action. If the condition is true, then the action is executed. Lifecycle management policies are applied to buckets and affect all objects in the bucket.

Conditions are often based on age. Once an object reaches a certain age, it can be deleted or moved to a lower-cost storage class. In addition to age, conditions can check the number of versions, whether the version is live, whether the object was created before a specific date, and whether the object is in a particular storage class.

You can delete an object or change its storage class. Both unversioned and versioned objects can be deleted. If the live version of a file is deleted, then instead of actually deleting it, the object is archived. If an archived version of an object is deleted, the object is permanently deleted.

You can also change the storage class of an object using lifecycle management. There are restrictions on which classes can be assigned. Multiregional and regional storage objects can be changed to nearline or coldline. Nearline can be changed only to coldline.

Configuring Cloud Storage

You can create buckets in Cloud Storage using the console. From the main menu, navigate to Storage and select Create Bucket. This will display a form similar to Figure 11.3.

FIGURE 11.3   Form to create a storage bucket from the console. Advanced options are displayed.

When creating a bucket, you need to supply some basic information, including a bucket name and storage class. You can optionally add labels and choose either Google-managed keys or customer-managed keys for encryption. You can also set a retention policy to prevent changes to files or deleting files before the time you specify.

Once you have created a bucket, you define a lifecycle policy. From the Storage menu in the console, choose the Browse option, as shown in Figure 11.4.

FIGURE 11.4   The list of buckets includes a link to define or modify lifecycle policies.

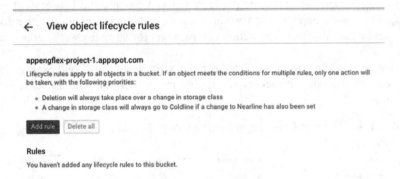

Notice that the Lifecycle column indicates whether a lifecycle configuration is enabled. Choose a bucket to create or modify a lifecycle and click None or Enabled in the Lifecycle column. This will display a form such as in Figure 11.5.

FIGURE 11.5   When creating a lifecycle policy, click the Add Rule option to define a rule.

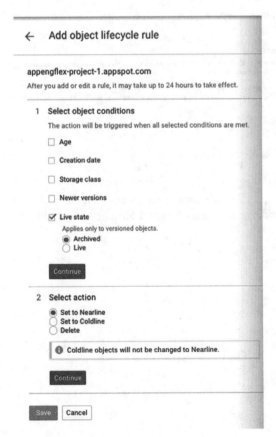

When you add a rule, you need to specify the object condition and the action. Condition options are Age, Creation Data, Storage Class, Newer Versions, and Live State. Live State applies to version objects, and you can set your condition to apply to either live or archived versions of an object. The action can be to set the storage class to either nearline or coldline.

Let's look at an example policy. From the Browser section of Cloud Storage in the console, you can see a list of buckets and their current lifecycle policies, as shown in Figure 11.6.

FIGURE 11.6   Listing of buckets in Cloud Storage Browser

Name	Default storage class ?	Location	Public access ?	Lifecycle ?
ace-exam-bucket1	Regional	US-WEST1	Per object	None
ace-exam-bucket2	Regional	US-CENTRAL1	Per object	None

Click the policy status of a bucket to create a lifecycle rule (see Figure 11.7).

FIGURE 11.7   Form to add a lifecycle rule to a bucket

←   View object lifecycle rules

ace-exam-bucket1

Lifecycle rules apply to all objects in a bucket. If an object meets the conditions for multiple rules, only one action will be taken, with the following priorities:

- Deletion will always take place over a change in storage class
- A change in storage class will always go to Coldline if a change to Nearline has also been set

[Add rule] [Delete all]

Rules

You haven't added any lifecycle rules to this bucket.

The Add Object Lifecycle Rule form appears as in Figure 11.8. In this form, you can specify the object conditions, such as Age and Storage Class, and action, such as Set To Nearline.

FIGURE 11.8   Add an object lifecycle rule to a bucket.

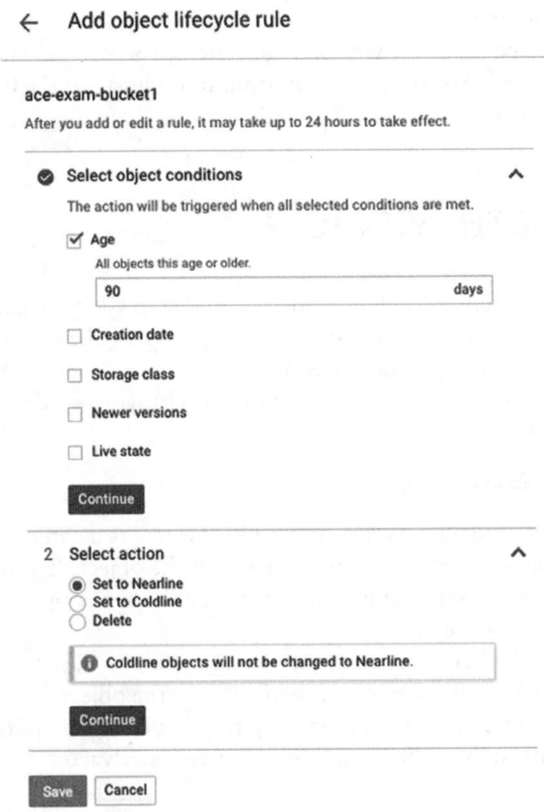

← **Add object lifecycle rule**

ace-exam-bucket1
After you add or edit a rule, it may take up to 24 hours to take effect.

☑ **Select object conditions**   ⌃
   The action will be triggered when all selected conditions are met.

   ☑ Age
      All objects this age or older.

      | 90 | days |

   ☐ Creation date

   ☐ Storage class

   ☐ Newer versions

   ☐ Live state

   Continue

2 **Select action**   ⌃
   ⦿ Set to Nearline
   ○ Set to Coldline
   ○ Delete

   ┌───┐
   │ ⓘ Coldline objects will not be changed to Nearline. │
   └───┘

   Continue

Save   Cancel

Storage Types When Planning a Storage Solution

When planning a storage solution, a factor to consider is the time required to access data.

Caches, like Memorystore, offer the fastest access time but are limited to the amount of memory available. Caches are volatile; when the server shuts down, the contents of the cache are lost. You should save the contents of the cache to persistent storage at regular intervals to enable recovery to the point in time when the contents of the cache were last saved.

Persistent storage is used for block storage devices, such as disks attached to VMs. GCP offers SSD and HDD drives. SSDs provide faster performance but cost more. HDDs are used when large volumes of data need to be stored in a file system but users of the data do not need the fastest access possible.

Object storage is used for storing large volumes of data for extended periods of time. Cloud Storage has both regional and multiregional storage classes and supports lifecycle management and versioning.

In addition to choosing an underlying storage system, you will also have to consider how data is stored and accessed. For this, it is important to understand the data models available and when to use them.

Storage Data Models

There are three broad categories of data models available in GCP: object, relational, and NoSQL. In addition, we will treat mobile optimized products like Cloud Firestore and Firebase as a fourth category, although these datastores use a NoSQL model. Their mobile supporting features are sufficiently important to warrant their own description.

Object: Cloud Storage

The object storage data model treats files as atomic objects. You cannot use object storage commands to read blocks of data or overwrite parts of the object. If you need to update an object, you must copy it to a server, make the change, and then copy the updated version back to the object storage system.

Object storage is used when you need to store large volumes of data and do not need fine-grained access to data within an object while it is in the object store. This data model is well suited for archived data, machine learning training data, and old Internet of Things (IoT) data that needs to be saved but is no longer actively analyzed.

Relational: Cloud SQL, Cloud Spanner, and BigQuery

Relational databases have been the primary data store for enterprises for decades. Relational databases support frequent queries and updates to data. They are used when it is important for users to have a consistent view of data. For example, if two users are reading data from a relational table at the same time, they will see the same data. This is not always the case with databases that may have inconsistencies between replicas of data, such as some NoSQL databases.

Relational databases, like Cloud SQL and Cloud Spanner, support database transactions. A transaction is a set of operations that is guaranteed to succeed or fail in its entirety—there is no chance that some operations are executed and others are not. For example, when a customer purchases a product, the count of the number of products available is decremented in the inventory table, and a record is added to a customer-purchased products table. With transactions, if the database fails after updating inventory but before updating the customer-purchased products table, the database will roll back the partially executed transaction when the database restarts.

Cloud SQL and Cloud Spanner are used when data is structured and modeled for relational databases. Cloud SQL is a managed database service that provides MySQL and PostgreSQL databases. Cloud SQL is used for databases that do not need to scale horizontally, that is, by adding additional servers to a cluster. Cloud SQL databases scale vertically, that is, by running on servers with more memory and more CPU. Cloud Spanner is used when you have extremely large volumes of relational data or data that needs to be globally distributed while ensuring consistency and transaction integrity across all servers.

Large enterprises often use Cloud Spanner for applications like global supply chains and financial services applications, while Cloud SQL is often used for web applications, business intelligence, and ecommerce applications.

Redshift ~ BigQuery is a service designed for a data warehouse and analytic applications. BigQuery is designed to store petabytes of data. BigQuery works with large numbers of rows and columns of data and is not suitable for transaction-oriented applications, such as ecommerce or support for interactive web applications.

Configuring Cloud SQL

You can create a Cloud SQL instance by navigating to Cloud SQL in the main menu of the console and selecting Create Instance. You will be prompted to choose either a MySQL or PostgreSQL instance, as shown in Figure 11.9.

FIGURE 11.9   Cloud SQL provides both MySQL and PostgreSQL instances.

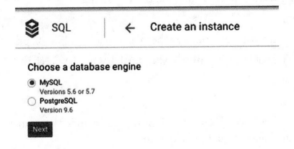

If you choose PostgreSQL, you are taken to the Configuration form. If you choose MySQL, you are prompted to choose either a First Generation or Second Generation MySQL instance (see Figure 11.10). Unless you need to use an older version of MySQL, a Second Generation instance is recommended. MySQL 2nd generation will provide greater capacity, optional high availability configurations, support for MySQL 5.7, and, in many cases, lower cost.

FIGURE 11.10   MySQL instances are available in First and Second Generation instances.

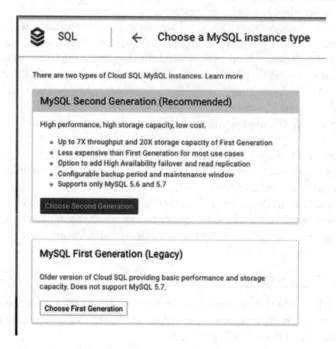

To configure a MySQL instance, you will need to specify a name, root password, region, and zone. The configuration options include the following:

- MySQL version.
- Connectivity, where you can specify whether to use a public or private IP address.
- Machine type. The default is a db-n1-standard-1 with 1 vCPU and 3.75GB of memory.
- Automatic backups.
- Failover replicas.
- Database flags. These are specific to MySQL and include the ability to set a database read-only flag and set the query cache size.
- Setting a maintenance time window.
- Labels.

Figure 11.11 shows the configuration form for MySQL second-generation, and Figure 11.12 shows the PostgreSQL configuration form.

FIGURE 11.11   Configuration form for a MySQL Second Generation instance

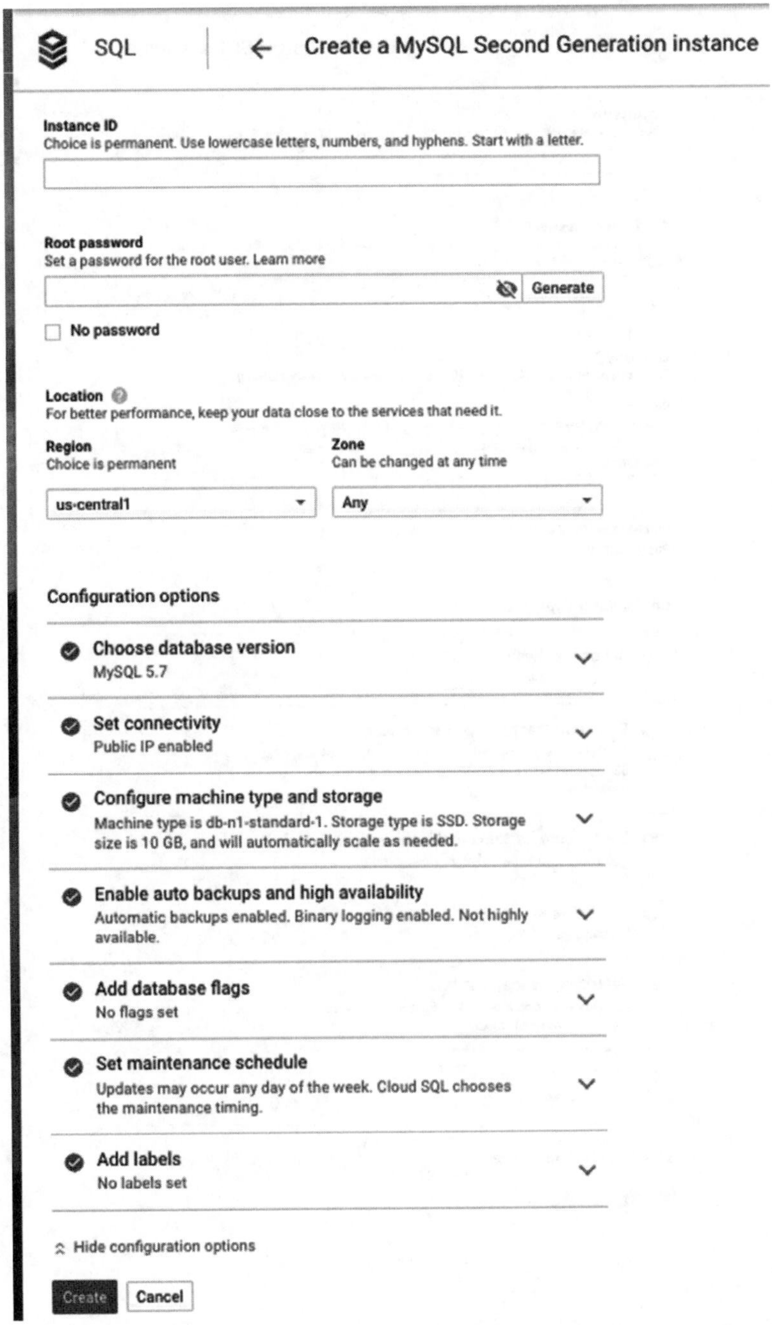

FIGURE 11.12 Configuration form for a PostgreSQL instance

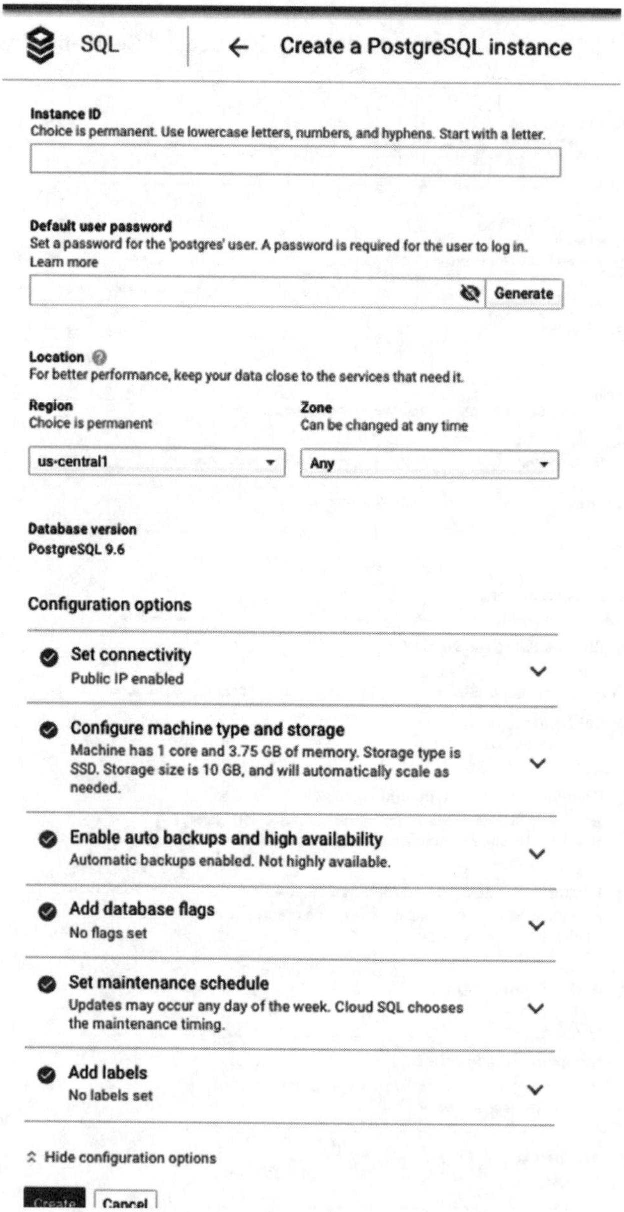

Configuring Cloud Spanner

If you need to create a global, consistent database with support for transactions, then you should consider Cloud Spanner. Given the advanced nature of Spanner, its configuration is surprisingly simple. In the console, navigate to Cloud Spanner and select Create Instance to display a form like Figure 11.13.

FIGURE 11.13 The Cloud Spanner configuration form in Cloud Console

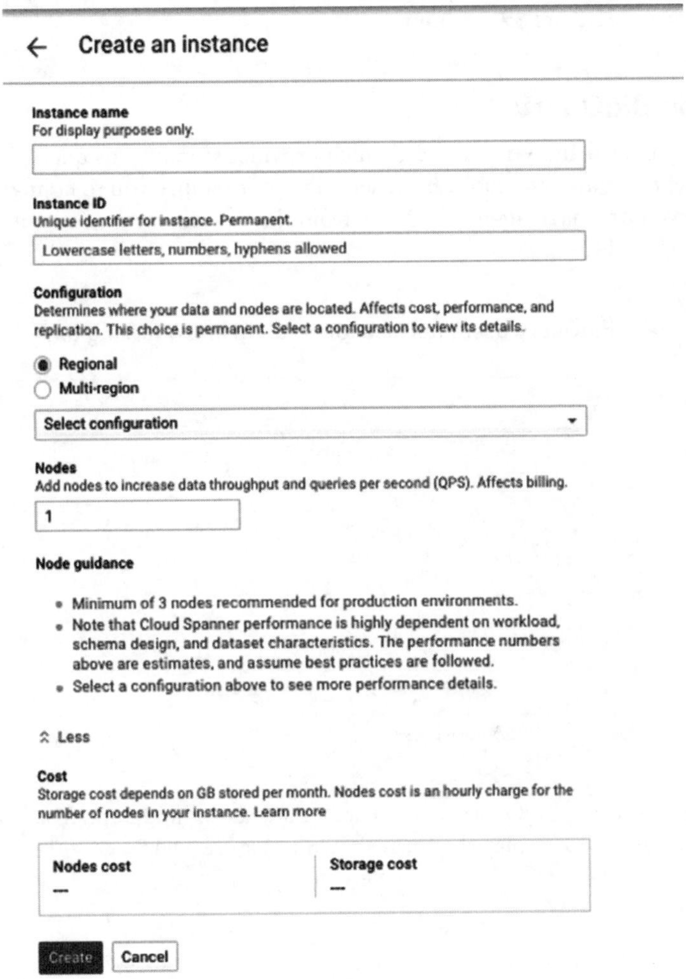

You need to provide an instance name, instance ID, and number of nodes.

You will also have to choose either a regional or multiregional configuration to determine where nodes and data are located. This will determine cost and replication storage location. If you select regional, you will choose from the list of available regions, such as us-west1, asia-east1, and europe-north1.

It should be noted that Cloud Spanner is significantly more expensive than Cloud SQL or other database options. A single regional node located in us-central1 costs $0.90 per hour, while a single multiregional node in nam3 costs $3 per hour. A single multiregional node in nam-eur-asia1 costs $9 per hour.

Configuring BigQuery

BigQuery is a managed analytics service, which provides storage plus query, statistical, and machine learning analysis tools. BigQuery does not require you to configure instances. Instead, when you first navigate to BigQuery from the console menu, you will see a form such as in Figure 11.14.

FIGURE 11.14   BigQuery user interface for creating and querying data

The first task for using BigQuery is to create a data set to hold data. You do this by clicking Create Dataset to display the form shown in Figure 11.15.

FIGURE 11.15   Form to create a dataset in BigQuery

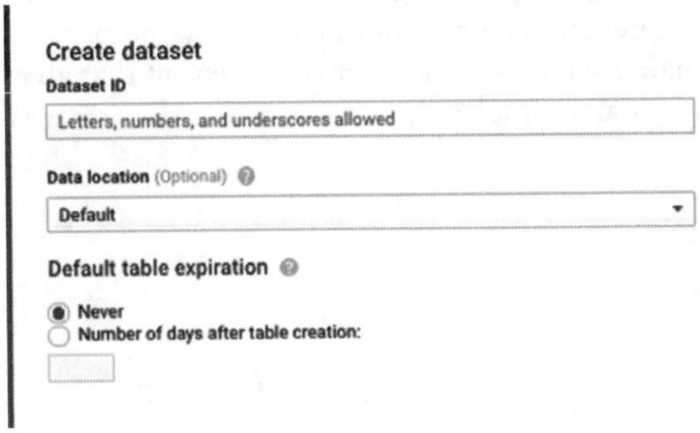

Create dataset
Dataset ID

Letters, numbers, and underscores allowed

Data location (Optional) ⊘

Default   ▼

Default table expiration ⊘

◉ Never
◯ Number of days after table creation:

When creating a data set, you will have to specify a name and select a region in which to store it. Not all regions support BigQuery. Currently you have a choice of nine locations across the United States, Europe, and Asia.

In Chapter 12, we will discuss how to load and query data in BigQuery and other GCP databases.

NoSQL: Datastore, Cloud Firestore, and Bigtable

NoSQL databases do not use the relational model and do not require a fixed structure or schema. Database schemas define what kinds of attributes can be stored. When no fixed schema is required, developers have the option to store different attributes in different records. GCP has three NoSQL options:

- Cloud Datastore
- Cloud Firestore
- Cloud Bigtable

Datastore Features   _Mongo_

Datastore is a document database. That does not mean it is used to store documents like spreadsheets or text files, but the data in the database is organized into a structure called a document. Documents are made up of sets of key-value pairs. A simple example is as follows:

```
{
book : "ACE Exam Guide",
      chapter: 11,
   length: 20,
   topic: "storage"
 }
```

This example describes the characteristics of a chapter in a book. There are four keys or properties in this example: book, chapter, length, and storage. This set of key-value pairs is called an entity in Datastore terminology. Entities often have properties in common, but since Datastore is a schemaless database, there is no requirement that all entities have the same set of properties. Here's an example:

```
{
book : "ACE Exam Guide",
        Chapter: 11,
    topic: "computing",
    number_of_figures: 8
  }
```

Datastore is a managed database, so users of the service do not need to manage servers or install database software. Datastore automatically partitions data and scales up or down as demand warrants.

Datastore is used for nonanalytic, nonrelational storage needs. It is a good choice for product catalogs, which have many types of products with varying characteristics or properties. It is also a good choice for storing user profiles associated with an application.

Datastore has some features in common with relational databases, such as support for transactions and indexes to improve query performance. The main difference is that Datastore does not require a fixed schema or structure and does not support relational operations, such as joining tables, or computing aggregates, such as sums and counts.

Configuring Datastore

Datastore, like BigQuery, is a managed database service that does not require you to specify node configurations. Instead, you can work from the console to add entities to the database. Figure 11.16 shows the initial form that appears when you first navigate to Datastore in Cloud Console.

FIGURE 11.16   The Datastore user interface allows you to create and query data.

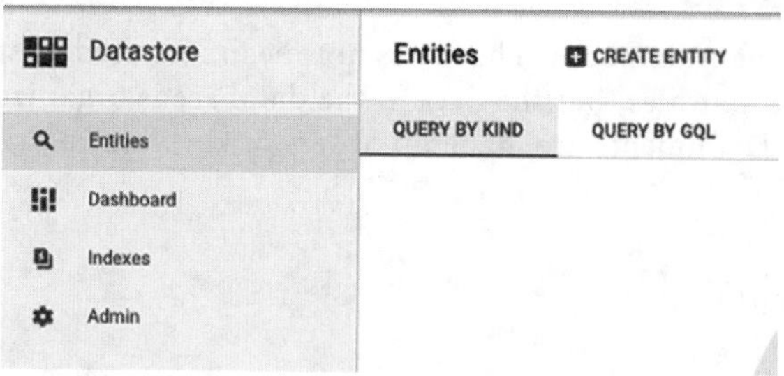

Select Create Entity to display a form to add data in a document data structure, as shown in Figure 11.17.

FIGURE 11.17   Adding entities to Datastore

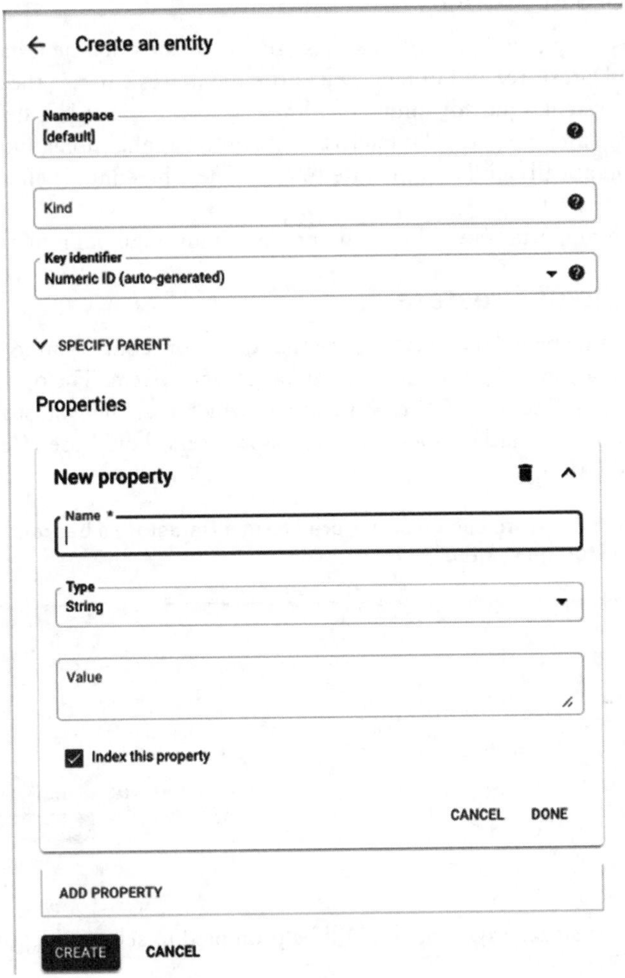

When creating an entity, you specify a namespace, which is a way to group entities much like schemas group tables in a relational database. You will need to specify a kind, which is analogous to a table in a relational database. Each entity requires a key, which can be an autogenerated numeric key or a custom-defined key.

Next, you will add one or more properties that have a names, types, and values. Types include string, date and time, Boolean, and other structured types like arrays.

Additional details on loading and querying data in Datastore are in Chapter 12.

Cloud Firestore Features

Cloud Firestore is a managed NoSQL database that uses the document data model. This is similar to Datastore, and in fact, Datastore databases can use the newer Cloud Firestore storage system. One advantage of Cloud Firestore is that it is designed for storing, synchronizing, and querying data across distributed applications, like mobile apps. Apps can be automatically updated in close to real time when data is changed on the backend.

Cloud Firestore supports transactions and provides multiregional replication.

Configuring Cloud Firestore

Cloud Firestore is a managed database service that does not require you to configure instances. You do, however, have to choose a data storage system. The options include using Datastore, using Firestore in Datastore mode (which uses the Datastore storage system,) or using Firestore in native mode. New Firestore users should use Firestore in native mode (see Figure 11.18).

FIGURE 11.18   Firestore can be configured to use Datastore's backend storage system or its newer native storage system.

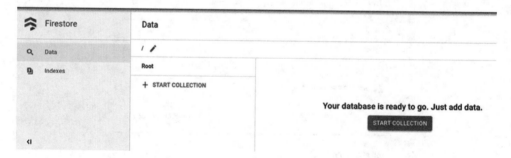

After selecting the storage system, you will be prompted to select a location for the database, as shown in Figure 11.19.

FIGURE 11.19 Selecting a location for a Firebase database

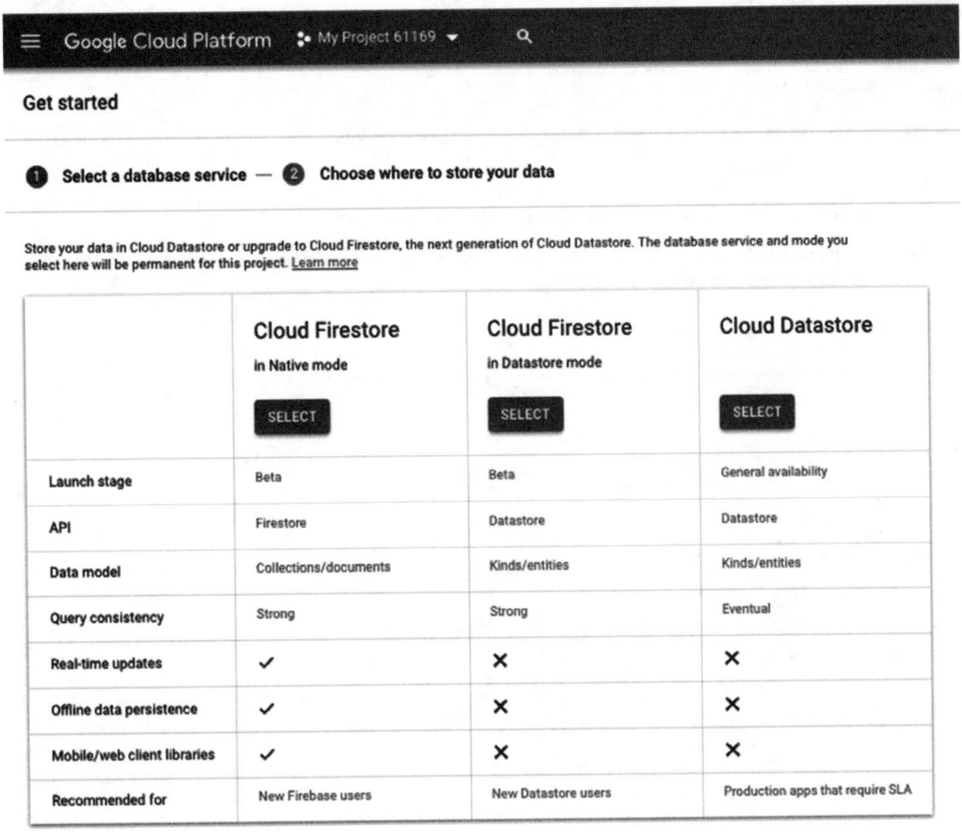

	Cloud Firestore in Native mode	Cloud Firestore in Datastore mode	Cloud Datastore
Launch stage	Beta	Beta	General availability
API	Firestore	Datastore	Datastore
Data model	Collections/documents	Kinds/entities	Kinds/entities
Query consistency	Strong	Strong	Eventual
Real-time updates	✓	✕	✕
Offline data persistence	✓	✕	✕
Mobile/web client libraries	✓	✕	✕
Recommended for	New Firebase users	New Datastore users	Production apps that require SLA

Firestore will create a database, which may take a few minutes. When the database is ready, you will see a display such as in Figure 11.20.

In Chapter 12, we will look into loading and querying data from Firestore.

Bigtable Features

Bigtable is another NoSQL database, but unlike Datastore, it is a wide-column database, not a document database. Wide-column databases, as the name implies, store tables that can have a large number of columns. Not all rows need to use all columns, so in that way it is like Datastore—neither require a fixed schema to structure the data.

Bigtable is designed for petabyte-scale databases. Both operational databases, like storing IoT data, and analytic processing, like data science applications, can effectively use Bigtable. This database is designed to provide consistent, low-millisecond latency. Bigtable runs in clusters and scales horizontally.

Bigtable is designed for applications with high data volumes and a high-velocity ingest of data. Time series, IoT, and financial applications all fall into this category.

FIGURE 11.20   Firestore database ready for use

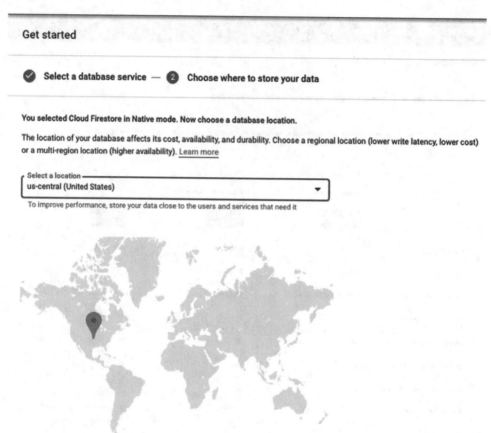

Configuring Bigtable

From Cloud Console, navigate to Bigtable and click Create Instance. This will display a form such as shown in Figure 11.21.

In this form, you will need to provide an instance name and an instance ID. Next, choose between production or development mode. Production clusters have a minimum of three nodes and provide for high availability. Development mode uses low-cost instances without replication or high availability. You will also need to choose either SSD or HDD for persistent disks used by the database.

Bigtable can support multiple clusters. For each cluster you will need to specify a cluster ID, a region and zone location, and the number of nodes in the cluster. The cluster can be replicated to improve availability.

In Chapter 12, we will describe how to load and query data in Bigtable.

FIGURE 11.21 Configuration form for Bigtable

Bigtable | ← Create an instance

A Cloud Bigtable instance is a container for your clusters. Learn more

Instance name
For display purposes only

Instance ID
ID is permanent

Lowercase letters, numbers and hyphens allowed

Instance type ⓘ
● Production (recommended)
  Minimum of 3 nodes. High availability. Cannot downgrade later.
○ Development
  Low-cost instance for development and testing. Does not provide high availability or replication. Can upgrade to Production later.

Storage type ⓘ
Choice is permanent. Applies to all clusters. Affects cost.
● SSD
  Lower latency and higher read QPS. Typically used for real-time serving use cases, such as ad serving and mobile app recommendations.
○ HDD
  Higher latency for random reads. Good performance on scans and typically used for batch analytics, such as machine learning or data mining.

Clusters

Cluster ⌃

Cluster ID
ID is permanent.

Lowercase letters, numbers and hyphens allowed

Location
Choice is permanent. Determines where cluster data is stored. To reduce latency and increase throughput, store your data near the services that need it.

Region   **Zone**
Select a region ▼   Select a zone ▼

Nodes
Add nodes to increase your cluster's capacity for data throughput, queries per second (QPS) and storage. Add enough to keep each cluster's CPU utilization under an average of 70% per node. Contact us if you need to increase your node quota. Learn more

3

Performance
Based on node count and storage type.
Adding a cluster increases read throughput, but not write throughput. Cloud Bigtable uses the additional write throughput for replication.

Reads: 30,000 QPS @ 6ms   or   Writes: 30,000 QPS @ 6ms   or   Scans: 660 MB/s

Storage: 7.5 TB

Done   Cancel

＋ Add replicated cluster

Monthly cost estimate

$1,593.50 per month (1,000 GB data, 3 nodes)
Hourly rate effectively $2.18

Try another storage size (per cluster)

1000   GB

Item	Estimated cost
▸ 1 cluster	$1,423.50/month
▸ 1000 GB SSD	$170.00/month
Total	$1,593.50

Node charges are for provisioned resources, regardless of node usage. The same node charges apply even if your instance is inactive. Learn more

Real World Scenario

The Need for Multiple Databases

Healthcare organizations and medical facilities store and manage a wide range of data about patients, their treatments, and the outcomes. A patient's medical records include demographic information, such as name, address, age, and so on. Medical records also store detailed information about medical conditions and diagnoses as well as treatment, such as drugs prescribed and procedures performed. This kind of data is highly structured. Transaction support and strong consistency are required. Relational databases, like Cloud SQL, are a good solution for this kind of application.

The medical data stored in transactional, relational databases is valuable for analyzing patterns in treatments and recovery. For example, data scientists could use medical records to identify patterns associated with re-admission to the hospital. However, transactional relational databases are not suited for analytics. A better option is to use BigQuery and build a data warehouse with data structured in ways that make it easier to analyze data. Data from the transactional system is extracted, transformed, and loaded into a Bigtable data set.

Choosing a Storage Solution: Guidelines to Consider

GCP offers multiple storage solutions. As a cloud engineer, you may have to help plan and implement storage solutions for a wide range of applications. The different storage solutions lend themselves to different use cases, and in many enterprise applications, you will find that you need two or more different storage products to support the full range of application requirements. Here are several factors to keep in mind when choosing storage solutions:

Read and Write Patterns   Some applications, such as accounting and retail sales applications, read and write data frequently. There are also frequent updates in these applications. They are best served by a storage solution such as Cloud SQL if the data is structured; however, if you need a global database that supports relational read/write operations, then Cloud Spanner is a better choice. If you are writing data at consistently high rates and in large volumes, consider Bigtable. If you are writing files and then downloading them in their entirety, Cloud Storage is a good option.

Consistency   Consistency ensures that a user reading data from the database will get the same data no matter which server in a cluster responds to the request. If you need strong consistency, which is always reading the latest data, then Cloud SQL and Cloud Spanner are good options. Datastore can be configured for strong consistency, but IO operations will take longer than if a less strict consistency configuration is used. Datastore is a good option if your data is unstructured; otherwise, consider one of the relational databases. NoSQL databases offer at least eventual consistency, which means some replicas may not be in sync for a short period of time. During those periods it is possible to read stale data. If your application can tolerate that, then you may find that less strict consistency requirements can lead to faster read and write operations.

Transaction Support   If you need to perform atomic transactions in your application, use a database that supports them. You may be able to implement transaction support in your application, but that code can be difficult to develop and maintain. The relational databases, Cloud SQL and Spanner, and Datastore provide transaction support.

Cost   The cost of using a particular storage system will depend on the amount of data stored, the amount of data retrieved or scanned, and per-unit charges of the storage system. If you are using a storage service in which you provision VMs, you will have to account for that cost as well.

Latency   Latency is the time between the start of an operation, like a request to read a row of data from a database, to the time it completes. Bigtable provides consistently low-millisecond operations. Spanner can have longer latencies, but with those longer latencies you get a globally consistent, scalable database.

In general, choosing a data store is about making tradeoffs. In an ideal world, we could have a low-cost, globally scalable, low-latency, strongly consistent database. We don't live in an ideal world. We have to give up one or more of those characteristics.

In the next chapter, you will learn how to use each of the storage solutions described here, with an emphasis on loading and querying data.

Summary

When planning cloud storage, consider the types of storage systems and types of data models. The storage systems provide the hardware and basic organizational structure used for storing data. The data models organize data into logical structures that determine how data is stored and queried within a database.

The main storage systems available in GCP are Memorystore, a managed cache service, and persistent disks, which are network-accessible disks for VMs in Compute Engine and Kubernetes Engine. Cloud Storage is GCP's object storage system.

The primary data models are object, relational, and NoSQL. NoSQL databases in GCP are further subdivided into document and wide-column databases. Cloud Storage uses an object data model. Cloud SQL and Cloud Spanner use relational databases for transaction processing applications. BigQuery uses a relational model for data warehouse and analytic applications. Datastore and Firebase are document databases. Bigtable is a wide-column table.

When choosing data storage systems, consider read and write patterns, consistency requirements, transaction support, cost, and latency.

Exam Essentials

Know the major storage system types, including caches, persistent disks, and object storage. Caches are used to improve application performance by reducing the need to read from databases on disk. Caches are limited by the amount of available memory. Persistent disks are network devices that are attached to VMs. Persistent disks may be attached to multiple VMs in read-only mode. Object storage is used for storing files for shared access and long-term storage.

Know the major kinds of data models.   Relational databases are used for transaction processing systems that require transaction support and strong consistency. Cloud SQL and Cloud Spanner are relational databases used for transaction processing applications. BigQuery uses a relational model but is designed for data warehouses and analytics. The object model is an alternative to a file system model. Objects, stored as files, are treated as atomic units. NoSQL data models include document data models and wide-column models. Datastore and Firebase are document model databases. Bigtable is a wide-column database.

Know the four storage classes in Cloud Storage.   Regional, multiregional, nearline, and coldline are the four storage classes. Multiregional class replicates data across regions. Regional storage replicates data across zones. Nearline is designed for infrequent access, less than once per month. Coldline storage is designed for archival storage, with files being accessed less than once per year. Both nearline and coldline storage incur retrieval charges in addition to charges based on the size of data.

Know that cloud applications may require more than one kind of data store.   For example, an application may need a cache to reduce latency when querying data in Cloud SQL, object storage for the long-term storage of data files, and BigQuery for data warehousing reporting and analysis.

Know that you can apply lifecycle configurations on Cloud Storage buckets.   Lifecycles are used to delete files and change storage class. Know that regional and multiregional class can be changed to nearline or coldline. Nearline storage can change to coldline. Regional class storage cannot be changed to multiregional, and multiregional cannot be changed to regional.

Know the characteristics of different data stores that help you determine which is the best option for your requirements.   Read and write patterns, consistency requirements, transaction support, cost, and latency are often factors.

Review Questions

You can find the answers in the Appendix.

1. You are tasked with defining lifecycle configurations on buckets in Cloud Storage. You need to consider all possible options for transitioning from one storage class to another. All of the following transitions are allowed except for one. Which one is that?

   A. Nearline to coldline

   B. Regional to nearline

   C. Multiregional to coldline

   D. Regional to multiregional

2. Your manager has asked for your help in reducing Cloud Storage charges. You know that some of the files stored in Cloud Storage are rarely accessed. What kind of storage would you recommend for those files?

   A. Nearline

   B. Regional

   C. Coldline

   D. Multiregional

3. You are working with a startup developing analytics software for IoT data. You have to be able to ingest large volumes of data consistently and store it for several months. The startup has several applications that will need to query this data. Volumes are expected to grow to petabyte volumes. Which database should you use?

   A. Cloud Spanner

   B. Bigtable

   C. BigQuery

   D. Datastore

4. A software developer on your team is asking for your help improving the query performance of a database application. The developer is using a Cloud SQL MySQL, Second Generation instance. Which options would you recommend?

   A. Memorystore and SSD persistent disks

   B. Memorystore and HDD persistent disks

   C. Datastore and SSD persistent disks

   D. Datastore and HDD persistent disks

5. You are creating a set of persistent disks to store data for exploratory data analysis. The disks will be mounted on a virtual machine in the us-west2-a zone. The data is historical data retrieved from Cloud Storage. The data analysts do not need peak performance and are more concerned about cost than performance. The data will be stored in a local relational database. Which type of storage would you recommend?

   A. SSDs

   B. HDDs

   C. Datastore

   D. Bigtable

6. Which of the following statements about Cloud Storage is not true?

   A. Cloud Storage buckets can have retention periods.

   B. Lifecycle configurations can be used to change storage class from regional to multiregional.

   C. Cloud Storage does not provide block-level access to data within files stored in buckets.

   D. Cloud Storage is designed for high durability.

7. When using versioning on a bucket, what is the latest version of the object called?

   A. Live version

   B. Top version

   C. Active version

   D. Safe version

8. A product manager has asked for your advice on which database services might be options for a new application. Transactions and support for tabular data are important. Ideally, the database would support common query tools. What databases would you recommend the product manager consider?

   A. BigQuery and Spanner

   B. Cloud SQL and Spanner

   C. Cloud SQL and Bigtable

   D. Bigtable and Spanner

9. The Cloud SQL service provides fully managed relational databases. What two types of databases are available in Cloud SQL?

   A. SQL Server and MySQL

   B. SQL Server and PostgreSQL

   C. PostgreSQL and MySQL

   D. MySQL and Oracle

10. Which of the following Cloud Spanner configurations would have the highest hourly cost?

    A. Located in us-central1

    B. Located in nam3

C. Located in us-west1-a

D. Located in nam-eur-asia1

11. Which of the following are database services that do not require you to specify configuration information for VMs?

   A. BigQuery only

   B. Datastore only

   C. Firebase and Datastore

   D. BigQuery, Datastore, and Firebase

12. What kind of data model is used by Datastore?

   A. Relational

   B. Document

   C. Wide-column

   D. Graph

13. You have been tasked with creating a data warehouse for your company. It must support tens of petabytes of data and use SQL for a query language. Which managed database service would you choose?

   A. BigQuery

   B. Bigtable

   C. Cloud SQL

   D. SQL Server

14. A team of mobile developers is developing a new application. It will require synchronizing data between mobile devices and a backend database. Which database service would you recommend?

   A. BigQuery

   B. Firestore

   C. Spanner

   D. Bigtable

15. A product manager is considering a new set of features for an application that will require additional storage. What features of storage would you suggest the product manager consider?

   A. Read and write patterns only

   B. Cost only

   C. Consistency and cost only

   D. None, they are all relevant considerations.

16. What is the maximum size of a Memorystore cache?

    A. 100GB

    B. 300GB

    C. 400GB

    D. 50GB

17. Once a bucket has its storage class set to coldline, what are other storage classes it can transition to?

    A. Regional

    B. Nearline

    C. Multi-regional

    D. None of the above

18. Before you can start storing data in BigQuery, what must you create?

    A. A data set

    B. A bucket

    C. A persistent disk

    D. An entity

19. What features can you configure when running a Second Generation MySQL database in Cloud SQL?

    A. Machine type

    B. Maintenance windows

    C. Failover replicas

    D. All of the above

20. A colleague is wondering why some storage charges are so high. They explain that they have moved all their storage to nearline and coldline storage. They routinely access most of the object on any given day. What is one possible reason the storage costs are higher than expected?

    A. Nearline and coldline incur access charges.

    B. Transfer charges.

    C. Multiregional coldline is more expensive.

    D. Regional coldline is more expensive.

Chapter

12

Deploying Storage in Google Cloud Platform

THIS CHAPTER COVERS THE FOLLOWING
OBJECTIVES OF THE GOOGLE ASSOCIATE
CLOUD ENGINEER CERTIFICATION EXAM:

✓ 3.4 Deploying and implementing data solutions

✓ 4.4 Managing data solutions

In this chapter, we will discuss how to create data storage systems in several Google Cloud Platform (GCP) products, including Cloud SQL, Cloud Datastore, BigQuery, Bigtable, Cloud Spanner, Cloud Pub/Sub, Cloud Dataproc, and Cloud Storage. You will learn how to create databases, buckets, and other basic data structures as well as how to perform key management tasks, such as backing up data and checking the status of jobs.

Deploying and Managing Cloud SQL

Cloud SQL is a managed relational database service. In this section, you will learn how to do the following:

- Create a database instance
- Connect to the instance
- Create a database
- Load data into the database
- Query the database
- Back up the database

We will use a MySQL instance in this section, but the following procedures are similar for PostgreSQL.

Creating and Connecting to a MySQL Instance

We described how to create and configure a MySQL instance in Chapter 11, but will review the steps here.

From the console, navigate to SQL and click Create Instance. Choose MySQL and then select Second Generation Instance type. This will lead to a form such as in Figure 12.1.

FIGURE 12.1   Creating a MySQL instance

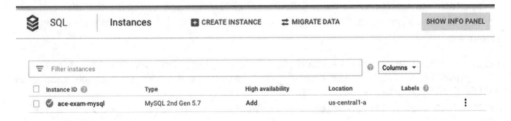

After a few minutes, the instance is created; the MySQL list of instances will look similar to Figure 12.2.

FIGURE 12.2   A listing of MySQL instances

After the database is created, you can connect by starting Cloud Shell and using the gcloud sql connect command. This command takes the name of the instance to connect to and optionally a username and password. It is a good practice to not specify a password in the command line. Instead, you will be prompted for it, and it will not be displayed as you type. You may see a message about whitelisting your IP address; this is a security measure and will allow you to connect to the instance from Cloud Shell.

To connect to the instance called ace-exam-mysql, use the following command:

```
gcloud sql connect ace-exam-mysql –user=root
```

This opens a command-line prompt to the MySQL instance, as shown in Figure 12.3.

FIGURE 12.3   Command-line prompt to work with MySQL after connecting using `gcloud sql connect`

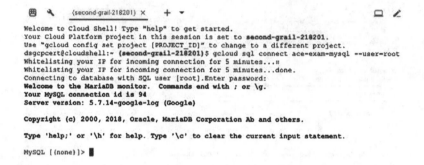

```
Welcome to Cloud Shell! Type "help" to get started.
Your Cloud Platform project in this session is set to second-grail-218201.
Use "gcloud config set project [PROJECT_ID]" to change to a different project.
dsgcpcert@cloudshell:~ (second-grail-218201)$ gcloud sql connect ace-exam-mysql --user=root
Whitelisting your IP for incoming connection for 5 minutes...⌐
Whitelisting your IP for incoming connection for 5 minutes...done.
Connecting to database with SQL user [root].Enter password:
Welcome to the MariaDB monitor.  Commands end with ; or \g.
Your MySQL connection id is 94
Server version: 5.7.14-google-log (Google)

Copyright (c) 2000, 2018, Oracle, MariaDB Corporation Ab and others.

Type 'help;' or '\h' for help. Type '\c' to clear the current input statement.

MySQL [(none)]>
```

Creating a Database, Loading Data, and Querying Data

In the MySQL command-line environment, you use MySQL commands, not `gcloud` commands. MySQL uses standard SQL, so the command to create a database is `CREATE DATABASE`. You indicate the database to work with (there may be many in a single instance) by using the `USE` command. For example, to create a database and set it as the default database to work with, use this:

```
CREATE DATABASE ace_exam_book;
USE ace_exam_book
```

You can then create a table using `CREATE TABLE`. Data is inserted using the `INSERT` command. For example, the following commands create a table called books and inserts two rows:

```
CREATE TABLE books (title VARCHAR(255), num_chapters INT, entity_id INT NOT NULL
\AUTO_INCREMENT, PRIMARY KEY (entity_id));INSERT INTO books (title,num_chapters)
VALUES ('ACE Exam Study Guide', 18);
INSERT INTO books (title,num_chapters) VALUES ('Architecture Exam Study Guide',
18);
```

To query the table, you use the `SELECT` command. Here's an example:

```
SELECT * from books;
```

This will list all the rows in the table, as shown in Figure 12.4.

FIGURE 12.4   Listing the contents of a table in MySQL

```
MySQL [ace_exam_book]> SELECT * FROM books;
+----------------------------+--------------+-----------+
| title                      | num_chapters | entity_id |
+----------------------------+--------------+-----------+
| ACE Exam Study Guide       |           18 |         1 |
| Architecture Exam Study Guide |        14 |         2 |
+----------------------------+--------------+-----------+
2 rows in set (0.04 sec)

MySQL [ace_exam_book]> █
```

Backing Up MySQL in Cloud SQL

Cloud SQL enables both on-demand and automatic backups.

To create an on-demand backup, click the name of the instance on the Instances page on the console. This will display the Instance Details page (see Figure 12.5).

FIGURE 12.5   A MySQL Instance Details page

Click the Backups tab to display the Create Backup option (see Figure 12.6).

FIGURE 12.6 Form used to click Create Backup

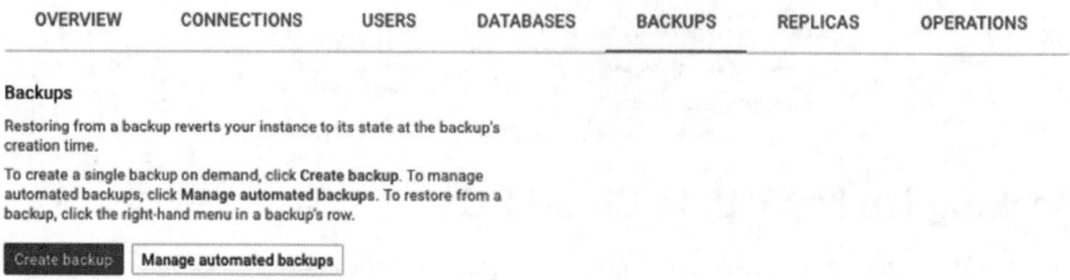

Clicking Create Backup opens a form like that shown in Figure 12.7.

FIGURE 12.7 Assign a description to a backup and create it.

Fill in the optional description and click Create. When the backup is complete, it will appear in the list of backups, as shown in Figure 12.8.

FIGURE 12.8   Listing of backups available for this instance

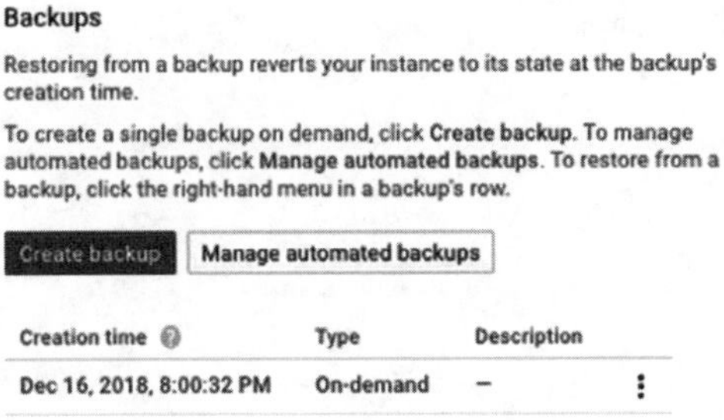

Backups

Restoring from a backup reverts your instance to its state at the backup's creation time.

To create a single backup on demand, click **Create backup**. To manage automated backups, click **Manage automated backups**. To restore from a backup, click the right-hand menu in a backup's row.

| Create backup | Manage automated backups |

Creation time ⓘ	Type	Description	
Dec 16, 2018, 8:00:32 PM	On-demand	—	⋮

You can also create a backup using the gcloud sql backups command, which has this form:

```
gcloud sql backups create --async --instance [INSTANCE_NAME]
```

Here, *[INSTANCE_NAME]* is the name, such as ace-exam-mysql and the --async parameter is optional.

To create an on-demand backup for the ace-exam-mysql instance, use the following command:

```
gcloud sql backups create --async --instance ace-exam-mysql
```

You can also have Cloud SQL automatically create backups.

From the console, navigate to the Cloud SQL Instance page, click the name of the instance, and then click Edit Instance. Open the Enabled Auto Backups section and fill in the details of when to create the backups (see Figure 12.9). You must specify a time range for when automatic backups should occur. You can also enable binary logging, which is needed for more advanced features, such as point-in-time recovery.

To enable automatic backups from the command line, use the gcloud command:

```
gcloud sql instances patch [INSTANCE_NAME] -backup-start-time [HH:MM]
```

For this example instance, you could run automatic backups at 1:00 a.m. with the following command:

```
gcloud sql instances patch ace-exam-mysql -backup-start-time 01:00
```

FIGURE 12.9   Enabling automatic backups in Cloud Console

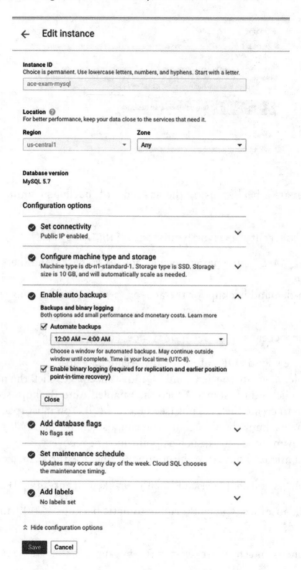

Deploying and Managing Datastore

Chapter 11 described how to initialize a Datastore document database. Now, you will see how to create entities and add properties to a document database. You'll also review backup and restore operations.

Adding Data to a Datastore Database

You add data to a Datastore database using the Entities option in the Datastore section of the console. The Entities data structure is analogous to a schema in relational databases.

You create an entity by clicking Create Entity and filling in the form that appears. Here you will need to fill in Kind, which is analogous to a table in a relational database, and Properties, as shown in Figure 12.10.

FIGURE 12.10   Adding data to a Datastore entity

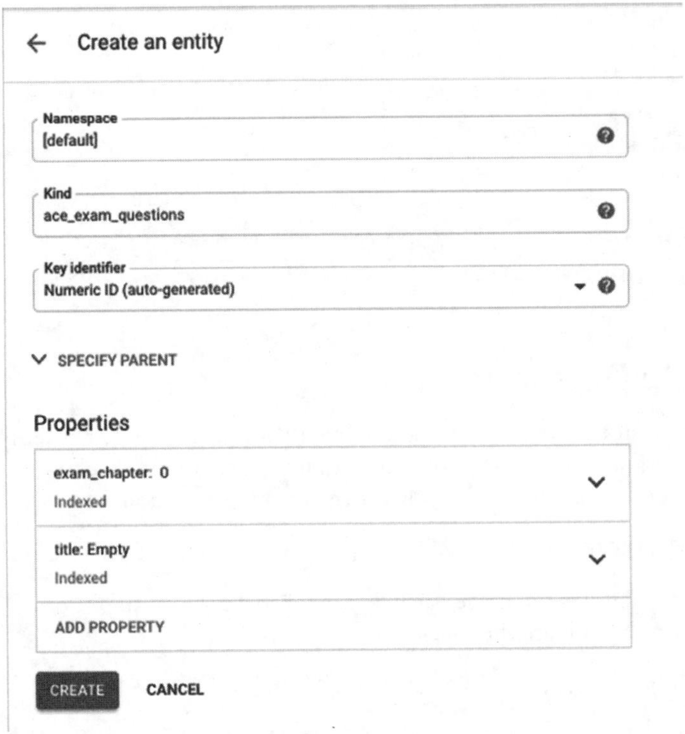

After creating entities, you can query the document database using GQL, a query language similar to SQL. Figure 12.11 shows an example query using the SELECT command.

FIGURE 12.11   Query data store using GGL, a SQL-like query language

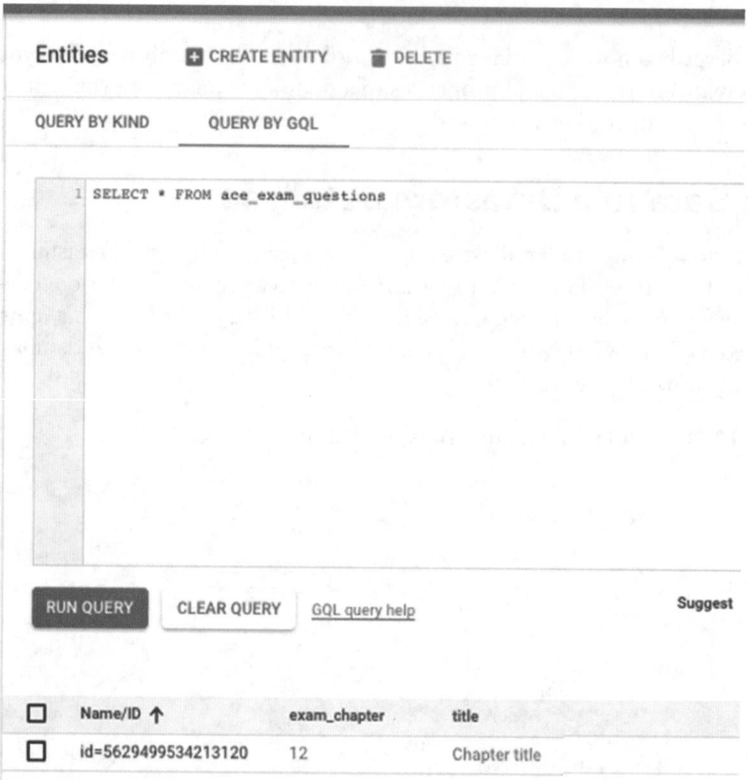

Backing Up Datastore

To back up a Datastore database, you need to create a Cloud Storage bucket to hold a backup file and grant appropriate permissions to users performing backup.

You can create a bucket for backups using the gsutil command.

```
gsutil mb gs://[BUCKET_NAME]/
```

Here, *[BUCKET_NAME]* is the name, such as ace_exam_backups. In our example, we use ace_exam_backups and create that bucket using the following:

```
gsutil mb gs://ace_exam_backups/
```

Users creating backups need the datastore.databases.export permission. If you are importing data, you will need datastore.databases.import. The Cloud Datastore Import Export Admin role has both permissions; see Chapter 17 for details on assigning roles to users.

The user with the Cloud Datastore Import Export Admin role can now make a backup using the following command:

```
gcloud -namespaces='[NAMESPACE]' gs://[BUCKET_NAME}
```

In this example, the command to create a backup is as follows:

```
gcloud datastore export -namespaces='(default)' gs://ace_exam_backups
```

To import a backup file, use the gcloud `datastore import` command:

```
gcloud datastore import gs://[BUCKET]/[PATH]/[FILE].overall_export_metadata
```

In our example, you can import using this:

```
gcloud datastore import gs://ace_exam_backups/[FILE].overall_export_metadata
```

Here, *[FILE]* is the filename assigned by the export process.

Deploying and Managing BigQuery

BigQuery is a fully managed database service, so Google takes care of backups and other basic administrative tasks. As a Cloud Engineer, you still have some administrative tasks when working with BigQuery. Two of those tasks are estimating the cost of a query and checking on the status of a job.

Estimating the Cost of Queries in BigQuery

In the console, choose BigQuery from the main navigation menu to display the BigQuery query interface, as shown in Figure 12.12.

FIGURE 12.12   The BigQuery user interface. Note that this is a beta version of the new interface; older versions will look different.

In this form you can enter a query in the Query Editor, such as a query about names and genders in the usa_1910_2013 table, as shown in Figure 12.13.

FIGURE 12.13   Example query with estimated amount of data scanned

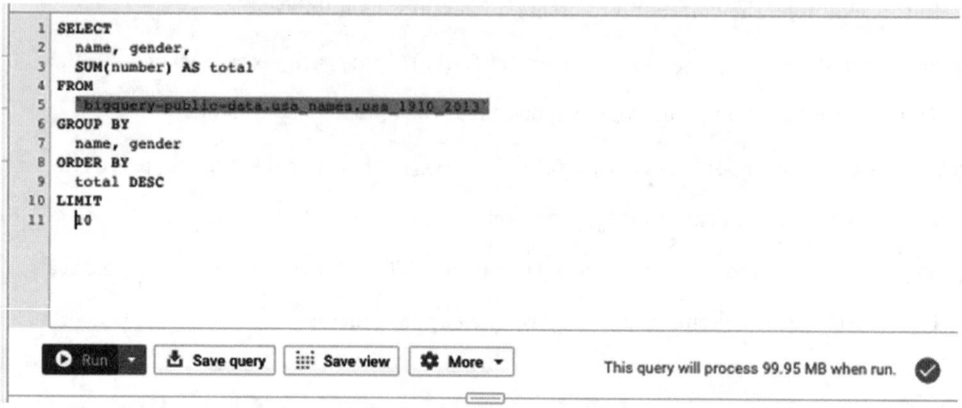

Notice in the lower-right corner that BigQuery provides an estimate of how much data will be scanned. You can also use the command line to get this estimate by using the bq command with the --dry-run option.

```
bq --location=[LOCATION] query --use_legacy_sql=false --dry_run [SQL_QUERY]
```

Here, *[Location]* is the location in which you created the data set you are querying, and *[SQL_QUERY]* is the SQL query you are estimating.

You can use this number with the Pricing Calculator to estimate the cost. The Pricing Calculator is available at https://cloud.google.com/products/calculator/. After selecting BigQuery, navigate to the On-Demand tab, enter the name of the table you are querying, set the amount of storage to 0, and then enter the size of the query in the Queries line of the Queries Pricing section. Be sure to use the same size unit as displayed in the BigQuery console. In our example, the unit of measure is megabytes. When you click Add To Estimate, the Pricing Calculator will display the cost (see Figure 12.14).

Viewing Jobs in BigQuery

Jobs in BigQuery are processes used to load, export, copy, and query data. Jobs are automatically created when you start any of these operations.

To view the status of jobs, navigate to the BigQuery console and click Job History in the menu to the left. This will display a list of jobs and their status. Notice, in Figure 12.15, that the top job in the list has a green bar, indicating that the job completed successfully. This is an example of an expanded view of a job entry. Below that is a single-line summary of a job that failed. The failure is indicated by the red icon next to the job description.

FIGURE 12.14   Using the Pricing Calculator to estimate the cost of a query

FIGURE 12.15   A listing of job statuses in BigQuery

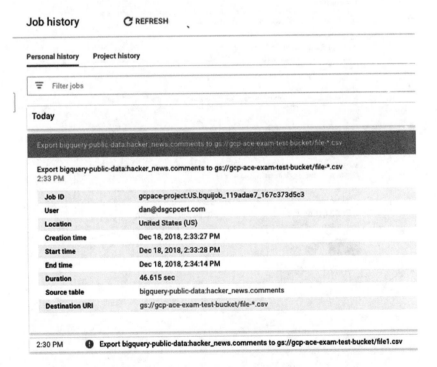

You could also view the status of a BigQuery job by using the bq show command. For example, to show the results of the successful export job shown in Figure 12.15, you could use this command:

```
bq --location=US show -j gcpace-project:US.bquijob_119adae7_167c373d5c3
```

Deploying and Managing Cloud Spanner

Now, let's turn our attention to Cloud Spanner, the global relational database. In this section, you will create a database, define a schema, insert some data, and then query it.

First, you will create a Cloud Spanner instance. Navigate to the Cloud Spanner form in the console and select Create Instance. This will display a form as shown in Figure 12.16.

FIGURE 12.16   Create a Cloud Spanner instance.

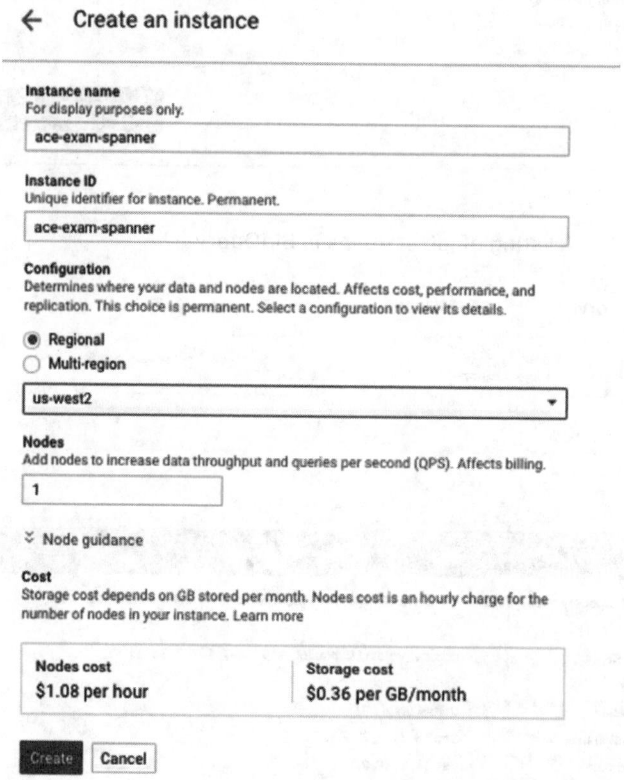

Next, you need to create a database in the instance. Select Create Database at the top of the Instance Details page, as shown in Figure 12.17.

FIGURE 12.17   Create a database within a Cloud Spanner instance.

When creating a database, you will need to use the SQL data definition language (DDL) to define the structure of tables. SQL DDL is the set of SQL commands for creating tables, indexes, and other data structures (see Table 12.1). In the example in Figure 12.18, you use a Singers table definition provided by Google in the Cloud Spanner Quickstart (https://cloud.google.com/spanner/docs/quickstart-console).

TABLE 12.1   SQL data definition commands

Command	Description
CREATE TABLE	Creates a table with columns and data types specified
CREATE INDEX	Creates an index on the specified column(s)
ALTER TABLE	Changes table structure
DROP TABLE	Removes the table from the database schema
DROP INDEX	Removes the index from the database schema

After executing the CREATE TABLE command, you will see a listing of the table structure, as in Figure 12.19.

FIGURE 12.18   Create a table within the database.

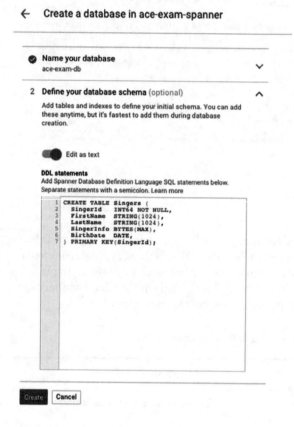

← Create a database in ace-exam-spanner

✓ **Name your database**
ace-exam-db   ⌄

2 **Define your database schema** (optional)   ⌃

Add tables and indexes to define your initial schema. You can add
these anytime, but it's fastest to add them during database
creation.

⬤ Edit as text

DDL statements
Add Spanner Database Definition Language SQL statements below.
Separate statements with a semicolon. Learn more

```
1  CREATE TABLE Singers (
2    SingerId   INT64 NOT NULL,
3    FirstName  STRING(1024),
4    LastName   STRING(1024),
5    SingerInfo BYTES(MAX),
6    BirthDate  DATE,
7  ) PRIMARY KEY(SingerId);
```

[Create] [Cancel]

FIGURE 12.19   List of table columns in the table

← Table details   🔍 QUERY   ➕ CREATE INDEX   ✏ EDIT SCHEMA   🗑 DELETE TABLE

Singers

Schema   Indexes   Data

Column	Type	Nullable
O⟶ SingerId	INT64	No
BirthDate	DATE	Yes
FirstName	STRING(1024)	Yes
LastName	STRING(1024)	Yes
SingerInfo	BYTES(MAX)	Yes

Show equivalent DDL

To add data to the table, select the Data table in the Table Details page, as shown in Figure 12.20.

FIGURE 12.20   Select the Data tab to insert data into the table.

When you add a row, you will see a form like the one in Figure 12.21, which shows the columns in the table. In this example, the columns are SingerID, BirthDate, FirstName, LastName, and SingerInfo.

FIGURE 12.21   Data entered into the table

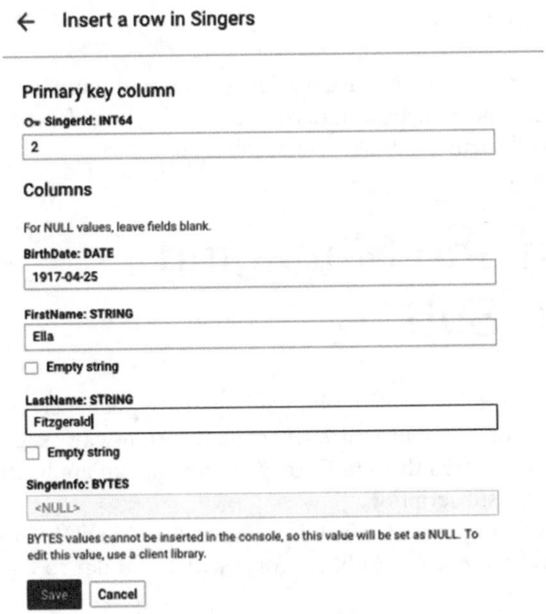

Finally, you can execute a query by selecting the query from the Table Details page (as shown in Figure 12.22).

FIGURE 12.22 Query a table from the Query form.

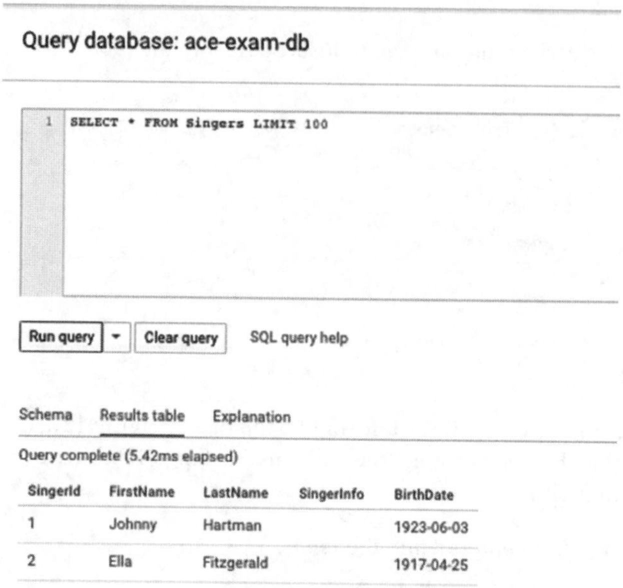

Query database: ace-exam-db

```
1  SELECT * FROM Singers LIMIT 100
```

| Run query | ▾ | | Clear query | SQL query help |

Schema   Results table   Explanation

Query complete (5.42ms elapsed)

SingerId	FirstName	LastName	SingerInfo	BirthDate
1	Johnny	Hartman		1923-06-03
2	Ella	Fitzgerald		1917-04-25

Cloud Spanner is a managed database service, so you will not have to patch, backup, or perform other basic data administration tasks. Your tasks, and those of data modelers and software engineers, will focus on design tables and queries.

Deploying and Managing Cloud Pub/Sub

There are two tasks required to deploy a Pub/Sub message queue: creating a topic and creating a subscription. A topic is a structure where applications can send messages. Pub/Sub receives the messages and keeps them until they are read by an application. Applications read messages by using a subscription.

The first step for working with Pub/Sub is to navigate to the Pub/Sub page in Cloud Console. The first time you use Pub/Sub, the form will be similar to Figure 12.23.

FIGURE 12.23   Create a Pub/Sub topic.

When you click Create a Topic, you will be prompted for a name for the topic, as in Figure 12.24.

FIGURE 12.24   Name a topic.

Create a topic

A topic forwards messages from publishers to subscribers.

Name ⓘ

projects/gcpace-project/topics/ ace-exam-topic

CANCEL   CREATE

You will see a list of topics displayed in the Topics page after creating the first topic, as shown in Figure 12.25.

FIGURE 12.25   List of topics

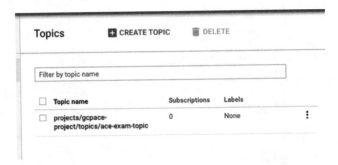

To create a subscription to a topic, click the three-dot icon at the end of the topic summary line in the listing. The menu that appears includes a Create Subscription option (see Figure 12.26). Click Create Subscription to create a subscription to that topic. This will display a form like that shown in Figure 12.27.

FIGURE 12.26   Creating a subscription to a topic

FIGURE 12.27   The form for creating a subscription

To create a subscription, specify a subscription name and delivery type. Subscriptions can be *pulled*, in which the application reads from a topic, or *pushed*, in which the subscription writes messages to an endpoint. If you want to use a push subscription, you will need to specify the URL of an endpoint to receive the message.

Once a message is read, the application reading the message acknowledges receiving the message. Pub/Sub will wait the period of time specified in the Acknowledgment Deadline parameter. The time to wait can range from 10 to 600 seconds.

You can also specify a retention period, which is the length of time to keep a message that cannot be delivered. After the retention period passes, messages are deleted from the topic.

When you complete creating a subscription, you will see a list of subscriptions like that shown in Figure 12.28.

FIGURE 12.28   A list of subscriptions

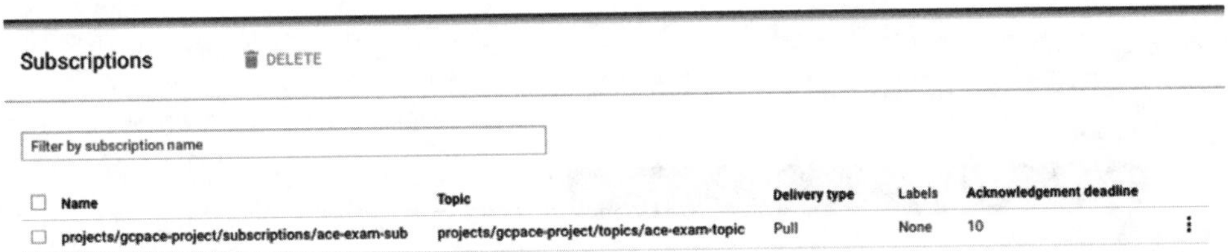

In addition to using the console, you can use gcloud commands to create topics and subscriptions. The commands to create topics and subscriptions are as follows:

```
gcloud pubsub topics create [TOPIC-NAME]
gcloud pubsub subscriptions create [SUBSCRIPTION-NAME] --topic [TOPIC-NAME]
```

Deploying and Managing Cloud Bigtable

As a Cloud Engineer, you may need to create a Bigtable cluster, or set of servers running Bigtable services, as well as create tables, add data, and query that data.

To create a Bigtable instance, navigate to the Bigtable console and click Create Instance. This will display a form like that shown in Figure 12.29. (See Chapter 11 for additional details on creating a Bigtable instance.)

FIGURE 12.29 Creating a Bigtable instance

Much of the work you will do with Bigtable is done at the command line.

To create a table, open a Cloud Shell browser and install the cbt command. Unlike relational databases, Bigtable is a NoSQL database and does not use the SQL command. Instead, the cbt command has subcommands to create tables, insert data, and query tables (see Table 12.2).

TABLE 12.2   cbt commands

Command	Description
createtable	Creates a table
createfamily	Creates a column family
read	Reads and displays rows
ls	Lists tables and columns

To configure cbt in Cloud Shell, enter these commands:

```
gcloud components update
gcloud components install cbt
```

Bigtable requires an environment variable called instance to be set by including it in a .cbt configuration file called .cbtrc, which is kept in the home directory.

For example, to set the instance to ace-exam-bigtable, enter this command at the command-line prompt:

```
echo instance = ace-exam-bigtable >> ~/.cbtrc
```

Now cbt commands will operate on that instance. To create a table, issue a command such as this:

```
cbt createtable ace-exam-bt-table
```

The ls command lists tables. Here's an example:

```
cbt ls
```

This will display a list of all tables. Tables contain columns, but Bigtable also has a concept of column families. To create a column family called colfam1, use the following command:

```
cbt createfamily ace-exam-bt-table colfam1
```

To set a value of the cell with the column colfam1 in a row called row1, use the following command:

```
cbt set ace-exam-bt-table row1 colfam1:col1=ace-exam-value
```

To display the contents of a table, use a read command such as this:

```
cbt read ace-exam-bt-table
```

The read command will generate output such as that shown in Figure 12.30.

FIGURE 12.30 Displaying table contents using the cbt read command

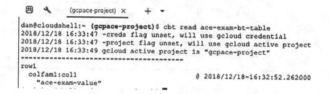

Deploying and Managing
Cloud Dataproc

Cloud Dataproc is Google's managed Apache Spark and Apache Hadoop service. Both Spark and Hadoop are designed for "big data" applications. Spark supports analysis and machine learning, while Hadoop is well suited to batch, big data applications. As a Cloud Engineer, you should be familiar with creating a Dataproc cluster and submitting jobs to run in the cluster.

To create a cluster, navigate to the Dataproc part of Cloud Console (see Figure 12.31).

FIGURE 12.31 Dataproc console page

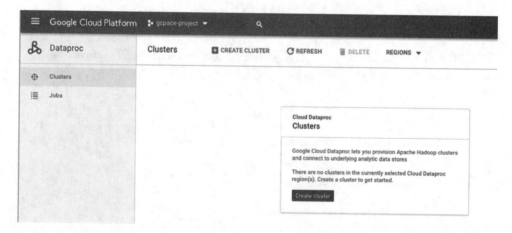

Create a Dataproc cluster by filling in the Create Cluster form. You will need to specify the name of the cluster and a region and zone. You'll also need to specify the cluster mode, which can be single node, standard, or high availability. Single node is useful for development. Standard has only one master node, so if it fails, the cluster becomes inaccessible. The high availability mode uses three masters.

You will also need to specify machine configuration information for the master nodes and the worker nodes. You'll specify CPUs, memory, and disk information. The cluster mode determines the number of master nodes, but you can choose the number of worker nodes. If you choose to expand the list of advanced options, you can indicate you'd like to use preemptible VMs and specify a number of preemptible VMs to run (see Figure 12.32).

FIGURE 12.32   Create a Dataproc cluster.

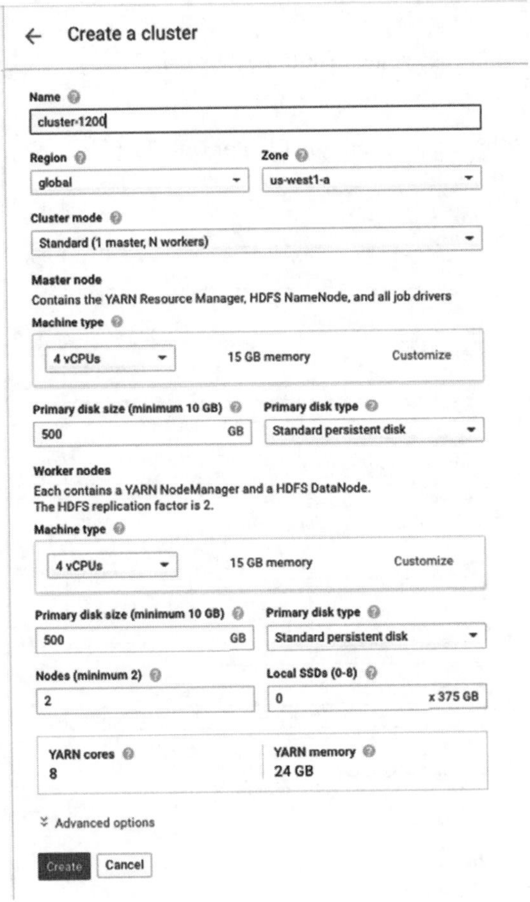

After you create a cluster, it will appear in the list of clusters, as in Figure 12.33.

FIGURE 12.33   Listing of Dataproc clusters

When the cluster is running, you can submit jobs using the Jobs form shown in Figure 12.34.

FIGURE 12.34   Submit a job from the Cluster Details page.

You will need to specify the cluster to run the job and the type of job, which can be either Spark, PySpark, SparkR, Hive, Spark SQL, Pig, or Hadoop. The JAR files are the Java programs that will be executed, and the Main Class or JAR is the name of the function or method that should be invoked to start the job. If you choose PySpark, you will submit a Python program; if you submit SparkR, you will submit an R program. When running Hive or SparkSQL, you will submit query files. You can also pass in optional arguments. Once the job is running, you will see it in the jobs listing page, as shown in Figure 12.35.

FIGURE 12.35   Listing of jobs

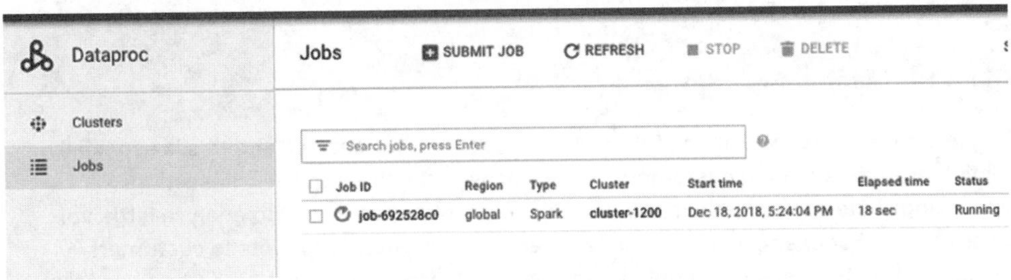

Double-clicking Jobs ID in the listing will display details of the job log (see Figure 12.36).

FIGURE 12.36   Logging detail of a running job

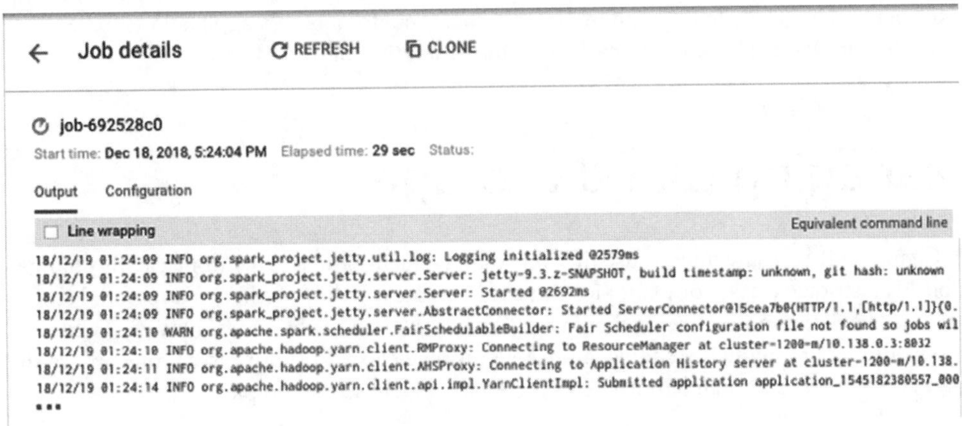

In addition to using the console, you can create a cluster using the gcloud dataproc clusters command. Here's an example:

```
gcloud dataproc clusters create cluster-bc3d --zone us-west2-a
```

This will create a default cluster in the us-west2-a zone. You can also specify additional parameters for machine types, disk configurations, and other cluster characteristics.

You use the gcloud dataproc jobs command to submit jobs from the command line. Here's an example:

```
gcloud dataproc jobs submit spark --cluster cluster-bc3d  --jar ace_exam_jar.jar
```

This will submit a job running the ace_exam_jar.jar program on the cluster-bc3d cluster.

Real World Scenario

Spark for Machine Learning

Retailers collect large volumes of data about shoppers' purchases, and this is especially helpful for understanding customers' preferences and interests. The transaction processing systems that collect much of this data are not designed to analyze large volumes of data. For example, if retailers wanted to recommend products to customers based on their interests, they could build machine learning models trained on their sales data. Spark has a machine learning library, called MLlib, that is designed for just this kind of problem. Engineers can export data from transaction processing systems, load it into Spark, and then apply a variety of machine learning algorithms, such as clustering and collaborative filtering, for recommendations. The output of these models includes products that are likely to be of interest to particular customers. It's applications like these that drive the adoption of Spark and other analytics platforms.

Managing Cloud Storage

In Chapter 11, you saw how to use lifecycle management policies to automatically change a bucket's storage class. For example, you could create a policy to change a regional storage class bucket to a nearline bucket after 90 days. There may be times, however, when you would like to manually change a bucket's storage class. In those cases, you can use the gsutil rewrite command and specify the -s flag. Here's an example:

```
gsutil rewrite -s [STORAGE_CLASS] gs://[PATH_TO_OBJECT]
```

Here, [STORAGE_CLASS] is the new storage class. It can be multi_regional, regional, nearline, or coldline.

It is not possible to change a bucket's storage class in the console.

Another common task with Cloud Storage is moving objects between buckets. You can do this using the gsutil mv command. The form of the command is as follows:

```
gsutil mv gs://[SOURCE_BUCKET_NAME]/[SOURCE_OBJECT_NAME] \
gs://[DESTINATION_BUCKET_NAME]/[DESTINATION_OBJECT_NAME]
```

Here, [SOURCE_BUCKET_NAME] and [SOURCE_OBJECT_NAME] are the original bucket name and filename, and [DESTINATION_BUCKET_NAME] and [DESTINATION_OBJECT_NAME] are the target bucket and filename, respectively.

The move command can also be used to rename an object, similar to the mv command in Linux. For an object in Cloud Storage, you can use this command:

```
gsutil mv gs://[BUCKET_NAME]/[OLD_OBJECT_NAME] gs://[BUCKET_NAME]/
[NEW_OBJECT_NAME]
```

You can also use the console to move and rename objects in a bucket. Navigate to the Cloud Storage section of the console and browse to a bucket, as shown in Figure 12.37. Click the three-dot icon at the end of the object description. This displays a list of operations, including renaming and moving.

FIGURE 12.37   Renaming and moving an object from the console

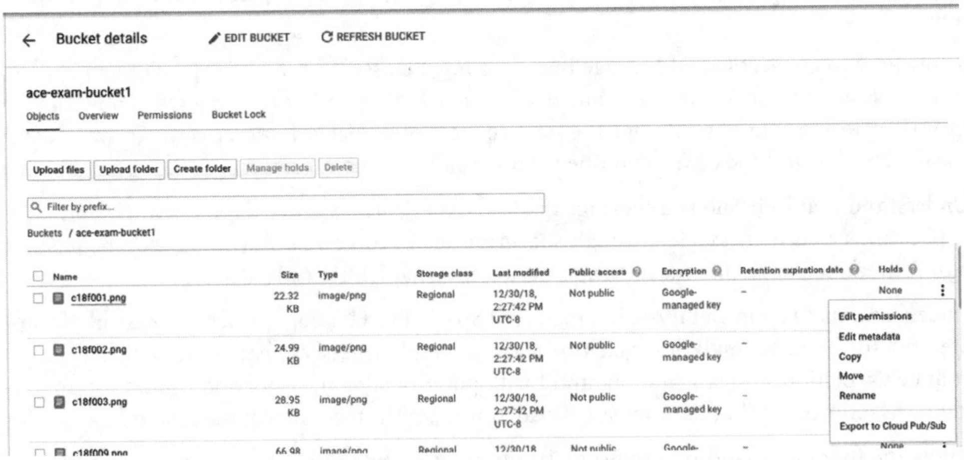

Summary

In this chapter, you learned how to perform basic deployment and management tasks for a number of GCP services, including Cloud SQL, Cloud Datastore, BigQuery, Bigtable, Cloud Spanner, Cloud Pub/Sub, Cloud Dataproc, and Cloud Storage. You have seen how to use the console and command-line tools. While gcloud is often used, several of the services have their own command-line tools. There was some discussion of how to create database structures, insert data, and query that data in the various database services. We also discussed basic Cloud Storage management operations, such as moving and renaming objects.

Exam Essentials

Understand how to initialize Cloud SQL and Cloud Spanner.   Cloud SQL and Cloud Spanner are the two managed relational databases for transaction processing systems. BigQuery is relational but designed for data warehouses and analytics. Understand the need to create databases and tables. Know that SQL is used to query these databases.

Understand how to initialize Cloud Datastore and Cloud Bigtable.   These are two NoSQL offerings. You can add small amounts of data to Cloud Datastore through the console and query it with a SQL-like language called GQL. Cloud Bigtable is a wide-column database that does not support SQL. Bigtable is managed with the cbt command-line tool.

Know how to export data from BigQuery, estimate the cost of a query, and monitor jobs in BigQuery.   BigQuery is designed to work with petabyte-scale data warehouses. SQL is used to query data. Know how to export data using the console. Understand that the bq command line, not gcloud, is the tool for working with BigQuery from the command line.

Know how to convert Cloud Storage bucket storage classes.   Lifecycle policies can change storage classes of buckets when events occur, such as a period of time passes. Know that gsutil rewrite is used to change the storage class of a bucket interactively. Know how to use the console and the command line to move and rename objects.

Understand that Pub/Sub is a message queue.   Applications write data to topics, and applications receive messages through subscriptions to topics. Subscriptions can be push or pull. Unread messages have a retention period after which they are deleted.

Understand that Cloud Dataproc is a managed Spark and Hadoop service.   These platforms are used for big data analytics, machine learning, and large-scale batch jobs, such as large volume extraction, transformation, and load operations. Spark is a good option for analyzing transaction data, but data must be loaded into Spark from its source system.

Know the four command-line tools: gcloud, gsutil, bq, and cbt.   gcloud is used for most products but not all. gsutil is used to work with Cloud Storage from the command line. If you want to work with BigQuery from the command line, you need to use bq. To work with Bigtable, you use the cbt command.

Review Questions

You can find the answers in the Appendix.

1. Cloud SQL is a fully managed relational database service, but database administrators still have to perform some tasks. Which of the following tasks do Cloud SQL users need to perform?

   A. Applying security patches

   B. Performing regularly scheduled backups

   C. Creating databases

   D. Tuning the operating system to optimize Cloud SQL performance

2. Which of the following commands is used to create a backup of a Cloud SQL database?

   A. `gcloud sql backups create`

   B. `gsutil sql backups create`

   C. `gcloud sql create backups`

   D. `gcloud sql backups export`

3. Which of the following commands will run an automatic backup at 3:00 a.m. on an instance called ace-exam-mysql?

   A. `gcloud sql instances patch ace-exam-mysql --backup-start-time 03:00`

   B. `gcloud sql databases patch ace-exam-mysql --backup-start-time 03:00`

   C. `cbt sql instances patch ace-exam-mysql --backup-start-time 03:00`

   D. `bq gcloud sql instances patch ace-exam-mysql --backup-start-time 03:00`

4. What is the query language used by Datastore?

   A. SQL

   B. MDX

   C. GQL

   D. DataFrames

5. What is the correct command-line structure to export data from Datastore?

   A. `gcloud datastore export '[NAMESPACE]' gs://[BUCKET_NAME]`

   B. `gcloud datastore export gs://[BUCKET_NAME]`

   C. `gcloud datastore export --namespaces='[NAMESPACE]' gs://[BUCKET_NAME]`

   D. `gcloud datastore dump --namespaces='[NAMESPACE]' gs://[BUCKET_NAME]`

6. When you enter a query into the BigQuery query form, BigQuery analyzes the query and displays an estimate of what metric?

   A. Time required to enter the query

   B. Cost of the query

   C. Amount of data scanned

   D. Number of bytes passed between servers in the BigQuery cluster

7. You want to get an estimate of the volume of data scanned by BigQuery from the command line. Which option shows the command structure you should use?

   A. `gcloud BigQuery query estimate [SQL_QUERY]`

   B. `bq --location=[LOCATION] query --use_legacy_sql=false --dry_run [SQL_QUERY]`

   C. `gsutil --location=[LOCATION] query --use_legacy_sql=false --dry_run [SQL_QUERY]`

   D. `cbt BigQuery query estimate [SQL_QUERY]`

8. You are using Cloud Console and want to check on some jobs running in BigQuery. You navigate to the BigQuery part of the console. Which menu item would you click to view jobs?

   A. Job History.

   B. Active Jobs.

   C. My Jobs.

   D. You can't view job status in the console; you have to use bq on the command line.

9. You want to estimate the cost of running a BigQuery query. What two services within Google Cloud Platform will you need to use?

   A. BigQuery and Billing

   B. Billing and Pricing Calculator

   C. BigQuery and Pricing Calculator

   D. Billing and Pricing Calculator

10. You have just created a Cloud Spanner instance. You have been tasked with creating a way to store data about a product catalog. What is the next step after creating a Cloud Spanner instance that you would perform to enable you to load data?

   A. Run `gcloud spanner update-security-patches`.

   B. Create a database within the instance.

   C. Create tables to hold the data.

   D. Use the Cloud Spanner console to import data into tables created with the instance.

11. You have created a Cloud Spanner instance and database. According to Google best practices, how often should you update VM packages using `apt-get`?

    A. Every 24 hours.

    B. Every 7 days.

    C. Every 30 days.

    D. Never, Cloud Spanner is a managed service.

12. Your software team is developing a distributed application and wants to send messages from one application to another. Once the consuming application reads a message, it should be deleted. You want your system to be robust to failure, so messages should be available for at least three days before they are discarded. Which GCP service is best designed to support this use case?

    A. Bigtable

    B. Dataproc

    C. Cloud Pub/Sub

    D. Cloud Spanner

13. Your manager asks you to set up a bare-bones Pub/Sub system as a sandbox for new developers to learn about messaging systems. What are the two resources within Pub/Sub you will need to create?

    A. Topics and tables

    B. Topics and databases

    C. Topics and subscriptions

    D. Tables and subscriptions

14. Your company is launching an IoT service and will receive large volumes of streaming data. You have to store this data in Bigtable. You want to explore the Bigtable environment from the command line. What command would you run to ensure you have command-line tools installed?

    A. `apt-get install bigtable-tools`

    B. `apt-get install cbt`

    C. `gcloud components install cbt`

    D. `gcloud components install bigtable-tools`

15. You need to create a table called `iot-ingest-data` in Bigtable. What command would you use?

    A. `cbt createtable iot-ingest-data`

    B. `gcloud bigtable tables create ace-exam-bt-table`

    C. `gcloud bigtable create tables ace-exam-bt-table`

    D. `gcloud create ace-exam-bt-table`

16. Cloud Dataproc is a managed service for which two big data platforms?

A. Spark and Cassandra

B. Spark and Hadoop

C. Hadoop and Cassandra

D. Spark and TensorFlow

17. Your department has been asked to analyze large batches of data every night. The jobs will run for about three to four hours. You want to shut down resources as soon as the analysis is done, so you decide to write a script to create a Dataproc cluster every night at midnight. What command would you use to create a cluster called `spark-nightly-analysis` in the `us-west2-a` zone?

A. `bq dataproc clusters create spark-nightly-analysis --zone us-west2-a`

B. `gcloud dataproc clusters create spark-nightly-analysis --zone us-west2-a`

C. `gcloud dataproc clusters spark-nightly-analysis --zone us-west2-a`

D. None of the above

18. You have a number of buckets containing old data that is hardly ever used. You don't want to delete it, but you want to minimize the cost of storing it. You decide to change the storage class to coldline for each of those buckets. What is the command structure that you would use?

A. `gcloud rewrite -s [STORAGE_CLASS] gs://[PATH_TO_OBJECT]`

B. `gsutil rewrite -s [STORAGE_CLASS] gs://[PATH_TO_OBJECT]`

C. `cbt rewrite -s [STORAGE_CLASS] gs://[PATH_TO_OBJECT]`

D. `bq rewrite -s [STORAGE_CLASS] gs://[PATH_TO_OBJECT]`

19. You want to rename an object stored in a bucket. What command structure would you use?

A. `gsutil cp gs://[BUCKET_NAME]/[OLD_OBJECT_NAME] gs://[BUCKET_NAME]/[NEW_OBJECT_NAME]`

B. `gsutil mv gs://[BUCKET_NAME]/[OLD_OBJECT_NAME] gs://[BUCKET_NAME]/[NEW_OBJECT_NAME]`

C. `gsutil mv gs://[OLD_OBJECT_NAME] gs://[NEW_OBJECT_NAME]`

D. `gcloud mv gs://[OLD_OBJECT_NAME] gs://[NEW_OBJECT_NAME]`

20. An executive in your company emails you asking about creating a recommendation system that will help sell more products. The executive has heard there are some GCP solutions that may be good fits for this problem. What GCP service would you recommend the executive look into?

A. Cloud Dataproc, especially Spark and its machine learning library

B. Cloud Dataproc, especially Hadoop

C. Cloud Spanner, which is a global relational database that can hold a lot of data

D. Cloud SQL, because SQL is a powerful query language

Chapter

13

Loading Data into Storage

THIS CHAPTER COVERS THE FOLLOWING
OBJECTIVES OF THE GOOGLE ASSOCIATE
CLOUD ENGINEER CERTIFICATION EXAM:

✓ 3.4 Deploying and implementing data solutions

In this chapter, we will delve into the details of loading and moving data into various storage and processing systems in Google Cloud Platform. We'll start by explaining how to load and move data in Cloud Storage using the console and the command line.

The bulk of the chapter will describe how to import and export data into data storage and analysis services, including Cloud SQL, Cloud Datastore, BigQuery, Cloud Spanner, Cloud Bigtable, and Cloud Dataproc. The chapter wraps up with a look into streaming data into Cloud Pub/Sub.

Loading and Moving Data to Cloud Storage

Cloud Storage is used for a variety of storage use cases, including long-term storage and archiving, file transfers, and data sharing. This section describes how to create storage buckets, load data into storage buckets, and move objects between storage buckets.

Loading and Moving Data to Cloud Storage Using the Console

Loading data into Cloud Storage is a common task and easily done using Cloud Console.

Navigate to the Cloud Storage page of Cloud Console. You will see either a list of existing buckets or an option to create a new bucket (see Figure 13.1).

FIGURE 13.1 The first step in loading data into Cloud Storage is to create a bucket.

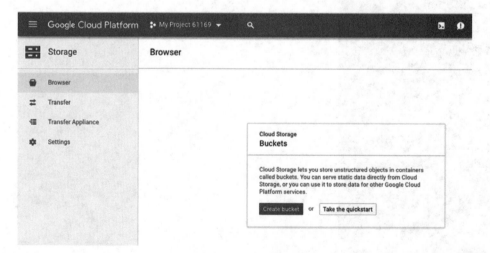

When you create a bucket, you are prompted to specify the storage class of the bucket and the region to store it in, as shown in Figure 13.2.

For the exam, remember that buckets are regional resources. Buckets are replicated across zones in the region.

FIGURE 13.2 Defining a regional bucket in us-west1

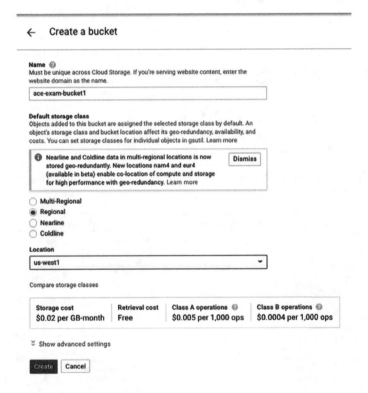

After you create a bucket, you see the Bucket Details page (see Figure 13.3). From here, you can upload individual files or folders.

FIGURE 13.3 From Bucket Details page, you can upload files and folders.

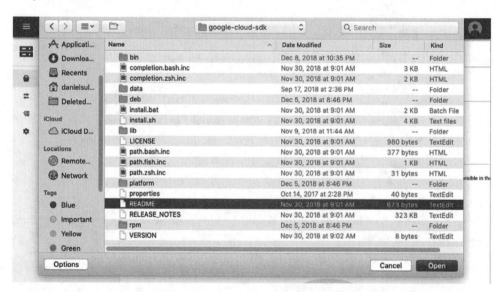

When you upload a file, you are prompted to do so using your client devices file system. Figure 13.4 shows a macOS Finder window for uploading files. You would see something similar on a Windows or Linux operating system.

FIGURE 13.4 Choosing the File Upload option prompts for a file using the client device file system tools.

When you upload a folder, you are also prompted by your local operating system tools (see Figure 13.5).

FIGURE 13.5 Choosing the Folder Upload option works similarly to File Upload; you are prompted for a folder using the client device file system tools.

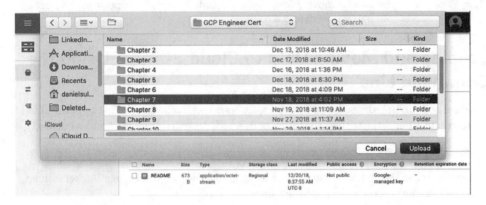

It's easy to move objects between buckets. Just click the three-dot option at the end of a line about an object to display a list of operations, which includes Move. Selecting Move will open a dialog form like that shown in Figure 13.6.

FIGURE 13.6 Objects can be moved by using the move command in the Operations menu.

Buckets / ace-exam-bucket1

	Name	Size	Type	Storage class	Last modified	Public access ⓘ	Encryption ⓘ	Retention expiration date ⓘ	Holds ⓘ	
☐	📁 Chapter 7/	—	Folder	—	—	Per object	—	—	·	⋮
☐	📄 README	673 B	application/octet-stream	Regional	12/20/18, 8:37:55 AM UTC-8	Not public	Google-managed key	—	None	⋮

Edit permissions
Edit metadata
Copy
Move
Rename

Export to Cloud Pub/Sub

When moving an object, you are prompted for a destination bucket and folder, as shown in Figure 13.7.

FIGURE 13.7 When moving an object in the console, you will be prompted for a destination bucket and folder.

Move object

Source
ace-exam-bucket1/README

Destination

📁 ace-exam-bucket1	Browse

◉ Keep source permissions ⓘ
◯ Use default permissions at destination ⓘ

⌄ gsutil equivalent

> You can move objects using the Move operation in the pop-up menu, but you cannot move a folder this way. Move is not an option in the pop-up-menu when selecting a folder.

Loading and Moving Data to Cloud Storage Using the Command Line

Loading and moving data can be done in the command line using the gsutil command.

To create a bucket, use the gsutil mb command; "mb" is short for "make bucket."

```
gsutil mb gs://[BUCKET_NAME]/
```

Keep in mind that bucket names must be globally unique. To create a bucket named ace-exam-bucket1, you would use the following command:

```
gsutil mb gs://ace-exam-bucket1/
```

To upload a file from your local device or a GCP virtual machine (VM), you can use the gsutil cp command to copy files. The command is as follows:

```
gsutil cp [LOCAL_OBJECT_LOCATION] gs://[DESTINATION_BUCKET_NAME]/
```

For example, to copy a file called README.txt from /home/mydir to the bucket ace-exam-bucket1, you'd execute the following command from your client device command line:

```
gsutil cp /home/mydir/README.txt gs://ace-exam-bucket1/
```

Similarly, if you'd like download a copy of your data from a Cloud Storage bucket to a directory on a VM, you could log into the VM using SSH and issue a command such as this:

```
gsutil cp gs://ace-exam-bucket1/README.txt /home/mydir/
```

In this example, the source object is on Cloud Storage, and the target file is on the VM from which you are running the command.

The gsutil tool has a move command; its structure is as follows:

```
gsutil mv gs://[SOURCE_BUCKET_NAME]/[SOURCE_OBJECT_NAME] \
        gs://[DESTINATION_BUCKET_NAME]/[DESTINATION_OBJECT_NAME]
```

To move the README.txt file from ace-exam-bucket1 to ace-exam-bucket2 and keep the same filename, you'd use this command:

```
gsutil mv gs://ace-exam-bucket1/README.txt  gs://ace-exam-bucket2/
```

Importing and Exporting Data

As a Cloud Engineer, you may need to perform bulk data operations, such as importing and exporting data from databases. These operations are done with command-line tools and sometimes the console. We will not look into how to programmatically insert data into databases; that is more of an application developer and database administrator task.

Importing and Exporting Data: Cloud SQL

To export a Cloud SQL database using the console, navigate to the Cloud SQL page of the console to list database instances, as in Figure 13.8.

FIGURE 13.8   Listing of database instances on the Cloud SQL page of the console

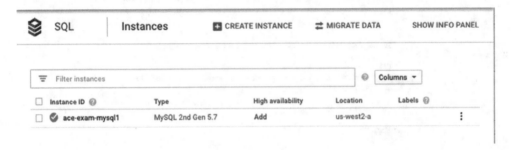

Open the Instance Detail page by double-clicking the name of the instance (see Figure 13.9).

FIGURE 13.9   The Instance Detail page has Import and Export tabs.

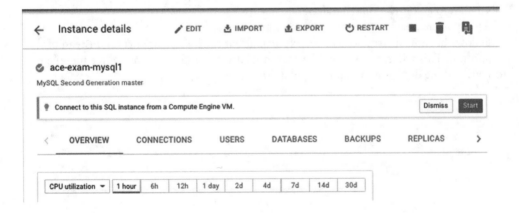

Select the Export tab to show the export database dialog. You will need to specify a bucket to store the backup file (see Figure 13.10).

FIGURE 13.10 Exporting a database requires a bucket to store the export file and a file format specification.

You will also need to choose SQL or CSV output. The SQL output is useful if you plan to import the data to another relational database. CSV is a good choice if you need to move this data into a nonrelational database.

After you create an export file, you can import it.

Follow the same instructions as for exporting, but choose the Import tab instead of the Export tab. This will show a form like that in Figure 13.11. Specify the source file, the file format, and the database to import the data to.

FIGURE 13.11 Importing a database requires a path to the bucket and object storing the export file, a file format specification, and a target database within the instance.

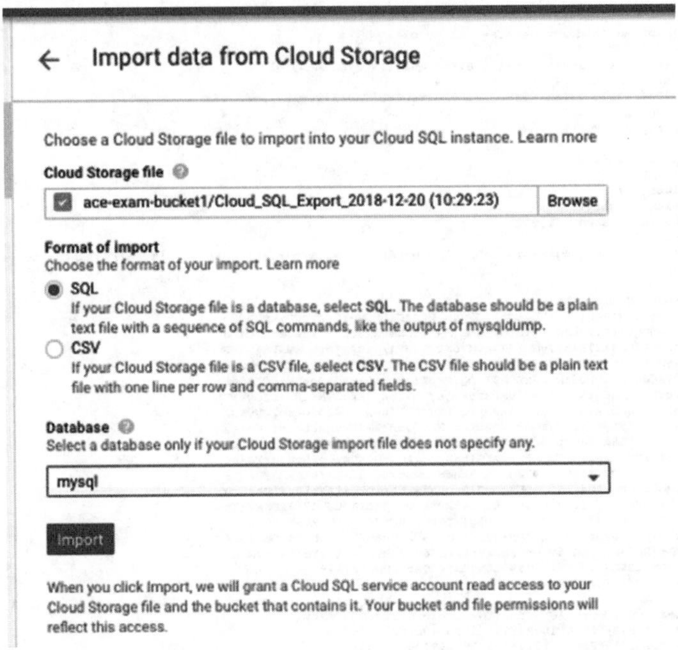

You can also create, import, and export a database using the command line. Use the gsutil command to create a bucket, such as this:

```
gsutil mb gs://ace-exam-bucket1/
```

You need to ensure that the service account can write to the bucket, so get the name of the service account by describing the instance with the following command:

```
gcloud sql instances describe [INSTANCE_NAME]
```

In this example, this command would be as follows:

```
gcloud sql instances describe ace-exam-mysql1
```

This will produce a detailed listing about the instance, including the service account email. See Figure 13.12 for an example of the output.

FIGURE 13.12 Details about a database instance generated by the `gcloud sql instances describe` command

```
$
$gcloud sql instances describe ace-exam-mysql1
backendType: SECOND_GEN
connectionName: phrasal-descent-215901:us-west2:ace-exam-mysql1
databaseVersion: MYSQL_5_7
etag: b37b029e41e738e0028eba63f8e37f3035c234006b770ef599c8289fcc69ea6d
gceZone: us-west2-a
instanceType: CLOUD_SQL_INSTANCE
ipAddresses:
- ipAddress: 35.235.110.75
  type: PRIMARY
kind: sql#instance
name: ace-exam-mysql1
project: phrasal-descent-215901
region: us-west2
selfLink: https://www.googleapis.com/sql/v1beta4/projects/phrasal-descent-215901/instances/ace-exam-mysql1
serverCaCert:
  cert: |-
    -----BEGIN CERTIFICATE-----
    MIIDITCCAgmgAwIBAgIBADANBgkqhkiG9w0BAQsFADBIMSMwIQYDVQQDExpHb29n
    bGUgQ2xvdWQgU1FMIFNlcnZlciBDQTEUMBIGA1UEChMLR29vZ2xlLCBJbmMxCzAJ
    BgNVBAYTAlVTMB4XDTE4MTIyMDE4MjQyNVoXDTI4MTIxNzE4MjUyNVowSDEjMCEG
    A1UEAxMaR29vZ2xlIENsb3VkIFNRTCBTZXJ2ZXIgQ0ExFDASBgNVBAoTC0dvb2ds
    ZSwgSW5jMQswCQYDVQQGEwJVUzCCASIwDQYJKoZIhvcNAQEBBQADggEPADCCAQoC
    qgEBAKFcYN3KQFgGgrAVEmUkpu8vKLXt6B+QeTNgN1bZj7KX439N8iHP+vIDy4MY
    irsOWUqimiEWqrR/xzqb4L1qtc8GxJMLFqfrEs+L7P/9GExYg0q8SO4To2vUvBNJ
    RQHwrp9Yxo4cfVAwFnkFPGyrGopgNqHqxiGZWYVdObE88P7VV6S9FDkwqf3Wglgx
    EfseqkpU5ucCyE8RGAgwMpd3/tEAQc+ir/eN9vg6J3KL96LeE5TCnn5WB9oTRUp8
    QfBvhk2HZ/fSUcE4Ez+5JCUlkkso0dXGIMX3/bm+1Qys0LADwvGpP0pHsgrPl/Wg
    YKRiU3XtW+jkG1MTT4JmLfAlOF8CAwEAAaMNMBQwEgYDVR0TAQH/BAgwBgEB/wIB
    ADANBgkqhkiG9w0BAQsFAAOCAQEAcEvQIPhCAh7XVEdriQxvIiAM+1JyzlUA4Kms
    QoPDzMryvjZVs2tad4f6es4H/Lu7az5mGR6kv3K2wBVjpLiJfUJbC7fRfCHM7rXp
    wWvCeeLiGiFFM8GhycvUA3i/yN26UAo5glxIQv01IHPmHrrQsTMORbeFQ0O0HcTl
    9zBKOvH80lp6X1eYGtv/h2wk0ZyMsUYsEf7hLg5O1SOs66/LLSxfhU0TxDhnlGE6
    WD9WJxDZmlRKT/81IO0gd6Y70gSrnxx8ZPw4Mi64QIqRF1s+115uVul1avhwN3U7
    3vhVKlqWDMXzJDGRyLU9qN/A9CYN5aDMvEsGxAQRgubOWHSrTA==
    -----END CERTIFICATE-----
  certSerialNumber: '0'
  commonName: C=US,O=Google\, Inc,CN=Google Cloud SQL Server CA
  createTime: '2018-12-20T18:24:25.497000+00:00'
  expirationTime: '2028-12-17T18:25:25.497000+00:00'
  instance: ace-exam-mysql1
  kind: sql#sslCert
  sha1Fingerprint: 7f5880321db93d5c4cfe952ef3566e2c5e12b6a6
serviceAccountEmailAddress: tnkknzut25bezoq72bjbfmo5hu@speckle-umbrella-30.iam.gserviceaccount.com
settings:
  activationPolicy: ALWAYS
  backupConfiguration:
    binaryLogEnabled: true
    enabled: true
    kind: sql#backupConfiguration
    replicationLogArchivingEnabled: false
    startTime: 06:00
  dataDiskSizeGb: '10'
  dataDiskType: PD_SSD
  ipConfiguration:
    ipv4Enabled: true
  kind: sql#settings
  maintenanceWindow:
    day: 0
    hour: 0
    kind: sql#maintenanceWindow
  pricingPlan: PER_USE
  replicationType: SYNCHRONOUS
  settingsVersion: '1'
  storageAutoResize: true
  storageAutoResizeLimit: '0'
  tier: db-n1-standard-1
state: RUNNABLE
```

With that you can use the gsutil acl ch command to change the access controls on the bucket to allow the service account to access the bucket. That command is as follows:

```
gsutil acl ch -u [SERVICE_ACCOUNT_ADDRESS]:W gs://[BUCKET_NAME]
```

The gsutil acl ch command changes access permissions. The -u parameter specifies the user. The :W option indicates that the user should have write access to the bucket. In our example, the command would be as follows:

```
gsutil acl ch -u tnkknzut25bezoq72bjbfmo5hu@spe-umbra-30.iam.gserviceaccount.com /
:W gs://ace-exam-bucket1
```

Now that the service account has write access to the bucket, you can create an export of a database using this command:

```
gcloud sql export sql [INSTANCE_NAME] gs://[BUCKET_NAME]/[FILE_NAME] \
                      --database=[DATABASE_NAME]
```

For example, the following command will export the MySQL database to a SQL dump file written to the ace-exam-bucket1 bucket:

```
gcloud sql export sql ace-exam-mysql1 \
              gs://ace-exam-buckete1/ace-exam-mysqlexport.sql \
              --database=mysql
```

If you prefer to export to a CSV file, you would change sql to csv in the above command. Here's an example:

```
gcloud sql export csv ace-exam-mysql1 gs://ace-exam-buckete1/ace-exam-mysql-export.csv \
                      --database=mysql
```

Importing to a database uses a similarly structured command.

```
gcloud sql import sql [INSTANCE_NAME] gs://[BUCKET_NAME]/[IMPORT_FILE_NAME] \
                      --database=[DATABASE_NAME]
```

Using the example database, bucket, and export file, you can import the file using this command:

```
gcloud sql import sql ace-exam-mysql1 gs://ace-exam-buckete1/ace-exam-mysql-export.sql \
                      --database=mysql
```

Importing and Exporting Data: Cloud Datastore

Importing and exporting data from Datastore is done through the command line. Datastore uses a namespace data structure to group entities that are exported. You will need to specify the name of the namespace used by the entities you are exporting. The default namespace is simply (default).

The Cloud Datastore export command is as follows:

```
gcloud datastore export --namespaces="(default)" gs://${BUCKET}
```

You can export to a bucket called ace-exam-datastore1 using this command:

```
gcloud datastore export --namespaces="(default)" gs://ace-exam-datastore1
```

The Cloud Datastore import command is as follows:

```
gcloud datastore import gs://${BUCKET}/[PATH]/[FILE].overall_export_metadata
```

The export process will create a folder named ace-exam-datastore1 using the data and time of the export. The folder will contain a metadata file and a folder containing the exported data. The metadata filename will use the same date and time used for the containing folder. The data folder will be named after the namespace of the exported Datastore database. An example import command is as follows:

```
gcloud datastore import gs://ace-exam-datastore1/2018-12-20T19:13:55_64324/
2018-12-20T19:13:55_64324.overall_export_metadata
```

Importing and Exporting Data: BigQuery

BigQuery users can export and import tables using Cloud Console and the command line.

To export a table using the console, navigate to the BigQuery console interface. Under Resources, open the data set containing the table you want to export. Click the table name to list the table description, as shown in Figure 13.13. Notice the Export option in the upper right.

FIGURE 13.13 Detailed list of a BigQuery table

At the far right, click Export to display a list of two export locations: Google Cloud Storage or Data Studio, which is an analysis tool in GCP (see Figure 13.14).

FIGURE 13.14   Choosing a target location for a BigQuery export

Selecting Cloud Storage displays a form like the one shown in Figure 13.15. Enter the bucket name to store the export file. Choose a file format. The options are CSV, Avro, and JSON. Choose a compression type. The options are None or Gzip for CSV and "deflate" and "snappy" for Avro.

File Formats

BigQuery offers several export file options. CSV, short for "comma-separated values," is a human-readable format suitable for small data sets that will be imported into tools that only support the CSV format. CSV is not optimized for storage, so it does not compress or use a more efficient encoding than text. It's not the best option when exporting large data sets.

JSON is also a human-readable format that has similar advantages and disadvantages to CSV. One difference is that JSON includes schema information with each record, while CSV uses an optional header row with column names at the beginning of the file to describe the schema.

Gzip is a widely used lossless compression utility.

Avro is a compact binary format that supports complex data structures. When data is saved in the Avro format, a schema is written to the file along with data. Schemas are defined in JSON. Avro is a good option for large data sets, especially when importing data into other applications that read the Avro format, including Apache Spark, which is available as a managed service in Cloud Dataproc. Avro files can be compressed using either the deflate or snappy utilities. Deflate produces smaller compressed files, but snappy is faster.

FIGURE 13.15   Specifying the output parameters for a BigQuery export operation

Export table to Google Cloud Storage

Select GCS location: ⓘ

| ☑ ace-exam-bucket2/ace-exam-bigquery-export | Browse |

Export format: **Compression:**

| CSV ▾ | None ▾ |

To export data from the command line, use the bq extract command. The structure is as follows:

```
bq extract --destination_format [FORMAT] --compression [COMPRESSION_TYPE]
--field_delimiter [DELIMITER] --print_header [BOOLEAN] [PROJECT_ID]:[DATASET].
[TABLE] gs://[BUCKET]/[FILENAME]
```

Here's an example:

```
bq extract --destination_format CSV --compression GZIP 'mydataset.mytable'
gs://example-bucket/myfile.zip
```

Remember, the command-line tool for working with BigQuery is bq, not gcloud.

To import data into BigQuery, navigate to the BigQuery console page and select a data set you'd like to import data into. Click a data set and then select the Create Table tab, as shown in Figure 13.16.

FIGURE 13.16   When viewing a data set, you have the option to create a table.

The Create Table form takes several parameters, including an optional source table, a destination project, the dataset name, the table type, and the table name (see Figure 13.17).

FIGURE 13.17   Creating a table in BigQuery

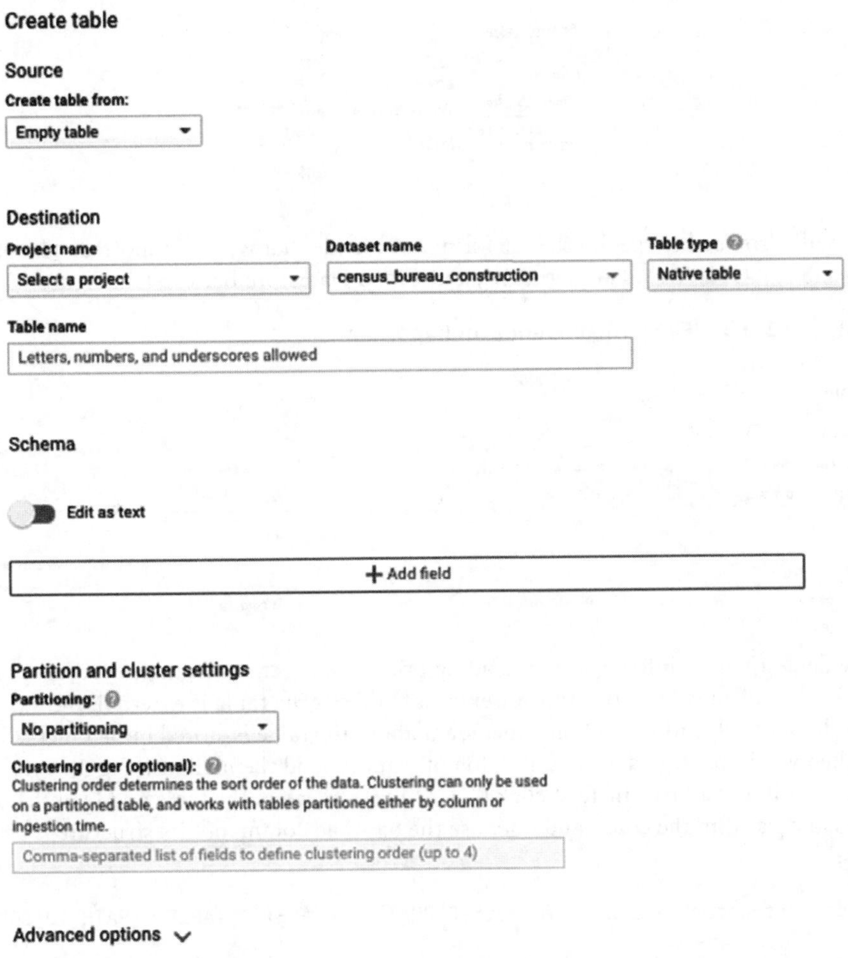

Create table

Source

Create table from:

Empty table ▾

Destination

Project name	Dataset name	Table type ⓘ
Select a project ▾	census_bureau_construction ▾	Native table ▾

Table name

Letters, numbers, and underscores allowed

Schema

◖ **Edit as text**

➕ Add field

Partition and cluster settings

Partitioning: ⓘ

No partitioning ▾

Clustering order (optional): ⓘ
Clustering order determines the sort order of the data. Clustering can only be used on a partitioned table, and works with tables partitioned either by column or ingestion time.

Comma-separated list of fields to define clustering order (up to 4)

Advanced options ⌄

The Create Table From field indicates where to find the source data, if any. This provides a way to create a table based on data in an existing table, but defaults to an empty table (see Figure 13.18).

FIGURE 13.18 Data can be imported from multiple kinds of locations.

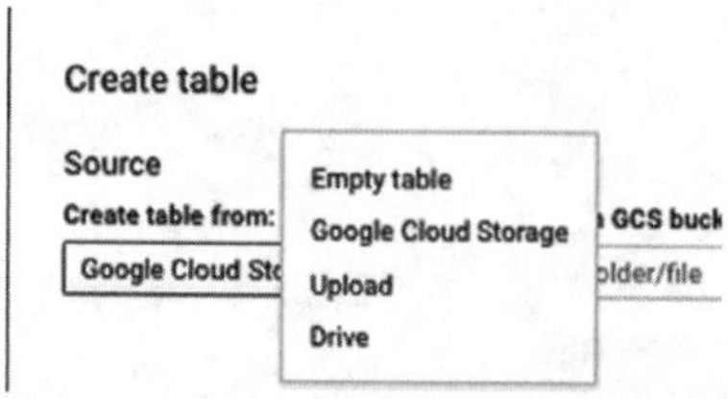

You will also need to specify the file format of the file that will be imported. The options include CSV, JSON, Avro, Parquet, PRC, and Cloud Datastore Backup (see Figure 13.19).

FIGURE 13.19 File format options for importing

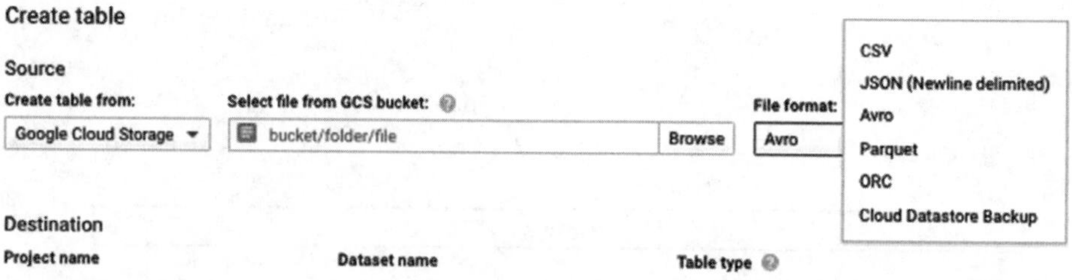

Provide destination information, including project, dataset name, table type, and table name. Table type may be native type or external table. If the table is external, the data is kept in the source location, and only metadata about the table is stored in BigQuery. This is used when you have large data sets and do not want to load them all into BigQuery.

After specifying all parameters, click Create Table to create the table and load the data.

To load data from the command line, use the bq load command. Its structure is as follows:

```
bq load --autodetect --source_format=[FORMAT] [DATASET].[TABLE] [PATH_TO_SOURCE]
```

The --autodetect parameter has bq load automatically detect the table schema from the source file. An example command is as follows:

```
bq load --autodetect --source_format=CSV mydataset.mytable gs://ace-exam-biquery/mydata.csv
```

Importing and Exporting Data: Cloud Spanner

Cloud Spanner users can import and export data using Cloud Console.

To export data from Cloud Spanner, navigate to the Cloud Spanner section of the console. You will see a list of Spanner instances, as shown in Figure 13.20.

FIGURE 13.20   Listing of Spanner instances

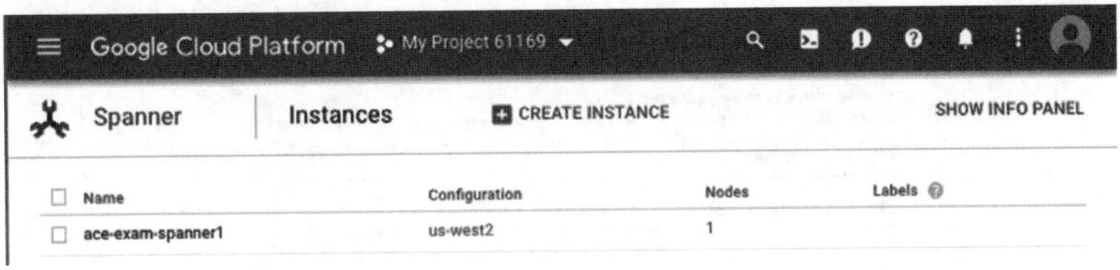

Click the name of the instance that is the source of data to export. This will show the Instance Detail page (see Figure 13.21).

FIGURE 13.21   Details of Spanner instance, with Import and Export tabs

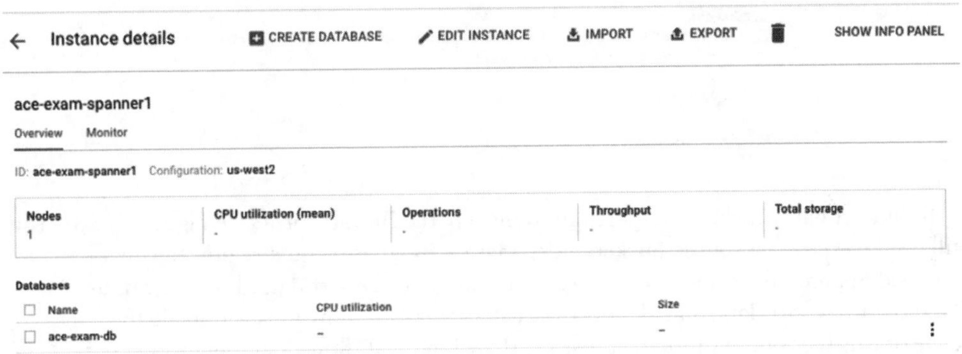

Click Export to show the Export form, as shown in Figure 13.22. You will need to enter a destination bucket, the database to export, and a region to run the job. Notice, you need to confirm that there will be charges for running Cloud Dataflow, and there may be data egress charges for data sent between regions.

FIGURE 13.22 Export form for Cloud Spanner

← **Export data from ace-exam-spanner1**

Use this workflow to export data from a Cloud Spanner database into a Google Cloud Storage bucket. Your database will export in the form of a folder containing Apache Avro files. Learn more

Before you get started: Cloud Spanner exports use multiple Cloud Platform products. Make sure you have the required permissions and/or quota in Cloud Spanner, Cloud Storage, Compute Engine, and Cloud Dataflow.

Choose where to store your export
Select a Cloud Storage bucket or folder to contain your export. Or enter a path manually.

| 📁 bucket/folder/ | Browse |

Choose a database to export
Select a Cloud Spanner database to export into your Cloud Storage bucket.

| Select a database ▾ |

Choose a region for the export job
This Cloud Spanner instance configuration is in **us-west2**. To avoid network egress charges, choose a region that overlaps with the configuration of this instance. Learn more

| Select a region ▾ |

Confirm charges
☐ I understand that this export will incur Cloud Dataflow charges at the standard rate, as well as possible network egress charges.

⌄ Pricing info

[Export] [Cancel]

To import data, click the Import tab to display the Import form (see Figure 13.23). You will need to specify a source bucket, a destination database, and a region to run a job.

Cloud Spanner does not have a `gcloud` command to export data, but you can use Dataflow to export data. The details of constructing Dataflow jobs is outside the scope of this section. For more details, see the Cloud Dataflow documentation at https://cloud.google.com/dataflow/docs/.

FIGURE 13.23   Import form for Cloud Spanner

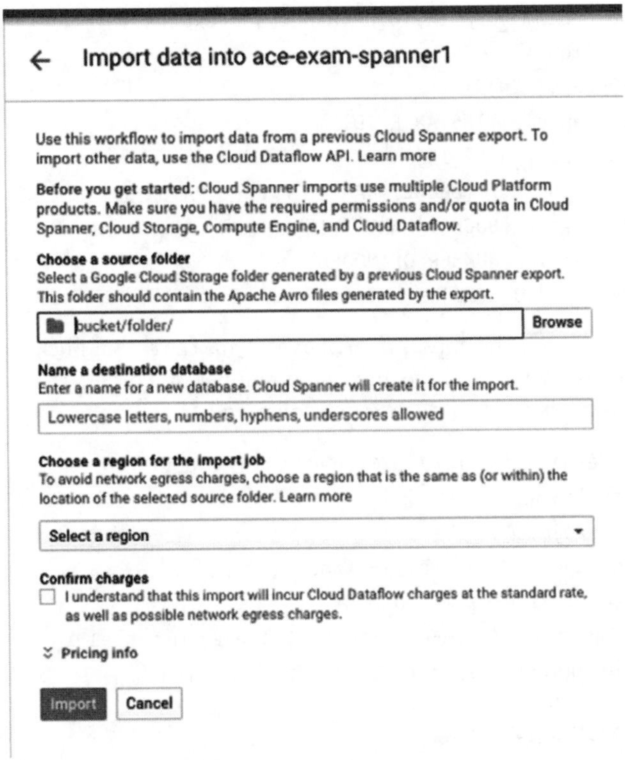

Importing and Exporting Data: Cloud Bigtable

Unlike other GCP databases, Cloud Bigtable does not have an Export and Import option in the Cloud Console or in gcloud. You have two other options: using a Java application for importing and exporting or using the HBase interface to execute HBase commands. The HBase commands are not included in Google documentation and will not be described in detail here. For more information, see the HBase documentation at https://hbase. apache.org/book.html/.

To export a Bigtable table, you will need to download a JAR file, which is a compiled program for the Java VM. The command to download the file is as follows:

```
curl -f -O http://repo1.maven.org/maven2/com/google/cloud/bigtable/bigtable-
beam-import/1.6.0/bigtable-beam-import-1.6.0-shaded.jar
```

To execute the export program, issue a command in the form of the following:

```
java -jar bigtable-beam-import-1.6.0-shaded.jar export \
    --runner=dataflow \
    --project=[PROJECT_ID] \
    --bigtableInstanceId=[INSTANCE_ID] \
    --bigtableTableId=[TABLE_ID] \
    --destinationPath=gs://[BUCKET_NAME]/[EXPORT_PATH] \
    --tempLocation=gs://[BUCKET_NAME]/[TEMP_PATH] \
    --maxNumWorkers=[10x_NUMBER_OF_NODES] \
    --zone=[DATAFLOW_JOB_ZONE]
```

You will need to specify the appropriate project_id, table_id, bucket information, a zone to run the Dataflow job, and the maximum number of workers to dedicate the export. The following is an example of the export command:

```
java -jar bigtable-beam-import-1.6.0-shaded.jar export \
    --runner=dataflow \
    --project=my-project \
    --bigtableInstanceId=ace-exam-instance \
    --bigtableTableId=ace-exam-table1 \
    --destinationPath=gs://ace-exam-bucket1/ace-exam-table1 \
    --tempLocation=gs://my-export-bucket/jar-temp \
    --maxNumWorkers=30 \
                  --zone=us-west2-a
```

To import data, you can use the same JAR file, but you will need to specify import instead of export in the command. There are some changes to the parameters, too, which are explained next. The import command structure is as follows:

```
java -jar bigtable-beam-import-1.6.0-shaded.jar import \
    --runner=dataflow \
    --project=[PROJECT_ID] \
    --bigtableInstanceId=[INSTANCE_ID] \
    --bigtableTableId=[TABLE_ID] \
    --sourcePattern='gs://[BUCKET_NAME]/[EXPORT_PATH]/part-*' \
    --tempLocation=gs://[BUCKET_NAME]/[TEMP_PATH] \
    --maxNumWorkers=[3x_NUMBER_OF_NODES] \
    --zone=[DATAFLOW_JOB_ZONE]
```

In addition to the parameters specified in the export command, the import command takes parameters to describe filename patterns that describe the files to import. Bigtable exports can be large enough to require multiple files to store all the data. You will also need to specify a bucket that can be used for temporary storage during the import.

The following is an example of the `import` command:

```
java -jar bigtable-beam-import-1.6.0-shaded.jar import \
    --runner=dataflow \
    --project=my-project \
    --bigtableInstanceId= ace-exam-instance \
    --bigtableTableId= ace-exam-table1 \
    --sourcePattern='gs://my-export-bucket/my-table/part-*' \
    --tempLocation=gs://my-export-bucket/jar-temp \
    --maxNumWorkers=10 \
    --zone=us-west2-a
```

Importing and Exporting Data: Cloud Dataproc

Cloud Dataproc is not a database like Cloud SQL or Bigtable; rather, it is a data analysis platform. These platforms are designed more for data manipulation, statistical analysis, machine learning, and other complex operations than for data storage and retrieval. Cloud Dataproc is not designed to be a persistent store of data. For that you should use Cloud Storage or persistent disks to store the data files you want to analyze.

Cloud Dataproc does have Import and Export commands to save and restore cluster configuration data. These commands are available, in beta, using `gcloud`.

To ensure you have access to beta commands in `gcloud`, issue the following command:

```
gcloud components install beta
```

The command to export a Dataproc cluster configuration is as follows:

```
gcloud beta dataproc clusters export [CLUSTER_NAME] --destination=[PATH_TO_EXPORT_FILE]
```

An example is as follows:

```
gcloud beta dataproc clusters export ace-exam-dataproc-cluster
--destination=gs://ace-exam-bucket1/mydataproc.yaml
```

To import a configuration file, use the `import` command:
```
gcloud beta dataproc clusters import [SOURCE_FILE]
```

For example, to import the file created in the previous export example, you could use the following:

```
gcloud beta dataproc clusters import gs://ace-exam-bucket1/mydataproc.yaml
```

Importing and exporting data are common operations. GCP provides console and command-line tools for most database services. There are also beta commands for exporting and importing cluster configuration data for Dataproc.

Streaming Data to Cloud Pub/Sub

So far in this chapter you have spent most of your time on moving data into and around Cloud Storage, along with importing and exporting data to databases. Let's now turn your attention to working with Cloud Pub/Sub, the messaging queue.

As a Cloud Engineer, you may need to create message queues for application developers. Although developers will most likely write services that use Pub/Sub, Cloud Engineers should be able to test Pub/Sub topics and subscriptions. We discussed how to create message queues in Chapter 12. Here our focus will be on creating messages on topics and receiving those messages through subscriptions.

The gcloud pubsub commands you will use are create, publish, and pull. To create a topic, you use the following command:

```
gcloud pubsub topics create [TOPIC_NAME]
```

The command to create a subscription is as follows:

```
gcloud pubsub subscriptions create --topic [TOPIC_NAME] [SUBSCRIPTION_NAME]
```

For example, to create a topic called ace-exam-topic1 and a subscription to that topic called ace-exam-sub1, you can use these commands:

```
gcloud pubsub topics create ace-exam-topic1
gcloud pubsub subscriptions create --topic=ace-exam-topic1 ace-exam-sub1
```

Now, to test whether the message queue is working correctly, you can send data to the topic using the following command:

```
cloud pubsub topics publish [TOPIC_NAME] --message [MESSAGE]
```

and then read that message from the subscription using the following:

```
gcloud pubsub subscriptions pull --auto-ack [SUBSCRIPTION_NAME]
```

To write a message to the topic and read it from the subscription you just created, you can use the following:

```
gcloud pubsub topics publish ace-exam-topic1 --message "first ace exam message"
gcloud pubsub subscriptions pull --auto-ack ace-exam-sub1
```

Real World Scenario

Decoupling Services Using Message Queues

One of the challenges with distributed systems is that sometimes one service cannot keep up with the inflow of data. This can create a backlog in services that depend on the lagging service.

For example, a sudden spike in traffic on a retail site may put a high load on an inventory tracking service, which updates inventory as customers add or remove items from their baskets. The inventory program may be slow to respond to a service that added an item to the cart. If that service is waiting for a response from the inventory service, it too will be delayed. This kind of synchronous communication is problematic when distributed systems are under load.

A better option is to decouple the direct connection between services. For example, the user interface could write a message to a Pub/Sub topic each time an item is added or removed from a customer's basket. The inventory management service can subscribe to this topic and update the inventory system as new messages come in. If the inventory system slows down, it will not affect the user interface because it is writing to a Pub/Sub topic, which can scale along with the load generated by the user interface.

Summary

In this chapter, you looked at the different ways you can load data into storage, database, and message queue systems. Cloud Storage is organized around objects in buckets. The gsutil command and Cloud Console can be used to upload data as well as move it between buckets. You saw that the gsutil cp command can be used to copy files between Cloud Storage and VMs.

The database services provide import and export utilities. Some, such as Cloud SQL and BigQuery, make these services available from both Cloud Console and the command line. Others, like Bigtable and Cloud Dataproc, have command-line options only.

Cloud Pub/Sub can be used to decouple applications and improve resiliency to spikes in load. You saw how to create a topic and subscriptions and how to push data to the message queue, where it can be read by subscribers.

Know that Cloud Spanner uses the Dataflow service for importing and exporting. There can be additional charges when using Dataflow and moving data between regions. There is no gcloud command for importing or exporting Cloud Spanner databases.

Exam Essentials

Know how to load data into and move data around Cloud Storage. Cloud Storage is widely used for a variety of use cases, including long-term storage and archiving, file transfers, and data sharing. Understand the structure of gsutil commands, which is different from gcloud. gsutil commands start with gsutil followed by an operation, such as copy or make bucket. Be sure to know the syntax of the copy (cp), move (mv), and make bucket (mb) commands. You can copy files from Cloud Storage to VMs, and vice versa. Also, know that the gsutil acl ch -u command is used to change permissions on objects.

Understand how import and export work with Cloud SQL. Importing and exporting data from databases are common operations. You can use the gsutil acl ch command to change permissions on a Cloud Storage bucket. You can perform imports and exports from the console and from the command line.

Know that you can export entities from a Cloud Datastore. Exports and imports are done at the level of namespaces. There isn't a Cloud Console option for exporting and importing from Datastore.

Understand how to export and import data from BigQuery. BigQuery has a range of options for the source of data to import. Data can be compressed when exported to save on space. BigQuery can export data in multiple formats, including CSV, JSON, and Avro. Know that the bq command is used for importing and exporting from the command line.

Remember that Bigtable and Cloud Dataproc are different from other import and export functions. Bigtable does not have a console or command-line feature to import or export data. A Java program is run from the command line to import or export data from Bigtable. Cloud Dataproc is different in that it is not designed as a persistent data store. It is a data analysis tool. When you export from Dataproc, you are exporting the cluster configuration, not data in the cluster.

Know that Pub/Sub is used to send messages between services. Pub/Sub allows for greater resiliency to fluctuations in load. If one service lags, its work can accumulate in a Pub/Sub queue without forcing the service that generates that data to wait.

Review Questions

You can find the answers in the Appendix.

1. Which of the following commands is used to create buckets in Cloud Storage?

   A. `gcloud storage buckets create`

   B. `gsutil storage buckets create`

   C. `gsutil mb`

   D. `gcloud mb`

2. You need to copy files from your local device to a bucket in Cloud Storage. What command would you use? Assume you have Cloud SDK installed on your local computer.

   A. `gsutil copy`

   B. `gsutil cp`

   C. `gcloud cp`

   D. `gcloud storage objects copy`

3. You are migrating a large number of files from a local storage system to Cloud Storage. You want to use the Cloud Console instead of writing a script. Which of the following Cloud Storage operations can you perform in the console?

   A. Upload files only

   B. Upload folders only

   C. Upload files and folders

   D. Compare local files with files in the bucket using the `diff` command

4. A software developer asks for your help exporting data from a Cloud SQL database. The developer tells you which database to export and which bucket to store the export file in, but hasn't mentioned which file format should be used for the export file. What are the options for the export file format?

   A. CSV and XML

   B. CSV and JSON

   C. JSON and SQL

   D. CSV and SQL

5. A database administrator has asked for an export of a MySQL database in Cloud SQL. The database administrator will load the data into another relational database and would to do it with the least amount of work. Specifically, the loading method should not require the database administrator to define a schema. What file format would you recommend for this task?

   A. SQL

   B. CSV

   C. XML

   D. JSON

6. Which command will export a MySQL database called `ace-exam-mysql1` to a file called `ace-exam-mysql-export.sql` in a bucket named `ace-exam-bucket1`?

   A. `gcloud storage export sql ace-exam-mysql1 gs://ace-exam-bucket1/ace-exam-mysql-export.sql \ --database=mysql`

   B. `gcloud sql export ace-exam-mysql1 gs://ace-exam-bucket1/ace-exam-mysql-export.sql \ --database=mysql`

   C. `gcloud sql export sql ace-exam-mysql1 gs://ace-exam-bucket1/ace-exam-mysql-export.sql \ --database=mysql`

   D. `gcloud sql export sql ace-exam-mysql1 gs://ace-exam-mysql-export.sql/ace-exam-bucket1/ \ --database=mysql`

7. As part of a compliance regimen, your team is required to back up data from your Datastore database to an object storage system. Your data is stored in the default namespace. What command would you use to export the default namespace from Datastore to a bucket called `ace-exam-bucket1`?

   A. `gcloud datastore export --namespaces="(default)" gs://ace-exam-bucket1`

   B. `gcloud datastore export --namespaces="(default)" ace-exam-bucket1`

   C. `gcloud datastore dump --namespaces="(default)" gs://ace-exam-bucket1`

   D. `gcloud datastore dump --namespaces="(default)" ace-exam-bucket1`

8. As required by your company's policy, you need to back up your Datastore database at least once per day. An auditor is questioning whether or not Datastore export is sufficient. You explain that the Datastore export command produces what outputs?

   A. A single entity file

   B. A metadata file

   C. A metadata file and a folder with the data

   D. A metadata file, an entity file, and a folder with the data

9. Which of the following file formats is not an option for an export file when exporting from BigQuery?

   A. CSV

   B. XML

   C. Avro

   D. JSON

10. Which of the following file formats is not supported when importing data into BigQuery?

    A. CSV

    B. Parquet

    C. Avro

    D. YAML

11. You have received a large data set from an Internet of Things (IoT) system. You want to use BigQuery to analyze the data. What command-line command would you use to make data available for analysis in BigQuery?

   A. `bq load --autodetect --source_format=[FORMAT] [DATASET].[TABLE] [PATH_TO_SOURCE]`

   B. `bq import --autodetect --source_format=[FORMAT] [DATASET].[TABLE] [PATH_TO_SOURCE]`

   C. `gloud BigQuery load --autodetect --source_format=[FORMAT] [DATASET]. [TABLE] [PATH_TO_SOURCE]`

   D. `gcloud BigQuery load --autodetect --source_format=[FORMAT] [DATASET]. [TABLE] [PATH_TO_SOURCE]`

12. You have set up a Cloud Spanner process to export data to Cloud Storage. You notice that each time the process runs you incur charges for another GCP service, which you think is related to the export process. What other GCP service might be incurring charges during the Cloud Spanner export?

   A. Dataproc

   B. Dataflow

   C. Datastore

   D. bq

13. As a developer on a project using Bigtable for an IoT application, you will need to export data from Bigtable to make some data available for analysis with another tool. What would you use to export the data, assuming you want to minimize the amount of effort required on your part?

   A. A Java program designed for importing and exporting data from Bigtable

   B. `gcloud bigtable table export`

   C. `bq bigtable table export`

   D. An import tool provided by the analysis tool

14. You have just exported from a Dataproc cluster. What have you exported?

   A. Data in Spark DataFrames

   B. All tables in the Spark database

   C. Configuration data about the cluster

   D. All tables in the Hadoop database

15. A team of data scientists has requested access to data stored in Bigtable so that they can train machine learning models. They explain that Bigtable does not have the features required to build machine learning models. Which of the following GCP services are they most likely to use to build machine learning models?

   A. Datastore

   B. Dataflow

   C. Dataproc

   D. DataAnalyze

16. The correct command to create a Pub/Sub topic is which of the following?

    A. `gcloud pubsub topics create`

    B. `gcloud pubsub create topics`

    C. `bq pubsub create topics`

    D. `cbt pubsub topics create`

17. Which of the following commands will create a subscription on the topic ace-exam-topic1?

    A. `gcloud pubsub create --topic=ace-exam-topic1 ace-exam-sub1`

    B. `gcloud pubsub subscriptions create --topic=ace-exam-topic1`

    C. `gcloud pubsub subscriptions create --topic=ace-exam-topic1 ace-exam-sub1`

    D. `gsutil pubsub subscriptions create --topic=ace-exam-topic1 ace-exam-sub1`

18. What is one of the direct advantages of using a message queue in distributed systems?

    A. It increases security.

    B. It decouples services, so if one lags, it does not cause other services to lag.

    C. It supports more programming languages.

    D. It stores messages until they are read by default.

19. To ensure you have installed beta `gcloud` commands, which command should you run?

    A. `gcloud components beta install`

    B. `gcloud components install beta`

    C. `gcloud commands install beta`

    D. `gcloud commands beta install`

20. What parameter is used to tell BigQuery to automatically detect the schema of a file on import?

    A. `--autodetect`

    B. `--autoschema`

    C. `--detectschema`

    D. `--dry_run`

21. The compression options deflate and snappy are available for what file types when exporting from BigQuery?

    A. Avro

    B. CSV

    C. XML

    D. Thrift

Chapter

14

Networking in the Cloud: Virtual Private Clouds and Virtual Private Networks

THIS CHAPTER COVERS THE FOLLOWING OBJECTIVES OF THE GOOGLE ASSOCIATE CLOUD ENGINEER CERTIFICATION EXAM:

✓ **2.4** Planning and configuring network resources

✓ **4.5** Managing networking resources

In this chapter we turn our attention to networking, starting with virtual private clouds (VPCs). You will learn how to create VPCs with default and custom subnets. You'll learn about creating custom network configurations in Compute Engine for cases when default network configurations do not meet your needs. Next, we will show how to configure firewall rules and create virtual private networks (VPNs).

Creating a Virtual Private Cloud with Subnets

VPCs are software versions of physical networks that link resources in a project. GCP automatically creates a VPC when you create a project. You can create additional VPCs and modify the VPCs created by GCP.

VPCs are global resources, so they are not tied to a specific region or zone. Resources, such as Compute Engine virtual machines (VMs) and Kubernetes Engine clusters, can communicate with each other, assuming traffic is not blocked by a firewall rule.

VPCs contain subnetworks, call *subnets*, which are regional resources. Subnets have a range of IP addresses associated with them. Subnets provide private internal addresses. Resources use these addresses to communicate with each other and with Google APIs and services.

In addition to VPCs associated with projects, you can create a shared VPC within an organization. The shared VPC is hosted in a common project. Users in other projects who have sufficient permissions can create resources in the shared VPC. You can also use VPC peering for interproject connectivity, even if an organization is not defined.

In this section, you will create a VPC with subnets using Cloud Console and gcloud, and then turn your attention to creating a shared VPC.

Creating a Virtual Private Cloud with Cloud Console

To create a VPC in Cloud Console, navigate to the VPC page, as shown in Figure 14.1.

Clicking Create VPC opens the form to create a VPC, as shown in Figure 14.2. Figure 14.2 shows that you can assign a name and description to a new VPC. It also shows a list of subnets that will be created in the VPC. When a VPC is created, subnets are created in each region. GCP chooses a range of IP addresses for each subnet when creating an auto mode network.

FIGURE 14.1   The VPC section of the Cloud Console

Name ∧	Region	Subnets	Mode	IP addresses ranges	Gateways	Firewall Rules	Global dynamic routing	Flow logs
default		18	Auto ▾			4	Off	
	us-central1	default		10.128.0.0/20	10.128.0.1			Off
	europe-west1	default		10.132.0.0/20	10.132.0.1			Off
	us-west1	default		10.138.0.0/20	10.138.0.1			Off
	asia-east1	default		10.140.0.0/20	10.140.0.1			Off
	us-east1	default		10.142.0.0/20	10.142.0.1			Off
	asia-northeast1	default		10.146.0.0/20	10.146.0.1			Off
	asia-southeast1	default		10.148.0.0/20	10.148.0.1			Off
	us-east4	default		10.150.0.0/20	10.150.0.1			Off
	australia-southeast1	default		10.152.0.0/20	10.152.0.1			Off

FIGURE 14.2   Form to create a VPC in Cloud Console, part 1

← **Create a VPC network**

Name ⓘ

ace-exam-vpc1

Description (Optional)

Example VPCX

Subnets

Subnets let you create your own private cloud topology within Google Cloud. Click
Automatic to create a subnet in each region, or click Custom to manually define the
subnets. Learn more

Subnet creation mode

Custom | **Automatic**

⚠ These IP address ranges will be assigned to each region in your VPC
network. When an instance is created for your VPC network, it will be
assigned an IP from the appropriate region's address range.

<< Previous | 1 | 2 | Next >>

Region	IP address range
us-central1	10.128.0.0/20
europe-west1	10.132.0.0/20
us-west1	10.138.0.0/20
asia-east1	10.140.0.0/20
us-east1	10.142.0.0/20
asia-northeast1	10.146.0.0/20
asia-southeast1	10.148.0.0/20
us-east4	10.150.0.0/20
australia-southeast1	10.152.0.0/20
europe-west2	10.154.0.0/20

<< Previous | 1 | 2 | Next >>

Alternatively, you can create one or more custom subnets by selecting the Custom tab in the Subnet section (Figure 14.3). This displays another form that allows you to specify a region and an IP address range. The IP range is specified in classless inter-domain routing (CIDR) notation. (See the sidebar "CIDR Notation Overview" on page 342 for details on how to specify IP address using that notation.) You can turn off Private Google Access. That allows VMs on the subnet to access Google services without assigning an external IP address to the VM. You can also turn on logging of network traffic by setting the Flow Logs option to on.

FIGURE 14.3   Creating a custom subnet

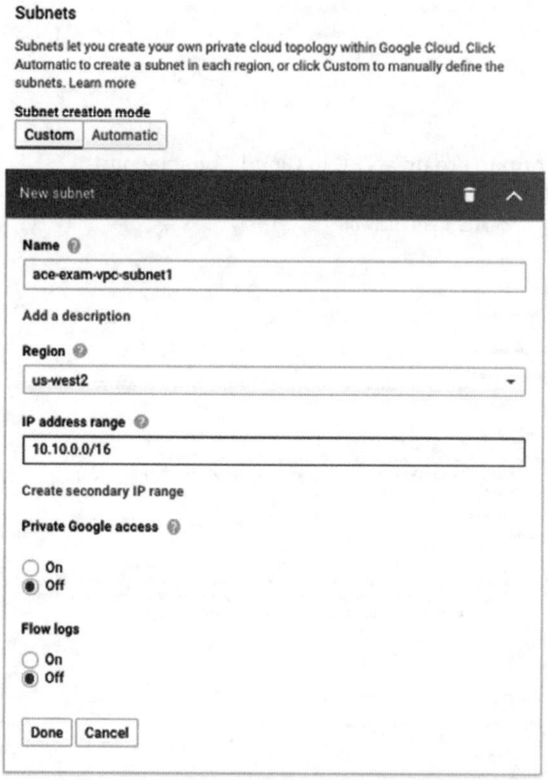

Subnets

Subnets let you create your own private cloud topology within Google Cloud. Click Automatic to create a subnet in each region, or click Custom to manually define the subnets. Learn more

Subnet creation mode

| Custom | Automatic |

New subnet

Name ⓘ

ace-exam-vpc-subnet1

Add a description

Region ⓘ

us-west2

IP address range ⓘ

10.10.0.0/16

Create secondary IP range

Private Google access ⓘ

○ On
⦿ Off

Flow logs

○ On
⦿ Off

| Done | Cancel |

Figure 14.4 shows the second part of the VPC form, which includes firewall rules, dynamic routing setting, and a DNS server policy. The Firewall Rules section lists rules that can be applied to the VPC. In the example in Figure 14.4, the rule allows ingress, which is incoming TCP traffic on port 22, to allow for SSH access. The IP range of 0.0.0.0/0 allows traffic from all source IP addresses.

FIGURE 14.4   Form to create a VPC in Cloud Console, part 2

Firewall rules ⊘
Select any of the firewall rules below that you would like to apply to this VPC network.
Once the VPC network is created, you can manage all firewall rules on the Firewall rules page.

☐ Name	Type	Targets	Filters	Protocols / ports	Action	Priority
☐ ace-exam-vpc1-allow-icmp ⊘	Ingress	Apply to all	IP ranges: 0.0.0.0/0	icmp	Allow	65534
☐ ace-exam-vpc1-allow-internal ⊘	Ingress	Apply to all	IP ranges: 10.128.0.0/9	all	Allow	65534
☐ ace-exam-vpc1-allow-rdp ⊘	Ingress	Apply to all	IP ranges: 0.0.0.0/0	tcp:3389	Allow	65534
☑ ace-exam-vpc1-allow-ssh ⊘	Ingress	Apply to all	IP ranges: 0.0.0.0/0	tcp:22	Allow	65534
ace-exam-vpc1-deny-all-ingress ⊘	Ingress	Apply to all	IP ranges: 0.0.0.0/0	all	Deny	65535
ace-exam-vpc1-allow-all-egress ⊘	Egress	Apply to all	IP ranges: 0.0.0.0/0	all	Allow	65535

Dynamic routing mode ⊘
⦿ Regional
   Cloud Routers will learn routes only in the region in which they were created
◯ Global
   Global routing lets you dynamically learn routes to and from all regions with a single
   VPN or interconnect and Cloud Router

DNS server policy (Optional)

No server policy ▾

The dynamic routing option determines what routes are learned. Regional routing will have Google Cloud Routers learn routes within the region. Global routing will enable Google Cloud Routers to learn routes on all subnetworks in the VPC.

The optional DNS server policy lets you choose a DNS policy that enables DNS name resolution provided by GCP or makes changes to name resolution order. (See Chapter 15 for more details.)

Once you have specified the parameters and created a VPC, it will appear in the VPC listing and show information about the VPC and its subnets, as shown in Figure 14.5.

FIGURE 14.5   Listing of VPCs and subnets

VPC networks   ⊞ CREATE VPC NETWORK   ↻ REFRESH

Name ∧	Region	Subnets	Mode	IP addresses ranges
ace-exam-vpc1		1	Custom	
	us-west2	ace-exam-vpc-subnet1		10.10.0.0/16
default		18	Auto ▾	
	us-central1	default		10.128.0.0/20
	europe-west1	default		10.132.0.0/20
	us-west1	default		10.138.0.0/20

Creating a Virtual Private Cloud with gcloud

The gcloud command to create a VPC is gcloud compute networks create. For example, to create a VPC in the default project with automatically generated subnets, you would use the following command:

```
gcloud compute networks create ace-exam-vpc1 --subnet-mode=auto
```

You can also configure custom subnets by creating a VPC network specifying the custom option and then creating subnets in that VPC. The first command to create a custom VPC called ace-exam-vpc1 is as follows:

```
gcloud compute networks create ace-exam-vpc1 --subnet-mode=custom
```

Next, you can create a subnet using the gcloud compute networks subnet create command. This command requires that you specify a VPC, the region, and the IP range. You can optionally turn on the Private Google Access and Flow Logs settings by adding the appropriate flags.

Here is an example command to create a subnet called ace-exam-vpc-subnet1 in the ace-exam-vpc1 VPC. This subnet is created in the us-west2 region with an IP range of 10.10.0.0/16. The Private IP Access and Flow Logs settings are turned on.

```
gcloud beta compute networks subnets create ace-exam-vpc-subnet1 --network=ace-
exam-vpc1 --region=us-west2 --range=10.10.0.0/16 --enable-private-ip-google-
access --enable-flow-logs
```

Understanding CIDR Notation

When you specify ranges of IP addresses, you use something called *classless inter-domain routing* (CIDR). The name stems from early IP networks that were defined into three fixed classes: A, B, and C. A classless network address structure was created to overcome the limitations of a class-based routing structure, particularly the lack of flexibility in creating different-sized subnets.

CIDR uses variable-length subnet masking (VLSM) to allow network administrators to define networks with the number of addresses that they need, not the fixed number that were allocated to the older class model interdomain routine.

CIDR addresses consist of two sets of numbers, a network address for identifying a subnet and a host identifier. These numbers are written out using CIDR notation, which consists of a network address and a network mask. Example network addresses, according to the RFC1918 specification are:

    10.0.0.0

    172.16,0.0

    192.168.0.0

CIDR notation adds a slash (/) and a number indicating how many bits of an IP address to allocate to the network mask, which determines which addresses are within the block of the address and which are not.

For example, 192.168.0.0/16 means that 16 bits of the 32 bits of an IP address are used to specify the network, and 16 bits are used to specify the host address. With 16 bits, you can create 2^{16} or 65,536 addresses.

The CIDR block 172.16.0.0/12 indicates that 12 bits are used for specifying the network, and 20 bits are used to specify host addresses. With 20 bits, you can create up to 1,048,576 addresses. In general, the smaller the number after the slash, the more addresses are available. You can experiment with CIDR block options using a CIDR calculator such as the one at www.subnet-calculator.com/cidr.php.

Creating a Shared Virtual Private Cloud Using gcloud

If you want to create a shared VPC, you can use the gcloud command gcloud compute shared-vpc.

Before executing commands to create a shared VPC, you will need to assign an org member the Shared VPC Admin role at the organization level or the folder level. To assign the Shared VPC Admin role, which uses the descriptor roles/compute.xpnAdmin, you would issue this command:

```
gcloud organizations add-iam-policy-binding [ORG_ID]
    --member='user:[EMAIL_ADDRESS]'
    --role="roles/compute.xpnAdmin"
```

[ORG_ID] is the organization identifier of the organization using the policy. You can find an organization ID with the command gcloud organizations list. If you prefer to assign the Shared VPC Admin role to a folder, you can use this command:

```
gcloud beta resource-manager folders add-iam-policy-binding [FOLDER_ID]
--member='user:[EMAIL_ADDRESS]'
--role="roles/compute.xpnAdmin"
```

[FOLDER_ID] is the identifier of the folder of the policy. You can get folder IDs by using this command:

```
gcloud beta resource-manager folders list --organization=[ORG_ID]
```

For more on roles and privileges, see Chapter 17.

Once you have set the Shared VPC Admin role at the organization level, you can issue the shared-vpc command:

```
gcloud compute shared-vpc enable [HOST_PROJECT_ID]
```

If you are sharing the VPC at the folder level, use this command:

```
gcloud beta compute shared-vpc enable [HOST_PROJECT_ID]
```

Now that the shared VPC is created, you can associate projects using the `gcloud compute shared-vpc associate-projects` command. At the organization level, you can use this command:

```
gcloud compute shared-vpc associated-projects add [SERVICE_PROJECT_ID] \
    --host-project [HOST_PROJECT_ID]
```

At the folder level, the command to associate folders is as follows:

```
gcloud beta compute shared-vpc associated-projects add [SERVICE_PROJECT_ID] \
    --host-project [HOST_PROJECT_ID]
```

Alternatively, VPC peering can be used for interproject traffic when an organization does not exist. VPC peering is implemented using the `gcloud compute networks peerings create` command. For example, you peer two VPCs by specifying peerings on each network. Here's an example:

```
gcloud compute networks peerings create peer-ace-exam-1 \
    --network ace-exam-network-A \
    --peer-project ace-exam-project-B \
    --peer-network ace-exam-network-B \
    --auto-create-routes
```

And then create a peering on the other network using:

```
gcloud compute networks peerings create peer-ace-exam-1 \
    --network ace-exam-network-B \
    --peer-project ace-exam-project-A \
    --peer-network ace-exam-network-A \
    --auto-create-routes
```

This peering will allow private traffic to flow between the two VPCs.

Deploying Compute Engine with a Custom Network

You can deploy a VM with custom network configurations using the console and the command line.

Navigate to the Compute Engine section of the console and open the Create Instance form, like that shown in Figure 14.6.

FIGURE 14.6   Preliminary form to create an instance in Cloud Console

Click Management, Security, Disks, Networking, Sole Tenancy to expand the optional forms and then click the Networking tab to display a form similar to Figure 14.7.

Note that in this form, you can set network tags. Click Add Network Interface to display a form like that shown in Figure 14.8. In this form you can choose a custom network. In this example, we are choosing ace-exam-vpc1, which we created earlier in the chapter. We also select a subnet in that form.

FIGURE 14.7   Networking configuration form

FIGURE 14.8   Form to add a custom network interface

From this form, you can also specify a static IP address or choose a custom ephemeral address using the Primary Internal IP setting. The External IP drop-down allows you to have an ephemeral external IP.

You can also create an instance to run in a particular subnet using the gcloud compute instances create command with Subnet and Zone parameters.

```
gcloud compute instances create [INSTANCE_NAME] --subnet [SUBNET_NAME] --zone
[ZONE_NAME]
```

Creating Firewall Rules for a Virtual Private Cloud

Firewall rules are defined at the network level and used to control the flow of network traffic to VMs.

Firewall rules allow or deny a kind of traffic on a port; for example, a rule may allow TCP traffic to port 22. They also are applied to traffic in one direction, either incoming (ingress) or outgoing (egress) traffic. It is important to note that the firewall is stateful which means if traffic is allowed in one direction and a connection established, it is allowed in the other direction. Firewalls rulesets are stateful so if a connection is allowed, like establishing a SSH connection on port 22, then all later traffic matching this rule is permitted as long as the connection is active. An active connection is one with at least one packet exchanged every ten minutes.

Structure of Firewall Rules

Firewall rules consist of several components:

- **Direction:** Either ingress or egress.
- **Priority:** Highest-priority rules are applied; any rule with a lower priority that matches are not applied. Priority is specified by an integer from 0 to 65535. 0 is the highest priority, and 65535 is lowest.
- **Action:** Either allow or deny. Only one can be chosen.
- **Target:** An instance to which the rule applies. Targets can be all instances in a network, instances with particular network tags, or instances using a specific service account.
- **Source/destination:** Source applies to ingress rules and specifies source IP ranges, instances with particular network tags, or instances using a particular service account. You can also use combinations of source IP ranges and network tags and combinations of source IP ranges and service accounts used by instances. The IP address 0.0.0.0/0 indicates any IP address. The Destination parameter uses only IP ranges.
- **Protocol and port:** A network protocol such as TCP, UDP, or ICMP and a port number. If no protocol is specified, then the rule applies to all protocols.
- **Enforcement status:** Firewall rules are either enabled or disabled. Disabled rules are not applied even if they match. Disabling is sometimes used to troubleshoot problems with traffic getting through when it should not or not getting through when it should.

All VPCs start with two implied rules: One allows egress traffic to all destinations (IP address 0.0.0.0/0), and one denies all incoming traffic from any source (IP address 0.0.0.0/0). Both implied rules have priority 65535, so you can create other rules with higher deny or allow traffic as you need. You cannot delete an implied rule.

When a VPC is automatically created, the default network is created with four network rules. These rules allow the following:

- Incoming traffic from any VM instance on the same network
- Incoming TCP traffic on port 22, allowing SSH
- Incoming TCP traffic on port 3389, allowing Microsoft Remote Desktop Protocol (RDP)
- Incoming Internet Control Message Protocol (ICMP) from any source on the network

The default rules all have priority 65534.

Creating Firewall Rules Using Cloud Console

To create or edit firewall rules, navigate to the VPC section of the console and select the Firewall option from the VPC menu (see Figure 14.9).

FIGURE 14.9 List of firewall rules in the VPC section of Cloud Console

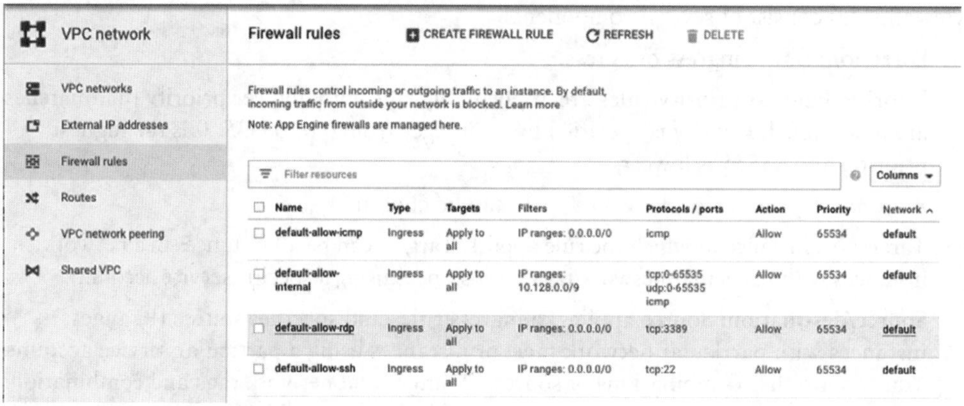

Click Create Firewall Rule to create a new firewall rule. This shows a form similar to Figure 14.10.

In this form, you specify a name and description of the firewall rule. You can choose to turn logging on or off. If it is on, logging information will be captured in Stackdriver. (See Chapter 18 for more on Stackdriver logging.) You also need to specify the network in the VPC to apply the rule to.

FIGURE 14.10   Create firewall rule form

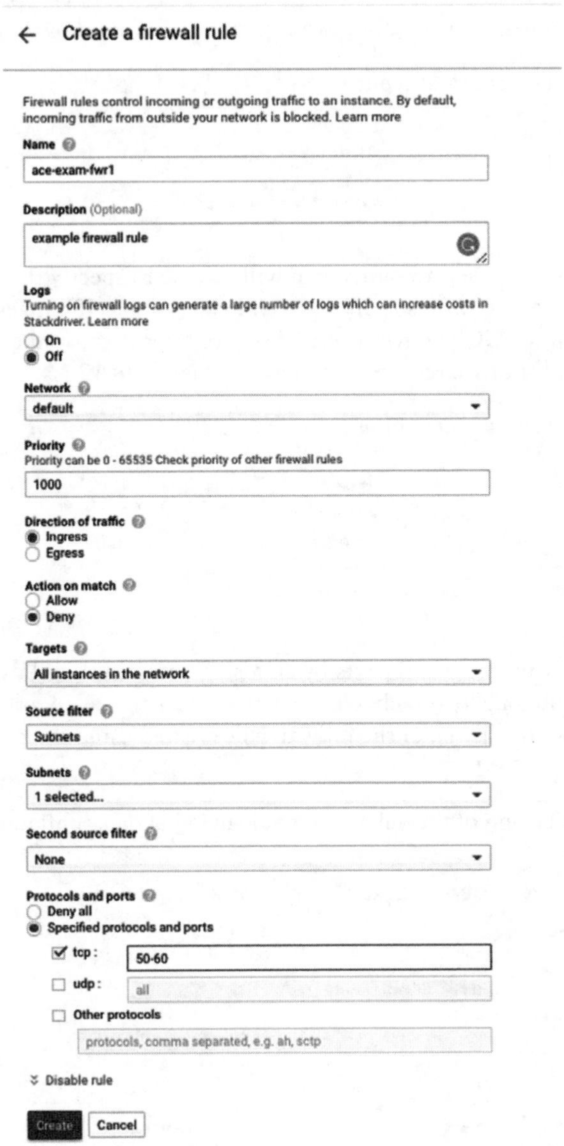

← **Create a firewall rule**

Firewall rules control incoming or outgoing traffic to an instance. By default, incoming traffic from outside your network is blocked. Learn more

Name ⊘

ace-exam-fwr1

Description (Optional)

example firewall rule

Logs
Turning on firewall logs can generate a large number of logs which can increase costs in Stackdriver. Learn more
○ On
⦿ Off

Network ⊘

default   ▾

Priority ⊘
Priority can be 0 - 65535 Check priority of other firewall rules

1000

Direction of traffic ⊘
⦿ Ingress
○ Egress

Action on match ⊘
○ Allow
⦿ Deny

Targets ⊘

All instances in the network   ▾

Source filter ⊘

Subnets   ▾

Subnets ⊘

1 selected...   ▾

Second source filter ⊘

None   ▾

Protocols and ports ⊘
○ Deny all
⦿ Specified protocols and ports
  ☑ tcp :   50-60
  ☐ udp :   all
  ☐ Other protocols
           protocols, comma separated, e.g. ah, sctp

⊻ Disable rule

[Create] Cancel

Next, you will need to specify a priority, direction, action, targets, and sources. Priority can be integers in the range from 0 to 65535. Direction can be ingress or egress. Action can be allow or deny. Targets are chosen from a drop-down list; the options are shown in Figure 14.11.

FIGURE 14.11   List of target types

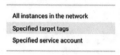

If you choose tags or service accounts, you will be able to specify the tags or the name of the service account. You can also specify source filters as either IP ranges, subnets, source tags, or service accounts. GCP allows a second source filter if you'd like to use a combination of conditions. A list of source filters is shown in Figure 14.12.

FIGURE 14.12   List of source filter types

Finally, you specify protocol and ports by choosing between the Allow All and Specified Protocols and Ports options. If you choose the latter, you can specify protocols and ports.

Figure 14.13 shows the listing of the firewall rule created using the parameters specified in Figure 14.10.

FIGURE 14.13   Listing of firewall rule created using earlier configuration

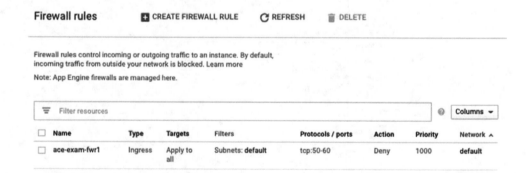

Creating Firewall Rules Using gcloud

The command for working with firewall rules from the command line is gcloud compute firewall-rules. With this command, you can create, delete, describe, update, and list firewall rules.

There are a number of parameters used with gcloud compute firewall-rules create:

- --action
- --allow
- --description
- --destination-ranges
- --direction
- --network
- --priority
- --source-ranges
- --source-service-accounts
- --source-tags
- --target-service-accounts
- --target-tags

For example, to allow all TCP traffic on ports 20000 to 25000, use this:

```
gcloud compute firewall-rules create ace-exam-fwr2 --network ace-exam-vpc1
--allow tcp:20000-25000
```

Creating a Virtual Private Network

VPNs allow you to securely send network traffic from the Google network to your own network. You can create a VPN using Cloud Console or the command line.

Creating a Virtual Private Network Using Cloud Console

To create a VPN using Cloud Console, navigate to the Hybrid Connectivity section of the console, as shown in Figure 14.14.

FIGURE 14.14   Hybrid Connectivity section of Cloud Console

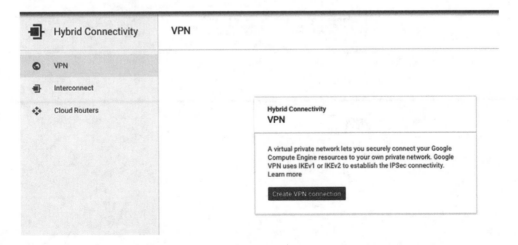

Click Create VPN Connection to display the form shown in Figure 14.15.

FIGURE 14.15   Create a VPN connection form

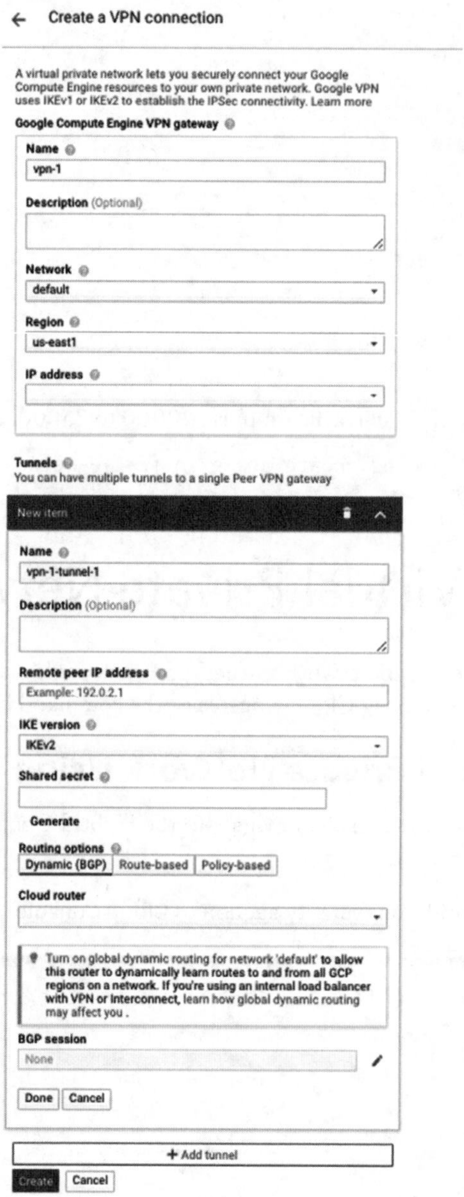

In this form, you specify a name and description of the VPN. In the section labeled Google Compute Engine VPN Gateway, you configure the GCP end of the VPN connection. This includes specifying a network, the region containing the network, and a static IP address. If you have not created an IP address, you create one by selecting Create IP Address from the drop-down menu for the IP Address parameter. It will display a dialog like the one in Figure 14.16.

FIGURE 14.16   Creating a static IP address

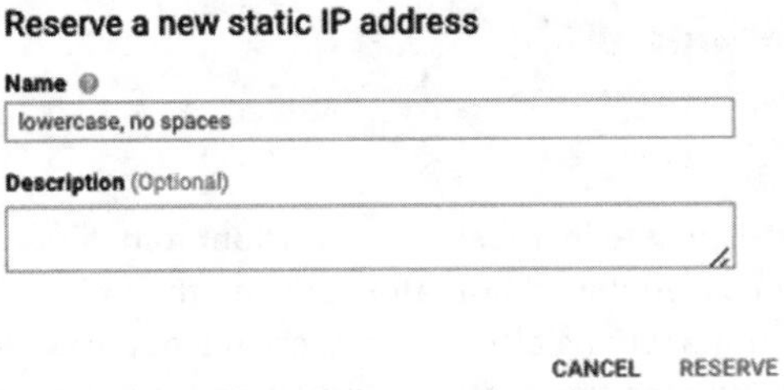

Reserve a new static IP address

Name ❓

lowercase, no spaces

Description (Optional)

CANCEL   RESERVE

In the Tunnels section, you configure the other network endpoint in the VPN. You specify a name, description, and IP address of the VPN gateway on your network. You can specify which version of the Internet Key Exchange (IKE) protocol to use. You will have to specify a shared secret, which is a secret string of characters, which your browser can create for you if you click Generate. You will need this shared secret when configuring your VPN endpoint.

In the Routing Options section, you can choose Dynamic, Route-Based, or Policy-Based Routing.

Dynamic routing uses the BGP protocol to learn routes in your networks. You will need to select or create a cloud router. If you have not created one, you can select Create Cloud Router from the drop-down list in the Cloud Router parameter. This will display a form like Figure 14.17.

FIGURE 14.17   Creating a cloud router

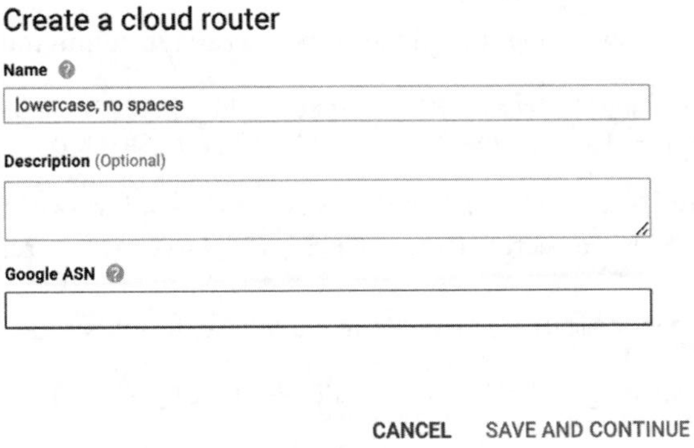

Create a cloud router

Name ❓

lowercase, no spaces

Description (Optional)

Google ASN ❓

CANCEL   SAVE AND CONTINUE

In that form, provide a name and description. You'll also need to specify a private autonomous system number (ASN) used by the BGP protocol. The ASN is a number in the range 64512–65534 or 4000000000–4294967294. Each cloud router you create will need a unique ASN.

If you choose route-based routing, you will need to enter the IP ranges of the remote network. If you choose policy-based routing, you will need to enter remote IP ranges, local subnetworks that will use the VPN, and local IP ranges.

 Real World Scenario

Analytics in the Cloud

Data science and data analysis are increasingly important to businesses. To derive insights from these practices, you need both the data and the tools. Data about customers, sales, and other kinds of transactions are often stored in a database in a company's data center. The tools analysts want to use, such as Spark and machine learning services, are readily available in the cloud. Many organizations have security practices to protect data and would not allow an analyst, for example, to download some data and then copy it over an unsecure Internet connection to the cloud. Instead, network and cloud engineers would create a VPN between the company's data center and GCP. This would ensure that network traffic between the data center and the cloud is encrypted. Analysts get access to the data and tools they need, and the information security professionals in the organization are able to protect the confidentiality and integrity of the data.

Creating a Virtual Private Network Using gcloud

To create a VPN at the command line, you can use these three commands:

- gcloud compute target-vpn-gateways
- gcloud compute forwarding-rule
- gcloud compute vpn-tunnels

The format of the gcloud compute target-vpn-gateways command is as follows:

```
gcloud compute vpn-tunnels create NAME --peer-address=PEER_ADDRESS --shared-
secret=SHARED_SECRET --target-vpn-gateway=TARGET_VPN_GATEWAY
```

NAME is the name of the tunnel. PEER_ADDRESS is the IPv4 address of the remote tunnel endpoint. SHARED_SECRET is a secret string. TARGET_VPN_GATEWAY is a reference to the target VPN gateway IP.

The format of gcloud compute forwarding-rule is as follows:

```
gcloud compute forwarding-rules create NAME --TARGET_SPECIFICATION=VPN_GATEWAY
```

NAME is the name of the forwarding rule. TARGET_SPECIFICATION is one of several target types, including target-instance, target-http-proxy, and --target-vpn-gateway. For additional details, see the documentation at https://cloud.google.com/sdk/gcloud/reference/compute/forwarding-rules/create.

The format of the gcloud compute vpn-tunnels command is as follows:

```
gcloud compute vpn-tunnels create NAME --peer-address=PEER_ADDRESS --shared-
secret=SHARED_SECRET --target-vpn-gateway=TARGET_VPN_GATEWAY
```

NAME is the name of the VPN tunnel, PEER_ADDRESS is the IPv4 address of the remote tunnel, SHARED_SECRET is a secret string, and TARGET_VPN_GATEWAY is a reference to a VPN gateway.

Summary

This chapter reviewed how to create VPCs and VPNs. VPCs define networks in the Google Cloud to link your GCP resources. VPNs in GCP are used to link your GCP networks to your internal networks. We discussed how to create VPCs, shared VPCs, and subnets. There was a description of CIDR notation. You also learned how to configure VMs with custom network connections. Next we reviewed firewall rules and how to create them. The chapter concluded with discussing the steps required to create a VPN.

Exam Essentials

Know that VPCs are logical data centers in the cloud and VPNs are secure connections between your VPC subnets and your internal network.   Your cloud resources are in a VPC. VPCs have subnets and routing rules for routing traffic between subnets. You control the flow of traffic using firewall rules.

Know that VPCs create subnets in each region when in auto mode.   You can create additional subnets. Each subnet has a range of IP addresses. Firewall rules are applied to subnets, also called networks. Routers can be configured to learn just regional routes or global routes.

Understand how to read and calculate CIDR notation.   CIDR notation represents a subnet mask and the size of available IP address in the IP range. The smaller the subnet mask size, which is the number after the slash in a CIDR block, the more IP addresses are available. The format of the CIDR address is an IP address followed by a slash, followed by the size of the subnet mask, for example 10.0.0.0/8.

Know that VPCs can be created using gcloud commands.   A VPC can be created with gcloud compute networks create. A shared VPC can be created using gcloud beta compute shared-vpc. Shared VPCs can be shared at the network or folder level. You will need to bind identity and access management (IAM) policies at the organizational or folder level to enable Shared VPC Admin roles. VPC peering can be used for interproject connectivity.

Understand that you can add network interfaces to a VM.   You can configure these interfaces to use a particular subnet. You can assign ephemeral or static IP addresses.

Know that firewall rules control the flow of network traffic.   Firewall rules consist of direction, priority, action, target, source/destination, protocols and port, and enforcement status. Firewall rules are applied to a subnet.

Know how to create a VPN with Cloud Console.   VPNs route traffic between your cloud resources and your internal network. VPNs include gateways, forwarding rules, and tunnels.

Review Questions

You can find the answers in the Appendix.

1. Virtual private clouds have a _____ scope.

   A. Zonal

   B. Regional

   C. Super-regional

   D. Global

2. You have been tasked with defining CIDR ranges to use with a project. The project includes 2 VPCs with several subnets in each VPC. How many CIDR ranges will you need to define?

   A. One for each VPC

   B. One for each subnet

   C. One for each region

   D. One for each zone

3. The legal department needs to isolate its resources on its own VPC. You want to have network provide routing to any other service available on the global network. The VPC network has not learned global routes. What parameter may have been missed when creating the VPC subnets?

   A. DNS server policy

   B. Dynamic routing

   C. Static routing policy

   D. Systemic routing policy

4. The command to create a VPC from the command line is:

   A. `gcloud compute networks create`

   B. `gcloud networks vpc create`

   C. `gsutil networks vpc create`

   D. `gcloud compute create networks`

5. You have created several subnets. Most of them are sending logs to Stackdriver. One subnet is not sending logs. What option may have been misconfigured when creating the subnet that is not forwarding logs?

   A. Flow Logs

   B. Private IP Access

   C. Stackdriver Logging

   D. Variable-Length Subnet Masking

6. At what levels of the resource hierarchy can a shared VPC be created?

   A. Folders and resources

   B. Organizations and project

   C. Organizations and folders

   D. Folders and subnets

7. You are using Cloud Console to create a VM that you want to exist in a custom subnet you just created. What section of the Create Instance form would you use to specify the custom subnet?

   A. Networking tab of the Management, Security, Disks, Networking, Sole Tenancy section

   B. Management tab of the Management, Security, Disks, Networking, Sole Tenancy section

   C. Sole Tenancy tab of Management, Security, Disks, Networking, Sole Tenancy

   D. Sole Tenancy tab of Management, Security, Disks, Networking

8. You want to implement interproject communication between VPCs. Which feature of VPCs would you use to implement this?

   A. VPC peering

   B. Interproject peering

   C. VPN

   D. Interconnect

9. You want to limit traffic to a set of instances. You decide to set a specific network tag on each instance. What part of a firewall rule can reference the network tag to determine the set of instances affected by the rule?

   A. Action

   B. Target

   C. Priority

   D. Direction

10. What part of a firewall rule determines whether a rule applies to incoming or outgoing traffic?

    A. Action

    B. Target

    C. Priority

    D. Direction

11. You want to define a CIDR range that applies to all destination addresses. What IP address would you specify?

    A. 0.0.0.0/0

    B. 10.0.0.0/8

    C. 172.16.0.0/12

    D. 192.168.0.0/16

12. You are using `gcloud` to create a firewall rule. Which command would you use?

   A. `gcloud network firewall-rules create`

   B. `gcloud compute firewall-rules create`

   C. `gcloud network rules create`

   D. `gcloud compute rules create`

13. You are using `gcloud` to create a firewall rule. Which parameter would you use to specify the subnet it should apply to?

   A. `--subnet`

   B. `--network`

   C. `--destination`

   D. `--source-ranges`

14. An application development team is deploying a set of specialized service endpoints and wants to limit traffic so that only traffic going to one of the endpoints is allowed through by firewall rules. The service endpoints will accept any UDP traffic and each endpoint will use a port in the range of 20000–30000. Which of the following commands would you use?

   A. `gcloud compute firewall-rules create fwr1 --allow=udp:20000-30000 --direction=ingress`

   B. `gcloud network firewall-rules create fwr1 --allow=udp:20000-30000 --direction=ingress`

   C. `gcloud compute firewall-rules create fwr1 --allow=udp`

   D. `gcloud compute firewall-rules create fwr1 --direction=ingress`

15. You have a rule to allow inbound traffic to a VM. You want it to apply only if there is not another rule that would deny that traffic. What priority should you give this rule?

   A. 0

   B. 1

   C. 1000

   D. 65535

16. You want to create a VPN using Cloud Console. What section of Cloud Console should you use?

   A. Compute Engine

   B. App Engine

   C. Hybrid Connectivity

   D. IAM & Admin

17. You are using Cloud Console to create a VPN. You want to configure the GCP end of the VPN. What section of the Create VPN form would you use?

    A. Tunnels

    B. Routing Options

    C. Google Compute Engine VPN

    D. IKE Version

18. You want the router on a tunnel you are creating to learn routes from all GCP regions on the network. What feature of GCP routing would you enable?

    A. Global dynamic routing

    B. Regional routing

    C. VPC

    D. Firewall rules

19. When you create a cloud router, what kind of unique identifier do you need to assign for the BGP protocol?

    A. IP address

    B. ASN

    C. Dynamic load routing ID

    D. None of the above

20. You are using `gcloud` to create a VPN. Which command would you use?

    A. `gcloud compute target-vpn-gateways` only

    B. `gcloud compute forwarding-rule` and `gcloud compute target-vpn-gateways` only

    C. `gcloud compute vpn-tunnels` only

    D. `gcloud compute forwarding-rule`, `gcloud compute target-vpn-gateways`, and `gcloud compute vpn-tunnels`

Chapter

15

Networking in the Cloud: DNS, Load Balancing, and IP Addressing

---

THIS CHAPTER COVERS THE FOLLOWING OBJECTIVES OF THE GOOGLE ASSOCIATE CLOUD ENGINEER CERTIFICATION EXAM:

✓ **2.4 Planning and configuring network resources**

✓ **3.5 Deploying and implementing networking resources**

✓ **4.5 Managing network resources**

This chapter continues the focus on networking, specifically configuring the Domain Name System (DNS), load balancing, and managing IP addresses. Cloud DNS is a managed service providing authoritative domain naming services. It is designed for high availability, low latency, and scalability. Load balancing services in Google Cloud Platform (GCP) offer five types of load balancers to address a range of needs. In this chapter, you will see how HTTP(S), SSL Proxy, TCP Proxy, Network TCP/UDP, and Internal TCP/UDP Network differ and when to use each. Cloud engineers should also be familiar with managing IP addresses, in particular managing Classless Inter-Domain Routing (CIDR) blocks and understanding how to reserve IP addresses. This chapter, in combination with Chapter 14, provides an overview of the networking topics covered on the Associate Cloud Engineer exam.

Configuring Cloud DNS

Cloud DNS is a Google service that provides domain name resolution. At the most basic level, DNS services map domain names, such as example.com, to IP addresses, such as 35.20.24.107. A managed zone contains DNS records associated with a DNS name suffix, such as aceexamdns1.com. DNS records contain specific details about a zone. For example, an A record maps a hostname to IP addresses in IPv4. AAAA records are used in IPv6 to map names to IPv6 addresses. CNAME records hold the canonical name, which contains alias names of a domain. In this section, you will learn how to configure DNS services in GCP, which consists of creating zones and adding records.

Creating DNS Managed Zones Using Cloud Console

To create a managed zone using Cloud Console, navigate to the Network Services section of the console. Click Cloud DNS. This displays a form like that in Figure 15.1.

Click Create Zone to display a form like the one shown in Figure 15.2.

First, select a zone type, which can be public or private.

Public zones are accessible from the Internet. These zones provide name servers that respond to queries from any source. Private zones provide name services to your GCP resources, such as virtual machines (VMs) and load balancers. Private zones respond only to queries that originate from resources in the same project as the zone.

In the form, provide a zone name and description. Specify the DNS name, which should be the suffix of a DNS name, such as aceexamdns1.com.

FIGURE 15.1   Network Services Cloud DNS page

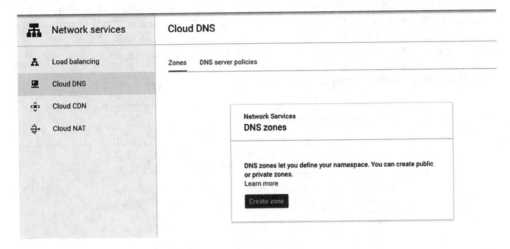

FIGURE 15.2   Create a public DNS zone.

← **Create a DNS zone**

A DNS zone is a container of DNS records for the same DNS name suffix. In Cloud DNS, all records in a managed zone are hosted on the same set of Google-operated authoritative name servers. Learn more

If you don't have a domain yet, purchase one through Google Domains.

Zone type ❔
○ Private
● Public

Zone name ❔

ace-exam-zone1

DNS name ❔

aceexamzone.com

DNSSEC ❔

Off ▼

Description (Optional)

After creating your zone, you can add resource record sets and modify the networks your zone is visible on.

Create   Cancel

You can enable DNSSEC, which is DNS security. It provides strong authentication of clients communicating with DNS services. DNSSEC is designed to prevent spoofing (a client appearing to be some other client) and cache poisoning (a client sending incorrect information to update the DNS server).

If you choose to create a private zone, a form such as Figure 15.3 appears.

FIGURE 15.3 Create a private DNS zone.

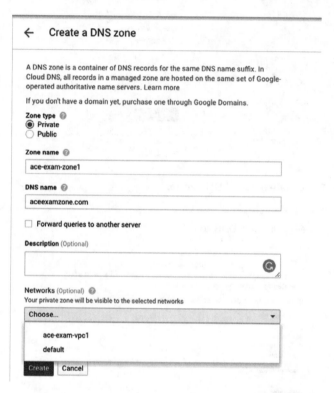

In addition to the parameters set for a public zone, you will need to specify the networks that will have access to the private zone.

After creating zones, the Cloud DNS page will list the zones, as shown in Figure 15.4.

Click the name of a zone to see its details. As shown in Figure 15.5, the zone details include a list of records associated with the zone. When a zone is created, NS and SOA records are added. NS is a *name server* record that has the address of an authoritative server that manages the zone information. SOA is a *start of authority* record, which has authoritative information about the zone. You can add other records, such as A and CNAME records.

FIGURE 15.4   List of DNS zones

FIGURE 15.5   List of records in a DNS zone

To add an A record, click Add Record Set to display a form like that in Figure 15.6.

Select A as a resource record type and specify an IPv4 address of the server that maps domain names to IP addresses for this zone.

The TTL, known as time to live, and TTL Unit parameters specify how long the record can live in a cache. This is the period of time DNS resolvers should cache the data before querying for the value again. DNS resolvers perform lookup operations mapping domain names to IP addresses. If you want to specify multiple IP addresses in the record, click Add Item to add other IP addresses.

FIGURE 15.6 Create an A record set.

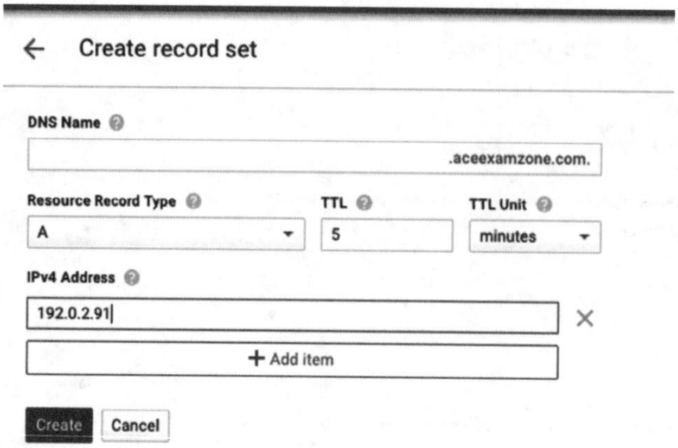

You can also add canonical name records using the Add Record Set form. In this case, select CNAME as the Resource Record Type, as shown in Figure 15.7.

FIGURE 15.7 Create a CNAME record.

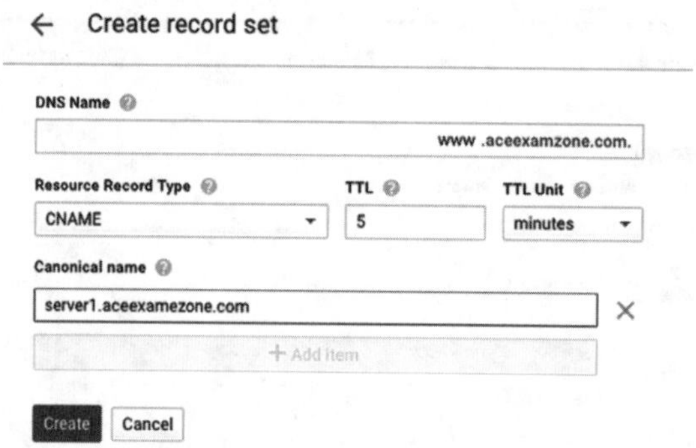

The CNAME record takes a name, or alias, of a server. The DNS name and TTL parameters are the same as in the A record example.

Also, DNS Forwarding is now available, which allows your DNS queries to be passed to an on-premise DNS server if you are using Cloud VPN or Interconnect.

Creating a DNS Managed Zones Using gcloud

To create DNS zones and add records, you will use gcloud beta dns managed-zones and gcloud dns record-sets transaction.

To create a managed public zone called ace-exam-zone1 with the DNS suffix aceexamzone .com, you use this:

```
gcloud beta dns managed-zones create ace-exam-zone1 --description= --dns-
name=aceexamzone.com.
```

To make this a private zone, you add the --visibility parameter set to private.

```
gcloud beta dns managed-zones create ace-exam-zone1 --description= --dns-
name=aceexamzone.com. --visibility=private --networks=default
```

To add an A record, you start a transaction, add the A record information, and then execute the transaction.

Transactions are started with gcloud dns record-sets transaction start. Record sets are added using gcloud dns record-sets transaction add, and transactions are completed using gcloud dns record-sets-transaction execute. Together, the steps are as follows:

```
gcloud dns record-sets transaction start --zone=ace-exam-zone1
gcloud dns record-sets transaction add 192.0.2.91 --name=aceexamzone.com. --ttl=300
--type=A --zone=ace-exam-zone1
gcloud dns record-sets transaction execute --zone=ace-exam-zone1.
```

To create a CNAME record, we would use similar commands:

```
gcloud dns record-sets transaction start --zone=ace-exam-zone1
gcloud dns record-sets transaction add server1.aceexamezone.com. --
name=www2.aceexamzone.com. --ttl=300 --type=CNAME --zone=ace-exam-zone1
gcloud dns record-sets transaction execute --zone=ace-exam-zone1
```

Configuring Load Balancers

Load balancers distribute workload to servers running an application. In this section, we will discuss the different types of load balancers and how to configure them.

Types of Load Balancers

Load balancers can distribute load within a single region or across multiple regions. The several load balancers offered by GCP are characterized by three features:

- Global versus regional load balancing
- External versus internal load balancing
- Traffic type, such as HTTP and TCP

Global load balancers are used when an application is globally distributed. Regional load balancers are used when resources providing an application are in a single region. There are three global load balancers:

- HTTP(S), which balances HTTP and HTTPS load across a set of backend instances
- SSL Proxy, which terminates SSL/TLS connections, which are secure socket layer connections. This type is used for non-HTTPS traffic.
- TCP Proxy, which terminates TCP sessions at the load balancer and then forwards traffic to backend servers.

The regional load balancers are as follows:

- Internal TCP/UDP, which balances TCP/UDP traffic on private networks hosting internal VMs
- Network TCP/UDP, which enables balancing based on IP protocol, address, and port. This load balancer is used for SSL and TCP traffic not supported by the SSL Proxy and TCP Proxy load balancers, respectively.

External load balancers distribute traffic from the Internet, while internal load balancers distribute traffic that originates within GCP. The Internal TCP/UDP load balancer is the only internal load balancer. The HTTP(S), SSL Proxy, TCP Proxy, and Network TCP/UDP load balancers are all external.

You will need to consider the traffic type too when choosing a load balancer. HTTP and HTTPS traffic needs to use external global load balancing. TCP traffic can use external global, external regional, or internal regional load balancers. UDP traffic can use either external regional or internal regional load balancing.

 Real World Scenario

Load Balancing and High Availability

Applications that need to be highly available should use load balancers to distribute traffic and to monitor the health of VMs in the backend. A company offering API access to customer data will need to consider how to scale up and down in response to changes in load and how to ensure high availability.

The combination of instance groups (Chapter 6) and load balancers solves both problems. Instance groups can manage autoscaling, and load balancers can perform health checks. If a VM is not functioning, the health checks will fail and take the failed VM out of rotation for traffic. Users of the API are less likely to get failed response codes when instance groups keep an appropriate number of VMs active and load balancers prevent any traffic from being routed to failed servers.

Configuring Load Balancers Using Cloud Console

To create a load balancer in Cloud Console, navigate to the Network Services section and select Load Balancing, as shown in Figure 15.8.

FIGURE 15.8   Network services, load balancing section

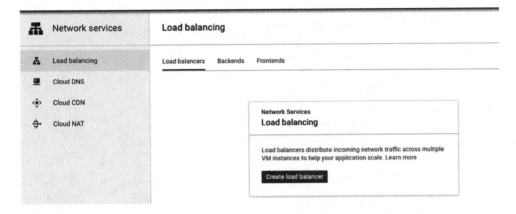

The first step to creating a load balancer is deciding on the type. In this example, you will create a TCP load balancer (see Figure 15.9).

FIGURE 15.9   Create A Load Balancer options

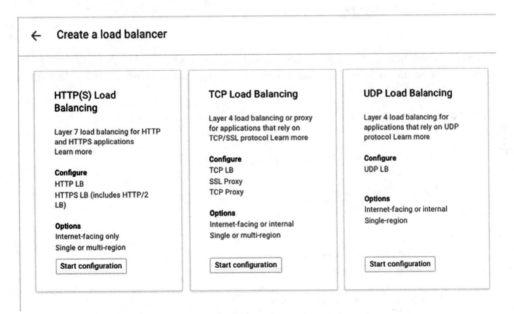

After selecting the TCP load balancer option, a form like Figure 15.10 appears. Select Only Between My VMs for private load balancing. This load balancer will be used in a single region, and you will not offload TCP or SSL processing.

FIGURE 15.10   Creating a TCP balancer

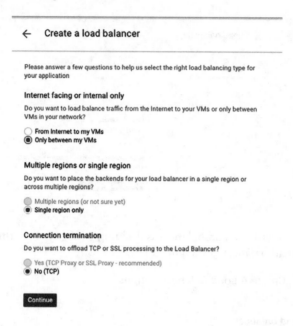

Now, you will begin a three-step process, as shown in Figure 15.11. You will configure the backend and the frontend and then review the configuration before creating the load balancer.

FIGURE 15.11   Three-step process to configure a load balancer

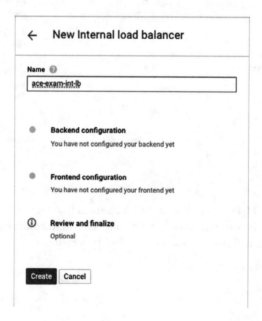

To configure the backend, you specify a name, a region, the network, and the backends. Backends are VMs that will have load distributed to them. In this example, two existing VMs are specified as backends (see Figure 15.12).

FIGURE 15.12   Configuring the backend

Backend configuration

Backend service

Name ⓘ

ace-exam-int-lb

Region ⓘ

us-central1   ▾

Network ⓘ

ace-exam-vpc3   ▾

Protocol: **TCP**

Backends

us-ig1 us-central1-b   ✎

us-ig2 us-central1-c   ✎

+ Add backend

Health check ⓘ

ace-exam-tcp-health-check (TCP)   ▾

port: 80, timeout: 5s, check interval: 5s, unhealthy threshold: 2 attempts

ⓘ The health check probes to your load balanced instances come from
addresses in range 130.211.0.0/22 and 35.191.0.0/16. You need to
manually configure firewall rules to allow these connections later.
Learn more

Session affinity ⓘ

None   ▾

⌄ Advanced configurations

You can configure a health check for the backend. This will bring up a separate form, as shown in Figure 15.13.

FIGURE 15.13   Creating a health check

Name ⊘

| ace-exam-tcp-health-check |

Description (Optional)

| |

| **Protocol** | | **Port** ⊘ |
| TCP | ▾ | 80 |

Port Specification ⊘

| Undefined | ▾ |

Proxy protocol ⊘

| NONE | ▾ |

| **Request** (Optional) ⊘ | **Response** (Optional) ⊘ |
| | |

Health criteria

Define how health is determined: how often to check, how long to wait for a response, and how many successful or failed attempts are decisive

| **Check interval** ⊘ | | **Timeout** ⊘ | |
| 5 | seconds | 5 | seconds |

| **Healthy threshold** ⊘ | | **Unhealthy threshold** ⊘ | |
| 2 | consecutive successes | 2 | consecutive failures |

In the health check, you specify a name, a protocol and port, and a set of health criteria. In this case, you check backends every 5 seconds and will wait for a response for up to 5 seconds. If you have two consecutive periods where the health check fails, then the server will be considered unhealthy and taken out of the load balancing rotation.

Next, you configure the frontend using the form in Figure 15.14. You specify a name, subnetwork, and an internal IP configuration, which in this case is ephemeral (see "Managing IP Addresses" on page 375 for more on types of IP addresses). You also specify the port that will have its traffic forwarded to the backend. In this example, you are forwarding traffic on port 80.

FIGURE 15.14 Configuring the frontend

The last step prior to creating the frontend is to review the configuration, as shown in Figure 15.15.

FIGURE 15.15 Reviewing the load balancer configuration

Review and finalize

Backend

Region: **us-central1** Network: **ace-exam-vpc3** Endpoint protocol: **TCP** Session affinity: **None** Health check: **ace-exam-tcp-health-check**

ˇ Advanced configurations

Instance group ^	Zone	Autoscaling
us-ig1	us-central1-b	Off
us-ig2	us-central1-c	Off

Frontend

Protocol ^	Subnetwork	IP:Ports	Service label ?
TCP	ace-exam-subnet2 (10.128.0.0/20)	AUTOMATIC:80	

After creating the load balancer, you will see the list of existing load balancers in the console (see Figure 15.16).

FIGURE 15.16   Listing of load balancers

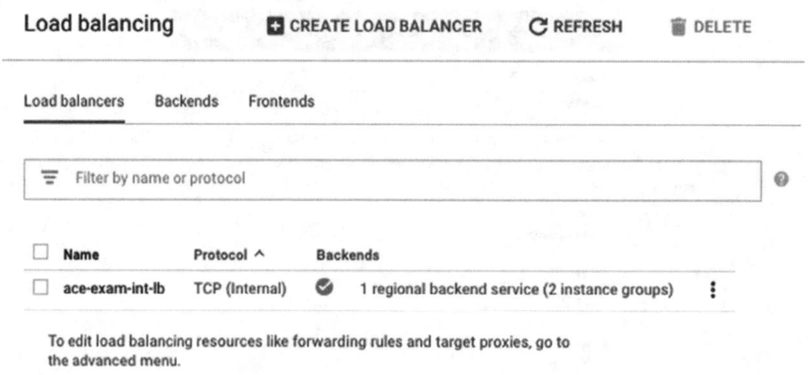

Configuring Load Balancers Using gcloud

In this section, we will review the steps needed to create a network load balancer. These are good options when you need to load balance protocols in addition to HTTP(S).

The gcloud compute forward-rules command is used to forward traffic that matches an IP address to the load balancer.

```
gcloud compute forwarding-rules create ace-exam-lb --port=80
--target-pool ace-exam-pool
```

This command routes traffic to any VM in the ace-exam-pool to the load balancer called ace-exam-lb.

Target pools are created using the gcloud compute target-pools create command. Instances are added to the target pool using the gcloud compute target-pools add-instances command. For example, to add VMs ig1 and ig2 to the target pool called ace-exam-pool, use the following command:

```
gcloud compute target-pools add-instances ace-exam-pool --instances ig1,ig2
```

Managing IP Addresses

The exam topics for the Associate Cloud Engineer certification specifically identifies two IP address–related topics: expanding CIDR blocks and reserving IP addresses.

> It is also important to understand the difference between ephemeral and static IP addresses. Static IP addresses are assigned to a project until they are released. These are used if you need a fixed IP address for a service, such as a website. Ephemeral IP addresses exist only as long as the resource is using the IP address, such as on a VM running an application only accessed by other VMs in the same project. If you delete or stop a VM, ephemeral addresses are released.

Expanding CIDR Blocks

CIDR blocks define a range of IP addresses that are available for use in a subnet. If you need to increase the number of addresses available, for example, if you need to expand the size of clusters running in a subnet, you can use the `gcloud compute networks subnets expand-ip-range` command. It takes the name of the subnet and a new prefix length. The prefix length determines the size of the network mask.

For example, to increase the number of addresses in ace-exam-subnet1 to 65,536, you set the prefix length to 16:

```
gcloud compute networks subnets expand-ip-range ace-exam-subnet1 --prefix-length 16
```

This assumes the prefix length was larger than 16 prior to issuing this command. The `expand-ip-range` command is used only to increase the number of addresses. You cannot decrease them, though. You would have to re-create the subnet with a smaller number of addresses.

Reserving IP Addresses

Static external IP addresses can be reserved using Cloud Console or the command line. To reserve a static IP address using Cloud Console, navigate to the Virtual Private Cloud (VPC) section of the console and select External IP Addresses.

This will display a form like the one shown in Figure 15.17.

FIGURE 15.17   List of reserved static IP addresses

Name	External Address	Region	Type ⌄	Version	In use by	Network Tier ❓	Labels
☐ ace-exam-reserved-static1	35.236.81.240	us-west2	Static	IPv4	⚠ None	Premium	**Change**
–	104.155.128.8	us-central1	Ephemeral ▾	IPv4	VM instance **ig-us-central1-1** (Zone b)		
–	35.184.156.97	us-central1	Ephemeral ▾	IPv4	VM instance **ig-us-central1-2** (Zone b)		
–	35.188.68.150	us-central1	Ephemeral ▾	IPv4	VM instance **ig-us-central1-4** (Zone c)		
–	35.226.112.140	us-central1	Ephemeral ▾	IPv4	VM instance **standalone-instance-1** (Zone b)		
–	35.238.227.246	us-central1	Ephemeral ▾	IPv4	VM instance **ig-us-central1-3** (Zone c)		

External IP addresses   ⊞ RESERVE STATIC ADDRESS   ↻ REFRESH   🗑 RELEASE STATIC ADDRESS   SHOW INFO PANEL

Click Reserve Static Address to display the form to reserve an IP address (see Figure 15.18).

When reserving an IP address, you will need to specify a name and optional description. You may have the option of using the lower-cost Standard service tier for networking, which uses the Internet for some transfer of data. The Premium tier routes all traffic over Google's global network. You will also need to determine whether the address is in IPv4 or IPv6 and whether it's regional or global. You can attach the static IP address to a resource as part of the reservation process, or you can keep it unattached.

Reserved addresses stay attached to a VM when it is not in use and stay attached until released. This is different from ephemeral addresses, which are released automatically when a VM shuts down.

To reserve an IP address using the command line, use the gcloud command gcloud beta compute addresses create. For example, to create a static IP address in the us-west2 region, which uses the Premium tier, use this command:

```
gcloud beta compute addresses create ace-exam-reserved-static1 --region=us-west2
--network-tier=PREMIUM
```

FIGURE 15.18   Reserving a static IP address

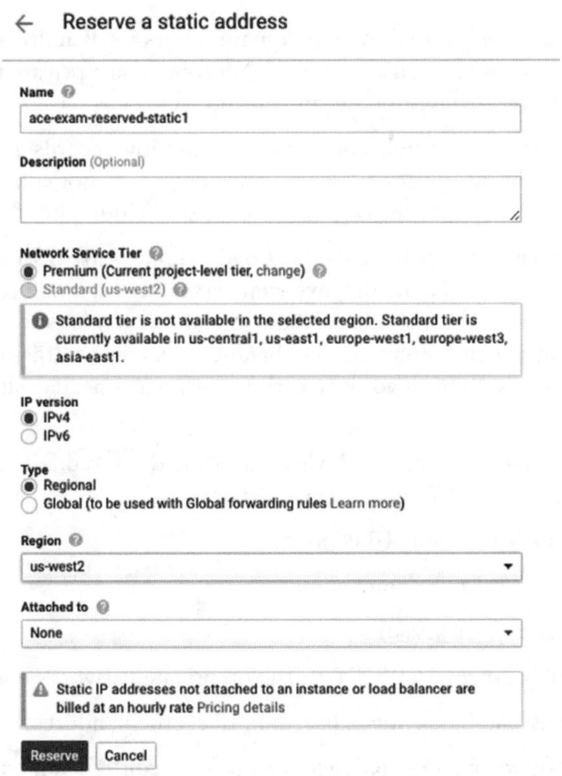

Summary

The Associate Cloud Engineer exam may test your knowledge of Cloud DNS, load balancing, and managing IP addresses. Cloud DNS is an authoritative name service for mapping domain names to IP addresses. You can set up public or private DNS zones. You will also need to be familiar with load balancing and the different types of load balancers. Some load balancers are regional, and some are global. Some are for internal use only, and others support external sources of traffic. The chapter also reviewed how to expand the number of addresses available in a subnet and discussed how to reserve IP addresses.

Exam Essentials

Understand that Cloud DNS is used to map domain names to IP addresses. If you want to support queries from the Internet, use a public DNS zone. Use a private DNS zone only if you want to accept queries from resources in your project.

Know that DNS entries, like example.com, can have multiple records associated with them. The A record specifies the address of a DNS resolver that maps domain names to IP addresses. CNAME records store the canonical name of the domain.

Know how load balancers are distinguished. Load balancers are distinguished based on global versus regional load balancing, external versus internal load balancing, and the protocols supported. Global balancers distribute load across regions, while regional load balancers work within a region. Internal load balancers balance traffic only from within GCP, not external sources. Some load balancers are protocol-specific, such as HTTP and SSL load balancers.

Know the five types of load balancers and when they should be used. The five are: HTTP(S), SSL Proxy, TCP Proxy, Internal TCP/UDP, and Network TCP/UDP.

HTTP(S) balances HTTP and HTTPS load.

SSL Proxy terminates SSL/TLS connections.

TCP Proxy terminates TCP sessions.

Internal TCP/UDP balances TCP/UDP traffic on private networks hosting internal VMs

Network TCP/UDP load balancing is based on IP protocol, address, and port.

Understand that configuring a load balancer can require configuring both the frontend and backend. The network load balancer can be configured by specifying a forwarding rule that routes traffic to the load balancer to VMs in the target pool.

Know how to increase the number of IP addresses in a subnet. Use the `gcloud compute network subnets expand-ip-range` command to increase IP addresses in a subnet. The number of addresses can only increase. The `expand-ip-range` command cannot be used to decrease the number of addresses.

Know how to reserve an IP address using the console and the `gcloud beta compute address create` command. Reserved IP addresses continue to be available to your project even if they are not attached to a resource. Know the difference between Premium and Standard tier network services.

Review Questions

You can find the answers in the Appendix.

1. What record type is used to specify the IPv4 address of a domain?

    A. AAAA

    B. A

    C. NS

    D. SOA

2. The CEO of your startup just read a news report about a company that was attacked by something called cache poisoning. The CEO wants to implement additional security measures to reduce the risk of DNS spoofing and cache poisoning. What would you recommend?

    A. Using DNSSEC

    B. Adding SOA records

    C. Adding CNAME records

    D. Deleting CNAME records

3. What do the TTL parameters specify in a DNS record?

    A. Time a record can exist in a cache before it should be queried again

    B. Time a client has to respond to a request for DNS information

    C. Time allowed to create a CNAME record

    D. Time before a human has to manually verify the information in the DNS record

4. What command is used to create a DNS zone in the command line?

    A. `gsutil dns managed-zones create`

    B. `gcloud beta dns managed-zones create`

    C. `gcloud beta managed-zones create`

    D. `gcloud beta dns create managed zones`

5. What parameter is used to make a DNS zone private?

    A. --private

    B. --visibility=private

    C. --private=true

    D. --status=private

6. Which load balancers provide global load balancing?

   A. HTTP(S) only

   B. SSL Proxy and TCP Proxy only

   C. HTTP(S), SSL Proxy, and TCP Proxy

   D. Internal TCP/UDP, HTTP(S), SSL Proxy, and TCP Proxy

7. Which regional load balancer allows for load balancing based on IP protocol, address, and port?

   A. HTTP(S)

   B. SSL Proxy

   C. TCP Proxy

   D. Network TCP/UDP

8. You are configuring a load balancer and want to implement private load balancing. Which option would you select?

   A. Only Between My VMs

   B. Enable Private

   C. Disable Public

   D. Local Only

9. What two components need to be configured when creating a TCP Proxy load balancer?

   A. Frontend and forwarding rule

   B. Frontend and backend

   C. Forwarding rule and backend only

   D. Backend and forwarding rule only

10. A health check is used to check what resources?

    A. Load balancer

    B. VMs

    C. Storage buckets

    D. Persistent disks

11. Where do you specify the ports on a TCP Proxy load balancer that should have their traffic forwarded?

    A. Backend

    B. Frontend

    C. Network Services section

    D. VPC

12. What command is used to create a network load balancer at the command line?

    A. `gcloud compute forwarding-rules create`

    B. `gcloud network forwarding-rules create`

    C. `gcloud compute create forwarding-rules`

    D. `gcloud network create forwarding-rules`

13. A team is setting up a web service for internal use. They want to use the same IP address for the foreseeable future. What type of IP address would you assign?

    A. Internal

    B. External

    C. Static

    D. Ephemeral

14. You are starting up a VM to experiment with a new Python data science library. You'll SSH via the server name into the VM, use the Python interpreter interactively for a while and then shut down the machine. What type of IP address would you assign to this VM?

    A. Ephemeral

    B. Static

    C. Permanent

    D. IPv8

15. You have created a subnet called sn1 using 192.168.0.0 with 65,534 addresses. You realize that you will not need that many addresses, and you'd like to reduce that number to 254. Which of the following commands would you use?

    A. `gcloud compute networks subnets expand-ip-range sn1 --prefix-length=24`

    B. `gcloud compute networks subnets expand-ip-range sn1 --prefix-length=-8`

    C. `gcloud compute networks subnets expand-ip-range sn1 --size=256`

    D. There is no command to reduce the number of IP addresses available.

16. You have created a subnet called sn1 using 192.168.0.0. You want it to have 14 addresses. What prefix length would you use?

    A. 32

    B. 28

    C. 20

    D. 16

17. You want all your network traffic to route over the Google network and not traverse the public Internet. What level of network service should you choose?

    A. Standard

    B. Google-only

    C. Premium

    D. Non-Internet

18. You have a website hosted on a Compute Engine VM. Users can access the website using the domain name you provided. You do some maintenance work on the VM and stop the server and restart it. Now users cannot access the website. No other changes have occurred on the subnet. What might be the cause of the problem?

   A. The restart caused a change in the DNS record.

   B. You used an ephemeral instead of a static IP address.

   C. You do not have enough addresses available on your subnet.

   D. Your subnet has changed.

19. You are deploying a distributed system. Messages will be passed between Compute Engine VMs using a reliable UDP protocol. All VMs are in the same region. You want to use the load balancer that best fits these requirements. Which kind of load balancer would you use?

   A. Internal TCP/UDP

   B. TCP Proxy

   C. SSL Proxy

   D. HTTP(S)

20. You want to use Cloud Console to review the records in a DNS entry. What section of Cloud Console would you navigate to?

   A. Compute Engine

   B. Network Services

   C. Kubernetes Engine

   D. Hybrid Connectivity

Chapter

16

Deploying Applications with Cloud Launcher and Deployment Manager

THIS CHAPTER COVERS THE FOLLOWING OBJECTIVES OF THE GOOGLE ASSOCIATE CLOUD ENGINEER CERTIFICATION EXAM:

✓ **3.6 Deploying a solution using Cloud Launcher**

✓ **3.7 Deploying an application using Deployment Manager**

Throughout this exam guide you have learned how to deploy computing, storage, and networking resources, and now you will turn your attention to deploying applications. Cloud Launcher is Google Cloud Platform's (GCP's) marketplace, where you can find preconfigured applications that are ready to deploy into the Google Cloud.

Google has given Cloud Launcher a new name: Marketplace. The Associate Cloud Engineer Certification guide refers to the service as Cloud Launcher, so we will continue to refer to it as Cloud Launcher in this chapter. You will see how to use Deployment Manager to configure templates, which can launch your own custom applications into Google Cloud. Cloud Launcher and Deployment Manager let users deploy applications and necessary compute, storage, and network resources without having to configure those resources themselves.

Deploying a Solution Using Cloud Launcher

Cloud Launcher is a central repository of applications and data sets that can be deployed to your GCP environment. Working with the Cloud Launcher is a two-step process: browsing for a solution that fits your needs and then deploying the solution.

Browsing Cloud Launcher and Viewing Solutions

To view the solutions available in Cloud Launcher, navigate to the Marketplace section. Marketplace is another name for the Cloud Launcher page in Cloud Console. This will display a page like that shown in Figure 16.1.

The main page of Cloud Launcher shows some featured solutions.

The solutions shown in Figure 16.1 include SAP HANA, a NVIDIA deep learning application, and a Palo Alto networks firewall package. There are also some popular open source systems, including a Linux, Apache, MySQL, and PHP (LAMP) stack and a WordPress blog platform.

FIGURE 16.1   Cloud Launcher main page

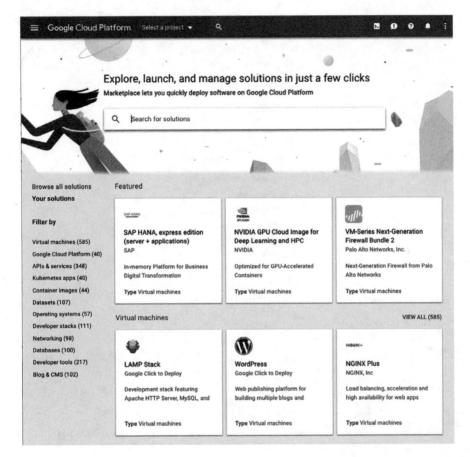

You can either search or browse by filter to see the list of solutions. Figure 16.2 shows the list of categories of available solutions.

You can narrow the set of solutions displayed on the main page by choosing a particular category. For example, if you filter to see only data sets, you will see a list of datasets such as that shown in Figure 16.3.

FIGURE 16.2   Filtering by category

FIGURE 16.3   Data sets available in Cloud Launcher

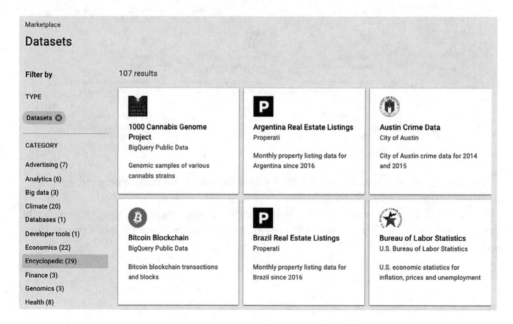

You can see a list of available operating systems in Figure 16.4.

FIGURE 16.4   Operating systems available in Cloud Launcher

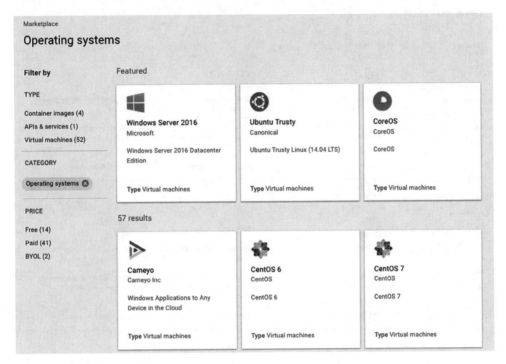

Notice that you can further filter the list of operating systems by license type. The license types are free, paid, and bring your own license (BYOL). Free operating systems include Linux and FreeBSD options. The paid operating systems include Windows operating systems and enterprise-supported Linux. You will be charged a fee based on your usage, and that charge will be included in your GCP billing. The BYOL option includes two supported Linux operating systems that require you to have a valid license to run the software. You are responsible for acquiring the license before running the software.

Figure 16.5 shows a sample of developer tools available in Cloud Launcher. These include WordPress, a backup and recovery application, and a document management system.

FIGURE 16.5   Developer tools available in Cloud Launcher

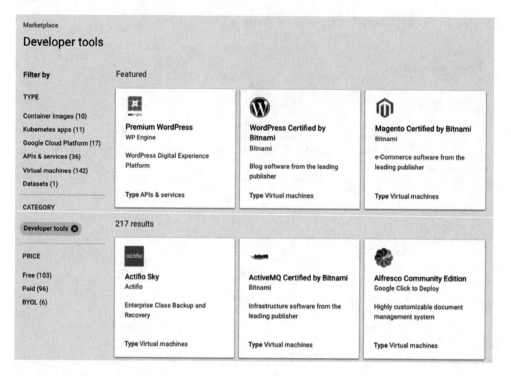

  Notice that there are two WordPress options. Cloud Launcher can have the same application provided by multiple vendors. It is best to review the description of each option to find the one best suited for your needs.

Let's take a look at the kind of information provided along with the solutions listed in Cloud Launcher. Figure 16.6 shows the bulk of the information available. It includes an overview, pricing information, and details about the contents of the package. There is also information on where the solution will run within the GCP.

The left side of the page lists the details of the contents of the solution. Figure 16.7 shows the contents of a WordPress package, which include Apache web server, MySQL, and PHP components. The list also specifies the operating system and the types of resources it will use.

FIGURE 16.6   Overview page of a WordPress solution

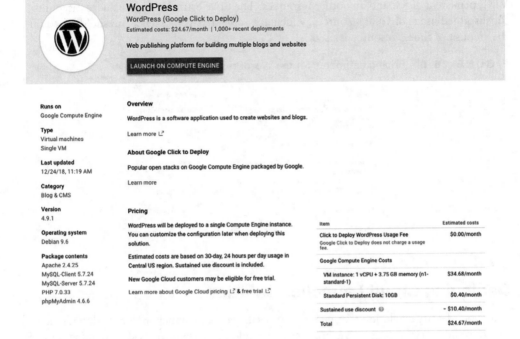

WordPress
WordPress (Google Click to Deploy)
Estimated costs: $24.67/month | 1,000+ recent deployments

Web publishing platform for building multiple blogs and websites

LAUNCH ON COMPUTE ENGINE

Runs on
Google Compute Engine

Type
Virtual machines
Single VM

Last updated
12/24/18, 11:19 AM

Category
Blog & CMS

Version
4.9.1

Operating system
Debian 9.6

Package contents
Apache 2.4.25
MySQL-Client 5.7.24
MySQL-Server 5.7.24
PHP 7.0.33
phpMyAdmin 4.6.6

Overview

WordPress is a software application used to create websites and blogs.

Learn more ⌐

About Google Click to Deploy

Popular open stacks on Google Compute Engine packaged by Google.

Learn more

Pricing

WordPress will be deployed to a single Compute Engine instance. You can customize the configuration later when deploying this solution.

Estimated costs are based on 30-day, 24 hours per day usage in Central US region. Sustained use discount is included.

New Google Cloud customers may be eligible for free trial.

Learn more about Google Cloud pricing ⌐ & free trial ⌐

Item	Estimated costs
Click to Deploy WordPress Usage Fee Google Click to Deploy does not charge a usage fee.	$0.00/month
Google Compute Engine Costs	
VM instance: 1 vCPU + 3.75 GB memory (n1-standard-1)	$34.68/month
Standard Persistent Disk: 10GB	$0.40/month
Sustained use discount ⍰	~ $10.40/month
Total	$24.67/month

FIGURE 16.7   Details of the contents of the solution package

Runs on
Google Compute Engine

Type
Virtual machines
Single VM

Last updated
12/24/18, 11:19 AM

Category
Blog & CMS

Version
4.9.1

Operating system
Debian 9.6

Package contents
Apache 2.4.25
MySQL-Client 5.7.24
MySQL-Server 5.7.24
PHP 7.0.33
phpMyAdmin 4.6.6

On the right side of the page is pricing information (see Figure 16.8). These are estimated costs for running the solution, as configured, for one month, which includes the costs of VMs, persistent disks, and any other resources. The price estimate also includes discounts for sustained usage of GCP resources, which are applied as you reach a threshold based on the amount of time a resource is used.

FIGURE 16.8   Pricing estimates for the WordPress solution

Item	Estimated costs
Click to Deploy WordPress Usage Fee Google Click to Deploy does not charge a usage fee.	$0.00/month
Google Compute Engine Costs	
VM instance: 1 vCPU + 3.75 GB memory (n1-standard-1)	$34.68/month
Standard Persistent Disk: 10GB	$0.40/month
Sustained use discount ⓘ	– $10.40/month
Total	$24.67/month

Deploying Cloud Launcher Solutions

After you identify a solution that meets your needs, you can launch it from Cloud Launcher. Go to the overview page of the product you would like to launch, as shown in Figure 16.9.

FIGURE 16.9   Launch a Cloud Launcher solution from the overview page of the product.

This will generate a form like the one shown in Figure 16.10.

The contents of the form will vary by application, but many parameters are common across solutions. In this form, you specify a name for the deployment, a zone, and the machine type, which is preconfigured. You must also specify an administrator email. You can optionally install a PHP tool called phpMyAdmin, which is helpful for administering WordPress and other PHP applications.

FIGURE 16.10   The launch form for a WordPress solution in Cloud Launcher

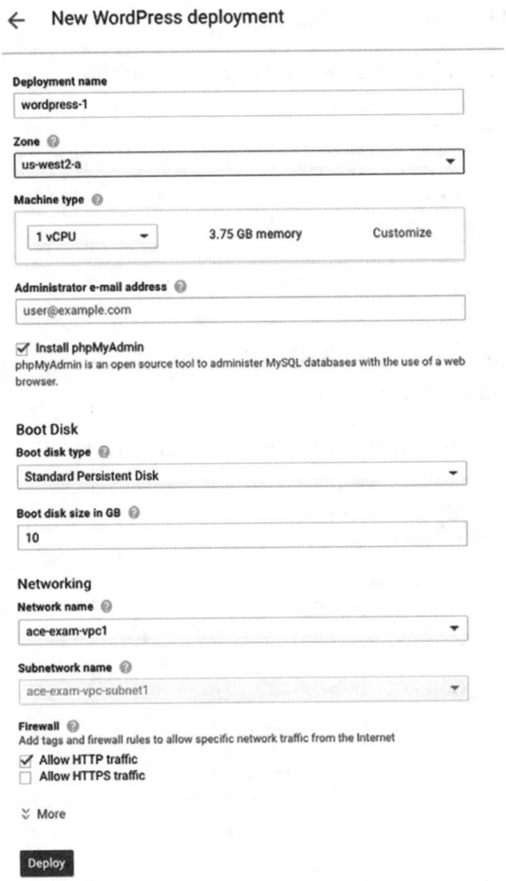

You can choose the type and size of the persistent disk. In this example, the solution will deploy to a 1 vCPU server with 3.75GB of memory and a 10GB boot disk using standard persistent disks. If you wanted, you could opt for an SSD disk for the boot disk. You can also change the size of the boot disk.

In the Networking section, you can specify the network and subnet to launch the VM. You can also configure firewall rules to allow HTTP and HTTPS traffic.

If you expand the More link below the Networking section, you will see options for configuring IP addresses (see Figure 16.11). You can choose to have an ephemeral external

IP or no external IP. If you are hosting a website, choose an external address so the site is accessible from outside the GCP project. Static IP is not an option. You can also specify source IP ranges for HTTP and HTTPS traffic.

FIGURE 16.11 Additional parameters for IP configuration

External IP

| Ephemeral |

Source IP ranges for HTTP traffic

| 0.0.0.0/0, 192.169.0.2/24 |

Source IP ranges for HTTPS traffic

| 0.0.0.0/0, 192.169.0.2/24 |

In addition to the parameters described earlier, the launch page will also display overview information, as shown in Figure 16.12.

FIGURE 16.12 Solution overview shown in the Launch form

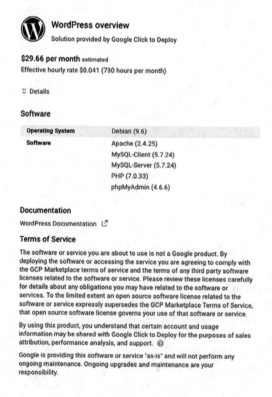

WordPress overview
Solution provided by Google Click to Deploy

$29.66 per month estimated
Effective hourly rate $0.041 (730 hours per month)

☆ Details

Software

Operating System	Debian (9.6)
Software	Apache (2.4.25)
	MySQL-Client (5.7.24)
	MySQL-Server (5.7.24)
	PHP (7.0.33)
	phpMyAdmin (4.6.6)

Documentation
WordPress Documentation ↗

Terms of Service

The software or service you are about to use is not a Google product. By deploying the software or accessing the service you are agreeing to comply with the GCP Marketplace terms of service and the terms of any third party software licenses related to the software or service. Please review these licenses carefully for details about any obligations you may have related to the software or services. To the limited extent an open source software license related to the software or service expressly supersedes the GCP Marketplace Terms of Service, that open source software license governs your use of that software or service.

By using this product, you understand that certain account and usage information may be shared with Google Click to Deploy for the purposes of sales attribution, performance analysis, and support. ⊘

Google is providing this software or service "as-is" and will not perform any ongoing maintenance. Ongoing upgrades and maintenance are your responsibility.

Click the Deploy button to launch the deployment. That will open Deployment Manager and show the progress of the deployment (see Figure 16.13).

FIGURE 16.13   Cloud Deployment Manager launching WordPress

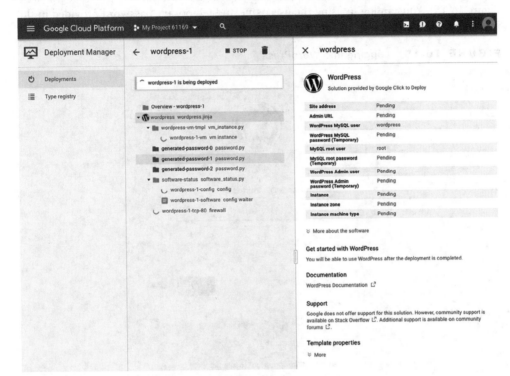

When the launching process completes, you will see summary information about the deployment and a button to launch the admin panel, as shown in Figure 16.14.

FIGURE 16.14   Information about the deployed WordPress instance

Clicking the Log Into The Admin Panel button brings you to the WordPress login (see Figure 16.15). You can log in using the username and temporary password provided in the information form after the deployment completes.

FIGURE 16.15   Logging into WordPress

Deploying an Application Using Deployment Manager   *Cloud Formation*

In addition to launching the solutions listed in Cloud Launcher, you can create your own solution configuration files so users can launch preconfigured solutions.

Deployment Manager Configuration Files

Deployment Manager configuration files are written in YAML syntax. The configuration files start with the word resources, followed by resource entities, which are defined using three fields:

- name, which is the name of the resource
- type, which is the type of the resource, such as compute.v1.instance

- properties, which are key-value pairs that specify configuration parameters for the resource. For example, a VM has properties to specify machine type, disks, and network interfaces.

 For information on YAML syntax, see the official documentation at https://yaml.org/start.html.

A simple example defining a virtual machine called ace-exam-deployment-vm starts with the following:

```
resources:
- type: compute.v1.instance
  name: ace-exam-deployment-vm
```

Next, you can add properties, such as the machine type, disk configuration, and network interfaces.

The properties section of the configuration file starts with the word properties. For each property, there is a single key-value pair or a list of key-value pairs. The machine type property has a single key-value pair, with the key being machineType. Disks have multiple properties, so following the term disks, there is a list of key-value pairs. Continuing the example of ace-exam-deployment-vm, the structure is as follows:

```
resources:
- type: compute.v1.instance
  name: ace-exam-deployment-vm
  properties:
      machineType: [MACHINE_TYPE_URL]
      disks:
[KEY]:[VALUE]
[KEY]:[VALUE]
```

In this example, machine type would be a URL to a Google API resource specification, such as the following:

```
https://www.googleapis.com/compute/v1/projects/[PROJECT_ID]/zones/
us-central1-f/machineTypes/f1-micro
```

Note that there is a reference to [PROJECT_ID], which would be replaced with an actual project ID in a configuration file. Disks have properties such as a deviceName, type, and Booleans indicating whether the disk is a boot disk or should be autodeleted. Let's continue the previous example by adding the machine type specification and some disk properties:

```
resources:
- type: compute.v1.instance
  name: ace-exam-deployment-vm
  properties:
```

```
    machineType: https://www.googleapis.com/compute/v1/projects/[PROJECT_ID]/
zones/us-central1-f/machineTypes/f1-micro
    disks:
    - deviceName: boot
      type: PERSISTENT
      boot: true
      autoDelete: true
```

Listing 16.1 shows the full configuration file from the Google Deployment Manager documentation. The following code is available at https://cloud.google.com/deployment-manager/docs/quickstart (source: https://github.com/GoogleCloudPlatform/deploymentmanager-samples/blob/master/examples/v2/quick_start/vm.yaml).

Listing 16.1: examples/v2/quick_start/vm.yaml

```
# Copyright 2016 Google Inc. All rights reserved.#
# Licensed under the Apache License, Version 2.0 (the "License");
# you may not use this file except in compliance with the License.
# You may obtain a copy of the License at
#
#      http://www.apache.org/licenses/LICENSE-2.0
#
# Unless required by applicable law or agreed to in writing, software
# distributed under the License is distributed on an "AS IS" BASIS,
# WITHOUT WARRANTIES OR CONDITIONS OF ANY KIND, either express or implied.
# See the License for the specific language governing permissions and
# limitations under the License.


# Put all your resources under 'resources:'. For each resource, you need:
# - The type of resource. In this example, the type is a Compute VM instance.
# - An internal name for the resource.
# - The properties for the resource. In this example, for VM instances, you add
#   the machine type, a boot disk, network information, and so on.
#
# For a list of supported resources,
# see https://cloud.google.com/deployment-manager/docs/configuration/
supported-resource-types

resources:
- type: compute.v1.instance
  name: quickstart-deployment-vm
  properties:
```

```
# The properties of the resource depend on the type of resource. For a list
# of properties, see the API reference for the resource.
zone: us-central1-f
# Replace [MY_PROJECT] with your project ID
machineType: https://www.googleapis.com/compute/v1/projects/[MY_PROJECT]/
zones/us-central1-f/machineTypes/f1-micro
  disks:
  - deviceName: boot
    type: PERSISTENT
    boot: true
    autoDelete: true
    initializeParams:
      # Replace [FAMILY_NAME] with the image family name.
      # See a full list of image families at
      # https://cloud.google.com/compute/docs/images#os-compute-support
      sourceImage: https://www.googleapis.com/compute/v1/projects/debian-
cloud/global/images/family/[FAMILY_NAME]
  # Replace [MY_PROJECT] with your project ID
  networkInterfaces:
  - network: https://www.googleapis.com/compute/v1/projects/[MY_PROJECT]/
global/networks/default
    # Access Config required to give the instance a public IP address
    accessConfigs:
    - name: External NAT
      type: ONE_TO_ONE_NAT
```

This configuration specifies a deployment named quickstart-deployment-vm, which will run in the us-central1-f zone. The deployment will use a f1-micro running a Debian distribution of Linux. An external IP address will be assigned.

Before executing this template, you would need to replace [MY_PROJECT] with your project ID and [FAMILY_NAME] with the name of a Debian image family, such as debian-9. You can find a list of images in the Compute Engine section of Cloud Console in the Images tab. You can also list images using the gcloud compute images list command.

Deployment Manager Template Files

If your deployment configurations are becoming complicated, you can use deployment templates. Templates are another text file you use to define resources and import those resources into configuration files. This allows you to reuse resource definitions in multiple places. Templates can be written in Python or Jinja2, a templating language.

For information on Jinja2 syntax, see the official documentation at http://jinja.pocoo.org/docs/2.10/.

As an Associate Cloud Engineer, you should know that Google recommends using Python to create template files unless the templates are relatively simple, in which case it is appropriate to use Jinja2.

Launching a Deployment Manager Template

You can launch a deployment template using the `gcloud deployment-manager deployments create` command. For example, to deploy the template from the Google documentation, use the following:

```
gcloud deployment-manager deployments create quickstart-deployment --config
vm.yaml
```

You can also describe the state of a deployment with the `describe` command, as follows:

```
gloud deployment-manager deployments describe quickstart-deployment
```

 Real World Scenario

Providing a Deployable Service

In large enterprises, different groups often want to use the same service, such as a data science application, to understand customer purchasing patterns. Product managers across the organization may want to use this. Software developers could create a single instance of the applications resources and have multiple users work with that one instance. This is a co-hosted structure. This has some advantages if you have a single DevOps team supporting all users.

Alternatively, you could allow each user or small group of users to have their own application instance. This has several advantages. Users could run the application in their own projects, simplifying allocating charges for resources, since the project would be linked to the users' billing accounts. Also, users could scale the resources up or down as needed for their use case.

A potential disadvantage is that users may not be comfortable configuring Google Cloud resources. Deployment Manager addresses that problem by making it relatively simple to deploy an application and resources in a repeatable process. Someone who can run a `gcloud deployment-manager` command could deploy application resources similar to the way users deploy applications from Cloud Launcher.

Summary

Cloud Launcher and Cloud Deployment Manager are designed to make it easier to deploy resources in GCP. Cloud Launcher is where third-party vendors can offer deployable applications based on proprietary or open source software. When an application is deployed from Cloud Launcher, resources such as VMs, storage buckets, and persistent disks are created automatically without additional human intervention. Deployment Manager gives cloud engineers the ability to define configuration files that describe the resources they would like to deploy. Once defined, cloud engineers can use gcloud commands to deploy the resources and list their status. The Deployment Manager is especially useful in organizations where you want to easily deploy resources without requiring users of those resources to understand the details of how to configure GCP resources.

Exam Essentials

Understand how to browse for solutions using the Cloud Launcher section of Cloud Console.   You can use filters to narrow your search to specific kinds of solutions, such as operating systems and developer tools. There may be multiple options for a single application, such as WordPress. This is because multiple vendors provide configurations. Review the description of each to understand which best fits your needs.

Know how to deploy a solution in Cloud Launcher.   Understand how to configure a Cloud Launcher deployment in Cloud Console. Understand that when you launch a solution, you may be prompted for application specific configurations. For example, with WordPress you may be prompted to install phpMyAdmin. You may also have the opportunity to configure common configuration attributes, such as the machine type and boot disk type.

Understand how to use the Deployment Manager section of the console to monitor deployment.   It may be a few minutes from the time you launch a configuration to the time it is ready to use. Note that once the application is ready, you may be provided additional information, such as a username and password to log in.

Know that Deployment Manager is a GCP service for creating configuration files that define resources to use with an application.   These configuration files use YAML syntax. They are made up of resource specifications that use key-value pairs to define properties of the resource.

Know that resources in a configuration file are defined using a name, type, and set of properties.   The properties vary by type. The machine type can be defined using just a URL that points to a type of machine available in a region. Disks have multiple properties, including a device name, a type, and whether the disk is a boot disk.

If your configuration files are getting long or complicated, you can modularize them using templates. Templates define resources and can be imported into other templates. Templates are text files written in Jinja2 or Python.

Know that you can launch a deployment configuration file using gcloud deployment-manager **deployments create.**   You can review the status of a deployment using gcloud deployment-manager deployments-describe.

Review Questions

1. What are the categories of Cloud Launcher solutions?

   A. Data sets only

   B. Operating systems only

   C. Developer tools and operating systems only

   D. Data sets, operating systems, and developer tools

2. What is the other name of Cloud Launcher?

   A. Cloud Deployment Manager

   B. Marketplace

   C. Cloud Tools

   D. Cloud Solutions: Third Party

3. Where do you navigate to launch a Cloud Launcher solution?

   A. Overview page of the solution

   B. Main Cloud Launcher page

   C. Network Services

   D. None of the above

4. You want to quickly identify the set of operating systems available in Cloud Launcher. Which of these steps would help with that?

   A. Use Google Search to search the Web for a listing.

   B. Use filters in Cloud Launcher.

   C. Scroll through the list of solutions displayed on the start page of Cloud Launcher.

   D. It is not possible to filter to operating systems.

5. You want to use Cloud Launcher to deploy a WordPress site. You notice there is more than one WordPress option. Why is that?

   A. It's a mistake. Submit a ticket to Google support.

   B. Multiple vendors may offer the same application.

   C. It's a mistake. Submit a ticket to the vendors.

   D. You will never see such an option.

6. You have used Cloud Launcher to deploy a WordPress site and would now like to deploy a database. You notice that the configuration form for the databases is different from the form used with WordPress. Why is that?

   A. It's a mistake. Submit a ticket to Google support.

   B. You've navigated to a different subform of Cloud Launcher.

   C. Configuration properties are based on the application you are deploying and will be different depending on what application you are deploying.

   D. This cannot happen.

7. You have been asked by your manager to deploy a WordPress site. You expect heavy traffic, and your manager wants to make sure the VM hosting the WordPress site has enough resources. Which resources can you configure when launching a WordPress site using Cloud Launcher?

   A. Machine type

   B. Disk type

   C. Disk size

   D. All of the above

8. You would like to define as code the configuration of a set of application resources. The GCP service for creating resources using a configuration file made up of resource specifications defined in YAML syntax is called what?

   A. Compute Engine

   B. Deployment Manager

   C. Marketplace Manager

   D. Marketplace Deployer

9. What file format is used to define Deployment Manager configuration files?

   A. XML

   B. JSON

   C. CSV

   D. YAML

10. A Deployment Manager configuration file starts with what term?

    A. Deploy

    B. Resources

    C. Properties

    D. YAML

11. Which of the following are used to define a resource in a Cloud Deployment Manager configuration file?

    A. type only

    B. properties only

    C. name and type only

    D. type, properties, and name

12. What properties may be set when defining a disk on a VM?

    A. A device name only

    B. A Boolean indicating a boot disk and a Boolean indicating autodelete

    C. A Boolean indicating autodelete only

    D. A device name, a Boolean indicating a boot disk, and a Boolean indicating autodelete

13. You need to look up what images are available in the zone in which you want to deploy a VM. What command would you use?

A. `gcloud compute images list`

B. `gcloud images list`

C. `gsutil compute images list`

D. `gcloud compute list images`

14. You want to use a template file with Deployment Manager. You expect the file to be complicated. What language would you use?

A. Jinja2

B. Ruby

C. Go

D. Python

15. What command launches a deployment?

A. `gcloud deployment-manager deployments create`

B. `gcloud cloud-launcher deployments create`

C. `gcloud deployment-manager deployments launch`

D. `gcloud cloud-launcher deployments launch`

16. A DevOps engineer is noticing a spike in CPU utilization on your servers. You explain you have just launched a deployment. You'd like to show the DevOps engineer the details of a deployment you just launched. What command would you use?

A. `gcloud cloud-launcher deployments describe`

B. `gcloud deployment-manage deployments list`

C. `gcloud deployment-manager deployments describe`

D. `gcloud cloud-launcher deployments list`

17. If you expand the More link in the Networking section when deploying a Cloud Launcher solution, what will you be able to configure?

A. IP addresses

B. Billing

C. Access controls

D. Custom machine type

18. What are the license types referenced in Cloud Launcher?

A. Free only

B. Free and Paid only

C. Free and Bring your own license (BYOL) only

D. Free, paid, and bring your own license

19. Which license type will add charges to your GCP bill when using Cloud Launcher with this type of license?

A. Free

B. Paid

C. BYOL

D. Chargeback

20. You are deploying a Cloud Launcher application that includes a LAMP stack. What software will this deploy?

A. Apache server and Linux only

B. Linux only

C. MySQL and Apache only

D. Apache, MySQL, Linux, and PHP

Chapter

17

Configuring Access and Security

THIS CHAPTER COVERS THE FOLLOWING OBJECTIVES OF THE GOOGLE ASSOCIATE CLOUD ENGINEER CERTIFICATION EXAM:

✓ **5.1 Managing Identity and Access Management (IAM)**

✓ **5.2 Managing service accounts**

✓ **5.3 Viewing audit logs for project and managed services**

Google Cloud engineers can expect to spend a significant amount of time working with access controls. This chapter provides instruction on how to perform several common tasks, including managing identity and access management (IAM) assignments, creating custom roles, managing service accounts, and viewing audit logs.

It is important to know that the preferred way of assigning permissions to users, groups, and service accounts is through the IAM system. However, Google Cloud did not always have IAM. Before that, permissions were granted using what are now known as primitive roles, which are fairly coarse-grained. Primitive roles may have more permissions than you want an identity to have. You can constrain permissions using scopes. In this chapter, we will describe how to use primitive roles and scopes as well as IAM. Going forward, it is a best practice to use IAM for access control.

Managing Identity and Access Management

When you work with IAM, there are a few common tasks you need to perform:

- Viewing account IAM assignments
- Assigning IAM roles
- Defining custom roles

Let's look at how to perform each of these tasks.

Viewing Account Identity and Access Management Assignments

You can view account IAM assignments in Cloud Console by navigating to the IAM & Admin section. In that section, select IAM from the navigation menu to display a form such as the one shown in Figure 17.1. The example in the figure shows a list of identities filtered by member name.

In this example, the user dan@gcpcert.com has three roles: App Engine Admin, BigQuery Admin, and Owner. App Engine Admin and BigQuery Admin are predefined IAM roles. Owner is a primitive role.

FIGURE 17.1   Permissions listing filtered by member

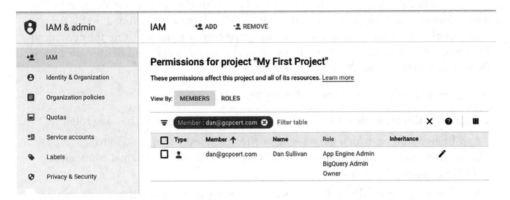

Primitive roles were used prior to IAM. There are three primitive roles: owner, editor, and viewer. Viewers have permission to perform read-only operations. Editors have viewer permissions and permission to modify an entity. Owners have editor permissions and can manage roles and permission on an entity. Owners can also set up billing for a project.

IAM roles are collections of permissions. They are tailored to provide identities with just the permissions they need to perform a task and no more. To see a list of users assigned a role, click the Roles tab in the IAM form. This will show a display similar to Figure 17.2.

FIGURE 17.2   List of identities assigned to App Engine Admin and Editor

IAM   +& ADD   -& REMOVE

Permissions for project "My First Project"

These permissions affect this project and all of its resources. Learn more

View By: MEMBERS   ROLES

	Role / Member ↑	Name	Inheritance
☐	▶ App Engine Admin (1)		
☐	▼ BigQuery Admin (1)		
☐	&dan@gcpcert.com	Dan Sullivan	✏ 🗑
☐	▶ Compute Engine Service Agent (1)		
☐	▼ Editor (3)		
☐	&494499262886-compute@developer.gserviceaccount.com	Compute Engine default service account	✏ 🗑
☐	&494499262886@cloudservices.gserviceaccount.com	Google APIs Service Agent ❓	✏ 🗑
☐	&service-494499262886@containerregistry.iam.gserviceaccount.com	Google Container Registry Service Agent ❓	✏ 🗑
☐	▶ Kubernetes Engine Service Agent (1)		
☐	▶ Owner (1)		

This form shows a list of roles with the number of identities assigned to that role in parentheses. Click the arrow next to the name of a role to display a list of identities with that role. Notice that both primitive and IAM predefined roles are included in this list.

You can also see a list of users and roles assigned across a project using the command gcloud projects get-iam-policy. For example, to list roles assigned to users in a project with the project ID ace-exam-project, use this:

```
gcloud projects get-iam-policy ace-exam-project
```

Predefined roles are grouped by service. For example, App Engine has five roles:

- App Engine Admin, which grants read, write, and modify permission to application and configuration settings. The role name used in gcloud commands is roles/appengine.appAdmin.

- App Engine Service Admin, which grants read-only access to configuration settings and write access to module-level and version-level settings. The role name used in gcloud commands is roles/appengine.serviceAdmin.

- App Engine Deployer, which grants read-only access to application configuration and settings and write access to create new versions. Users with only the App Engine Deployer role cannot modify or delete existing versions. The role name used in gcloud commands is roles/appengine.deployer.

- App Engine Viewer, which grants read-only access to application configuration and settings. The role name used in gcloud commands is roles/appengine.appViewer.

- App Engine Code Viewer, which grants read-only access to all application configurations, settings, and deployed source code. The role name used in gcloud commands is roles/appengine.codeViewer.

> Although you do not have to know all of them, it helps to review predefined roles to understand patterns of how they are defined. For more details, see the Google Cloud documentation at: https://cloud.google.com/iam/docs/understanding-roles.

Assigning Identity and Access Management Roles to Accounts and Groups

To add IAM roles to accounts and groups, navigate to the IAM & Admin section of the console. Select IAM from the menu. Click the Add link at the top to display a form like that shown in Figure 17.3.

Specify the name of a user or group in the parameter labeled New Members. Click Select A Role to add a role. You can add multiple roles. When you click the down arrow in the Role parameter, you will see a list of services and their associated roles. You can choose the roles from that list. See Figure 17.4 for an example of a subset of the list, showing the roles for BigQuery.

FIGURE 17.3   The Add option in IAM is where you can assign users or groups one or more roles.

Add members, roles to "My First Project" project

Enter one or more members below. Then select a role for these members to grant them access to your resources. Multiple roles allowed. Learn more

New members

dan@gcpcert.com ⊗   ❓

Role

Editor   ▼   🗑

Edit access to all resources.

Role

Cloud Spanner Admin   ▼   🗑

Full control of Cloud Spanner resources.

Role

Stackdriver Account Editor   ▼   🗑

Read/write access to manage Stackdriver account structure.

Select a role   ▼   🗑

＋ ADD ANOTHER ROLE

SAVE   CANCEL

FIGURE 17.4   The drop-down list in the Roles parameters shows available roles grouped by service.

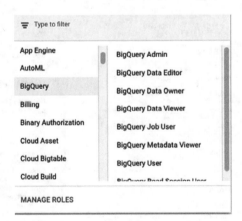

≡ Type to filter

App Engine	BigQuery Admin
AutoML	BigQuery Data Editor
BigQuery	BigQuery Data Owner
Billing	BigQuery Data Viewer
Binary Authorization	BigQuery Job User
Cloud Asset	BigQuery Metadata Viewer
Cloud Bigtable	BigQuery User
Cloud Build	BigQuery Read Session User

MANAGE ROLES

If you want to know which of the fine-grained permissions are granted when you assign a role, you can list those permissions at the command line or in the console. You can also see what permissions are assigned to a role using the command gcloud iam roles describe. For example, Figure 17.5 shows the list of permissions in the App Engine Deployer role.

FIGURE 17.5   An example listing permissions using the gcloud iam roles describe command

```
$gcloud iam roles describe roles/appengine.deployer
description: Necessary permissions to deploy new code to App Engine, and remove old
    versions.
etag: AA==
includedPermissions:
- appengine.applications.get
- appengine.instances.get
- appengine.instances.list
- appengine.operations.get
- appengine.operations.list
- appengine.services.get
- appengine.services.list
- appengine.versions.create
- appengine.versions.delete
- appengine.versions.get
- appengine.versions.list
- resourcemanager.projects.get
- resourcemanager.projects.list
name: roles/appengine.deployer
stage: GA
title: App Engine Deployer
```

You can also use Cloud Console to view permissions. Navigate to the IAM & Admin section and select Roles from the menu. This displays a list of roles. Click the checkbox next to a role name to display a list of permissions on the right, as shown in Figure 17.6 for App Engine Deployer.

FIGURE 17.6   An example listing of permissions available for App Engine Deployer using Cloud Console

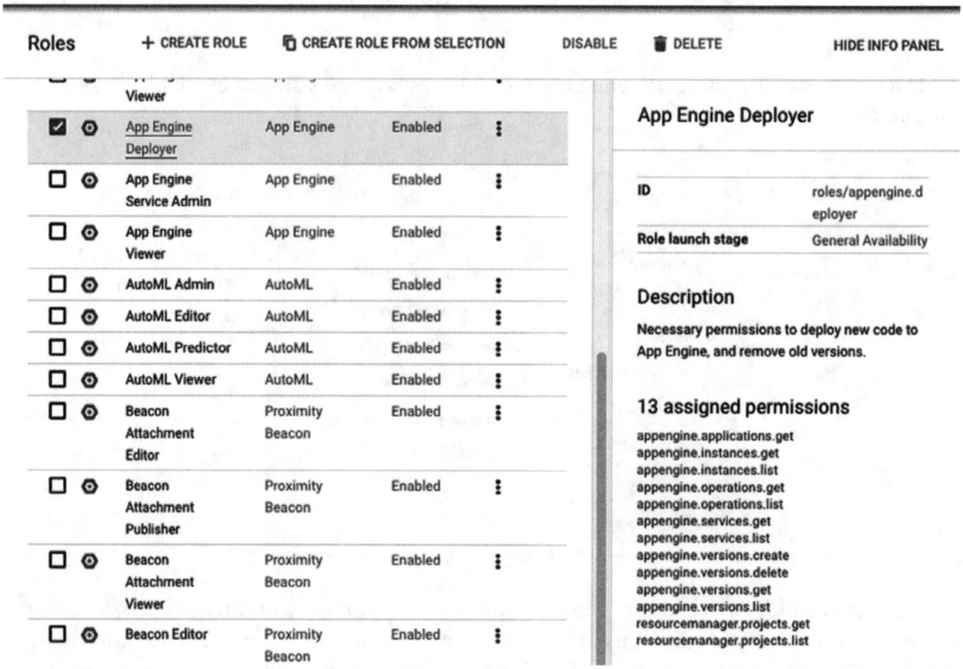

You can assign roles to a member in a project using the following command:

```
gcloud projects add-iam-policy-binding [RESOURCE-NAME] --member user:[USER-
EMAIL] --role [ROLE-ID]
```

For example, to grant the role App Engine Deployer to a user identified by jane@acexam.com, you could use this:

```
gcloud projects add-iam-policy-binding ace-exam-project --member user:jane@
aceexam.com --role roles/appengine.deployer
```

 Real World Scenario

IAM Roles Support Least Privilege and Separation of Duties

Two security best practices are assigning least privileges and maintaining a separation of duties. The principle of least privileges says you grant only the smallest set of permissions that is required for a user or service account to perform their required tasks. For example, if users can do everything they need to do with only read permission to a database, then they should not have write permission.

In the case of separation of duties, the idea is that a single user should not be able to perform multiple sensitive operations that together could present a risk. In high-risk domains, such as finance or defense, you would not want a developer to be able to modify an application and deploy that change to production without review. A malicious engineer, for example, could modify code in a finance application to suppress application logging when funds are transferred to a bank account controlled by the malicious engineer. If that engineer were to put that code in production, it could be some time before auditors discover that logging has been suppressed and there may have been fraudulent transactions.

IAM roles support least privilege by assigning minimal permissions to predefined roles. It also supports separation of duties by allowing some users to have the ability to change code and others to deploy code.

Another common security practice is defense in depth, which applies multiple, overlapping security controls. That is also a practice that should be adopted. IAM can be applied as one of the layers of defense.

Defining Custom Identity and Access Management Roles

If the set of predefined IAM roles does not meet your needs, you can define a custom role.

To define a custom role in Cloud Console, navigate to the Roles option in the IAM & Admin section of the console. Click the Create Role link at the top of the page. This will display a form like that shown in Figure 17.7.

FIGURE 17.7   Creating a role in Cloud Console

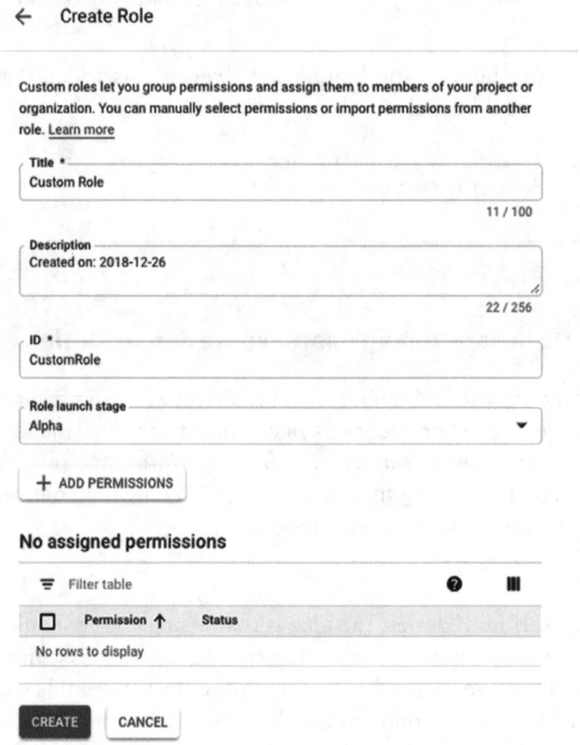

←   **Create Role**

Custom roles let you group permissions and assign them to members of your project or organization. You can manually select permissions or import permissions from another role. Learn more

Title *
Custom Role

11 / 100

Description
Created on: 2018-12-26

22 / 256

ID *
CustomRole

Role launch stage
Alpha   ▼

+ ADD PERMISSIONS

No assigned permissions

≡ Filter table   ❓   ▥

☐   Permission ↑   Status

No rows to display

CREATE   CANCEL

In this form you can specify a name for the custom role, a description, an identifier, a launch stage, and a set of permissions. The launch stage options are as follows: Alpha, Beta, General Availability, and Disabled.

You can click Add Permissions to display a list of permissions. The list in Figure 17.8 is filtered to include only permissions in the App Engine Admin role.

Although the list includes all permissions in the role, not all permissions are available for use in a custom role. For example, `appengine.runtimes.actAsAdmin` is not available for custom roles. When a permission is not available, its status is listed as Not Supported. Permissions that are available for use are listed as Supported, so in the example all other permissions are available. Check the boxes next to the permissions you want to include in your custom role. Click Add to return to the Create Role form, where the list of permissions will now include the permissions you selected (see Figure 17.9).

FIGURE 17.8 List of available permissions filtered by role

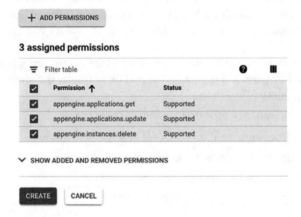

FIGURE 17.9 The permissions section of the Create Role form with permissions added

You can also define a custom role using the gcloud iam roles create command. The structure of that command is as follows:

```
gcloud iam roles create [ROLE-ID] --project [PROJECT-ID] --title [ROLE-TITLE] \
--description [ROLE-DESCRIPTION] --permissions [PERMISSIONS-LIST] --stage [LAUNCH-STAGE]
```

For example, to create a role that has only App Engine application update permission, you could use the following command:

```
gcloud iam roles create customAppEngine1 --project ace-exam-project
--title='Custom Update App Engine' \
--description='Custom update' --permissions=appengine.applications.update
--stage=alpha
```

Managing Service Accounts

Service accounts are used to provide identities independent of human users. Service accounts are identities that can be granted roles. Service accounts are assigned to VMs, which then use the permissions available to the service accounts to carry out tasks.

Three things cloud engineers are expected to know how to do are working with scopes, assigning service accounts to VMs, and granting access to a service account to another project.

Managing Service Accounts with Scopes

Scopes are permissions granted to a VM to perform some operation. Scopes authorize the access to API methods. The service account assigned to a VM has roles associated with it. To configure access controls for a VM, you will need to configure both IAM roles and scopes. We have discussed how to manage IAM roles, so now we will turn our attention to scopes.

A scope is specified using a URL that starts with https://www.googleapis.com/auth/ and is then followed by permission on a resource. For example, the scope allowing a VM to insert data into BigQuery is as follows:

```
https://www.googleapis.com/auth/bigquery.insertdata
```

The scope that allows viewing data in Cloud Storage is as follows:

```
https://www.googleapis.com/auth/devstorage.read_only
```

And to write to Compute Engine logs, use this:

```
https://www.googleapis.com/auth/logging.write
```

An instance can only perform operations allowed by both IAM roles assigned to the service account and scopes defined on the instance. For example, if a role grants only read-only access to Cloud Storage but a scope allows write access, then the instance will not be able to write to Cloud Storage.

To set scopes in an instance, navigate to the VM instance page in Cloud Console. Stop the instance if it is running. On the Instance Detail page, click the Edit link. At the bottom of the Edit page, you will see the Access Scopes section, as shown in Figure 17.10.

FIGURE 17.10   Access Scopes section in VM instance details edit page

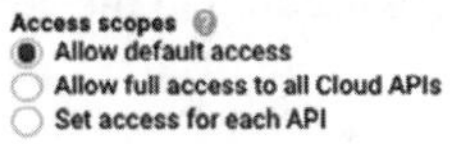

The options are Allow Default Access, Allow Full Access To All Cloud APIs, and Set Access For Each API. Default access is usually sufficient. If you are not sure what to set, you can choose Allow Full Access, but be sure to assign IAM roles to limit what the instance can do. If you want to choose scopes individually, choose Set Access For Each API. This will display a list of services and scopes like that shown in Figure 17.11.

FIGURE 17.11   A partial list of services and scopes that can be individually configured

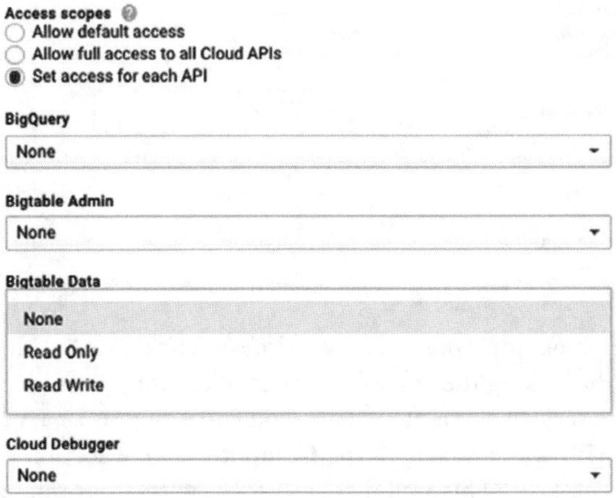

You can also set scopes using the gcloud compute instances set-service-account command. The structure of the command is as follows:

```
gcloud compute instances set-service-account [INSTANCE_NAME] \
    [--service-account [SERVICE_ACCOUNT_EMAIL] | [--no-service-account] \
    [--no-scopes | --scopes [SCOPES,...]]
```

An example scope assignment using gcloud is as follows:

```
gcloud compute instances set-service-account ace-instance \
    --service-account examadmin@ace-exam-project.iam.gserviceaccount.com \
    --scopes compute-rw,storage-ro
```

Assigning a Service Account to a Virtual Machine Instance

You can assign a service account to a VM instance. First, create a service account by navigating to the Service Accounts section of the IAM & Admin section of the console. Click Create Service Account to display a form like that shown in Figure 17.12.

FIGURE 17.12   Creating a service account in the console

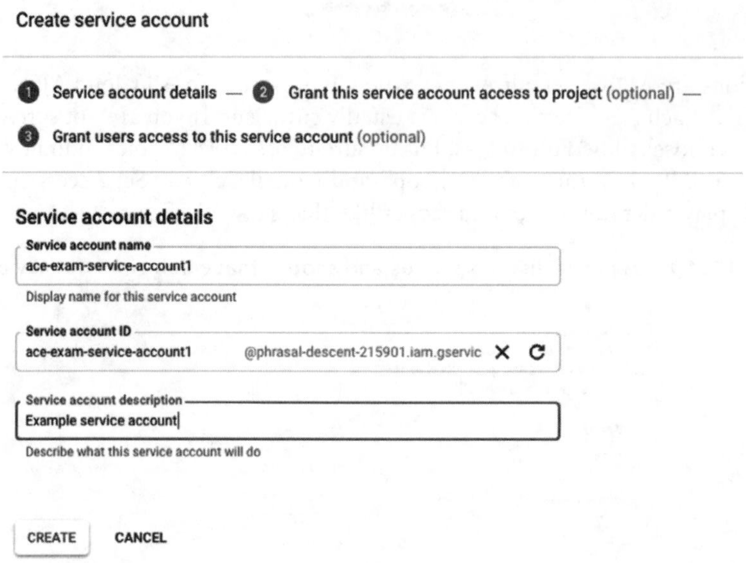

After specifying a name, identifier, and description, click Create. Next, you can assign roles as described earlier, using the console or `gcloud` commands. Once you have assigned the roles you want the service account to have, you can assign it to a VM instance.

Navigate to the VM Instances page in the Compute Engine section of the console. Select a VM instance and click Edit. This will display a form with a parameter for the instance. Scroll down to see the parameter labeled Service Account (see Figure 17.13).

FIGURE 17.13   Section of Edit Instance page showing the Service Account parameter

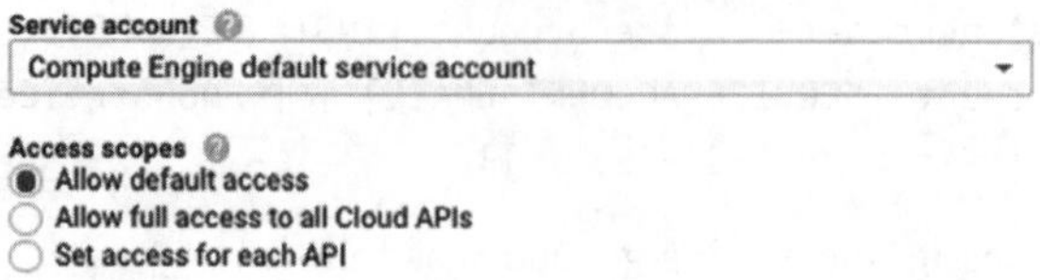

From the drop-down list, select the service account you want assigned to that instance, as shown in Figure 17.14.

FIGURE 17.14   List of service accounts that can be assigned to the instance

You can also specify a service instance at the command line when you create an instance using the gcloud compute instance create command. It has the following structure:

```
gcloud compute instances create [INSTANCE_NAME]  --service-account [SERVICE_
ACCOUNT_EMAIL]
```

To grant access to a project, navigate to the IAM page of the console and add a member. Use the service accounts email as the entity to add.

Viewing Audit Logs

To view audit logs, navigate to the Stackdriver Logging page in Cloud Console. This will show a listing like that in Figure 17.15.

FIGURE 17.15   Default listing of the Stackdriver Logging page

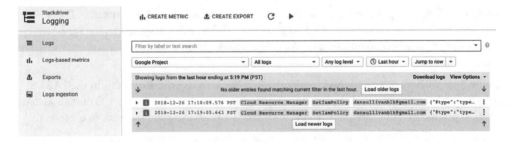

Notice you can select the resource, types of logs to display, the log level, and the period of time from which to display entities.

For additional information on logging, see Chapter 18.

Summary

Access controls in GCP are managed using IAM, primitive roles, and scopes. The three primitive roles are owner, editor, and viewer. They provide coarse-grained access controls to resources. Scopes are access controls that apply to instances of VMs. They are used to limit operations that can be performed by an instance. The set of operations that an instance can perform is determined by the scopes assigned and the roles assigned to a service account used by the instance. IAM provides predefined roles. These roles are grouped by service. The roles are designed to provide the minimal set of permissions needed to carry out a logical task, such as writing to a bucket or deploying an App Engine application. When predefined roles do not meet your needs, you can define custom roles.

Service accounts are used to enable VMs to perform operations with a set of permissions. The permissions are granted to service accounts through the roles assigned to the service account. You can use the default service account provided by GCP for an instance or you can assign your own.

Exam Essentials

Know the three types of roles: primitive, predefined, and custom.   Primitive roles include owner, editor, and viewer. These were developed prior to the release of IAM. Predefined roles are IAM roles. Permissions are assigned to these roles, and then the roles are assigned to users, groups, and service accounts. Custom roles include permissions selected by the user creating the custom role.

Understand that scopes are a type of access control applied to VM instances.   The VM can only perform operations allowed by scopes and IAM roles assigned to the service account of the instance. You can use IAM roles to constrain scopes and use scopes to constrain IAM roles.

Know how to view roles assigned to identities.   You can use the Roles tab in the IAM & Admin section of the console to list the identities assigned particular roles. You can also use `gcloud projects get-iam-policy` command to list roles assigned to users in a project.

Understand that IAM roles support separation of duties and the principle of least privilege. Primitive roles did not support least privilege and separation of duties because they are too coarse-grained. Separation of duties ensures that two or more people are required to complete a sensitive task.

Know how to use `gcloud iam roles describe` **to view details of a role, including permissions assigned to a role.**   You can also view users granted roles by drilling down into a role in the Roles page of the IAM & Admin section of the console. When working with IAM, you will be using the `gcloud` command when working from the command line.

Understand the different options for accessing scopes when creating an instance.   The options are Default Access, Full Access, and Set Access for Each API. If you aren't sure which to use, you can grant full access, but be sure to limit what the instance can do by assigning roles that constrain allowed operations.

Know that Stackdriver Logging collects logging events.   They can be filtered and displayed in the Logging section of Cloud Console. You can filter by resource, type of log, log level, and period of time to display.

Review Questions

You can find the answers in the Appendix.

1.   What does IAM stand for?

   A.   Identity and Authorization Management

   B.   Identity and Access Management

   C.   Identity and Auditing Management

   D.   Individual Access Management

2.   When you navigate to IAM & Admin in Cloud Console, what appears in the main body of the page?

   A.   Members and roles assigned

   B.   Roles only

   C.   Members only

   D.   Roles and permissions assigned

3.   Why are primitive roles classified in a category in addition to IAM?

   A.   They are part of IAM.

   B.   They were created before IAM.

   C.   They were created after IAM.

   D.   They are not related to access control.

4.   A developer intern is confused about what roles are used for. You describe IAM roles as a collection of what?

   A.   Identities

   B.   Permissions

   C.   Access control lists

   D.   Audit logs

5.   You want to list roles assigned to users in a project called ace-exam-project. What gcloud command would you use?

   A.   `gcloud iam get-iam-policy ace-exam-project`

   B.   `gcloud projects list ace-exam-project`

   C.   `gcloud projects get-iam-policy ace-exam-project`

   D.   `gcloud iam list ace-exam-project`

6. You are working in the form displayed after clicking the Add link in the IAM form of IAM & Admin in Cloud Console. There is a parameter called New Members. What items would you enter in that parameter?

   A. Individual users only

   B. Individual users or groups

   C. Roles or individual users

   D. Roles or groups

7. You have been assigned the App Engine Deployer role. What operations can you perform?

   A. Write new versions of an application only

   B. Read application configuration and settings only

   C. Read application configuration and settings and write new configurations

   D. Read application configuration and settings and write new versions

8. You want to list permissions in a role using Cloud Console. Where would you go to see that?

   A. IAM & Admin; select Roles. All permissions will be displayed.

   B. IAM & Admin; select Roles. Check the box next to a role to display the permissions in that role.

   C. IAM & Admin; select Audit Logs.

   D. IAM & Admin; select Service Accounts and then Roles.

9. You are meeting with an autidor to discuss security practices in the cloud. The auditor asks how you implement several best practices. You describe how IAM predefined roles help to implement which security best practice(s)?

   A. Least privilege

   B. Separation of duties

   C. Defense in depth

   D. Options A and B

10. What launch stages are available when creating custom roles?

    A. Alpha and beta only

    B. General availability only

    C. Disabled only

    D. Alpha, beta, general availability, and disabled

11. The gcloud command to create a custom role is what?

    A. `gcloud project roles create`

    B. `gcloud iam roles create`

    C. `gcloud project create roles`

    D. `gcloud iam create roles`

12. A DevOps engineer is confused about the purpose of scopes. Scopes are access controls that are applied to what kind of resources?

   A. Storage buckets

   B. VM instances

   C. Persistent disks

   D. Subnets

13. A scope is identified using what kind of identifier?

   A. A randomly generated ID

   B. A URL beginning with `https://www.googleserviceaccounts/`

   C. A URL beginning with `https://www.googleapis.com/auth/`

   D. A URL beginning with `https://www.googleapis.com/auth/PROJECT_ID]`

14. A VM instance is trying to read from a Cloud Storage bucket. Reading the bucket is allowed by IAM roles granted to the service account of the VM. Reading buckets is denied by the scopes assigned to the VM. What will happen if the VM tries to read from the bucket?

   A. The application performing the read will skip over the read operation.

   B. The read will execute because the most permissive permission is allowed.

   C. The read will not execute because both scopes and IAM roles are applied to determine what operations can be performed.

   D. The read operation will succeed, but a message will be logged to Stackdriver Logging.

15. What are the options for setting scopes in a VM?

   A. Allow Default Access and Allow Full Access only

   B. Allow Default Access, Allow Full Access, and Set Access for Each API

   C. Allow Full Access or Set Access For Each API only

   D. Allow Default Access and Set Access For Each API only

16. What gcloud command would you use to set scopes?

   A. `gcloud compute instances set-scopes`

   B. `gcloud compute instances set-service-account`

   C. `gcloud compute service-accounts set-scopes`

   D. `gcloud compute service-accounts define-scopes`

17. What gcloud command would you use to assign a service account when creating a VM?

   A. `gcloud compute instances create [INSTANCE_NAME]`
        `--service-account [SERVICE_ACCOUNT_EMAIL]`

   B. `gcloud compute instances create-service-account`
        `[INSTANCE_NAME][SERVICE_ACCOUNT_EMAIL]`

   C. `gcloud compute instances define-service-account`
        `[INSTANCE_NAME][SERVICE_ACCOUNT_EMAIL]`

   D. `gcloud compute create instances-service-account`
        `[INSTANCE_NAME][SERVICE_ACCOUNT_EMAIL]`

18. What GCP service is used to view audit logs?

   A. Compute Engine

   B. Cloud Storage

   C. Stackdriver Logging

   D. Custom logging

19. What options are available for filtering log messages when viewing audit logs?

   A. Period time and log level only

   B. Resource, type of log, log level, and period of time only

   C. Resource and period of time only

   D. Type of log only

20. An auditor needs to review audit logs. You assign read-only permission to a custom role you create for auditors. What security best practice are you following?

   A. Defense in depth

   B. Least privilege

   C. Separation of duties

   D. Vulnerability scanning

Chapter

18

Monitoring, Logging, and Cost Estimating

THIS CHAPTER COVERS THE FOLLOWING OBJECTIVES OF THE GOOGLE ASSOCIATE CLOUD ENGINEER CERTIFICATION EXAM:

✓ **4.6 Monitoring and logging**

✓ **2.1 Planning and estimating GCP product use using the Pricing Calculator**

Monitoring system performance is an essential part of cloud engineering. In this chapter, you will learn about Stackdriver, a GCP service for resource monitoring, logging, tracing, and debugging. You will start by creating alerts based on resource metrics and custom metrics. Next, you will turn your attention to logging with a discussion of how to create log sinks to store logging data outside of Stackdriver. You'll also see how to view and filter log data. Stackdriver includes diagnostic tools such as Cloud Trace and Cloud Debugger, which you'll learn about as well. We'll close out the chapter with a review of the Pricing Calculator for estimating the cost of GCP resources and services.

Monitoring with Stackdriver

Stackdriver is a service for collecting performance metrics, logs, and event data from our resources. Metrics include measurements such as the average percent CPU utilization over the past minute and the number of bytes written to a storage device in the last minute. Stackdriver includes many predefined metrics. Some examples are shown in Table 18.1 that you can use to assess the health of your resources and, if needed, trigger alerts to bring your attention to resources or services that are not meeting service-level objectives.

TABLE 18.1   Example Stackdriver metrics

GCP Product	Metric
Compute Engine	CPU utilization
Compute Engine	Disk bytes read
BigQuery	Execution times
Bigtable	CPU load
Cloud Functions	Execution count

Stackdriver works in hybrid environments with support for GCP, Amazon Web Services, and on-premise resources.

Creating Alerts Based on Resource Metrics

Metrics are defined measurements on a resource collected at regular intervals. Metrics return aggregate values, such as the maximum, minimum, or average value of the item measured, which could be CPU utilization, amount of memory used, or number of bytes written to a network interface.

For this example, assume you are working with a VM that has Apache Server and PHP installed. To monitor and collect metrics, you need to install the Stackdriver agent for monitoring. Since you are installing the monitoring agent, you'll install the logging agent at the same time because you'll need that later. To install the Stackdriver monitoring and logging agents on a Linux VM, execute the following command at the shell prompt (note, these are not gcloud commands):

```
curl -sSO https://dl.google.com/cloudagents/install-monitoring-agent.sh
sudo bash install-monitoring-agent.sh
curl -sSO https://dl.google.com/cloudagents/install-logging-agent.sh
sudo bash install-logging-agent.sh --structured
```

VMs with agents installed collect monitoring and logging data and send it to Stackdriver. Stackdriver needs a Workspace to store the data.

To create a Workspace and initialize it, navigate to the Stackdriver Monitoring section of Cloud Console. If a Workspace does not exist for your project, a form such as that shown in Figure 18.1 will appear.

FIGURE 18.1   Initial form used to create a Workspace in Stackdriver

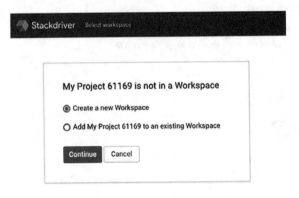

Next, select a project to monitor, as shown in Figure 18.2.

FIGURE 18.2 Selecting a project for the Workspace

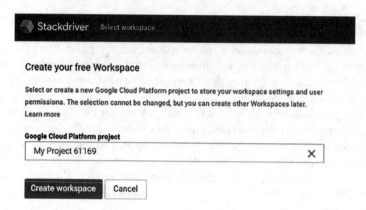

If you want to monitor multiple projects in a Workspace, you can optionally select other projects, as shown in Figure 18.3.

FIGURE 18.3 Optionally adding other projects to monitor

Add Google Cloud Platform projects to monitor optional

Add Google Cloud Platform projects to monitor as part of this Workspace. You can edit this selection later in workspace settings. Learn more

> 🔍 Pr|

Select all None

- ☑ My Project 61169 (phrasal-descent-215901) ❷
- ☐ AppEngFlex-Project-1 (appengflex-project-1) ❷

1 projects selected

Continue

If you want to monitor AWS resources in a Workspace, you can optionally select them as well, as shown in Figure 18.4.

FIGURE 18.4   Optionally monitoring AWS resources

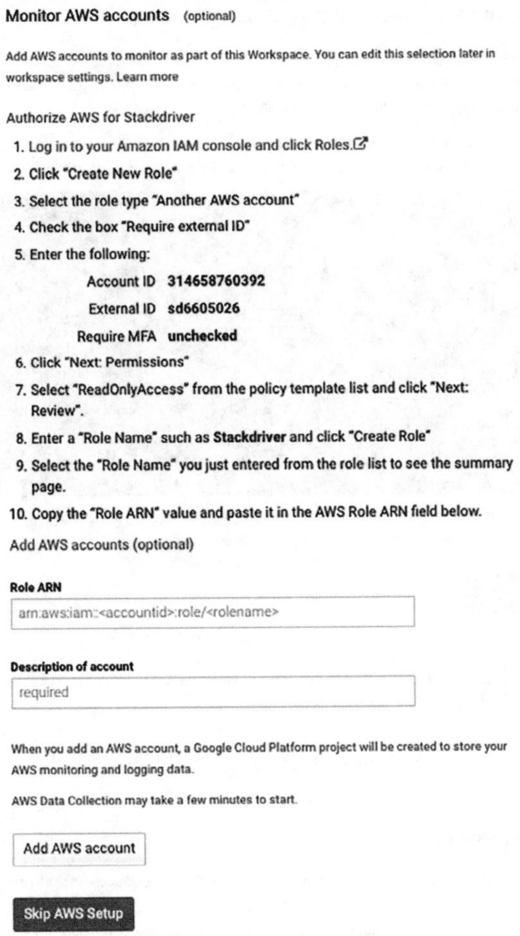

Monitor AWS accounts   (optional)

Add AWS accounts to monitor as part of this Workspace. You can edit this selection later in workspace settings. Learn more

Authorize AWS for Stackdriver

1. Log in to your Amazon IAM console and click Roles.

2. Click "Create New Role"

3. Select the role type "Another AWS account"

4. Check the box "Require external ID"

5. Enter the following:

       Account ID   **314658760392**

       External ID   **sd6605026**

       Require MFA   **unchecked**

6. Click "Next: Permissions"

7. Select "ReadOnlyAccess" from the policy template list and click "Next: Review".

8. Enter a "Role Name" such as **Stackdriver** and click "Create Role"

9. Select the "Role Name" you just entered from the role list to see the summary page.

10. Copy the "Role ARN" value and paste it in the AWS Role ARN field below.

Add AWS accounts (optional)

Role ARN

arn:aws:iam::<accountid>:role/<rolename>

Description of account

required

When you add an AWS account, a Google Cloud Platform project will be created to store your AWS monitoring and logging data.

AWS Data Collection may take a few minutes to start.

Add AWS account

Skip AWS Setup

The next step in the initialization process lists commands to install agents (see Figure 18.5).

FIGURE 18.5 Listing of instructions to install agents on servers to be monitored

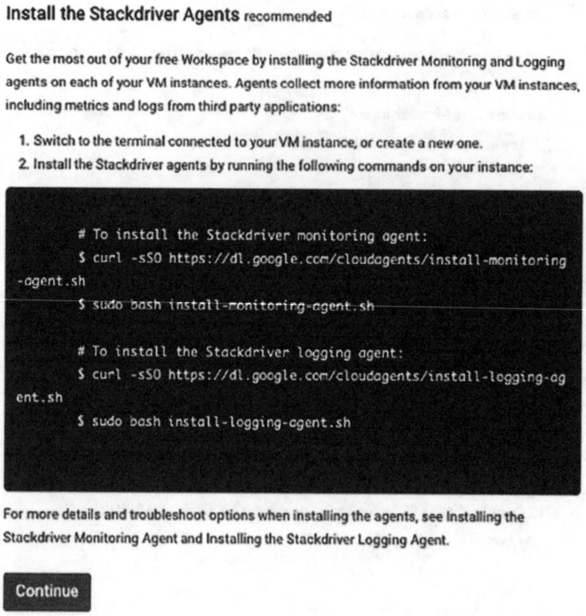

Install the Stackdriver Agents recommended

Get the most out of your free Workspace by installing the Stackdriver Monitoring and Logging agents on each of your VM instances. Agents collect more information from your VM instances, including metrics and logs from third party applications:

1. Switch to the terminal connected to your VM instance, or create a new one.
2. Install the Stackdriver agents by running the following commands on your instance:

```
# To install the Stackdriver monitoring agent:
$ curl -sSO https://dl.google.com/cloudagents/install-monitoring
-agent.sh
$ sudo bash install-monitoring-agent.sh

# To install the Stackdriver logging agent:
$ curl -sSO https://dl.google.com/cloudagents/install-logging-ag
ent.sh
$ sudo bash install-logging-agent.sh
```

For more details and troubleshoot options when installing the agents, see Installing the Stackdriver Monitoring Agent and Installing the Stackdriver Logging Agent.

Continue

Stackdriver will mail daily or weekly reports if you opt email to have them emailed to you (see Figure 18.6).

FIGURE 18.6 Listing of email reporting options

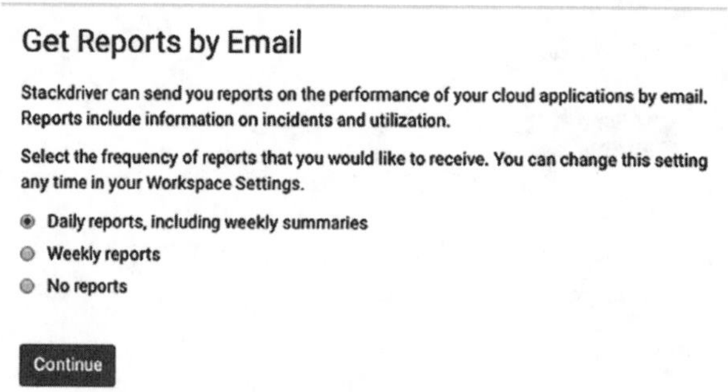

Get Reports by Email

Stackdriver can send you reports on the performance of your cloud applications by email. Reports include information on incidents and utilization.

Select the frequency of reports that you would like to receive. You can change this setting any time in your Workspace Settings.

- ◉ Daily reports, including weekly summaries
- ○ Weekly reports
- ○ No reports

Continue

When the initialization process is done, a form similar to the one shown in Figure 18.7 appears, which lists some common tasks, such as adding metrics and viewing release notes.

FIGURE 18.7 The Stackdriver Workspace initialization is complete.

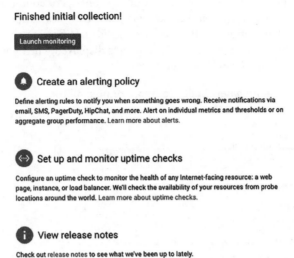

After the Workspace is initialized, navigate to Stackdriver Monitoring to display a Monitoring Overview page, similar to Figure 18.8.

FIGURE 18.8 Monitoring Overview page in Stackdriver

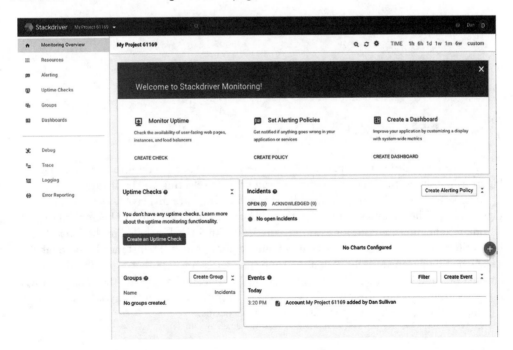

At this point, Stackdriver agents are installed and you have a Workspace available.

Next, create a policy to monitor a metric. A policy consists of conditions that determine when to issue an alert or notification, for example when CPU utilization is greater than 80 percent for more than 5 minutes. Policies also include notification channels and optional documentation, as shown in Figure 18.9. This form is displayed when you click Create Policy from the Monitoring Overview page.

FIGURE 18.9   Creating a new policy for monitoring a metric

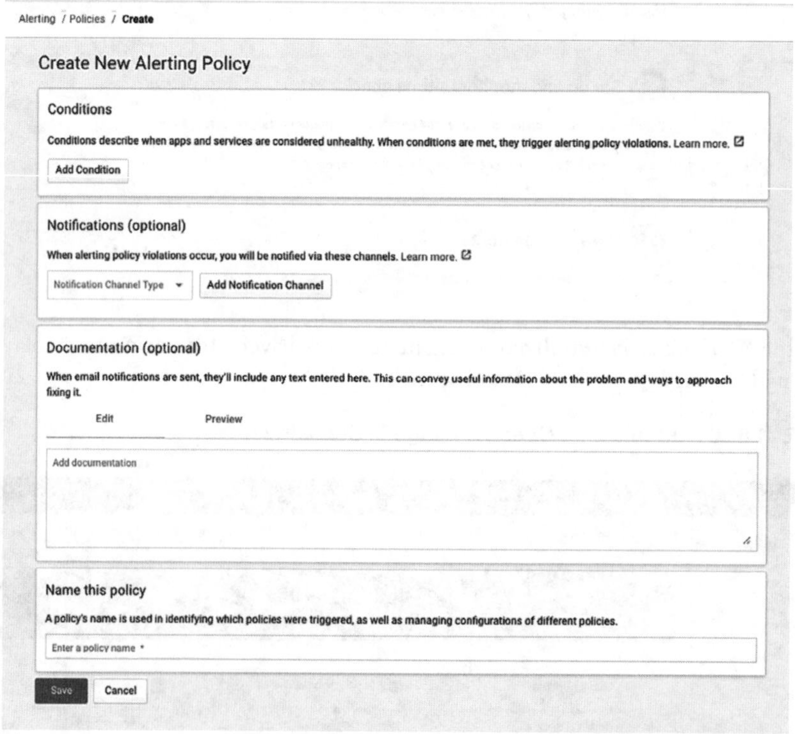

Click Add Condition to display a form where you can specify condition parameters. Figure 18.10 shows the Metric Condition form prior to selecting CPU utilization.

After selecting CPU utilization, additional parameters are displayed, as shown in Figure 18.11. The condition will check the CPU utilization status. It will be applied to VMs that match the filter criteria, for example, any VM with a label included in the filter. The filter criteria include VM features such as zone, region, project ID, instance ID, and labels. The Group By parameter allows you to group time series, or data that is produced at regular intervals and has a fixed format, for example by zone, and aggregate the values so there are fewer time series to display. This is especially helpful, for example, if you want to have a group of VMs in a cluster appear as a single time series.

FIGURE 18.10   Selecting a CPU utilization metric

FIGURE 18.11   Additional parameters to configure CPU utilization monitoring

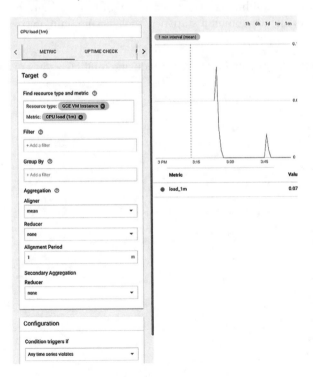

Agents send data from monitored resources to Stackdriver in streams. To perform checks on the streamed data, the data points need to be aggregated at specific time intervals. For example, data points may be received every 20 seconds but for monitoring purposes, we check the average CPU utilization per minute. Consider a stream of CPU utilization metrics that come in to Stackdriver over a 1-minute period. It is useful to consolidate those measures into a single value, like the average, maximum, or minimum value for the set of measures for that minute. This process of grouping data into regular-sized buckets of time is called aligning. Figure 18.12 shows some of the functions, including min, max, and mean, that can be applied to data that arrives within a time bucket.

FIGURE 18.12 Optional aggregates for Aligner

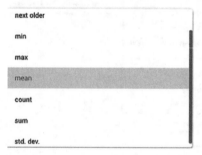

In addition to aligning time series, when you aggregate, you can specify a reducer, which is a function for combining values in a group of time series to produce a single value. The reducers include common statistics, such as sum, min, max, and count (see Figure 18.13).

FIGURE 18.13 Aggregate functions for reducing multiple values to a single value

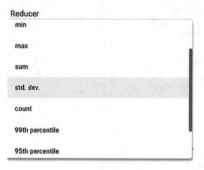

Next, you need to specify when a condition should trigger, as shown in Figure 18.14. This could be anytime you see a value that exceeds the specified threshold, or it could be only if the measured value exceeds a threshold for an extended period of time. For example, you may only want to trigger an alert on CPU utilization if it is above a threshold for more than five minutes. This can help prevent too many alerts from being generated just because there is an occasional but short-term spike in CPU utilization.

FIGURE 18.14   Specifying a threshold above which an alert is triggered

Configuration

Condition triggers if

Any time series violates ▾

Condition	Threshold	For
is above ▾	80	3 minutes ▾

A policy can have one or more notification channels. Channels include email notification as well as Slack, Google Cloud Console (mobile), and popular DevOps tools such as PagerDuty, HipChat, and Campfire (see Figure 18.15).

FIGURE 18.15   Specifying notification channels

Notifications (optional)

When alerting policy violations occur, you will be notified via these channels. Learn more. ☑

Campfire   ation Channel

Google Cloud Console (mobile)

Email

HipChat   de any text entered here. This can convey useful information :

PagerDuty

PagerDuty Sync

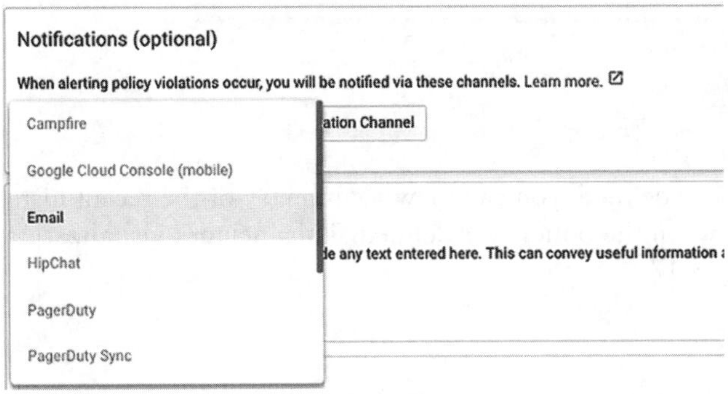

The documentation parameter, shown in Figure 18.16, is optional but recommended. The documentation will be included in notifications, which can help DevOps engineers understand the problem and provide information on how to resolve the issue.

FIGURE 18.16 Adding documentation and a policy name along with a condition and notification specifications

After policies are defined, you can view a summary of the recent history of the metric back to the time when the policy was defined. This includes visualizations such as those shown in Figure 18.17.

FIGURE 18.17   The status of the policy and a display of CPU load in the recent past

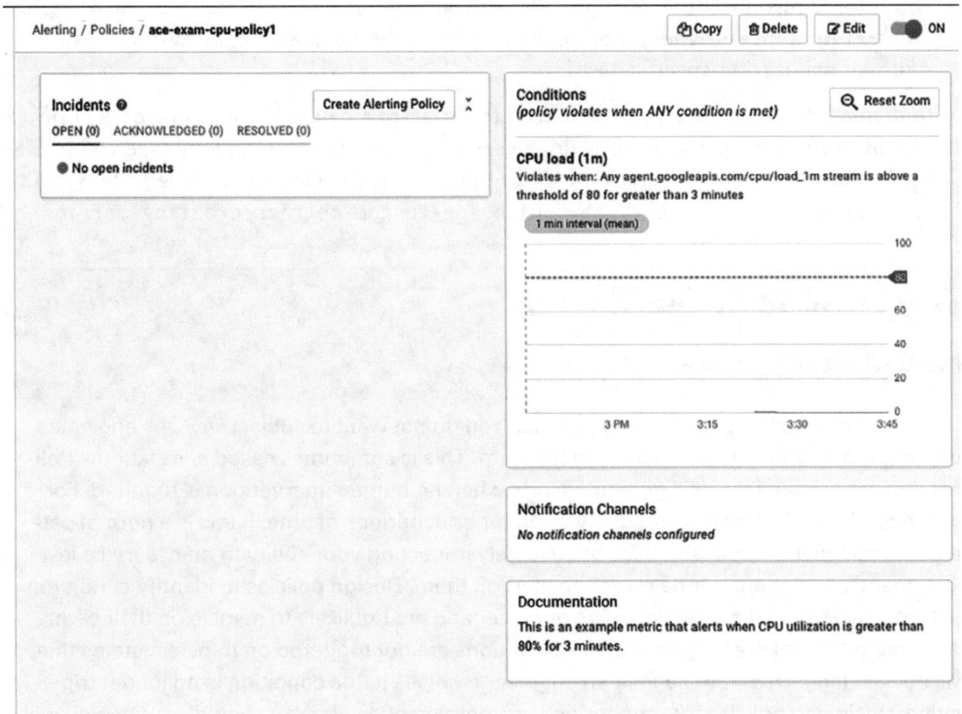

Creating Custom Metrics

If there is an application-specific metric you would like to monitor, you can create custom metrics. Custom metrics are like predefined metrics, except you create them. The names of custom metrics start with custom.googleapis.com/, so they are easy to recognize by name. The most important difference is that you can decide what time series data to write to the custom metric.

There are two ways to create custom metrics: using OpenCensus, an open source monitoring library (https://opencensus.io/) or using Stackdriver's Monitoring API. OpenCensus provides a higher-level, monitoring-focused API, while the Stackdriver Monitoring API is lower-level.

When you define a custom metric, you will need to specify the following:

- A type name that is unique within the project
- A project
- A display name and description
- A metric kind, such as a gauge, delta, or cumulative metric. Gauges are measures at a point in time, deltas capture the change over an interval, and cumulative are accumulated values over an interval.

- Metric labels
- Monitored resource objects to include with time series data points. These provide the context for a measurement. For example, you could include an application instance ID with an application-specific metric.

To define a custom metric, you will need to program a call to the monitoring API or use the OpenCensus library. How this is done varies by the programming language you use. See Google's Stackdriver documentation for examples using C#, Go, Java, Node.js, PHP, and Python (https://cloud.google.com/monitoring/custom-metrics/creating-metrics).

 Real World Scenario

Too Many Monitors Are As Bad As Too Few

Be careful when crafting monitoring policies. You do not want to subject DevOps engineers to so many alerts that they begin to ignore them. This is sometimes called alert fatigue. Policies that are too sensitive will generate alerts when no human intervention is required. For example, CPU utilization may regularly spike for brief periods of time. If this is a normal pattern for your environment and it is not adversely impacting your ability to meet service level agreements, then there is little reason to alert on them. Design policies to identify conditions that actually require the attention of an engineer and are not likely to resolve on their own. Use thresholds that are long enough so conditions are not triggered on transient states that will not last long. Often by the time an engineer resolves it, the condition is no longer triggering. Designing policies for monitoring is something of an art. You should assume you will need multiple iterations to tune your policies to find the right balance of generating just the right kinds of useful alerts without also generating alerts that are not helpful.

Logging with Stackdriver

Stackdriver Logging is a service for collecting, storing, filtering, and viewing log and event data generated in GCP and in Amazon Web Services. Logging is a managed service, so you do not need to configure or deploy servers to use the service.

The Associate Cloud Engineering Exam guidelines note three logging tasks a cloud engineer should be familiar with:

- Configuring log sinks
- Viewing and filtering logs
- Viewing message details

We'll review each of these in this section.

Configuring Log Sinks

Stackdriver Logging retains log data for 30 days. This is sufficient if you use logs to diagnose operational issues but rarely view the logs after a few days. This is often not enough.

Your organization may need to keep logs longer to comply with government or industry regulations. You may also want to analyze logs to gain insight into application performance. For these use cases, it is best to export logging data to a long-term storage system like Cloud Storage or BigQuery.

The process of copying data from Logging to a storage system is called exporting, and the location to which you write the log data is called a sink. You can create a log sink by navigating to the Logging section of Cloud Console and selecting the Exports option from the Logging menu, as shown in Figure 18.18.

FIGURE 18.18   Logging Export form in Cloud Console

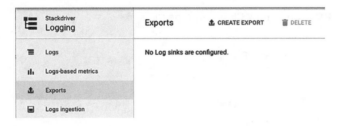

Click Create Export to open a form to create a log sink. The form prompts for three parameters:

- Sink name
- Sink service
- Sink destination

You can make up a sink name, as in Figure 18.19. The sink service is one of the following:

- BigQuery
- Cloud Storage
- Cloud Pub/Sub
- Custom Destination

FIGURE 18.19   Creating a BigQuery log sink

If you choose BigQuery as your service, the sink destination will be an existing BigQuery data set or a new data set, as shown in Figure 18.19. When log data is exported to BigQuery, it is organized into tables based on the log name and timestamps. For example, a syslog exported on January 2, 2019, would have the name syslog_20190102. The tables have columns storing the timestamp, log name, and text payload or log message.

If you choose Cloud Storage, you can export logs to an existing bucket or you can create a new bucket (see Figure 18.20). When log data is exported to Cloud Storage, Logging writes a set of files to the sink bucket. Files are organized hierarchically by log type and date. For example, if a syslog is exported on January 2, 2019, to a bucket named ace-exam-log-sink1, the path to the file would be `ace-exam-log-sink1/syslog/2019/01/02/`.

FIGURE 18.20 Creating a Cloud Storage log sink

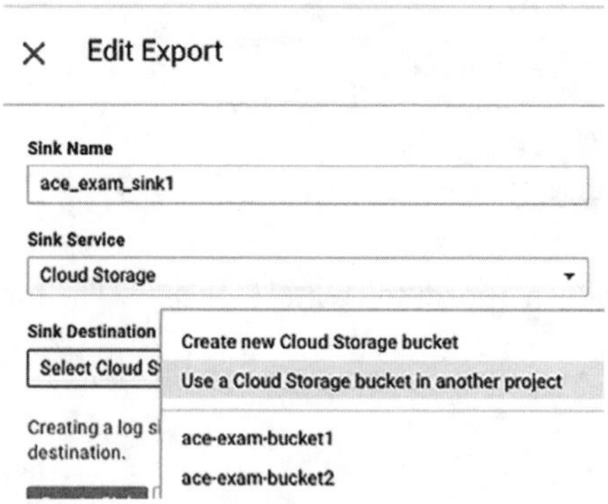

If you choose Cloud Pub/Sub, then you can choose between creating a topic or using an existing one, as shown in Figure 18.21. When log data is exported to Cloud Pub/Sub, the data is encoded in base64 in an object structure known as a LogEntry. LogEntries contain the logname, timestamp, textPayload, and resource properties, such as `type`, `instance_id`, `zone`, and `project_id`.

FIGURE 18.21 Creating a Pub/Sub log sink

A custom destination is used to specify the name of a project, other than the current project, that is hosting the sink. If you choose to create a new object as a sink, you will be prompted to name the new sink, as shown in Figure 18.22.

FIGURE 18.22 Specifying the name of a new BigQuery data set

Create new BigQuery dataset

Name

ace_exam_sink_dataset2

CANCEL   CREATE

After a sink is created, you will receive a message such as the one shown in Figure 18.23, with details on the newly created sink.

FIGURE 18.23 Confirmation that a new sink has been created

Sink created

Export sink **ace-exam-sink1** was successfully created.

A unique service account, **p601440046466-274027@gcp-sa-logging.iam.gserviceaccount.com**, has been created with permissions to write logs to the destination, **storage.googleapis.com/ace-exam-bucket1**.

CLOSE

Viewing and Filtering Logs

To view the contents of logs, navigate to the Stackdriver Logging section of the console and select Logs in the Logging menu, as shown in Figure 18.24.

FIGURE 18.24 Listing of log entries in Cloud Console

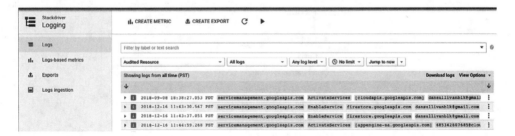

Notice that at the top of the form there are several options for filtering log messages, including filtering by the following:

- Label or text search
- Resource type
- Log type
- Log level
- Time limit

There is also an option to jump to the latest entries by selecting Jump To Now.

You can use the label or text search to filter on text strings or labels in log messages. For example, Figure 18.25 shows a set of log entries filtered by the text Monitoring. Stackdriver will add types such as text: as needed.

FIGURE 18.25   Log entries that contain the text string Monitoring

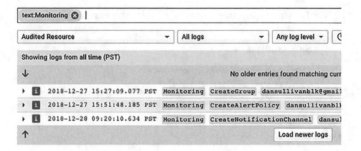

The resource type drop-down box (see Figure 18.26) provides a list of GCP resource types, including any audited resources, VM instances, subnetworks, projects, and databases.

FIGURE 18.26   Partial list of resource types for filtering logs

The drop-down box labeled All Logs lets you filter by log type (see Figure 18.27).

FIGURE 18.27   Example listing of logs generating entries in Stackdriver Logging

The next option, Any Log Level, shows log message levels, such as Error, Info, Warning, and Debug (see Figure 18.28).

FIGURE 18.28   A list of log levels that can be used to filter log entries displayed

The time selection filter shows No Limit by default. The drop-down (see Figure 18.29) includes several time spans and allows for a custom time limit.

FIGURE 18.29   Predefined time span options for filtering log entries

If you choose Custom, you can select start and end dates, as shown in Figure 18.30.

FIGURE 18.30   Form for specifying a custom time range for filtering log entries

Viewing Message Details

Each log entry is displayed as a single line when you view the contents of logs. Notice the triangle icon at the left end of the line. If you click that icon, the line will expand to show additional detail. For example, Figure 18.31 shows a log entry expanded one level.

FIGURE 18.31   A log entry expanded one level

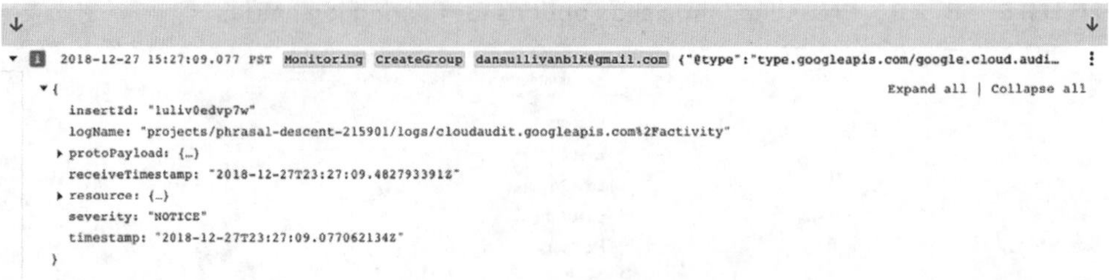

In the case of the first-level expansion, you see high-level information such as insertId, logName, and receiveTimestamp. You also see other structured data elements, such as protoPayload and resources. Figure 18.32 shows the protoPayload structure expanded.

FIGURE 18.32 A log entry with the protoPayload structure expanded

```
▼ ⓘ  2018-12-27 15:27:09.077 PST  Monitoring  CreateGroup  dansullivanblk@gmail.com  {"@type":"
  ▼ {
      insertId: "1uliv0edvp7w"
      logName: "projects/phrasal-descent-215901/logs/cloudaudit.googleapis.com%2Factivity"
    ▼ protoPayload: {
        @type: "type.googleapis.com/google.cloud.audit.AuditLog"
      ▶ authenticationInfo: {…}
      ▶ authorizationInfo: [1]
        methodName: "google.monitoring.v3.GroupService.CreateGroup"
      ▶ request: {…}
      ▶ requestMetadata: {…}
        resourceName: "projects/phrasal-descent-215901"
      ▶ response: {…}
        serviceName: "monitoring.googleapis.com"
      }
      receiveTimestamp: "2018-12-27T23:27:09.482793391Z"
    ▶ resource: {…}
      severity: "NOTICE"
      timestamp: "2018-12-27T23:27:09.077062134Z"
    }
```

You can continue to drill down individually into each structure if there is a triangle at the left. For example, in the protoPayload structure, you could drill down into authenticationInfo, authorizationInfo, and requestMetadata, among others. Alternatively, you could click the Expand All link in the upper-right corner of the log entry listing to expand all structures (see Figure 18.33).

FIGURE 18.33 A partial listing of a fully expanded log entry

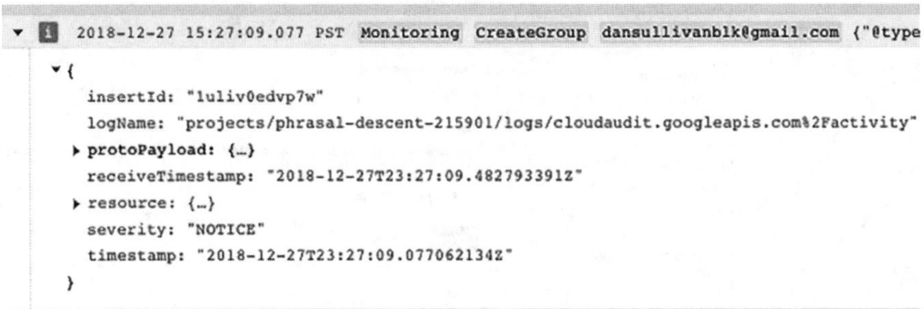

```
▼ ⓘ  2018-12-27 15:27:09.077 PST  Monitoring  CreateGroup  dansullivanblk@gmail.com  {"@type
  ▼ {
      insertId: "1uliv0edvp7w"
      logName: "projects/phrasal-descent-215901/logs/cloudaudit.googleapis.com%2Factivity"
    ▶ protoPayload: {…}
      receiveTimestamp: "2018-12-27T23:27:09.482793391Z"
    ▶ resource: {…}
      severity: "NOTICE"
      timestamp: "2018-12-27T23:27:09.077062134Z"
    }
```

Stackdriver Logging is used to collect log data and events and store them for up to 30 days. Logs can be exported to Cloud Storage, BigQuery, and Cloud Pub/Sub. Cloud Console provides a logging interface that provides multiple ways to filter and search log entries.

Using Cloud Diagnostics

Google Cloud Platform provides diagnostic tools that software developers can use to collect information about the performance and functioning of their applications. Specifically, developers can use Cloud Trace and Cloud Debug to collect data as their applications execute.

Overview of Cloud Trace

Cloud Trace is a distributed tracing system for collecting latency data from an application. This helps developers understand where applications are spending their time and to identify cases where performance is degrading. Figure 18.34 shows the overview page of the Cloud Trace service.

FIGURE 18.34   Overview of Cloud Trace

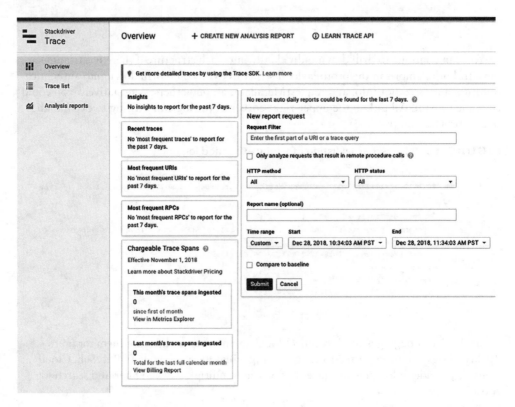

From the Cloud Trace console, you can list traces generated by applications running in a project. Traces are generated when developers specifically call Cloud Trace from their applications. In addition to seeing lists of traces, you can create reports that filter trace data according to report criteria (see Figure 18.35).

FIGURE 18.35   Creating a report using Cloud Trace data

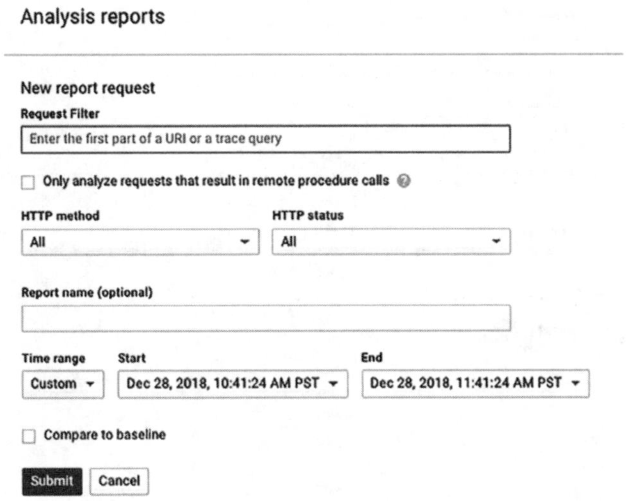

Analysis reports

New report request
Request Filter

Enter the first part of a URI or a trace query

☐ Only analyze requests that result in remote procedure calls ⃝

HTTP method   **HTTP status**

All   ▾   All   ▾

Report name (optional)

Time range   **Start**   **End**

Custom ▾   Dec 28, 2018, 10:41:24 AM PST ▾   Dec 28, 2018, 11:41:24 AM PST ▾

☐ Compare to baseline

Submit   Cancel

In addition to filtering on time and trace query, you can filter on HTTP method (see Figure 18.36) and return status (see Figure 18.37).

FIGURE 18.36   Filtering trace data by HTTP method

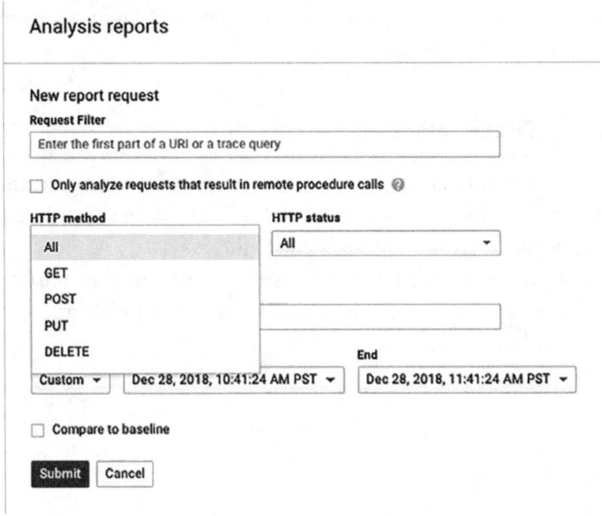

Analysis reports

New report request
Request Filter

Enter the first part of a URI or a trace query

☐ Only analyze requests that result in remote procedure calls ⃝

HTTP method   **HTTP status**

All   All   ▾

GET

POST

PUT

DELETE   End

Custom ▾   Dec 28, 2018, 10:41:24 AM PST ▾   Dec 28, 2018, 11:41:24 AM PST ▾

☐ Compare to baseline

Submit   Cancel

FIGURE 18.37 Filtering trace data by response code

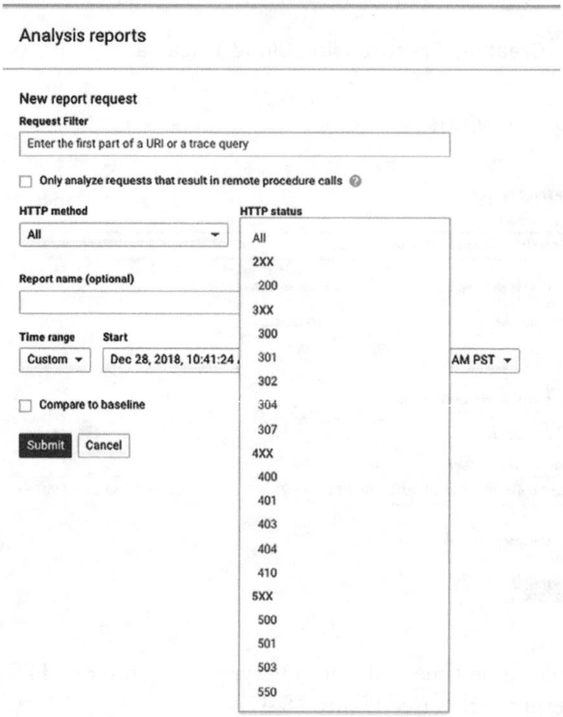

For the purpose of the Associate Cloud Engineering exam, remember that Cloud Trace is a distributed tracing application that helps developers and DevOps engineers identify sections of code that are performance bottlenecks.

Overview of Cloud Debug

Cloud Debug is an application debugger for inspecting the state of a running program. Like Cloud Trace, this is a tool typically used by software developers, but it is helpful for cloud engineers to be familiar with Cloud Debug's capabilities.

Cloud Debug allows developers to insert log statements or take snapshots of the state of an application. The service is enabled by default on App Engine and can be enabled for Compute Engine and Kubernetes Engine.

To view Cloud Debug, navigate to Cloud Debug in Cloud Console to display a page like the one shown in Figure 18.38.

FIGURE 18.38 Overview page of Cloud Debug

Selecting a program file displays the contents of the file. For example, Figure 18.39 shows the contents of a file called main.py.

FIGURE 18.39 Code listing of sample Python program provided by Google

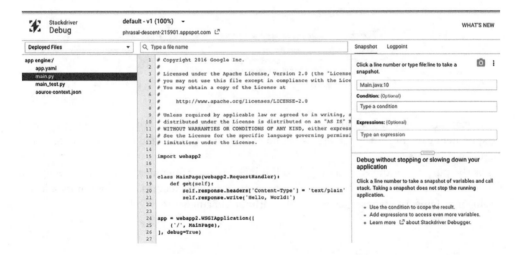

In this interface, you can click a line of code to have a snapshot taken when that line executes. In Figure 18.40 the light blue arrow on line 20 indicates where Cloud Debug will take the snapshot.

FIGURE 18.40 Setting a snapshot to be taken when line 20 executes

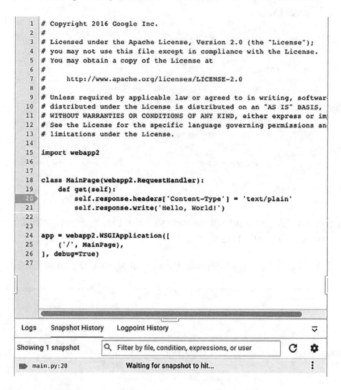

You can also inject a logpoint, which is a log statement that is written to the log when the statement executes. In Figure 18.41 a line of code has been added to create a logpoint and print a message.

For the purpose of the Associate Cloud Engineer exam, remember that Cloud Debug is used to take snapshots of the status of a program while it executes, and logpoints allow developers to inject log messages on the fly without altering source code.

FIGURE 18.41   Code with a logpoint injected

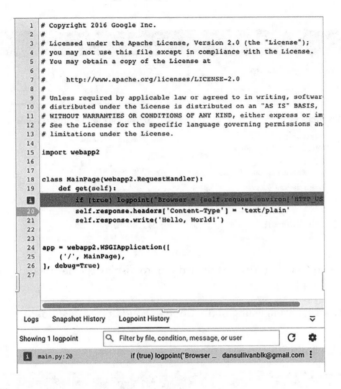

Viewing Google Cloud Platform Status

In addition to understanding the state of your applications and services, cloud engineers need to be aware of the status of GCP services. You can find this status in the Google Cloud Status Dashboard.

To view the status of Google Cloud services, navigate to the home page in Cloud Console and find the Google Cloud Platform Status card on the home page (see Figure 18.42). You can also find the dashboard at https://status.cloud.google.com/.

FIGURE 18.42   The Cloud Console home page has a card linking to the Cloud Status Dashboard.

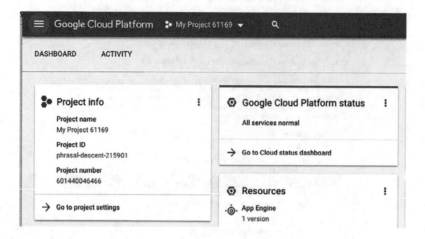

Click the Go To Cloud Status Dashboard link to display the dashboard. An example is shown in Figure 18.43.

FIGURE 18.43   Partial listing of the Google Cloud Status Dashboard

Google Cloud Status Dashboard

This page provides status information on the services that are part of Google Cloud Platform. Check back here to view the current status of the services listed below. If you are experiencing an issue not listed here, please contact Support. Learn more about what's posted on the dashboard in this FAQ. For additional information on these services, please visit cloud.google.com.

	December 21	22	23	24	25	26	27	28	
Google App Engine									✔
Google Compute Engine									✔
Google Cloud Storage	ⓘ								✔
Google BigQuery									✔
Google Cloud Dataproc									✔
Google Cloud Datastore									✔
Cloud Developer Tools									✔
Google Cloud DNS									✔
Google Cloud Functions									✔

The dashboard lists GCP services on the left side. The columns represent days in the recent past. The content of each cell indicates the status. If there is a green check mark, the service is up and running. If there is an orange icon, for example as in the Cloud Storage row and December 21 column, then there was a disruption in the service. Click the orange icon to display additional details, as shown in Figure 18.44.

FIGURE 18.44   Example description of service interruption

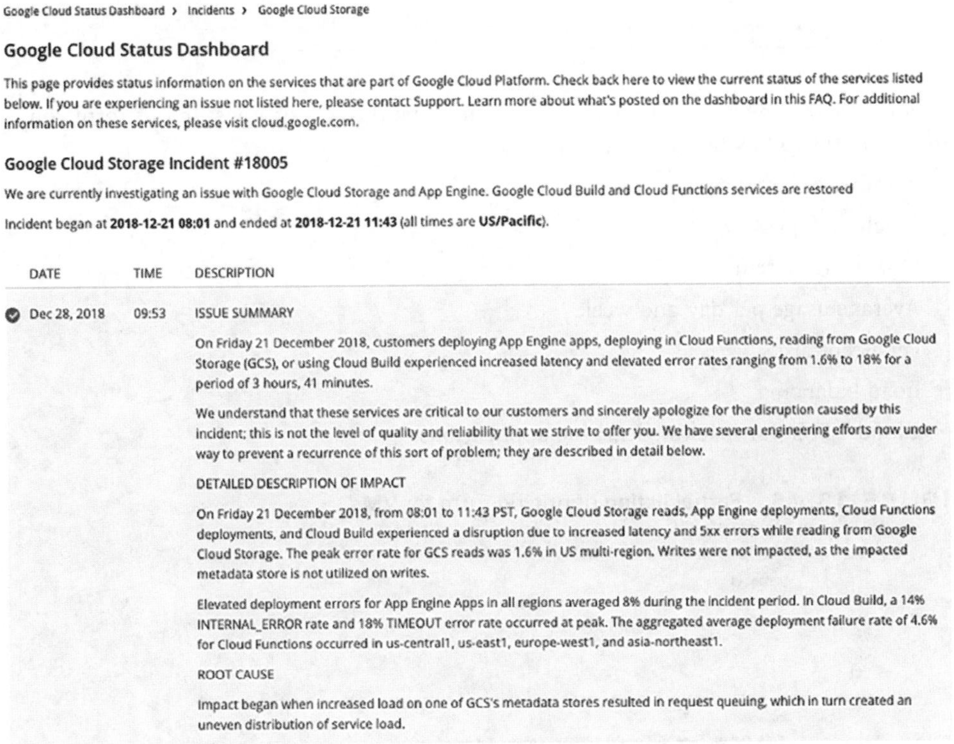

Google Cloud Status Dashboard > Incidents > Google Cloud Storage

Google Cloud Status Dashboard

This page provides status information on the services that are part of Google Cloud Platform. Check back here to view the current status of the services listed below. If you are experiencing an issue not listed here, please contact Support. Learn more about what's posted on the dashboard in this FAQ. For additional information on these services, please visit cloud.google.com.

Google Cloud Storage Incident #18005

We are currently investigating an issue with Google Cloud Storage and App Engine. Google Cloud Build and Cloud Functions services are restored

Incident began at **2018-12-21 08:01** and ended at **2018-12-21 11:43** (all times are **US/Pacific**).

DATE	TIME	DESCRIPTION
✓ Dec 28, 2018	09:53	ISSUE SUMMARY

On Friday 21 December 2018, customers deploying App Engine apps, deploying in Cloud Functions, reading from Google Cloud Storage (GCS), or using Cloud Build experienced increased latency and elevated error rates ranging from 1.6% to 18% for a period of 3 hours, 41 minutes.

We understand that these services are critical to our customers and sincerely apologize for the disruption caused by this incident; this is not the level of quality and reliability that we strive to offer you. We have several engineering efforts now under way to prevent a recurrence of this sort of problem; they are described in detail below.

DETAILED DESCRIPTION OF IMPACT

On Friday 21 December 2018, from 08:01 to 11:43 PST, Google Cloud Storage reads, App Engine deployments, Cloud Functions deployments, and Cloud Build experienced a disruption due to increased latency and 5xx errors while reading from Google Cloud Storage. The peak error rate for GCS reads was 1.6% in US multi-region. Writes were not impacted, as the impacted metadata store is not utilized on writes.

Elevated deployment errors for App Engine Apps in all regions averaged 8% during the incident period. In Cloud Build, a 14% INTERNAL_ERROR rate and 18% TIMEOUT error rate occurred at peak. The aggregated average deployment failure rate of 4.6% for Cloud Functions occurred in us-central1, us-east1, europe-west1, and asia-northeast1.

ROOT CAUSE

Impact began when increased load on one of GCS's metadata stores resulted in request queuing, which in turn created an uneven distribution of service load.

Using the Pricing Calculator

Google provides a Pricing Calculator to help GCP users understand the costs associated with the services and configuration of resources they choose to use. The Pricing Calculator is an online tool at https://cloud.google.com/products/calculator/.

With the Pricing Calculator you can specify the configuration of resources, the time they will be used, and, in the case of storage, the amount of data that will be stored. Other parameters can be specified too. Those will vary according to the service you are calculating charges for.

For example, Figure 18.45 shows some of the services available to use with the Pricing Calculator. Currently, there are almost 40 services available in the Pricing Calculator.

FIGURE 18.45 Pricing Calculator banner with a partial display of services available

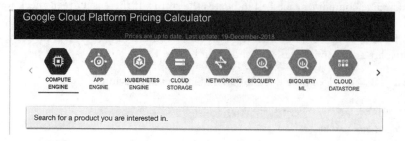

Figure 18.46 shows part of the form for estimating the cost of VMs. In this form you can specify the following:

- Number of instances
- Machine types
- Operating system
- Average usage per day and week
- Persistent disks
- Load balancing
- Cloud TPUs (for machine learning applications)

FIGURE 18.46 Partial listing of pricing form for VMs

Instances

Number of instances *

What are these instances for?

Operating System / Software
Free: Debian, CentOS, CoreOS, Ubuntu, or other User Provided OS

VM Class
Regular

Instance type
f1-micro   (vCPUs: shared, RAM: 0.60 GB)

☐ Add GPUs.

GPUs aren't available for shared vCPUs.
Local SSD
0

Datacenter location
Iowa (us-central1)

Committed usage
None

Average hours per day each server is running *
24   hours   per day

Average days per week each server is running *
7

After you enter data into the form, the Pricing Calculator will generate an estimate, such as that shown in Figure 18.47.

FIGURE 18.47   Example price estimate for 2 n1-standard-1 VMs

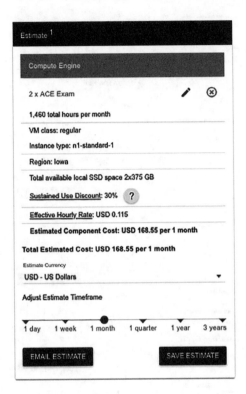

Different resources will require different parameters for an estimate. For example, Figure 18.48 shows estimating the price of a Kubernetes cluster, which requires details about VMs, persistent disks, and load balancers.

Figure 18.49 shows a further example, this time for BigQuery. For that service, you need to specify the location of your data, the amount of data stored, the amount streamed in, and the volume of data scanned when executing queries. The table parameter is where you indicate which BiqQuery table you are querying. Storage Pricing and Query Pricing both accept numeric values for the amount of data stored in the table (GBs) and the volume scanned during queries (TBs). Also, there is an option for flat rate pricing if you spend more than $40,000 per month.

FIGURE 18.48   Form for estimating the price of a Kubernetes cluster

FIGURE 18.49   The parameters required to estimate the cost of storing and querying BigQuery data

The Pricing Calculator allows you to estimate the price of multiple services and then generate a total estimate for all services.

Summary

Cloud engineers are responsible for monitoring the health and performance of applications and cloud services. GCP provides multiple tools, including monitoring, logging, debugging, and tracing services.

Stackdriver Monitoring allows you to define alerts on metrics, such as CPU utilization, so that you can be notified if part of your infrastructure is not performing as expected. Stackdriver Logging collects, stores, and manages log entries. Log data that needs to be stored more than 30 days can be exported to Cloud Storage, BigQuery, or Cloud Pub/Sub. Cloud Trace provides distributed tracing services to identify slow-running parts of code. Cloud Debug provides for creating snapshots of running code and injecting log messages without altering source code.

You can always get the status of GCP services at the Google Cloud Status Dashboard at `https://status.cloud.google.com/`.

The Pricing Calculator is designed to help you estimate the cost of almost 40 services in the GCP.

Exam Essentials

Understand the need for monitoring and the role of metrics.   Metrics provide data on the state of applications and infrastructure. We create conditions, like CPU exceeding 80 percent for 5 minutes, to trigger alerts. Alerts are delivered by notification channels. GCP has a substantial number of predefined metrics, but you can create custom metrics as well.

Stackdriver Logging collects, stores, filters, and displays log data.   Logs can come from virtually any source. Logging keeps log data for 30 days. If you need to keep log data longer than that, then you need to export the data to a log sink. Log sinks may be a Cloud Storage bucket, a BigQuery data set, or a Cloud Pub/Sub topic.

Know how to filter logs.   Logs can contain a large amount of data. Use filters to search for text or labels, limit log entries by log type and severity, and restrict the time range to a period of interest.

Log entries are hierarchical. Stackdriver Logging shows a single line summary for a log entry by default, but you can drill down into the details of a log entry. Use the Expand All and Collapse All options to quickly view or hide the full details of a log entry.

Cloud Trace is a distributed tracing service.   Software developers include Cloud Tracer code in their applications to record trace data. Trace data can be viewed as individual traces, or you can create reports that include parameters specifying a subset of traces to include.

Cloud Debug is used to analyze running code by taking snapshots or injecting logpoints. Snapshots show the stack, or execution context, at a point in the execution of a program. Logpoints are log statements injected into running code but do not require changes to source code.

GCP publishes the status of services in the Google Cloud Platform Status page. It includes a list of all services, their current status, and the status over the near past. If there is an incident in a service, you will find additional details on the impact and root cause of the problem.

The Pricing Calculator is used to estimate the cost of resources and services in the GCP. It is available at https://cloud.google.com/products/calculator/.

There is a separate calculator for each service. Each service has its own set of parameters for estimating costs. The Pricing Calculator allows you to estimate the cost of multiple services and generate a total estimate for all those services.

Review Questions

1. What Stackdriver service is used to generate alerts when the CPU utilization of a VM exceeds 80 percent?

   A. Logging

   B. Monitoring

   C. Cloud Trace

   D. Cloud Debug

2. You have just created a virtual machine, and you'd like Stackdriver Monitoring to alert you via email whenever the CPU average utilization exceeds 75 percent for 5 minutes. What do you need to do to the VM to have this happen?

   A. Install a Stackdriver workspace

   B. Install the Stackdriver monitoring agent on the VM

   C. Edit the VM configuration in Cloud Console and check the Monitor With Stackdriver checkbox

   D. Set a notification channel

3. Stackdriver can be used to monitor resources where?

   A. In Google Cloud Platform only

   B. In Google Cloud Platform and Amazon Web Services only

   C. In Google Cloud Platform and on premises data centers

   D. In Google Cloud Platform, Amazon Web Services, and on premises data centers

4. Grouping a set of metrics that arrive in a period of time into regular-sized buckets is called what?

   A. Aggregation

   B. Alignment

   C. Minimization

   D. Consolidation

5. You have created a condition of CPU utilization, and you want to receive notifications. Which of the following are options?

   A. Email only

   B. PagerDuty only

   C. Hipchat and PagerDuty

   D. Email, PagerDuty, and Hipchat

6. When you create a policy to notify you of a potential problem with your infrastructure, you can specify optional documentation. Why would you bother putting documentation in that form?

    A. It is saved to Cloud Storage for future use.

    B. It can help you or a colleague understand the purpose of the policy.

    C. It can contain information that would help someone diagnose and correct the problem.

    D. Options B and C.

7. What is alert fatigue, and why is it a problem?

    A. Too many alert notifications are sent for events that do not require human intervention, and eventually DevOps engineers begin to pay less attention to notifications.

    B. Too many alerts put unnecessary load on your systems.

    C. Too few alerts leave DevOps engineers uncertain of the state of your applications and infrastructure.

    D. Too many false alerts

8. How long is log data stored in Stackdriver Logging?

    A. 7 days

    B. 15 days

    C. 30 days

    D. 60 days

9. You need to store log entries for a longer period of time than Stackdriver Logging retains them. What is the best option for preserving log data?

    A. There is no option; once the data retention period passes, Stackdriver Logging deletes the data.

    B. Create a log sink and export the log data using Stackdriver Logging's export functionality.

    C. Write a Python script to use the Stackdriver API to write the data to Cloud Storage.

    D. Write a Python script to use the Stackdriver API to write the data to BigQuery.

10. Which of the following are options for logging sinks?

    A. Cloud Storage bucket only

    B. BigQuery dataset and Cloud Storage bucket only

    C. Cloud Pub/Sub topic only

    D. Cloud Storage bucket, BigQuery dataset, and Cloud Pub/Sub topic

11. Which of the following can be used to filter log entries when viewing logs in Stackdriver Logging?

    A. Label or text search only

    B. Resource type and log type only

C. Time and resource type only

D. Label or text search, resource type, log type, and time

12. Which of the following is not a standard log level that can be used to filter log viewings?

A. Critical

B. Halted

C. Warning

D. Info

13. You are viewing log entries and spot one that looks suspicious. You are not familiar with the kind of log entry, and you want to see the complete details of the log entry as quickly as possible. What would you do?

A. Drill down one by one into each structure in the log entry.

B. Click Expand all to show all details.

C. Write a Python script to reformat the log entry.

D. Click the Show Detail link next to the log entry.

14. What Stackdriver service is best for identifying where bottlenecks exist in your application?

A. Monitoring

B. Logging

C. Trace

D. Debug

15. There is a bug in a microservice. You have reviewed application outputs but cannot identify the problem. You decide you need to step through the code. What Stackdriver service would you use to give you insight into the status of the services at particular points in execution?

A. Monitoring

B. Logging

C. Trace

D. Debug

16. You believe there may be a problem with BigQuery in the us-central zone. Where would you go to check the status of the BigQuery service for the quickest access to details?

A. Email Google Cloud Support.

B. Check `https://status.cloud.google.com/`.

C. Check `https://bigquery.status.cloud.google.com/`.

D. Call Google tech support.

17. You would like to estimate the cost of GCP resources you will be using. Which services would require you to have information on the virtual machines you will be using?

    A. Compute Engine and BigQuery

    B. Compute Engine and Kubernetes Engine

    C. BigQuery and Kubernetes Engine

    D. BigQuery and Cloud Pub/Sub

18. You are generating an estimate of the cost of using BigQuery. One of the parameters is Query Pricing. You have to specify a value in TB units. What is the value you are specifying?

    A. The amount of data stored in BigQuery

    B. The amount of data returned by the query

    C. The amount of data scanned by the query

    D. The amount of data in Cloud Storage bucket

19. Why do you need to specify the operating system to be used when estimating the cost of a VM?

    A. All operating systems are charged a fixed rate.

    B. Some operating systems incur a cost.

    C. It's not necessary; it is only included for documentation.

    D. To estimate the cost of Bring Your Own License configurations.

20. You want to create a custom metric for use in Stackdriver Monitoring but do not want to use the low-level Stackdriver API. What is an alternative open source option for working with custom metrics?

    A. Prometheus

    B. OpenCensus

    C. Grafana

    D. Nagios

Appendix

Answers to Review Questions

Chapter 1: Overview of Google Cloud Platform

1.   B. The basic unit for purchasing computing resources is the virtual machine (VM). A physical server underlies VMs, but the resources of a physical server are allocated to VMs. Blocks and subnets are not relevant to the fundamental unit of computing.

2.   D. When using managed clusters, the cloud provider will monitor the health of nodes in the cluster, set up networking between nodes in the cluster, and configure firewall and other security controls.

3.   B. App Engine is a serverless platform for running applications, while Cloud Functions is a service for executing short-running functions in response to events. Kubernetes Engine is a managed cluster service, and both Kubernetes Engine and Compute Engine require you to configure servers.

4.   B. Object storage, like Cloud Storage, provides redundantly stored objects without limits on the amount of data you can store, which makes option B correct. Since file system functionality is not required, option D is not a good option. Block storage could be used, but you would have to manage your own replication to ensure high availability. Caches are transient, in-memory storage and are not high-availability, persistent storage systems.

5.   D. Block sizes in a block storage system can vary; therefore, option D is the correct answer. Block size is established when a file system is created. 4KB block sizes are commonly used in Linux.

6.   C. Firewalls in Google Cloud Platform (GCP) are software-defined network controls that limit the flow of traffic into and out of a network or subnetwork, so option C is the correct answer. Routers are used to move traffic to appropriate destinations on the network. Identity access management is used for authenticating and authorizing users; it is not relevant to network controls between subnetworks. IP address tables are not a security control.

7.   C. Option C is correct because specialized services in GCP are serverless. Google manages the compute resources used by the services. There is no need for a user to allocate or monitor VMs.

8.   B. Option B is correct; investing in servers works well when an organization can accurately predict the number of servers and other equipment it will need for an extended period and can utilize that equipment consistently. Startups are not established businesses with histories that can guide expected needs in three to five years. It does not matter if a budget is fixed or variable; investing in servers should be based on demand for server capacity.

9.   B. The characteristics of the server, such as the number of virtual servers, the amount of memory, and the region where you run the VM, influence the cost, so option B is correct. Time of day is not a factor, nor is the type of application you run on the VM.

10.   D. Cloud Vision is one of GCP's specialized services. Users of the service do not need to configure any VMs to use the service.

11. B. Containers give the most flexibility for using the resources of a cluster efficiently and orchestration platforms reduce the operations overhead, which makes option B correct. Running in a single cluster is not recommended because if the server fails, all services will be down. Using two VMs with one read-only is not useful. Read-only servers are sometimes used with databases, but there was no mention of databases in the question. Using a small VM and upgrading when it is no longer able to keep up with the workload delivers poor-quality service to users and should be avoided.

12. D. All of the operations are available to a system administrator after creating a VM, so option D is correct.

13. A. Option A is correct; Cloud Filestore is based on Network Filesystem (NSF), which is a distributed file management system. The other options are file systems supported by Linux but are not the foundation of Cloud Filestore.

14. A. When you create a network, it is treated as a virtual private cloud, which makes option A correct. Resources are added to the VPC and are not accessible outside the VPC unless you explicitly configure them to be. A subdomain is related to web domains and not related to GPC network configuration. Clusters, such as Kubernetes clusters, may be in your network, but are not a characteristic of the network.

15. D. Caches use memory, and that makes them the fastest storage type for reading data, so option D is right. Caches are data stores on the backend of distributed systems, not the clients. A cache would have no effect on client-side JavaScript execution. Caches do not store data in a cache if power is lost; the data would have to be reloaded. Caches can get out of sync with the system of truth because the system of truth could be updated, but the cache may not be updated. Caches have faster read times than SSDs and HDDs.

16. B. Option B is correct; cloud providers have large capacity and can quickly allocate those resources to different customers. With a mix of customers and workloads, they can optimize the allocation of resources. Option A is incorrect; cloud providers do not take resources from one customer to give them to another, with the exception of preemptible instances. Option C is incorrect; cloud providers usually offer discounts for increased use.

17. C. Specialized services are monitored by Google so users do not have to monitor them; therefore, option C is correct. Specialized services provide a specific compute functionality but do not require the user to configure any resources. They also provide APIs.

18. B. Attached drives are block storage devices. Cloud Storage is the object storage service and does not attach directly to a VM. NoSQL is a type of database, not a storage system. Attached drives may be either SSDs or hard drives.

19. C. Databases require persistent storage on block devices. Object storage does not provide data block or file system storage, making option C the correct answer. Data storage is not a type of storage system. Caches are often used with databases to improve read performance, but they are volatile and are not suitable for persistently storing data files.

20. B. All three services are serverless, so the user does not need to configure VMs; therefore, option B is correct. Cloud Storage is charged based on time and size of data stored. App Engine Standard and Cloud Functions are not restricted to just the Go language.

Chapter 2: Google Cloud Computing Services

1. C. Cloud Load Balancing distributes workloads within and across regions, provides health checks, and implements autoscaling. Cloud DNS provides domain name services, such as translating a URL like www.example.com to an IP address. Cloud Spanner is a distributed relational database but does not implement workload distribution. Cloud CDN distributes content across regions to reduce latency when delivering content to users across the globe.

2. C. App Engine flexible environments allow you to run containers on the App Engine PaaS. Kubernetes Engine is an orchestration platform for running containers. Both provide container management services. The App Engine standard environment runs applications in language-specific sandboxes and is not a general container management system. Cloud Functions is a serverless service for running code in response to events. It does not provide container services.

3. D. Options A and B are both correct answers. The Apigee API platform provides policy-based rate-limiting and routing services to help accommodate spikes in traffic. It also provides OAuth 2.0 and SAML authentication. It does not provide version control; Cloud Source Repositories is the service user for version control.

4. A. Cloud Armor builds on GCP's load balancing services to provide the ability to allow or restrict access based on IP address, deploy rules to counter cross-site scripting attacks, and provide countermeasures to SQL injection attacks. Cloud CDN is a content distribution service, not a security service. Identity Access Management is a security service, but it is for authentication and authorization, not denial-of-service mitigation. Virtual private clouds are used to restrict network access to an organization's resources, but it does not have features to mitigate denial-of-service attacks. Also, Cloud CDN acts as a first line of defense in the case of DDoS attacks.

5. A. This is a good use case for preemptible VMs because they could reduce the cost of running the second application without the risk of losing work. Since tasks are deleted from the queue only after they are completed if a preemptible VM is shut down before completing the task, another VM can perform the task. Also, there is no harm in running a task more than once, so if two VMs do the same task, it will not adversely affect the output of the application. DataProc and Spanner are not appropriate products for this task.

6. B. Cloud Memorystore is the only GCP designed to cache data in memory. Cloud SQL is a relational database service and might be a good option for the backend database. Cloud Spanner is a global relational database and is a good option when you need a globally consistent database. Cloud Datastore is a document database suitable for product catalogs, user profiles, and other semistructured data.

7. D. All three of the services listed, Compute Engine, Cloud Storage, and network firewalls, can be managed and configured using Cloud SDK.

8. D. Cloud Functions is a serverless product, no configuration is required.

9. D. The Stackdriver Logging product is used to consolidate and manage logs generated by applications and servers.

10. B. The data analytics set of specialized services includes products that help with extraction, transformation, and loading (ETL) and work with both batch and streaming data. The Apigee API platform is used for managing APIs and does not meet the needs described. AI and machine learning might be useful for analyzing data in the data warehouse, but the services in that set are not always helpful for ETL operations. Cloud SDK is used to control services but by itself is not directly able to perform the operations needed.

11. B. Bigtable is designed to accept billions of rows of data. Collecting data from 100,000 sensors every 5 seconds will generate 6,000,000 data points every minute, or 8,640,000,000 data points per day. Spanner is a relational database and supports transactions, but they are not needed. Cloud SQL MySQL and Cloud SQL PostgreSQL would be difficult to scale to this level of read and write performance.

12. A. Cloud Firestore is a mobile database service that can synchronize data between mobile devices and centralized storage. Spanner is a global relational database for large-scale applications that require transaction support in highly scaled databases. Datastore and Cloud SQL could be used but would require more custom development to synchronize data between mobile devices and the centralized data store.

13. B. A computationally intensive application obviously requires high CPUs, but the fact that there are many mathematical calculations indicates that a GPU should be used. You might consider running this in a cluster, but the work is not easily distributed over multiple servers, so you will need to have a single server capable of handling the load. Immediate access to large amounts of data indicates that a high-memory machine should be recommended.

14. B. Identities are abstractions of users. They can also represent characteristics of processes that run on behalf of a human user or a VM in the GCP. Identities are not related to VM IDs. Roles are collections of privileges that can be granted to identities. Option D is synonymous with option C.

15. C. Cloud Natural Language Processing provides functionality for analyzing text. Cloud Text Miner does not exist. Cloud ML is a general-purpose machine learning service that could be applied to text analysis but would require knowledge of language processing, which the client does not have. Cloud Vision is for image processing.

16. B. Both options B and D would meet the need of running Spark, which would give the data scientists access to the machine library they need. However, option D requires that they manage and monitor the cluster of servers, which would require more DevOps and administration work than if they used the Dataproc service. Option C, BigQuery, is a scalable database, not a platform for running Spark. Cloud Spark is a fictitious product and does not exist in the GCP.

17. B. Option B is correct. Spanner supports ANSI 2011 standard SQL and global transactions. Cloud SQL supports standard SQL but does not have global transaction. Datastore and Bigtable are NoSQL databases.

18. A. Dataproc is designed to execute workflows in both batch and streaming modes, which makes option A correct. BigQuery is a data warehouse service. Datastore is a document database. AutoML is a machine learning service.

19. C. App Engine standard environment provides a serverless Python sandbox that scales automatically, so option C is correct. App Engine flexible environment runs containers and requires more configuration. Cloud Engine and Kubernetes Engine both require significant management and monitoring.

20. D. Error reporting consolidates crash information, which makes Error Reporting the right answer. Monitoring collects metrics on application and server performance. Logging is a log management service. Dataproc is not part of Stackdriver; it is a managed Hadoop and Spark service.

Chapter 3: Projects, Service Accounts, and Billing

1. A. Option A, the correct answer, separates the two main applications into their own folders and further allows separating private insurance from government payer, but using folders for each. This satisfies the regulatory need to keep the government payer software isolated from other software. Option B does not include an organization, which is the root of the resource hierarchy. Option C is not flexible with regard to differences in constraints on different applications. Option D is false because option A does meet the requirements.

2. C. Resource hierarchies have a single organization at the root, which makes option C correct. Below that, there are folders that can contain other folders or projects. Folders can contain multiple folders and multiple projects.

3. B. Service accounts are designed to give applications or VMs permission to perform tasks. Billing accounts are for associating charges with a payment method. Folders are part of resource hierarchies and have nothing to do with enabling an application to perform a task. Messaging accounts are a fictitious option.

4. B. Inherited policies can be overridden by defining a policy at a folder or project level. Service accounts and billing accounts are not part of the resource hierarchy and are not involved in overriding policies.

5. E. All of the listed types of constraints are supported in policies.

6. B. Option B is the correct answer because Publisher is not a primitive role. Owner, Editor, and Viewer are the three primitive privileges in GCP.

7. D. Primitive roles only include the Owner, Editor, and View permissions. Predefined roles are designed for GCP products and services, like App Engine and BigQuery. For a custom application, you can create sets of privileges that give the user with that role as much permission as needed but not more.

8. D. Users should have only the privileges that are needed to carry out their duties. This is the principle of least privilege. Rotation of duties is another security principle related to having different people perform a task at a different times. Defense in depth is the practice of using multiple security controls to protect the same asset. Option B is not a real security principal.

9. A. A resource hierarchy has only one organization, which makes option A correct. You can, however, create multiple folders and projects within a resource hierarchy.

10. B. In option B, the correct answer, the billing account is used to specify payment information and should be used to set up automatic payments. Service accounts are used to grant privileges to a VM and are not related to billing and payments. Resource accounts and credit accounts do not exist.

11. C. GCP offers a free service level for many products, which makes option C the correct answer. You can use these services without having to set up a billing account. Google charges for serverless products, such as Cloud Functions and App Engine, when customers exceed the amount allowed under the free tier.

12. D. Stackdriver Workspaces are linked to projects, not individual resources like VM instances, clusters, or App Engine apps, so option D is correct. Options A, B, and C all incorrectly indicate that Workspaces are associated with individual compute resources.

13. D. Large enterprises should use invoicing when incurring large charges, which makes option D the right answer. A self-service account is appropriate only for amounts that are within the credit limits of credit cards. Since the subdivisions are independently managed and have their own budgets, each should have its own billing accounts.

14. A. When a user is granted `iam.serviceAccountUser` at the project level, that user can manage all service accounts in the project, so option A is correct. If a new service account is created, they will automatically have privilege to manage that service account. You could grant `iam.serviceAccountUser` to the administrator at the service account level, but that would require setting the role for all service accounts. If a new service account is created, the application administrator would have to grant `iam.serviceAccountUser` to the other administrator on the new service account. `iam.serviceProjectAccountUser` is a fictional role.

15. C. When a service account is created, Google generates encrypted keys for authentication, making option C correct. Usernames and passwords are not an option for service accounts. Two-factor authentication is an authentication practice that requires two forms of authentication, such as a username password pair and a code from an authentication device. Biometrics cannot be used by services and is not an option.

16. B. Service accounts are resources that are managed by administrators, but they also function as identities that can be assigned roles, which makes option B the correct answer. Billing accounts are not related to identities. Projects are not identities; they cannot take on roles. Roles are resources but not identities. They can take on privileges, but those privileges are used only when they are attached to an identity.

17. B. Predefined roles are defined for a particular product, such as App Services or Compute Engine, so option B is the right answer. They bundle privileges often needed together when managing or using a service. Primitive roles are building blocks for other roles. Custom roles are created by users to meet their particular needs; Application roles is a fictitious role.

18. B. By default all users in an organization can create projects, which makes option B correct. The role `resourcemanager.projects.create` is the role that allows users to create projects. The billing account is not associated with creating projects.

19. D. The maximum number of organizations is determined on a per-account basis by Google, so option D is the correct answer. If you need additional organizations, you can contact Google and ask for an increase in your limit.

20. B. Users with the Organization IAM role are not necessarily responsible for determining what privileges should be assigned to users. That is determined based on the person's role in the organization and the security policies established within the organization, which makes option B correct.

Chapter 4: Introduction to Computing in Google Cloud

1. B. The App Engine standard environment can run Python applications, which can autoscale down to no instances when there is no load and thereby minimize costs. Compute Engine and the App Engine flexible environment both require more configuration management than the App Engine standard environment. Kubernetes Engine is used when a cluster of servers is needed to support large or multiple applications using the same computing resources.

2. A. Database servers require high availability to respond to queries from users or applications. Preemptible machines are guaranteed to shut down in at most 24 hours. A batch processing job with no fixed time requirements could use preemptible machines as long as the VM is restarted. High-performance computing clusters can use preemptible machines because work on a preemptible machine can be automatically rescheduled for another node on the cluster when a server is preempted. D is incorrect because there is a correct answer in the set of options.

3. A. VMs are created in projects, which are part of the resource hierarchy. They are also located in geographic regions and data centers, so a zone is specified as well. Usernames and admin roles are not specified during creation. The billing account is tied to a project and so does not have to be specified when the VM is created. Cloud storage buckets are created independently of VMs. Not all VMs will make use of storage buckets.

4. C. Compute Engine can run Docker containers if you install Docker on the VM. Kubernetes and the App Engine flexible environment support Docker containers. The App Engine standard environment provides language-specific runtime environments and does not allow customers to specify custom Docker images for use.

5. B. The name of the file that is used to build and configure a Docker container is `Dockerfile`.

6. D. Kubernetes uses 25 percent of memory up to 4GB and then slightly less for the next 4GB, and it continues to reduce the percentage of additional memory down to 2 percent of memory over 128GB.

7. B. Kubernetes provides load balancing, scaling, and automatic upgrading of software. It does not provide vulnerability scanning. GCP does have a Cloud Security Scanner product, but that is designed to work with App Engine to identify common application vulnerabilities.

8. D. The scenario described is a good fit for Kubernetes. Each of the groups of services can be structured in pods and deployed using Kubernetes deployment. Kubernetes Engine manages node health, load balancing, and scaling. App Engine Standard Edition has language-specific sandboxes and is not a good fit for this use case. Cloud Functions is designed for short-running event processing and is not the kind of continuous processing needed in this scenario. Compute Engine could meet the requirements of this use case, but it would require more effort on the part of application administrators and DevOps professionals to configure load balancers, monitor health, and manage software deployments.

9. B. This is an ideal use case for Cloud Functions. The cloud function is triggered by a file upload event. The cloud function calls the image processing service. With this setup, the two services are independent. No additional servers are required. Option A violates the requirement to keep the services independent. Options C and D incur more management overhead and will probably cost more to operate than option B.

10. D. Each invocation of a cloud function runs in a secure, isolated runtime environment. There is no need to check whether other invocations are running. With the Cloud Functions service, there is no way for a developer to control code execution at the process or thread level.

11. A. You would create a custom image after you installed the custom code, in this case the encryption library. A public image does not contain custom code, but it could be used as the base that you add custom code to. Both CentOS and Ubuntu are Linux distributions. You could use either as the base image that you add custom code to, but on their own, they do not have custom code.

12. B. Projects are the lowest level of the resource hierarchy. The organization is at the top of the hierarchy, and folders are between the organization and projects. VM instances are not part of the resource hierarchy.

13. D. All Google regions have the same level of service level agreement, so reliability is the same. Costs may differ between regions. Regulations may require that data stay within a geographic area, such as the European Union. Latency is a consideration when you want a region that is close to end users or data you will need is already stored in a particular region.

14. B. Compute Engine Admin Role is the role that gives users complete control over instances. Options A and C are fictitious roles. Compute Engine Security Admin gives users the privileges to create, modify, and delete SSL certificates and firewall rules.

15. D. Preemptible VMs will be terminated after 24 hours. Google does not guarantee that preemptible VMs will be available. Once an instance is started as a preemptible machine, it cannot migrate to a regular VM. You could, however, save a snapshot and use that to create a new regular instance.

16. C. Custom VMs can have up to 64 CPUs and up to 6.5GB of memory per vCPU.

17. C. The C programming language is not supported in the App Engine standard environment. If you need to run a C application, it can be compiled and run in a container running in the App Engine flexible environment.

18. B. Kubernetes reserves CPU capacity according to the following schedule:

   1. 6 percent of the first core

   2. 1 percent of the next core (up to two cores)

   3. 0.5 percent of the next two cores (up to four cores)

   4. 0.25 percent of any cores above four cores

19. B. The only states a Kubernetes deployment can be in are progressing, completed, and failed.

20. A. Cloud Functions is best suited for event-driven processing, such as a file being uploaded to Cloud Storage or an event being writing to a Pub/Sub queue. Long-running jobs, such as loading data into a data warehouse, are better suited to Compute Engine or App Engine.

Chapter 5: Computing with Compute Engine Virtual Machines

1. C. You should verify the project selected because all operations you perform will apply to resources in the selected project, making option C the correct answer. You do not need to open Cloud Shell unless you want to work with the command line, and if you did, you should verify that the project is correctly selected first. Logging into a VM using SSH is one of the tasks that requires you to be working with the correct project, so logging in via SSH should not happen before verifying the project. The list of VMs in the VM Instance window is a list of VMs in the current project. You should verify which project you are using to ensure you are viewing the set of VMs you think you are using.

2. A. You will need to set up billing if it is not already enabled when you start using the console, so option A is the right answer. You may create a project, but you will be able to do this only if billing is enabled. You do not need to create a storage bucket to work with the console. Specifying a default zone is not a one-time task; you may change zones throughout the life of your project.

3. B. The name of the VM, the region and zone, and the machine type can all be specified in the console along with other parameters, so option B is correct. Option A is missing required parameters. A CIDR block is a range of IP addresses that is associated with a subnet and not needed to create a VM. An IP address is assigned automatically so it is not required.

4. B. Different zones may have different machine types available, so you will need to specify a region first and then a zone to determine the set of machine types available. If the machine type does not appear in the list, it is not available in that zone. This makes option B the correct answer. Options A and C are incorrect. Subnets and IP addresses are not related to the machine types available. Unless you are specifying a custom machine type, you do not specify the amount of memory; that is defined by the machine type, so option D is incorrect.

5. C. Labels and descriptions are for helping us track our own attributes of resources; GCP does not need them to perform its tasks. As the number of servers grows, it can become difficult to track which VMs are used for which applications and services, so option C is the correct answer. Labels and a general description will help administrators track numbers of VMs and their related costs. Options A and B are used for security and storage but do not help with managing multiple VMs. Option D is only partially correct. Descriptions are helpful but so are labels.

6. A. The Availability Policy section within the Management tab is where you set preemptibility, so option A is correct. Identity And API Access is used to control the VM's access to Google Cloud APIs and which service account is used with the VM. Sole Tenancy is used if you need to run your VMs on physical servers that only run your VMs. Networking is used to set network tags and change the network interface.

7. B. Shield VM is an advanced set of security controls that includes Integrity Monitoring, a check to ensure boot images have not been tampered with, which makes option B the right answer. Firewalls are used to control ingress and egress of network traffic to a server or subnet. Project-wide SSH keys are used for authenticating users across servers within a project. Boot disk integrity check is a fictional feature.

8. C. Block size is not an option in the Additional Disks dialog, so option C is correct. Encryption key management, disk type, and the option of specifying a source image are all available options.

9. B. Using version-controlled scripts is the best approach of the four options. Scripts can be documented with reasons for the changes and they can be run repeatedly on different machines to implement the same change. This reduces the chance of error when manually entering a command. Option A does not help to improve documenting why changes were made. Option C could help improve documentation, but executable scripts are precise and accurate reflections of what was executed. Notes may miss details. Option D is not advisable. You could become a bottleneck to making changes, changes cannot be made when you are unavailable, and your memory may not be a reliable way to track all configuration changes.

10. A. gcloud compute instances is the start of commands for administering Compute Engine resources, making option A the right answer. Option B, gcloud instances, is missing the compute keyword that indicates we are working with Compute Engine. Option C has switched the order of compute and instances. Option D is false because option A is the correct answer.

11. B. Option B follows the pattern of the glcoud command, which is hierarchical and starts with the glcoud name of the service, in this case compute for Compute Engine, followed by the next level down, which in this case is instances. Finally, there is the action or verb, in this case list. Option A is missing the term instances to indicate you are working with VM instances. Option C is missing the compute keyword to indicate you are working with Compute Engine. Option D is missing the compute instance keyword and has switched the order of instances and list.

12. B. The correct format is to use the --labels parameter and specify the key followed by an equal sign followed by the value in option B. Options A and C have the wrong character separating the key and value. Option D is incorrect because it is possible to specify labels in the command line.

13. C. The two operations you can specify when using the book disk configuration are adding a new disk and attaching an existing disk, so option C is correct. Reformatting an existing disk is not an option, so options A, B, and D cannot be the correct answer.

14. B. 10 GB of data is small enough to store on a single disk. By creating an image of a disk with the data stored on it, you can specify that source image when creating a VM. Option A would require the data scientist to copy the data from Cloud Storage to a disk on the VM. Option C would similarly require copying the data. Option D would load data into a database, not a file system as specified in the requirements.

15. B. In the Network tab of the VM form, you can add another network interface, so option B is correct. GCP sets the IP address, so option A is incorrect. There is no option to specify a router or change firewall rules on the Network tab, so options C and D are incorrect.

16. A. The correct option is boot-disk-type, which is option A. The other three options are not parameters to the gcloud compute instances command.

17. A. Option A is the correct command. It is the only option that includes a correct machine type and properly specifies the name of the instance. Option B uses the --cpus parameter, which does not exist. Option C uses the parameter instance-name, which does not exist. The instance name is passed as an argument and does not need a parameter name. Option D is incorrect because machine type n1-4-cpu is not a valid machine type.

18. C. Option C is the correct command, which is gcloud compute instances, to indicate you are working with VMs, followed by the stop command and the name of the VM. Option A is incorrect because halt is not an option. Option B is incorrect because -terminate is not a parameter. Option D is missing the word instances, which indicates you are working with VMs.

19. B. SSH is service for connecting to a remote server and logging into a terminal window. Once logged in, you would have access to a command line, so option B is the right answer. FTP is a file transfer protocol and does not allow you to log in and perform system administration tasks. RDP is a protocol used to remotely access Windows servers, not Ubuntu, which is a Linux distribution. `ipconfig` is a command-line utility for configuring IP stacks on a device and does not allow you to log into a remote server.

20. A. All of the statements in option A are true and relevant to billing and costs. Option B is correct that VMs are billed in 1-second increments, but the only preemptible VMs are shut down within 24 hours of starting. Option C is incorrect because discounts are not limited to some regions. Option D is incorrect because VMs are not charged for a minimum of 1 hour.

Chapter 6: Managing Virtual Machines

1. A. The Compute Engine page is where you have the option of creating a single VM instance, so option A is the correct answer. App Engine is used for containers and running applications in language-specific runtime environments. Kubernetes Engine is used to create and manage Kubernetes clusters. Cloud Functions is where you would create a function to run in Google's serverless cloud function environment.

2. B. Instances can be stopped, and when they are, then you cannot connect to them via SSH, which makes option B the correct answer. Starting the instance will enable SSH access. Option A is not correct because you can log into preemptible machines. Option C is incorrect because there is no No SSH option. Option D is incorrect because the SSH option can be disabled.

3. B. The Reset command can be used to restart a VM; thus, option B is correct. The properties of the VM will not change, but data in memory will be lost. There is no Reboot, Restart, Shutdown, or Startup option in the console.

4. C. Labels, members of a managed instance group, and status are all available for filtering, so option C is the correct answer. You can also filter by internal IP, external IP, zone, network, deletion protection, and member of a managed or unmanaged instance group.

5. A. To function properly, the operating system must have GPU libraries installed, so option A is correct. The operating system does not have to be Ubuntu based, and there is no need to have at least eight CPUs in an instance before you can attach and use a GPU. Available disk space does not determine if a GPU is used or not.

6. A. If you add a GPU to a VM, you must set the instance to terminate during maintenance, which makes option A the correct response. This is set in the Availability Policies section of the VM configuration form. The instance does not need to be preemptible and it can have non-boot disks attached. The instance is not required to run Ubuntu 14.02 or later.

7.   B. When you first create a snapshot, GCP will make a full copy of the data on the persistent disk. The next time you create a snapshot from that disk, GCP will only copy the data that has changed since the last snapshot. Option A is incorrect; GCP does not store a full copy of the second snapshot. Option C is incorrect; the first snapshot is not deleted automatically. Option D is incorrect, subsequent snapshots do not incur 10 percent overhead.

8.   D. To work with snapshots, a user must be assigned the Compute Storage Admin role, which makes option D the correct answer. The other options are fictitious roles.

9.   C. Images can be created from four sources, namely, disks, snapshots, cloud storage files, or another image, so option C is the right answer. Database export files are not sources for images.

10.   B. Deprecated marks the image as no longer supported and allows you to specify a replacement image to use going forward, making option B the correct answer. Deprecated images are available for use but may not be patched for security flaws or have other updates. The other options are fictitious features of images.

11.   C. The base command for working with instances is gcloud compute instances, which makes option C the correct answer. The list command is used to show details of all instances. By default, output is in human-readable form, not json. Using the --format json option forces the output to be in JSON format. --output is not a valid option.

12.   B. --async causes information about the start process to be displayed; therefore, option B is correct. --verbose is an analogous parameter in many Linux commands. --describe provides details about an instance but not necessarily the startup process. --details is not a valid parameter.

13.   C. The command to delete an instance is gcloud compute instances delete followed by the name of the instance, so option C is correct. Option A is incorrect because there is no instance parameter. Option B is incorrect because that command stops but does not delete the instance. Option D is missing instances in the command, which is required to indicate what type of entity is being deleted.

14.   A. gcloud compute instances is the base command followed by delete, the name of the instance, and --keep-disks=boot, so option A is correct. There is no --save-disk parameter. Option C is wrong because filesystem is not a valid value for the keep-disk parameter. Option D is missing the instances option which is required in the command.

15.   B. The correct answer is option B, which is to use the describe command. Option A will show some fields but not all. Options C and D are incorrect because there is no detailed parameter.

16.   B. Instance groups are sets of VMs that can be configured to scale and are used with load balancers, which contribute to improving availability, so option B is correct. Preemptible instances are not highly available because they can be shut down at any time by GCP. Cloud Storage is not a Compute Engine component. GPUs can help improve throughput for math-intensive operations but do not contribute to high availability.

17. B. An instance group template is used to specify how the instance group should be created, which makes option B the correct answer. Option A is incorrect because instances are created automatically when an instance group is created. Boot disk images and snapshots do not have to be created before creating an instance group.

18. B. The command to delete an instance group is `gcloud compute instance-template delete`, so option B is correct. Option A incorrectly includes the term `instances`. Option C is in incorrect order. Option D is wrong because `instance-template` is in the wrong position and is plural in the option.

19. C. You can configure an autoscaling policy to trigger adding or removing instances based on CPU utilization, monitoring metric, load balancing capacity, or queue-based workloads. Disk, network latency, and memory can trigger scaling if monitoring metrics on those resources are configured. So, option C is correct.

20. B. Unmanaged instance groups are available for limited use cases such as this. Unmanaged instance groups are not recommended in general. Managed instance groups are the recommended way to use instance groups, but the two different configurations prevents their use. Preemptible instances and GPUs are not relevant to this scenario.

Chapter 7: Computing with Kubernetes

1. C. Kubernetes creates instance groups as part of the process of creating a cluster, which makes option C the correct answer. Stackdriver, not instance groups, is used to monitor the health of nodes and to create alerts and notifications. Kubernetes creates pods and deployments; they are not provided by instance groups.

2. A. A Kubernetes cluster has a single cluster master and one or more nodes to execute workloads, so option A is the correct answer. Stackdriver is not part of the Kubernetes cluster; it is a separate GCP service. Kubernetes does not require instances with at least four vCPUs; in fact, the default node configuration uses one vCPU.

3. C. Pods are single instances of a running process in a cluster, so option C is correct. Pods run containers but are not sets of containers. Application code runs in containers that are deployed in pods. Pods are not controllers, so they cannot manage communication with clients and Kubernetes services.

4. B. Services are applications that provide API endpoints that allow applications to discover pods running a particular application, making option B correct. Options A and C, if they could be coded using the API designed for managing clusters, would require more code than working with services and are subject to changes in a larger set of API functions. Option D is not an actual option.

5. C. ReplicaSets are controllers that are responsible for maintaining the correct number of pods, which makes option C the correct answer. Deployments are versions of application code running on a cluster. Stackdriver is a monitoring and logging service that monitors but does not control Kubernetes clusters. Jobs is an abstraction of workloads and is not tied to the number of pods running in a cluster.

6. B. Multizone/multiregion clusters are available in Kubernetes Engine and are used to provide resiliency to an application, so option B is correct. Option A refers to instance groups that are a feature of Compute Engine, not directly of Kubernetes Engine. Option C is incorrect; regional deployments is a fictitious term. Load balancing distributes load and is part of Kubernetes by default. If load is not distributed across zones or regions, it does not help to add resiliency across data centers.

7. A. Option A is the best answer. Starting with an existing template, filling in parameters, and generating the gcloud command is the most reliable way. Option D may work, but multiple parameters that are needed for your configuration may not be in the script you start with. There may be some trial and error with this option. Options B and C may lead to a solution but could take some time to complete.

8. A. The correct command is option A. Option B has beta in the wrong position. Option C is missing beta. Option D is missing the --num-nodes parameter name.

9. C. Time to Live is not an attribute of deployments, so option C is the correct answer. Application name, container image, and initial command can all be specified.

10. B. Deployment configuration files created in Cloud Console are saved in YAML format. CSV, TSV, and JSON are not used.

11. C. The kubectl command is used to control workloads on a Kubernetes cluster once it is created, so option C is correct. Options A and B are incorrect because gcloud is not used to manipulate Kubernetes processes. Option D is wrong because beta is not required in kubectl commands.

12. C. Option C is the correct command. Option A uses the term upgrade instead of scale. Option B incorrectly uses gcloud. Option D uses the incorrect parameter pods.

13. D. Stackdriver is a comprehensive monitoring, logging, alerting, and notification service that can be used to monitor Kubernetes clusters.

14. B. Workspaces are logical structures for storing information about resources in a project that are being monitored, so option B is correct. Stackdriver works with logs, but a log is not required before starting to use Stackdriver. Pods and ReplicaSets are part of Kubernetes, not Stackdriver.

15. C. The Stackdriver Instance Detail page includes time-series charts on CPU usage, network traffic, and disk I/O.

16. B. When creating an alert policy, you can specify conditions, notifications, and documentation, making option B the correct answer. Options A and D are incorrect because there is no Time to Live attribute on policies. Option C is wrong because it does not include notifications and documentation.

17. A. Alerts can have multiple channels, so Option A is correct. Channels include email, webhooks, and SMS text messaging as well as third-party tools such as PagerDuty, Campfire, and Slack. There is no need for multiple alerts with individual notifications. Option C is ad hoc and would require additional maintenance overhead. Option D does not meet requirements.

18. B. Alerts are assigned to instances or sets of instances; therefore, option B is correct. Option A is incorrect because it does not include groups. Option C is incorrect because it does not include instances. Option D is wrong because alerts are not assigned to pods.

19. A. All interactions with the cluster are done through the master using the Kubernetes API. If an action is to be taken on a node, the command is issued by the cluster master, so option A is the correct answer. Options B and D are incorrect because they are controllers within the cluster and do not impact how commands are received from client devices. Option C is incorrect because kubectl, not gcloud, is used to initiate deployments.

20. A. Services provide a level of indirection to accessing pods. Pods are ephemeral. Clients connect to services, which can discover pods. ReplicaSets and StatefulSets provide managed pods. Alerts are for reporting on the state of resources.

Chapter 8: Managing Kubernetes Clusters

1. B. When on the Cloud Console pages, you can click the cluster name to see a Details page, so option B is the correct answer. Typing the name of cluster in the search bar does not always return cluster details; it can return instance group details. There is no such command as gcloud cluster details.

2. D. You can find the number of vCPUs on the cluster listing in the Total Cores column or on the Details page in the Node Pool section in the size parameter, making option D correct. The Labels section does not have vCPU information.

3. B. The correct command includes gcloud container to describe the service, clusters to indicate the resource you are referring to, and list to indicate the command, which makes option B the correct answer. Options A and C are not valid commands.

4. B. It is likely you do not have access privileges to the cluster. The gdcloud container clusters get-credentials command is the correct command to configure kubectl to use GCP credentials for the cluster, so option B is the right option. Options A, C, and D are invalid commands.

5. C. Clicking the Edit button allows you to change, add, or remove labels, so option C is the correct answer. The Connect button is on the cluster listing page, and the Deploy button is for creating new deployments. There is no way to enter labels under the Labels section when displaying details.

6. D. When resizing, the `gcloud container clusters resize` command requires the name of the cluster and the node pool to modify. The size is required to specify how many nodes should be running. Therefore, option D is correct.

7. B. Pods are used to implement replicas of a deployment. It is a best practice to modify the deployments, which are configured with a specification of the number of replicas that should always run, so option B is the correct answer. Option A is incorrect; you should not modify pods directly. Options C and D are incorrect because they do not change the number of pods running an application.

8. C. Deployments are listed under Workloads, making option C the correct answer. The Cluster option shows details about clusters but does not have details on deployments. Storage shows information about persistent volumes and storage classes. Deployments is not an option.

9. B. There are four actions available for deployments (Autoscale, Expose, Rolling Update, and Scale), so option B is correct. Add, Modify, and Delete are not options.

10. C. Since deployments are managed by Kubernetes and not GCP, we need to use a `kubectl` command and not a `gcloud` command, which makes option C correct. Option D is incorrect because it follows the `gcloud` command structure, not the `kubectl` command structure. The `kubectl` command has the verb, like `get`, before the resource type, like `deployments`, for example.

11. D. You can specify container image, cluster name, and application name along with the labels, initial command, and namespace; therefore, option D is the correct answer.

12. A. The Deployment Details page includes services, so option A is the correct answer. Containers are used to implement services; service details are not available there. The Clusters Detail page does not contain information on services running in the cluster.

13. A. `kubectl run` is the command used to start a deployment. It takes a name for the deployment, an image, and a port specification. The other options are not valid `kubectl` commands.

14. A. Option A shows the correct command, which is `kubectl delete service ml-classifier-3`. Option B is missing the service term. Options C and D cannot be correct because services are managed by Kubernetes, not GCP.

15. C. The Container Registry is the service for managing images that can be used in other services, including Kubernetes Engine and Compute Engine, making option C correct. Both Compute Engine and Kubernetes Engine use images but do not manage them. There is no service called Container Engine.

16. A. Images are managed by GCP, so the correct command will be a `gcloud` command, so option A is the correct answer. Option B is incorrect because the verb is placed before the resource. Options C and D are incorrect because `kubectl` is for managing Kubernetes resources, not GCP resources like container images.

17. B. The correct command is `gcloud container images describe`, which makes option B the right answer. `describe` is the `gcloud` verb or operation for showing the details of an object. All other options are invalid commands.

18. B. The `kubectl expose deployment` command makes a service accessible, so option B is the correct answer. IP addresses are assigned to VMs, not services. The command `gcloud` does not manage Kubernetes services, so option C is incorrect. Option D is incorrect because making a service accessible is not a cluster-level task.

19. B. Autoscaling is the most cost-effective and least burdensome way to respond to changes in demand for a service, so option B is the correct answer. Option A may run nodes even when they are not needed. Option C is manually intensive and requires human intervention. Option D reduces human intervention but does not account for unexpected spikes or lulls in demand.

20. B. Cloud engineers working with Kubernetes will need to be familiar with working with clusters, nodes, pods, and container images. They will also need to be familiar with deployment. Option B is the correct answer because the other options are all missing an important component of Kubernetes that cloud engineers will have to manage.

Chapter 9: Computing with App Engine

1. B. Versions support migration. An app can have multiple versions, and by deploying with the `--migrate` parameter, you can migrate traffic to the new version, so option B is the correct answer. Services are a higher-level abstraction and represent the functionality of a microservice. An app may have multiple services, but they serve different purposes. Instances execute code in a version. Instances may be added and removed as needed, but they will run only one version of a service. Instance groups are part of Compute Engine and are not an App Engine component.

2. A. Autoscaling enables setting a maximum and minimum number of instances, which makes option A correct. Basic scaling does not support maximum and minimum instances. Option C is not recommended because it is difficult to predict when load will peak and even if the schedule is predictable today, it may change over time. Option D is wrong; there is no instance detection option.

3. B. Application is the top-level component, so option B is the correct answer. Applications have one or more services. Services have one or more versions. Versions are executed on one or more instances when the application is running.

4. B. The correct command is `gcloud app deploy`, which is option B. Options A and C are incorrect because `gcloud components` commands are used to install `gcloud` commands for working with parts of App Engine, such as the Python runtime environment. Option D is incorrect; you do not need to specify instance in the command.

5. B. The `app.yaml` file is used to configure an App Engine application, which makes option B correct. The other options are not files used to configure App Engine.

6. **A.** A project can support only one App Engine app, so option A is the right answer. If you'd like to run other applications, they will need to be placed in their own projects.

7. **C.** The correct answer is option C because the correct parameter is `--no-promote`. Option A uses `no-traffic`, which is not a valid parameter to the `gcloud app deploy` command. Option B does not get the code out and could release the code too early if there is a delay in getting the press release out. Option D does not meet the requirements of getting the code out as soon as possible.

8. **B.** App Engine applications are accessible from URLs that consist of the project name followed by `appspot.com`, so option B is correct. Option A is incorrect because the domain is not `appengine.com`. Options C and D are incorrect because the names of services are not used to reference the application as a whole.

9. **A.** `max_concurrent_requests` lets you specify the maximum number of concurrent requests before another instance is started, which makes option A correct. `target_throughput_utilization` functions similarly but uses a 0.05 to 0.95 scale to specify maximum throughput utilization. `max_instances` specifies the maximum number of instances but not the criteria for adding instances. `max_pending_latency` is based on the time a request waits, not the number of requests.

10. **C.** Basic scaling only allows for idle time and maximum instances, so option C is the right answer. `min_instances` is not supported. `target_throughput_utilization` is an autoscaling parameter, not a basic scaling parameter.

11. **C.** The `runtime` parameter specifies the language environment to execute in, which makes option C correct. The script to execute is specified by the `script` parameter. The URL to access the application is based on the project name and the domain `appspot.com`. There is no parameter for specifying the maximum time an application can run.

12. **A.** Resident instances are used with manual scaling while dynamic instances are used with autoscaling and basic scaling, so option A is the correct answer. There are no persistent, stable, or nonresident types of App Engine instances.

13. **A.** Using dynamic instances by specifying autoscaling or basic scaling will automatically adjust the number of instances in use based on load, so option A is correct. Option B is incorrect because autoscaling and basic scaling only create dynamic instances. Options C and D are incorrect because manual scaling will not adjust instances automatically, so you may continue to run more instances than needed at some points.

14. **A.** The correct answer is `gcloud app services set-traffic`. Option B is incorrect because the term `instances` is not needed. Option C is incorrect because it does not specify the term `services`. Option D is incorrect because that would require changes on the client's part.

15. **A.** `--split-traffic` is the parameter used to specify the method for splitting traffic, which makes option A correct. Valid options are `cookie`, `ip`, and `random`. All other options are not valid parameters to the `gcloud app services set-traffic` command.

↗ Conflicts with Chapter

16. B. `--split` is the parameter for specifying a list of instances and the percent of traffic they should receive, so option B is the right answer. The other options are not valid parameters for the `gcloud app services set-traffic` command.

17. C. `--migrate` is the parameter for specifying that traffic should be moved or migrated to the newer instance, which makes option C the correct answer. The other options are not valid parameters for the `gcloud app services set-traffic` command.

18. D. From the App Engine console you can view the list of services and versions as well as information about the utilization of each instance.

19. D. All three methods listed, IP address, HTTP cookie, and random splitting, are allowed methods for splitting traffic.

20. B. The cookie used for splitting in App Engine is called GOOGAPPUID, which makes option B the correct answer. Options A, C, and D are not valid names.

Chapter 10: Computing with Cloud Functions

1. C. App Engine is designed to support multiple tightly coupled services comprising an application, making option C the correct answer. This is unlike Cloud Functions, which is designed to support single-purpose functions that operate independently and in response to isolated events in the Google Cloud and complete within a specified period of time. Compute Engine is not a serverless option. Cloud Storage is not a computing product.

2. C. A timeout period that is too low would explain why the smaller files are processed in time but the largest are not, which makes option C the right answer. If only 10 percent of the files are failing, then it is not a syntax error or the wrong runtime selected, as in options A and B. Those errors would affect all files, not just the largest ones. Similarly, if there was a permission problem with the Cloud Storage bucket, it would affect all files.

3. B. Those actions are known as events in Google Cloud terminology; thus, option B is the correct answer. An incident may be a security or performance-related occurrence, but those are unrelated to the expected and standardized actions that constitute events. A trigger is a declaration that a certain function should execute when an event occurs. A log entry is related to applications recording data about significant events. Log entries are helpful for monitoring and compliance, but in themselves are not event-related actions.

4. C. The correct answer is option C because SSL is a secure protocol for remotely accessing servers. It is used, for example, to access instances in Compute Engine. It does not have events that can be triggered using Cloud Functions. The three GCP products listed do generate events that can have triggers associated with them.

5. C. Cloud Functions supports three runtimes: Node.js 6, Node.js 8, and Python. Go and Node.js 5 are not supported runtimes.

6. D. HTTP requests using GET, POST, DELETE, PUT, and OPTIONS can invoke an HTTP trigger in Cloud Functions, so option C is the right answer.

7. D. The correct answer, option D, shows the four events supported in Cloud Storage.

`google.storage.object.finalize`

`google.storage.object.delete`

`google.storage.object.archive`

`google.storage.object.metadataUpdate`

8. C. There is no option to specify the file type to apply the function to, so option C is correct. You can, however, specify the bucket to which the function is applied. You could only save files or the types you want processed in that bucket, or you could have your function check file type and then execute the rest of the function or not, based on type. All the other options listed are parameters to a Cloud Storage function.

9. D. Cloud Functions can have between 128MB and 2GB of memory allocated, which makes option D the correct answer. The default is 256MB.

10. B. By default Cloud Functions can run for up to 1 minute before timing out, so option B is correct. You can, however, set the `timeout` parameter for a cloud function for periods of up to 9 minutes before timing out.

11. B. Python Cloud Functions is currently in beta. The standard set of gcloud commands does not include commands for alpha or beta release features by default. You will need to explicitly install beta features using the `gcloud components install beta` command, so option B is the right answer. Option A will install standard gcloud commands. Options C and D are not valid gcloud commands.

12. A. The correct trigger in option A is `google.storage.object.finalize`, which occurs after a file is uploaded. Option B is not a valid trigger name. Option C triggers when a file is archived, not uploaded. Option D is triggered when some metadata attribute changes, but not necessarily only after a file uploads.

13. C. The three parameters are `runtime`, `trigger-resource`, and `trigger-event`, as listed in option C. All must be set, so options A and B are incorrect. `file-type` is not a parameter to creating a cloud function on Cloud Storage, so option D is incorrect.

14. A. The correct answer is option A, `gcloud functions delete`. Option B references components, which is incorrect. You do need to reference components when installing or updating gcloud commands but not when deleting a cloud function, so options B and C are incorrect. Option D is incorrect because the GCP entity type, in this case `functions`, comes before the name of the operation, in this case `delete`, in a gcloud command.

15. B. Messages are stored in a text format, base64, so that binary data can be stored in the message in a text format, so option B is correct. Option A is incorrect; it is needed to map from a binary encoding to a standard text encoding. Option C is incorrect because the function does not pad with extra characters to make them the same length. Option D is incorrect; it does not change dictionary data types into list data types.

16. C. Option C is correct because it includes the name of the function, the runtime environment, and the name of the Pub/Sub topic. Option A is incorrect because it's missing both the runtime and the topic. Option B is incorrect because it is missing the topic. Option D is incorrect because the runtime specification is incorrect; you have to specify `python37` and not `python` as the runtime.

17. B. There is only one type of event that is triggered in Cloud Pub/Sub, and that is when a message is published, which is option B. Option A is incorrect; Cloud Pub/Sub has one event type that can have a trigger. Option C is incorrect; Cloud Pub/Sub does not analyze the code to determine when it should be run. Option D is incorrect; you do not have to specify an event type with Cloud Pub/Sub functions.

18. B. The correct answer is option B because it uses a Cloud Storage finalize event to trigger conversion if needed. There is minimal delay between the time the file is uploaded and when it is converted. Option A is a possibility but would require more coding than option B. Option C is not a good option because files are not converted until the batch job runs. Option D is incorrect because you cannot create a cloud function for Cloud Pub/Sub using a finalize event. That event is for Cloud Storage, not Cloud Pub/Sub.

19. D. All of the options are available along with zip from Cloud Storage.

20. A. The HTTP trigger allows for the use of POST, GET, and PUT calls, so option A is the correct answer. Webhook and Cloud HTTP are not valid trigger types. Option D is incorrect because option A is the correct answer.

Chapter 11: Planning Storage in the Cloud

1. D. Once a bucket is created as either regional or multiregional, it cannot be changed to the other, so option D is correct. Nearline to coldline and regional to nearline are both allowed, as is multiregional to coldline.

2. C. The goal is to reduce cost, so you would want to use the least costly storage option. Coldline has the lowest per-gigabyte charge at $0.07/GB/month, so option C is correct. Nearline is the next lowest followed by regional. Multiregional has the highest per-gigabyte charge. Both nearline and coldline have access charges, but those are not considered in this question.

3. B. Bigtable is a wide-column database that can ingest large volumes of data consistently, so option B is correct. It also supports low-millisecond latency, making it a good choice for supporting querying. Cloud Spanner is a global relational database that is not suitable for high-speed ingestion of large volumes of data. Datastore is an object data model and not a good fit for IoT or other time series data. BigQuery is an analytics database and not designed for ingestion of large volumes of data in short periods of time.

4.   A. Option A is correct because Memorystore is a managed Redis cache. The cache can be used to store the results of queries. Follow-on queries that reference the data stored in the cache can read it from the cache, which is much faster than reading from persistent disks. SSDs have significantly lower latency than hard disk drives and should be used for performance-sensitive applications like databases. Options B and D are incorrect because HDD persistent disks do give the best performance with respect to IOPS. Options C and D are incorrect because Datastore is a managed NoSQL database and would not have any impact on SQL query performance.

5.   B. HDDs are the better choice for persistent disks for a local database when performance is not the primary concern and you are trying to keep costs down, so option B is correct. Option A is wrong because SSDs are more expensive and the users do not need the lowest latency available. Options C and D are wrong; both of those are other databases that would not be used to store data in a local relational database.

6.   B. Lifecycle configurations can change storage class from regional to nearline or coldline. Once a bucket is created as regional or multiregional, it cannot be changed to the other, so option B is the right answer. Option A is true; you can set retention periods when creating a bucket. Option C is true; Cloud Storage does not provide file system–like access to internal data blocks. Option D is true because Cloud Storage is highly durable.

7.   A. The most recent version of an object is called the live version, so option A is correct. Options B and C are incorrect; top and active are not terms used to refer to versions. Option D is incorrect because option A is correct.

8.   B. Both Cloud SQL and Spanner are relational databases and are well suited for transaction-processing applications, so option B is right. Option A is incorrect because BigQuery is relational, but it is designed for data warehousing and analytics, not transaction processing. Options C and D are incorrect because Bigtable a wide-column NoSQL database, not a relational database.

9.   C. Both MySQL and PostgreSQL are Cloud SQL options so Option C is correct. Options A and B are incorrect, SQL Server is not a Cloud SQL option. Option D is incorrect because Oracle is not a Cloud SQL option. You could choose to run SQL Server or Oracle on your instances but you would have to manage them, unlike Cloud SQL managed databases.

10.   D. The multiregional and multi-super-regional location of nam-eur-aisa1 is the most expensive, which makes option D the right answer. Option A is a region that costs less than the multi-super-regional nam-eur-asia1. Option C is incorrect; that is a zone, and Spanner is configured to regions or super regions. Option B is incorrect; it is only a single super region, which cost less than deploying to multiple super regions.

11.   D. BigQuery, Datastore, and Firebase are all fully managed services that do not require you to specify configuration information for VMs, which makes option D correct. Cloud SQL and Bigtable require you to specify some configuration information for VMs.

12.   B. Datastore is a document database, which makes option B correct. Cloud SQL and Spanner are relational databases. Bigtable is a wide-column database. Google does not offer a managed graph database.

13. A. BigQuery is a managed service designed for data warehouses and analytics. It uses standard SQL for querying, which makes option A the right answer. Bigtable can support the volume of data described, but it does not use SQL as a query language. Cloud SQL is not the best option to scale to tens of petabytes. SQL Server is a relational database from Microsoft; it is not a GCP-managed database service.

14. B. Firestore is a document database that has mobile supporting features, like data synchronization, so option B is the right answer. BigQuery is for analytics, not mobile or transactional applications. Spanner is a global relational database but does not have mobile-specific features. Bigtable could be used with mobile devices, but it does not have mobile-specific features like synchronization.

15. D. In addition to read and write patterns, cost, and consistency, you should consider transaction support and latency, which makes option D correct.

16. B. Option B is correct because Memorystore can be configured to use between 1GB and 300GB of memory.

17. D. Once a bucket is set to coldline, it cannot be changed to another storage class; thus, option D is correct. Regional and multiregional can change to nearline and coldline. Nearline buckets can change to coldline.

18. A. To use BigQuery to store data, you must have a data set to store it, which makes option A the right answer. Buckets are used by Cloud Storage, not BigQuery. You do not manage persistent disks when using BigQuery. An entity is a data structure in Datastore, not BigQuery.

19. D. With a second-generation instance, you can configure the MySQL version, connectivity, machine type, automatic backups, failover replicas, database flags, maintenance windows, and labels, so option D is correct.

20. A. Access charges are used with nearline and coldline storage, which makes option A correct. There is no transfer charge involved. Options C and D do not refer to actual storage classes.

Chapter 12: Deploying Storage in Google Cloud Platform

1. C. Creating databases is the responsibility of database administrators or other users of Cloud SQL, so option C is correct. Google applies security patches and performs other maintenance, so option A is incorrect. GCP performs regularly scheduled backups, so option B is incorrect. Database administrators need to schedule backups, but GCP makes sure they are performed on schedule. Cloud SQL users can't SSH into a Cloud SQL server, so they can't tune the operating system. That's not a problem; Google takes care of that.

2. A. Cloud SQL is controlled using the gcloud command; the sequence of terms in gcloud commands is gcloud followed by the service, in this case SQL; followed by a resource, in this case backups, and a command or verb, in this case create. Option A is the correct answer. Option B is incorrect because gsutil is used to work with Cloud Storage, not Cloud SQL. Option C is wrong because the order of terms is incorrect; backups comes before create. Option D is incorrect because the command or verb should be create.

3. A. Option A is the correct answer. The base command is gcloud sql instances patch, which is followed by the instance name and a start time passed to the --backup-start-time parameter. Option B is incorrect because databases is not the correct resource to reference; instances is. Option C uses the cbt command, which is for use with Bigtable, so it is incorrect. Similarly, Option D is incorrect because it uses the bq command, which is used to manage BigQuery resources.

4. C. Datastore uses a SQL-like query language called GQL, so option C is correct. Option A is incorrect; SQL is not used with this database. Option B is incorrect; MDX is a query language for online analytic processing (OLAP) systems. Option D is incorrect because DataFrames is a data structure used in Spark.

5. C. Option C is the correct command. It has the correct base command, gcloud datastore export, followed by the --namespaces parameter and the name of a Cloud Storage bucket to hold the export file. Option A is incorrect because the --namespaces parameter name is missing. Option B is incorrect because it is missing a namespace. Option D is incorrect because it uses the command or verb dump instead of export.

6. C. Option C is correct; BigQuery displays an estimate of the amount of data scanned. This is important because BigQuery charges for data scanned in queries. Option A is incorrect; knowing how long it took you to enter a query is not helpful. Option B is incorrect; you need to use the scanned data estimate with the Pricing Calculator to get an estimate cost. Option D is incorrect; you do not create clusters in BigQuery as you do with Bigtable and Dataproc. Network I/O data is not displayed.

7. B. Option B shows the correct bq command structure, which includes location and the --dry_run option. This option calculates an estimate without actually running the query. Options A and C are incorrect because they use the wrong command; gcloud and gsutil are not used with BigQuery. Option D is also wrong. cbt is a tool for working with Bigtable, not BigQuery. Be careful not to confuse the two because their names are similar.

8. A. Option A is correct; the menu option is Job History. Options B and C are incorrect; there is no Active Jobs or My Jobs option. Job History shows active jobs, completed jobs, and jobs that generated errors. Option D is incorrect; you can get job status in the console.

9. C. BigQuery provides an estimate of the amount of data scanned, and the Pricing Calculator gives a cost estimate for scanning that volume of data. Options A, B, and C are incorrect; the Billing service tracks charges incurred. It is not used to estimate future or potential charges.

10. B. Option B is correct; the next step is to create a database within the instance. Once a database is created, tables can be created, and data can be loaded into tables. Option A is incorrect; Cloud Spanner is a managed database, so you do not need to apply security patches. Option C is incorrect because you can't create tables without first having created a database. Option D is incorrect; no tables are created that you could import data into when an instance is created.

11. D. Option D is correct because there is no need to apply patches to the underlying compute resources when using Cloud Spanner. because Google manages resources used by Cloud Spanner. Updating packages is a good practice when using VMs, for example, with Compute Engine, but it is not necessary with a managed service.

12. C. This use case is well suited to Pub/Sub, so option C is correct. It involves sending messages to the topic, and the subscription model is a good fit. Pub/Sub has a retention period to support the three-day retention period. Option A is incorrect; Bigtable is designed for storing large volumes of data. Dataproc is for processing and analyzing data, not passing it between systems. Cloud Spanner is a global relational database. You could design an application to meet this use case, but it would require substantial development and be costly to run.

13. C. Pub/Sub works with topics, which receive and hold messages, and subscriptions, which make messages available to consuming applications; therefore, option C is correct. Option A is incorrect; tables are data structures in relational databases, not message queues. Similarly, option B is wrong because databases exist in instances of database management systems, not messaging systems. Option D is wrong because tables are not a resource in messaging systems.

14. C. The correct command is `gcloud components install cbt` to install the Bigtable command-line tool, so option C is correct. Options A and B are incorrect; `apt-get` is used to install packages on some Linux systems but is not specific to GCP. Option D is incorrect; there is no such command as `bigtable-tools`.

15. A. You would need to use a `cbt` command, which is the command-line tool for working with Bigtable, so option A is correct. All other options reference `gcloud` and are therefore incorrect.

16. B. Cloud Dataproc is a managed service for Spark and Hadoop, so option B is correct. Cassandra is a big data distributed database but is not offered as a managed service by Google, so options A and C are incorrect. Option D is incorrect because TensorFlow is a deep learning platform not included in Dataproc.

17. B. The correct command is `gcloud dataproc clusters create` followed by the name of the cluster and the a `--zone` parameter. Option B is correct. Option A is incorrect because bq is the command-line tool for BigQuery, not Dataproc. Option C is a gcloud command missing a verb or command, so it is incorrect. Option D is wrong because option B is the correct answer.

18. B. gsutil is the correct command, so option B is correct. Option A is incorrect because gcloud commands are not used to manage Cloud Storage. Similarly, options C and D are incorrect because they use commands for Bigtable and BigQuery, respectively.

19. B. The command in option B correctly renames an object from an old name to a new name. Option A is incorrect because it uses a cp command instead of mv. Option C does not include bucket names, so it is incorrect. Option D uses gcloud, but gsutil is the command-line tool for working with Cloud Storage.

20. A. Dataproc with Spark and its machine learning library are ideal for this use case, so option A is correct. Option B suggests Hadoop, but it is not a good choice for machine learning applications. Option C is incorrect because Spanner is designed as a global relational database with support for transaction processing systems, not analytic and machine learning systems. Option D is incorrect. SQL is a powerful query language, but it does not support the kinds of machine learning algorithms needed to solve the proposed problem.

Chapter 13: Loading Data into Storage

1. C. gsutil is the command-line utility for working with Cloud Storage. It is one of the few GCP services that does not use gcloud. (BigQuery and Bigtable are others.) Option C is the correct answer because mb, short for "make bucket," is the verb that follows gsutil to create a bucket. Options A and D are wrong because they use gcloud instead of gsutil. Option B is wrong because it uses gsutil with a command syntax used by gcloud.

2. B. The correct answer is option B; gsutil is the command to copy files to Cloud Storage. Option A is incorrect; the verb is cp, not copy. Options C and D are wrong because gsutil, not gcloud, is the command-line utility for working with Cloud Storage.

3. C. From the console, you can upload both files and folders. Options A and B are incorrect because they are missing an operation that can be performed in the console. Option D is incorrect because there is no diff operation in Cloud Console.

4. D. When exporting a database from Cloud SQL, the export file format options are CSV and SQL, which makes option D correct. Option A is incorrect because XML is not an option. Options B and C are incorrect because JSON is not an option.

5. A. Option A, SQL format, exports a database as a series of SQL data definition commands. These commands can be executed in another relational database without having to first create a schema. Option B could be used, but that would require mapping columns to columns in a schema that was created before loading the CSV, and the database administrator would like to avoid that. Options C and D are incorrect because they are not export file format options.

6. C. Option C is the correct command, gcloud sql export sql, indicating that the service is Cloud SQL, the operation is export, and the export file format is SQL. The filename and target bucket are correctly formed. Option A is incorrect because it references gcloud storage, not gcloud sql. Option B is incorrect because it is missing an export file format parameter. Option D is incorrect because the bucket name and filename are in the wrong order.

7.   A. Option A uses the correct command, which is `gcloud datastore export` followed by a namespace and a bucket name. Option B is incorrect because the bucket name is missing `gs://`. Options C and D are incorrect because they use the command `dump` instead of `export`. The bucket name in option D is missing `gs://`.

8.   C. The export process creates a metadata file with information about the data exported and a folder that has the data itself, so option C is correct. Option A is incorrect because export does not produce a single file; it produces a metadata file and a folder with the data. Option B is incorrect because it does not include the data folder. Option D is incorrect because the correct answer is option C.

9.   B. Option B is correct because XML is not an option in BigQuery's export process. All other options are available.

10.   D. Option D is correct because YAML is not a file storage format; it used for specifying configuration data. Options A, B, and C are all supported import file types.

11.   A. The correct command is bq load in option A. The `autodetect` and `source_format` parameters and path to source are correctly specified in all options. Option B is incorrect because it uses the term `import` instead of `load`. Options C and D are incorrect because they use `gcloud` instead of `bq`.

12.   B. The correct answer is B because Dataflow is a pipeline service for processing streaming and batch data that implements workflows used by Cloud Spanner. Option A is incorrect; Dataproc is a managed Hadoop and Spark service, which is used for data analysis. Option C is incorrect; Datastore is a NoSQL database. Option D is incorrect because bq is used with BigQuery only.

13.   A. Bigtable data is exported using a compiled Java program, so option A is correct. Option B is incorrect; there is no `gcloud` Bigtable command. Option C is incorrect; bq is not used with Bigtable. Option D is incorrect because it does not export data from Bigtable.

14.   C. Exporting from Dataproc exports data about the cluster configuration, which makes option C correct. Option A is incorrect; data in DataFrames is not exported. Option B is incorrect; Spark does not have tables for persistently storing data like relational databases. Option D is incorrect; no data from Hadoop is exported.

15.   C. The correct answer is option C; the service Dataproc supports Apache Spark, which has libraries for machine learning. Options A and B are incorrect, neither is an analysis or machine learning service. Option D, DataAnalyze, is not an actual service.

16.   A. The correct command in option A uses `gcloud` followed by the service, in this case `pubsub`, followed by the resource, in this case `topics`; and finally the verb, in this case `create`. Option B is incorrect because the last two terms are out of order. Options C and D are incorrect because they do not use `gcloud`. bq is the command-line tool for BigQuery. cbt is the command-line tool for Bigtable.

17.   C. The correct answer, option C, uses `gcloud pubsub subscriptions create` followed by the topic and the name of the subscription. Option A is incorrect because it is missing the term `subscriptions`. Option B is incorrect because it is missing the name of the subscription. Option D is incorrect because it uses `gsutil` instead of `gcloud`.

18. B. Using a message queue between services decouples the services, so if one lags it does not cause other services to lag, which makes option B correct. Option A is incorrect because adding a message queue does not directly mitigate any security risks that might exist in the distributed system, such as overly permissive permissions. Option C is incorrect; adding a queue is not directly related to programming languages. Option D is incorrect; by default, message queues have a retention period.

19. B. The correct answer is B, gcloud components followed by install and then beta. Option A is incorrect because beta and install are in the wrong order. Options C and D are wrong because commands is used instead of components.

20. A. The correct parameter name is autodetect, which is option A. Options B and C are not actually valid bq parameters. Option D is a valid parameter, but it returns the estimated size of data scanned to when executing a query.

21. A. Avro supports Deflate and Snappy compression. CSV supports Gzip and no compression. XML and Thrift are not export file type options.

Chapter 14: Networking in the Cloud: Virtual Private Clouds and Virtual Private Networks

1. D. Virtual private clouds are global, so option D is correct. By default, they have subnets in all regions. Resources in any region can be accessed through the VPC. Options A, B, and C are all incorrect.

2. B. IP ranges are assigned to subnets, so option B is correct. Each subnet is assigned an IP range for its exclusive use. IP ranges are assigned network structures, not zones and regions. VPCs can have multiple subnets but each subnet has its own address range.

3. B. Option B is correct; dynamic routing is the parameter that specifies whether routes are learned regionally or globally. Option A is incorrect; DNS is a name resolution service and is not involved with routing. Option C is incorrect; there is no static routing policy parameter. Option D is incorrect because global routing is not an actual option.

4. A. The correct answer is gcloud compute networks create, which is option A. Option B is incorrect; networks vpc is not a correct part of the command. Option C is incorrect because gsutil is the command used to work with Cloud Storage. Option D is incorrect because there is no such thing.

5. A. The Flow Log option of the create vpc command determines whether logs are sent to Stackdriver, so option A is correct. Option B, Private IP Access, determines whether an external IP address is needed by a VM to use Google services. Option C is incorrect because Stackdriver Logging is the service, not a parameter used when creating a subnet. Option D is incorrect because variable-length subnet masking has to do with CIDR addresses, not logging.

6. C. Shared VPCs can be created at the organization or folder level of the resource hierarchy, so option C is correct. Options A and B are incorrect; shared VPCs are not created at the resource or project levels. Option D is incorrect; shared VPCs are not applied at subnets, which are resources in the resource hierarchy.

7. A. The correct answer is the Networking tab of the Management, Security, Disks, Networking, Sole Tenancy section of the form, which makes option A correct. The Management tab is not about subnet configurations. Option D is incorrect because it does not lead to Sole Tenancy options.

8. A. VPC is used for interproject communications. Option B is incorrect; there is no interproject peering. Options C and D are incorrect; they have to do with linking on-premise networks with networks in GCP.

9. B. The target can be all instances in a network, instances with particular network tags, or instances using a specific service account, so option B is correct. Option A is incorrect; action is either allow or deny. Option C is incorrect; priority determines which of all the matching rules is applied. Option D is incorrect; it specifies whether the rule is applied to incoming or outgoing traffic.

10. D. Direction specifies whether the rule is applied to incoming or outgoing traffic, which makes option D the right answer. Option A is incorrect; action is either allow or deny. Option B is incorrect; target specifies the set of instances that the rule applies to. Option C is incorrect; priority determines which of all matching rules is applied.

11. A. The 0.0.0.0/0 matches all IP addresses, so option A is correct. Option B represents a block of 16,777,214 addresses. Option C represents a block of 1,048,574 addresses. Option D represents a block of 65,534. You can experiment with CIDR block options using a CIDR calculator such as the one at www.subnet-calculator.com/cidr.php.

12. B. The product you are working with is compute and the resource you are creating is a firewall rule, so option B is correct. Options A and C references network instead of compute. Option D references rules instead of firewall-rules.

13. B. The correct parameter is network, which makes option B correct. Option A is incorrect; subnet is not a parameter to gcloud to create a firewall. Option C is incorrect; destination is not a valid parameter. Option D is incorrect; source-ranges is for specifying sources of network traffic the rule applies to.

14. A. The rule in option A uses the correct gcloud command and specifies the allow and direction parameters. Option B is incorrect because it references gcloud network instead of gcloud compute. Option C is incorrect because it does not specify the port range. Option D is incorrect because it does not specify the protocol or port range.

15. D. Option D is correct because it is the largest number allowed in the range of values for priorities. The larger the number, the lower the priority. Having the lowest priority will ensure that other rules that match will apply.

16. C. The VPC create option is available in the Hybrid Connectivity section, so option C is correct. Compute Engine, App Engine, and IAM & Admin do not have features related to VPNs.

17. C. The Google Compute Engine VPN is where you specify information about the Google Cloud end of the VPN connection, so option C is correct. You specify name, description, network, region, and IP address. Option A is incorrect because tunnels are about the connections between the cloud and the remote network. Option B is incorrect; Routing Options is about how to configure routers. Option D is incorrect; IKE Version is about exchanging secret keys.

18. A. Option A is correct because global dynamic routing is used to learn all routes on a network. Option B is incorrect; regional routing would learn only routes in a region. Options C and D are incorrect because they are not used to configure routing options.

19. B. The autonomous system number (ASN) is a number used to identify a cloud router on a network, so option B is correct. IP addresses are not unique identifiers for the BGP protocol. Option C is incorrect; there is no dynamic load routing ID. Option D is incorrect because option B is correct.

20. D. When using gcloud to create a VPN, you need to create forwarding rules, tunnels, and gateways, so all the gcloud commands listed would be used.

Chapter 15: Networking in the Cloud: DNS, Load Balancing, and IP Addressing

1. B. The A record is used to map a domain name to an IPv4 address, so option B is correct. Option A is incorrect because the AAAA record is used for IPv6 addresses. Option C is incorrect; NS is a name server record. Option D is incorrect; SOA is a start of authority record.

2. A. DNSSEC is a secure protocol designed to prevent spoofing and cache poisoning, so option A is correct. Options B and C are incorrect because SOA and CNAME records contain data about the DNS record; they are not an additional security measure. Option D is incorrect because deleting a CNAME record does not improve security.

3. A. The TTL parameters specify the time a record can be in a cache before the data should be queried again, so option A is correct. Option B is incorrect; this time period is not related to timeouts. Option C is incorrect; the TTLs are not related to time restriction on data change operations. Option D is not correct; there is no manual review required.

4. B. The correct answer, Option B, is gcloud beta dns managed-zones create. Option A is incorrect, it uses the gsutil command which is used to work with Cloud Storage. Option C is incorrect, it is missing the term dns. Option D is incorrect, the ordering of terms is incorrect.

5. B. The visibility parameter is the parameter that can be set to private, so option B is correct. Option A is not a valid parameter. Option C is incorrect; private is not a parameter. Similarly, option D is incorrect; status is not a valid parameter for making a DNS zone private.

6. C. The three global load balancers are HTTP(S), SSL Proxy, and TCP Proxy, so option C is correct. Options A and B are missing at least one global load balancer. Option D is incorrect because Internal TCP/UD is a regional load balancer.

7. D. Network TCP/UDP enables balancing based on IP protocol, address, and port, so option D is correct. Options A, B, and C are all global load balancers, not regional ones.

8. A. In the console there is an option to select between From Internet To My VMs and Only Between My VMs. This is the option to indicate private or public, so option A is correct. Options B, C, and D are all fictitious parameters.

9. B. TCP Proxy load balancers require you to configure both the frontend and backendthe , so option B is correct. Options A and D are incorrect because they are missing one component. Option C is incorrect; forwarding rules are the one component specified with network load balancing. There is no component known as a traffic rule.

10. B. Health checks monitor the health of VMs used with load balancers, so option B is correct. Option A is incorrect, nearline storage is a type of Cloud Storage. Option C and D are incorrect; storage devices or buckets are not health checked.

11. B. You specify ports to forward when configuring the frontend, so option B is correct. The backend is where you configure how traffic is routed to VMs. Option C is incorrect; Network Services is a high-level area of the console. Option D is incorrect; VPCs are not where you specify load balancer configurations.

12. A. The correct answer, option A, is `gcloud compute forwarding-rules create`. Option B is incorrect; the service should be `compute`, not `network`. Option C is incorrect; `create` comes after `forwarding-rules`. Option D is incorrect because it has the wrong service, and the verb is in the wrong position.

13. C. Static addresses are assigned until they are released, so option C is correct. Options A and B are incorrect because internal and external addresses determine whether traffic is routed into and out of the subnet. External addresses can have traffic reach them from the Internet; internal addresses cannot. Option D is incorrect; ephemeral addresses are released when a VM shuts down or is deleted.

14. A. An ephemeral address is sufficient, since resources outside the subnet will not need to reach the VM and you can SSH into the VM from the console, so option A is correct. Option B is incorrect because there is no need to assign a permanent address, which would then have to be released. Option C is incorrect; there is no Permanent type. Option D is incorrect; there is no IPv8 address.

15. D. You cannot reduce the number of addresses using any of the commands, so option D is correct. Option A is incorrect because the prefix length specified in the expand-ip-range command must be a number less than the current length. If there are 65,534 addresses, then the prefix length is 16. Option B is incorrect for the same reason, and the prefix length cannot be a negative number. Option C is incorrect; there is no --size parameter.

16. B. The prefix length specifies the length in bits of the subnet mask. The remaining bits of the IP address are used for device addresses. Since there are 32 bits in an IP address, you subtract the length of the mask to get the number of bits used to represent the address. 16 is equal to 2^4, so you need 4 bits to represent 14 addresses. 32-4 is 28, so option B is the correct answer. Option A would leave 1 address, option C would provide 4,094 addresses, and option D would provide 65,534.

17. C. Premium is the network service level that routes all traffic over the Google network, so option C is correct. Option A is incorrect; the Standard tier may use the public Internet when routing traffic. Options B and D are incorrect; there are no service tiers called Google-only or non-Internet.

18. B. Stopping and starting a VM will release ephemeral IP addresses, so option B is correct. Use a static IP address to have the same IP address across reboots. Option A is incorrect; rebooting a VM does not change a DNS record. Option C is incorrect because if you had enough addresses to get an address when you first started the VM and you then released that IP address, there should be at least one IP address assuming no other devices are added to the subnet. Option D is incorrect because no other changes, including changes to the subnet, were made.

19. A. Internal TCP/UDP is a good option. It is a regional load balancer that supports UDP, so option A is correct. Options B, C, and D are all global load balancers. Option B supports TCP, not UDP. Option D supports HTTP and HTTPS, not UDP.

20. B. Network Services is the section of Cloud Console that has the Cloud DNS console, so option B is correct. Option A is incorrect; Compute Engine does not have DNS management forms. Neither does option C, Kubernetes Engine. Option D is related to networking, but the services in Hybrid Connectivity are for services such as VPNs.

Chapter 16: Deploying Applications with Cloud Launcher and Deployment Manager

1. D. Categories of solutions include all of the categories mentioned, so option D is correct. Others include Kubernetes Apps, API & Services, and Databases.

2. B. The Cloud Launcher is also known as Marketplace, so option B is correct. Option A is incorrect because the Cloud Deployment Manager is used to create deployment templates. Options C and D are fictional names of services.

3. A. You launch a solution by clicking the Launch on Compute Engine link in the overview page, so option A is correct. Option B is incorrect; the main page has summary information about the products. Option C is incorrect; Network Services is unrelated to this topic. Option D is incorrect because option A is the correct answer.

4. B. Cloud Launcher has a set of predefined filters, including filtering by operating system, so option B is correct. Option A may eventually lead to the correct information, but it is not efficient. Option D is incorrect because it is impractical for such a simple task.

5. B. Multiple vendors may offer configurations for the same applications, so option B is correct. This gives users the opportunity to choose the one best suited to their requirements. Options A and C are incorrect; this is a feature of Cloud Launcher. Option D is incorrect because option B is the correct answer.

6. C. Cloud Launcher will display configuration options appropriate for the application you are deploying, so option C is correct. For example, when deploying WordPress, you will have the option of deploying an administration tool for PHP. Option A is incorrect; this is a feature of Cloud Launcher. Option B is incorrect; you are not necessarily on the wrong form. Option D is incorrect; this is a feature of Cloud Launcher.

7. D. You can change the configuration of any of the items listed, so option D is correct. You can also specify firewall rules to allow both HTTP and HTTPS traffic or change the zone in which the VM runs.

8. B. Deployment Manager is the name of the service for creating application resources using a YAML configuration file, so option B is correct. Option A is incorrect, although you could use scripts with `gcloud` commands to deploy resources in Compute Engine. Options C and D are incorrect because those are fictitious names of products.

9. D. Configuration files are defined in YAML syntax, so option D is correct. Options A, B, and C are all incorrect; configuration files are defined in YAML.

10. B. Configuration files define resources and start with the term resources, so option B is correct. Options A, B, and C are all incorrect. Those terms do not start the configuration file.

11. D. All three, `type`, `properties`, and `name`, are used when defining resources in a Cloud Deployment Manager configuration file, so option D is correct.

12. D. All three can be set; specifically, the keys are `deviceName`, `boot`, and `autodelete`. Option D is correct.

13. A. Option A is the correct command. Option B is incorrect; it is missing the term `compute`. Option C is incorrect; `gsutil` is the command for working with Cloud Storage. Option D is incorrect because the terms `list` and `images` are in the wrong order.

14. D. Google recommends using Python for complicated templates, so option D is correct. Option A is incorrect because Jinja2 is recommended only for simple templates. Options B and C are incorrect; neither language is supported for templates.

15. A. The correct answer is `gcloud deployment-manager deployments create`, so option A is correct. Options B and D are incorrect; the service is not called `cloud-launcher` in the command. Option C is incorrect; `launch` is not a valid verb for this command.

16. C. The correct answer is gcloud deployment-manager deployments describe, so option C is correct. Options A and D are incorrect; cloud-launcher is not the name of the service. Option B is incorrect; list displays a brief summary of each deployment. describe displays a detailed description.

17. A. You will be able to configure IP addresses, so option A is correct. You cannot configure billing or access controls in Deployment Manager, so options B and C are incorrect. You can configure the machine type, but that is not the More section of Networking.

18. D. The correct answer is option D because free, paid, and BYOL are all license options used in Cloud Launcher.

19. B. The paid license types include payment for the license in your GCP charges, so option B is correct. The free license type does not incur charges. The BYOL license type requires you to work with the software vendor to get and pay for a license. There is no such license type as chargeback, so option D is incorrect.

20. D. LAMP is short for Linux, Apache, MySQL, and PHP. All are included when installing LAMP solutions, so option D is correct.

Chapter 17: Configuring Access and Security

1. B. IAM stands for Identity and Access Management, so option B is correct. Option A is incorrect; the A does not stand for authorization, although that is related. Option C is incorrect; the A does not stand for auditing, although that is related. Option D is incorrect. IAM also works with groups, not just individuals.

2. A. Members and their roles are listed, so option A is correct. Options B and C are incorrect because they are missing the other main piece of information provided in the listing. Option D is incorrect; permissions are not displayed on that page.

3. B. Primitive roles were created before IAM and provided coarse-grained access controls, so option B is correct. Option A is incorrect; they are used for access control. Option C is incorrect; IAM is the newer form of access control. Option D is incorrect; they do provide access control functionality.

4. B. Roles are used to group permissions that can then be assigned to identities, so option B is correct. Option A is incorrect; roles do not have identities, but identities can be granted roles. Option C is incorrect; roles do not use access control lists. Option D is incorrect; roles do not include audit logs. Logs are collected and managed by Stackdriver Logging.

5. C. The correct answer is gcloud projects get-iam-policy ace-exam-project, so option C is correct. Option A is incorrect because the resource should be projects and not iam. Option B is incorrect; list does not provide detailed descriptions. Option D is incorrect because iam and list are incorrectly referenced.

6. B. New members can be users, indicated by their email addresses, or groups, so option B is correct. Option A is incorrect; it does not include groups. Options C and D are incorrect because roles are not added there.

7. D. Deployers can read application configurations and settings and write new application versions, so option D is correct. Option A is incorrect because it is missing the ability to read configurations and settings. Option B is incorrect because it is missing writing new versions. Option C is incorrect because it references writing new configurations.

8. B. The correct steps are navigating to IAM & Admin, selecting Roles, and then checking the box next to a role, so option B is correct. Option A is incorrect; all roles are not displayed automatically. Option C is incorrect; audit logs do not display permissions. Option D is incorrect; there is no Roles option in Service Accounts.

9. D. Predefined roles help implement both least privilege and separation of duties, so option D is correct. Predefined roles do not implement defense in depth by themselves but could be used with other security controls to implement defense in depth.

10. D. The four launch stages available are alpha, beta, general availability, and disabled, so option D is correct.

11. B. The correct answer, option B, is `gcloud iam roles create`. Option A is incorrect because it references `project` instead of `iam`. Option C is incorrect because it references `project` instead of `iam`, and the terms `create` and `roles` are out of order. Option D is incorrect because the terms `create` and `roles` are out of order.

12. B. Scopes are permissions granted to VM instances, so option B is correct. Scopes in combination with IAM roles assigned to service accounts assigned to the VM instance determine what operations the VM instance can perform. Options A and C are incorrect; scopes do not apply to storage resources. Option D is incorrect; scopes do not apply to subnets.

13. C. Scope identifiers start with `https://www.googleapis.com/auth/` and are followed by a scope-specific name, such as `devstorage.read_only` or `logging.write`, so option C is correct. Option A is incorrect; scope IDs are not randomly generated. Option B is incorrect; the domain name is not `googleserviceaccounts`. Option D is incorrect; scopes are not linked directly to projects.

14. C. Both scopes and IAM roles assigned to service accounts must allow an operation for it to succeed, so option C is correct. Option A is incorrect; access controls do not affect the flow of control in applications unless explicitly coded for that. Option B is incorrect; the most permissive permission is not used. Option D is incorrect; the operation will not succeed.

15. B. The options for setting scopes are: Allow Default Access, Allow Full Access, and Set Access For Each API, so option B is correct. Option A is incorrect; it is missing Set Access For Each API. Option C is incorrect; it is missing Allow Default Access. Option D is incorrect; it is missing Allow Full Access.

16. B. The correct command is `gcloud compute instances set-service-account`, so option B is correct. Option A is incorrect; there is no `set-scopes` command verb. Option C is incorrect; the command verb is not `set-scopes`. Option D is incorrect; there is no command verb `define-scopes`.

17. A. You can assign a service account when creating a VM using the `create` command. Option B is incorrect; there is no `create-service-account` command verb. Option C is incorrect; there is no `define-service-account` command verb. Option D is incorrect; there is no `instances-service-account` command; also, `create` should come at the end of the command.

18. C. Stackdriver Logging collects, stores, and displays log messages, so option C is correct. Option A is incorrect; Compute Engine does not manage logs. Option B is incorrect; Cloud Storage is not used to view logs, although log files can be stored there. Option D is incorrect; custom logging solutions are not GCP services.

19. B. Logs can be filtered by resource, type of logs, log level, and period of time only, so option B is correct. Options A, C, and D are incorrect because they are missing at least one option.

20. B. This is an example of assigning the least privilege required to perform a task, so option B is correct. Option A is incorrect; defense in depth combines multiple security controls. Option C is incorrect because it is having different people perform sensitive tasks. Option D is incorrect; vulnerability scanning is a security measure applied to applications that helps reveal potential vulnerabilities in an application that an attacker could exploit.

Chapter 18: Monitoring, Logging, and Cost Estimating

1. B. The Monitoring service is used to set a threshold on metrics and generate alerts when a metric exceeds the threshold for a specified period of time, so option B is correct. Option A is incorrect; Logging is for collecting logged events. Option C is incorrect; Cloud Trace is for application tracing. Option D is incorrect; Debug is used to debug applications.

2. B. You must install the monitoring agent on the VM. The agent will collect data and send it to Stackdriver, so option B is correct. Option A is incorrect because a Workspace is not installed on a VM; it is created in Stackdriver. Option C is incorrect; there is no Monitor With Stackdriver check box in the VM configuration form. Option D is incorrect because you set notification channels in Stackdriver, not on a VM.

3. D. Stackdriver can monitor resources in GCP, AWS, and in on-premise data centers, so option D is correct. Options A through C are incorrect because they do not include two other correct options.

4. B. Aligning is the process of separating data points into regular buckets, so option B is correct. Option A is incorrect; aggregation is used to combine data points using a statistic, such as mean. Options C and D are incorrect; they are not processes related to processing streams of metric data.

5. D. All three options are valid notification channels in Stackdriver Monitoring, so option D is correct. PagerDuty and HipChat are popular DevOps tools.

6. D. The documentation is useful for documenting the purpose of the policy and for providing guidance for solving the problem, so option D is correct. Option A is incorrect; where a policy is stored is irrelevant to its usefulness. Options B and C alone are partially correct, but option D is a better answer.

7. A. Alert fatigue is a state caused by too many alert notifications being sent for events that do not require human intervention, so option A is correct. This creates the risk that eventually DevOps engineers will begin to pay less attention to notifications. Option B is incorrect, although it is conceivable that too many alerts could adversely impact performance, but that is not likely. Option C is a potential problem, too, but that is not alert fatigue. Option D is incorrect because too many true alerts contribute to alert fatigue.

8. C. Stackdriver Logging stores log entries for 30 days, so option C is correct.

9. B. The best option is to use Stackdriver Logging's export functionality to write log data to a log sink, so option B is correct. Option A is incorrect; there is a way to export data. Options C and D are incorrect because writing a custom script would take more time to develop and maintain than using Logging's export functionality.

10. D. All three, Cloud Storage buckets, BigQuery data sets, and Cloud Pub/Sub topics, are available as sinks for logging exports, so option D is correct.

11. D. All of the options listed can be used to filter, so option D is correct. Log level is another option as well.

12. B. The correct answer, option B, is halted. There is no such standard log level status. Statuses include Critical, Error, Warning, Info, and Debug.

13. B. The fastest way to see the details is to expand all levels of structured data in the entry, so option B is correct. Option A would show the details, but it is not the fastest way. Option C is more time-consuming than using the functionality built into Stackdriver Logging. Option D is incorrect; there is no such link.

14. C. Cloud Trace is a distributed tracing application that provides details on how long different parts of code run, so option C is correct. Option A is incorrect; monitoring is used to notify DevOps engineers when resources are not functioning as expected. Option B is incorrect; Logging is for collecting, storing, and viewing log data, and although log entries might help diagnose bottlenecks, it is not specifically designed for that. Option D is incorrect; Debug is used to generate snapshots and inject logpoints.

15. D. Debug is used to generate snapshots that provide a view of the status of an application at a particular point in its execution, so option D is correct. Option A is incorrect; monitoring is used to notify DevOps engineers when resources are not functioning as expected. Option B is incorrect; Logging is for collecting, storing, and viewing log data. Option C is incorrect because Cloud Trace is a distributed tracing application that provides details on how long different parts of code run.

16. B. The Google Cloud Status Dashboard at https://status.cloud.google.com/ has information on the status of GCP services, so option B is correct. Options A and B might lead to information, but they would take longer. Option C is not a link to a source of information on BigQuery.

17. B. Both Compute Engine and Kubernetes Engine will require details about the VMs' configurations, so option B is correct. The other options are incorrect because BigQuery and Cloud Pub/Sub are serverless services.

18. C. Query pricing in BigQuery is based on the amount of data scanned, so option C is correct. Option A is incorrect; the amount of data storage is specified in the Storage Pricing section. Option B is incorrect; query pricing is not based on the volume of data returned. Option D is incorrect because this is not related to Cloud Storage. Option D is incorrect because option C is correct.

19. B. Some operating systems, like Microsoft Windows Server, require a license, so option B is correct. Google sometimes has arrangements with vendors to collect fees for using proprietary software. Option A is incorrect; there is no fixed rate charge for operating systems. Option C is incorrect; the information is sometimes needed to compute charges. Option D is incorrect because if you Bring Your Own License, there is no additional license charge.

20. B. OpenCensus is a library for developing custom metrics that can be used with Stackdriver Logging, so option B is correct. Option A is incorrect; Prometheus is an open source monitoring tool, but it is not used to define custom metrics in Stackdriver Monitoring. Option C is incorrect; Grafana is a visualization tools for Prometheus. Option D is incorrect; Nagios is an open source monitoring and alerting service, but it is not used for defining custom metrics in Stackdriver Logging.

Index

L

M

N

O

W-Z

Z

Architecting with Google Cloud Platform Specialization

First Month FREE

This multi-course Specialization introduces the comprehensive and flexible infrastructure and platform services on the Google Cloud Platform. Through a combination of presentations, demos, and hands-on labs, participants explore networks, systems, and applications services. This Specialization also covers deploying practical solutions like securely-interconnected networks, customer-supplied encryption keys, security and access management, quotas, billing, and resource monitoring.

Redeem your free month here:
www.coursera.org/promo/ACEstudyguide

19 - 570501

Google Cloud | **coursera** | SYBEX®
A Wiley Brand

Comprehensive Online Learning Environment

Register to gain one year of FREE access to the online interactive test bank to help you study for your Google Associate Cloud Engineer certification exam—included with your purchase of this book! All of the chapter review questions, the practice tests in this book are included in the online test bank so you can practice in a timed and graded setting.

Register and Access the Online Test Bank

To register your book and get access to the online test bank, follow these steps:

1. Go to bit.ly/SybexTest (this address is case sensitive)!
2. Select your book from the list.
3. Complete the required registration information, including answering the security verification to prove book ownership. You will be emailed a pin code.
4. Follow the directions in the email or go to www.wiley.com/go/sybextestprep.
5. Enter the pin code you received and click the "Activate PIN" button.
6. On the Create an Account or Login page, enter your username and password, and click Login. A "Thank you for activating your PIN!" message will appear. If you don't have an account already, create a new account.
7. Click the "Go to My Account" button to add your new book to the My Products page.